Demystifying
Serials Cataloging

Recent Titles in Libraries Unlimited
Third Millennium Cataloging Series
Susan Lazinger and Sheila Intner, Series Editors

Using the Open Archives Initiative Protocol for Metadata Harvesting
Timothy W. Cole and Muriel Foulonneau

Subject Access to a Multilingual Museum Database: A Step-by-Step Approach
to the Digitization Process
Allison Siffre Guedalia Kupietzky

Moving Image Cataloging: How to Create and How to Use a Moving Image Catalog
Martha M. Yee

Collection-level Cataloging: Bound-with Books
Jain Fletcher

Practical Strategies for Cataloging Departments
Rebecca L. Lubas, Editor

Demystifying FRAD: Functional Requirements for Authority Data
Qiang Jin

FRSAD: Conceptual Modeling of Aboutness
Maja Žumer, Marcia Lei Zeng, and Athena Salaba

Demystifying Serials Cataloging

A Book of Examples

FANG HUANG GAO, HEATHER TENNISON, AND
JANET A. WEBER

Third Millennium Cataloging
SUSAN LAZINGER AND SHEILA INTNER, SERIES EDITORS

 LIBRARIES UNLIMITED

AN IMPRINT OF ABC-CLIO, LLC
Santa Barbara, California • Denver, Colorado • Oxford, England

Library of Congress Cataloging-in-Publication Data

Gao, Fang Huang.
   Demystifying serials cataloging : a book of examples / Fang Huang Gao, Heather Tennison, and Janet A. Weber.
      pages cm. — (Third millennium cataloging)
   Includes bibliographical references and index.
   ISBN 978-1-59884-596-9 (pbk.) — ISBN 978-1-61069-281-6 (e-book) (print)
1. Cataloging of serial publications—Handbooks, manuals, etc. 2. Cataloging of serial publications—Problems, exercises, etc.
I. Tennison, Heather. II. Weber, Janet A. III. Title.
Z695.7G36   2012
025.3′432—dc23   2012020397

ISBN: 978-1-59884-596-9
EISBN: 978-1-61069-281-6

16 15 14 13 12   1 2 3 4 5

This book is also available on the World Wide Web as an eBook.
Visit www.abc-clio.com for details.

Libraries Unlimited
An Imprint of ABC-CLIO, LLC

ABC-CLIO, LLC
130 Cremona Drive, P.O. Box 1911
Santa Barbara, California 93116-1911

This book is printed on acid-free paper ∞

Manufactured in the United States of America

Contents

General Introduction to Serials Cataloging

I. OVERVIEW

The dynamic nature of serials cataloging can provide interesting challenges. Some people find serials cataloging so complicated that they avoid it. However, with so many resources exhibiting seriality, including updating websites, loose-leaf publications, and databases, a basic knowledge of serials cataloging is helpful in understanding today's complicated bibliographic universe.

Serials are an important component of this universe and are essential not only for research and enlightenment but also for entertainment. To provide the best access to serials, we should always bear in mind why we catalog. We must strive to help users navigate within and beyond the catalog to find, identify, select, and obtain the serials resource they desire. These are the users tasks defined in the *Functional Requirements for Bibliographic Records* (FRBR), published in 1998 by the International Federation of Library Associations and Institutions (IFLA).[1] In addition, the first principle of the Statement of International Cataloguing Principles (ICP), published in 2009 by IFLA, is "to serve the convenience of catalogue users." Other principles include common usage, representation, accuracy, sufficiency and necessity, significance, economy, consistency and standardization, and integration.[2] These principles reflect the influences of the great minds and traditions in cataloging throughout history—from Sir Anthony Panizzi, Charles Ammi Cutter, Seymour Lubetzky, and Shiyali Ramamrita Ranganathan to the Paris Principles and FRBR. Ranganathan's Five Laws of Library Science—books are for use, every reader his book, every book its reader, save the time of the reader, and the library is a growing organism—continue to have great impact on the development of our profession and on library practices.[3] The term *book* used by Ranganathan is now understood to cover all library resources, including serials.

Through case studies, this book will attempt to answer such questions as: What are serials? How can we catalog serials and make them accessible so our users can find them easily? Where do serials fit in with other categories of resources in the bibliographic universe and what makes serials unique? How should these unique features be reflected in serials bibliographic description? Through these examples it is hoped that catalogers—whether new to serials or just needing a refresher—will not only grasp the important concepts and rules relating to serials cataloging but will also learn how to apply these rules when creating bibliographic records while developing cataloger's judgment.

II. DEFINING SERIALS

In the bibliographic world, a dichotomy has existed between serials and monographs. In the *Anglo-American Cataloging Rules* (AACR), a serial is defined as "a publication issued in successive parts bearing numerical or chronological designations and intended to be continued indefinitely. Serials include periodicals, newspapers, annuals (reports, yearbooks, etc.), the journals, memoirs, proceedings, transactions, etc., of societies, and numbered monographic series," while a monograph is defined as "a work, collection, or other writing that is not a serial."[4]

This dichotomy continued with the *Anglo-American Cataloguing Rules* (2nd edition) (AACR2), which defines a monograph as "a nonserial item, i.e., an item either complete in one part or complete, or intended to be completed, in a finite number of separate parts," while a serial is defined as "a publication in any medium issued in successive parts bearing numeric or chronological designations and intended to be continued indefinitely. Serials include periodicals; newspapers; annuals (reports, yearbooks, etc.); the journals, memoirs, proceedings, transactions, etc., of societies; and numbered monographic series."[5] Not included in the list are loose-leaf publications.

Complicating matters further, in this era of proliferating electronic resources, the continuing and changing nature is not unique to "traditional serials" (i.e., serials in print) anymore. Online databases, websites, discussion lists, blogs, and tweets are all ongoing, with content being constantly updated through addition, deletion, and replacement. Like loose-leaf publications, online databases and websites are revised at regular or irregular intervals or they can be updated continually. For example, some serials in print become databases when they go online; the Internet address for an electronic publication may be changed without warning and the earlier issues of an electronic serial may disappear altogether, making it impossible to trace the bibliographic history of that serial. These new forms of publications do not fit within the traditional definitions of serials and monographs and thus pose special challenges to catalogers.

AACR2 provides no guidelines for describing these publications. To address the inadequacy of AACR2, efforts have been made to revise AACR2. Recommendations were presented in the April 1999 report to the Joint Steering Committee (JSC) for Revision of AACR, "Revising AACR2 to Accommodate Seriality," prepared by Jean Hirons, with the assistance of Regina Reynolds and Judy Kuhagen and the CONSER AACR Review Task Force.[6]

The JSC report presents a new type of publication model, shown below, to accommodate a broader range of publications that display seriality.[7]

In this model, two broad categories of resources are defined: finite and continuing resources. Finite resources are complete or intended to be completed (e.g., monographs), and continuing resources are intended to be continued over time with no predetermined conclusion (e.g., serials, loose-leaf publications, databases, etc.). Under continuing resources, there are two subcategories based on type of issuance: successively issued and integrating. The former includes publications issued successively in discrete parts, such as series and e-journals. The latter includes loose-leaf publications, databases, and websites, for which updated materials do not remain discrete as issues or parts but are integrated into the whole.

Based on this model, some existing terms in AACR2 have been revised and updated, while new terms have been introduced in the 2002 revision of the AACR2.[8]

Representation of Bibliographic Resources

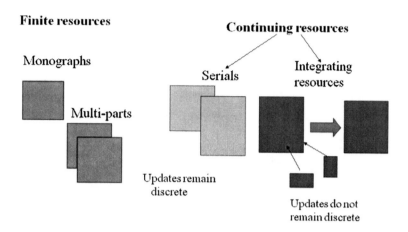

- **Monograph:** A bibliographic resource that is complete in one part or intended to be completed within a finite number of parts.

- **Continuing Resource:** A bibliographic resource that is issued over time with no predetermined conclusion. Continuing resources include serials and ongoing integrating resources.

- **Integrating Resource:** A bibliographic resource that is added to or changed by means of updates that do not remain discrete and are integrated into the whole. Integrating resources can be finite or continuing. Examples of integrating resources include updating loose leafs and updating websites.

- **Serial:** A continuing resource issued in a succession of discrete parts, usually bearing numbering, that has no predetermined conclusion. Examples of serials include journals, magazines, electronic journals, continuing directories, annual reports, newspapers, and monographic series.

As can be seen from AACR, AACR2, and the 2002 revision of AACR2, the definition of serials has not changed much. There are three basic elements that define a serial: (1) issuance in a succession of discrete parts, (2) the presence of numeric, alphabetic, or chronological designations, (3) the likelihood to be continued indefinitely. Before any given resource is cataloged, one must first decide whether the resource should be cataloged as a monograph, an integrating resource, or a serial. Although serials and integrating resources display seriality, they are different types of continuing resources and therefore have different cataloging rules. The focus of this book is on cataloging serials only.

Serials have long been recognized as resources with their own special characteristics. They are prone to changes in titles, publication frequency, issuing body/publisher, and numbering pattern. They are sometimes accompanied by special issues, supplements, and nonprint materials, such as CD-ROMs, in the course of their lifetime. Kathryn Henderson, professor emerita of the Graduate School of Library and Information Science at the University of Illinois at Urbana-Champaign, summarizes the changing nature of serials vividly when she describes serials as having "personalities of their own." She likens serials to humans:

Between "life" and "death" many things can happen to serials as to humans—some live calm, consistent, orderly lives; others find life to be turbulent, inconsistent, changeable; some "marry" (merge); some "divorce" (split). Some even have "offspring." Some are "resurrected," or "born again."[9]

With so many variations, it can be difficult for a serials cataloger to know where to start. What are the cataloging conventions and rules for cataloging serials? What is the source for description? What is the best way to deal with changes in title, publisher, place of publication, frequency, enumeration, etc.? Before we attempt to answer these questions, a brief review of serials cataloging rules, including changes over time, will be beneficial, as it will help us understand how we have arrived where we are now and to see how the previous rules have influenced current serials cataloging practices.

III. CHANGES IN SERIALS CATALOGING CONVENTIONS

The rules governing serials cataloging have changed over time, as reflected in the major Anglo-American cataloging codes: the *A.L.A. Cataloging Rules for Author and Title Entries* of 1949 (ALA Rules), the *Anglo-American Cataloging Rules, North American Text* of 1967 (AACR), the *Anglo-American Cataloguing Rules* (2nd ed.) of 1978 (AACR2), and AACR2, 2002 revision. We will look at how these codes deal with the entry of serials, title differentiation, and title changes.[10]

A. Entry of Serials

The entry of serials is linked directly to the concept of authorship. Most serials are entered under title because few serials are of personal authorship. However, when corporate authorship is involved, things become complicated. According to *A.L.A Rules*, serials—together with collections—are identified as "material in which the responsibility for the intellectual content is so divided that no one of the contributors can be considered the chief author." For these materials, "preference is given to entry under title when it is distinctive or when it is the least variable element and it is, of course, the only possible entry when no editorial or publishing responsibility is apparent" (Rule 5). Although separate rules for entry are provided for different types of serial publications, such as periodicals, newspapers, almanacs, yearbooks, and directories, Rule 5 calls for entry under title for all types. There are some exceptions where serials are entered under corporate body, such as the instruction to "enter a telephone directory issued by a telephone company under the name of the company."[11]

In AACR, serials not issued by a corporate body and not of personal authorship are entered under title (Rule 6A). Although AACR attempted to avoid special rules for different types of publications, Rule 6B again called for the determination of main entry based on the type of serial publication when a corporate body is involved. Some serials issued by or under the authority of a corporate body were to be entered under the corporate body, while other serials such as periodicals, bibliographies, directories, almanacs, and yearbooks—although also issued by or under the authority of a corporate body—were to be entered under title. There was an exception for the latter (i.e., "If the title (exclusive of the subtitle) includes the name or the abbreviation of the name of the corporate body, or consists solely of a generic term that requires the name of the body for adequate identification of the serial, enter it under the body").[12] The difficulties of applying these rules have been explained by Glasby:

As some of you may remember this rule for entry of serials issued by a corporate body was most difficult to apply as one was trying continually to determine whether something was a directory and could go under title or whether some titles were, indeed, generic terms so could go under corporate body.[13]

According to Maxwell, between the publication of AACR in 1961 and AACR2 in 1978, serials catalogers preferring title entry for all serials advocated a change in the rules regarding entry of serials. The recommended change was intended to address the complexity of AACR1 Rule 6. However, this change was not accepted. Chapter 21 of AACR2 continues to be used to determine entry of serials. Therefore, choice of entry for serials is the same as the choice of entry for monographs, with only a few exceptions (found in Chapter 21) that specifically address serials.[14]

B. Unique identification of Serials

Different serials sometimes have the same title (*Art Journal* published by the College Art Association of America and *Art Journal* published by the Saskatchewan Society for Education through Art), and serials sometimes have generic titles (*Report* issued by the Southampton Archaeological Research Committee and *Report* issued by the Association of American Railroads). In these cases, a mechanism is needed to differentiate nondistinctive titles. A uniform title fulfills this need when used as a means to distinguish serials with the same title. Uniform titles in AACR2 serve two functions: They bring together the various manifestations (e.g., editions, translations) of a work appearing under various titles, and they differentiate between two or more works published under identical titles proper.[15] According to AACR2 Chapter 25.5B1, the uniform title is constructed by adding a qualifier to the title proper.[16]

The Library of Congress Rule Interpretation of AACR2 25.5B provides detailed information with regard to the choice of qualifying term and the form of qualifying term for serials entered under title and serials entered under a name heading.[17] For serials entered under title, when the title proper is a "generic" title (i.e., it consists solely of an indication of type of publication and/or periodicity), the heading for the body issuing or publishing the serial is used as the qualifier. For other "nongeneric" titles, a cataloger should use judgment in determining the most appropriate qualifier for the serial being cataloged. Possible qualifiers are corporate body, date of publication, descriptive data elements (such as edition statement), General Material Designations (GMD), physical medium, and place of publication. If needed, more than one qualifier can be used to make the uniform title unique.

For serials entered under a name heading, a cataloger should use judgment in choosing the most appropriate qualifier for the serial being cataloged. Possible qualifiers are date of publication or descriptive data elements (e.g., edition statement or any word(s) that will serve to distinguish one serial or series from another). More than one qualifier should be used if needed to make the uniform title unique.

The CONSER Standard Record (CSR), created for the simplification and efficiency of serials cataloging, makes uniform titles used to distinguish between serials a nonrequired data element. The two exceptions where a uniform title would still be required by CSR guidelines are when it is needed to distinguish between monographic series (although not required to resolve conflicts involving an online series and another medium) or when needed to differentiate "generic" titles.[18]

In Resource Description and Access (RDA), the term *uniform title* has been changed to *preferred title*. The "preferred title for the work" is defined as the "title or form of title chosen as the basis for the authorized access point representing that work."[19]

C. Title Changes

Throughout cataloging history, three methods have been used to handle serials title changes: earliest entry cataloging, latest entry cataloging, and successive entry cataloging. Earliest entry cataloging calls for a single bibliographic record with notes containing the full history of the subsequent title changes of that serial.[20] The title statement contains the earliest title of the serial, and added entries for the later titles are provided as access points. Earliest entry was replaced by latest entry cataloging with the publication of *A.L.A. Rules* in 1949.

Latest entry cataloging also uses a single bibliographic record, with the history of a serial's titles recorded in the notes area. However, it differs from earliest entry cataloging in that the title statement contains the latest title used by the serial. Earlier title variations are described in notes fields and included as added entries to provide access. This method was used until the Library of Congress adopted successive entry cataloging in 1971. Latest entry cataloging can be illustrated with selected fields from the bibliographic record for *The Dance Magazine*. The latest title is entered in the 245 field and the earliest title—*Dance Lovers Magazine*—in the 247 field. The 547 field provides the title's history.

OCLC #664432420

245	0	4	The Dance magazine
246	1	0	Dance magazine of the stage and screen, ǂf [Nov. 1930-Feb. 1931]
247	1	1	Dance lovers magazine, ǂf Nov. 1923-Dec. 1925
260			New York, N.Y.: ǂb Dance Publications,
300			v. : ǂb ill; ǂc 30-33 cm.
310			Monthly.
362	1		Began publication with v. 1 in Nov. 1923.
547			TITLE HISTORY: Dance lovers magazine, -v. 5, no. 2 (Dec. 1925), The Dance magazine, v. 5, no. 3-v. 17, no. 2 (Jan. 1926-Dec. 1931).
500			[Nov. 1930-Feb. 1931] has cover title: The Dance magazine of stage and screen.
500			Publisher and place of publication varies.

Latest entry cataloging was replaced when AACR, published in 1967, prescribed the exclusive use of successive entry cataloging, an idea which had originally been proposed by Cutter in 1876.[21] In successive entry cataloging, a separate bibliographic record is created each time a serial undergoes a major title change. Notes in the linking fields (field 780 and field 785) in each record link the current title to the bibliographic record(s) for the immediate preceding and/or succeeding title(s) only.

Successive entry cataloging is illustrated by the bibliographic records for *ALCTS Newsletter*, which has a previous title—*RTSD Newsletter*—and a later title—*ALCTS Newsletter Online*—which exists only in electronic format.

OCLC #20820888

Type: a	ELvl:	Srce: c	GPub:	Ctrl:	Lang: eng
BLvl: s	Form:	Conf: 0	Freq: b	MRec:	Ctry: ilu
S/L: 0	Orig:	EntW:	Regl: x	Alph: a	
Desc: a	SrTp: p	Cont:	DtSt: d	Dates: 1990	, 1998

245	0	0	ALCTS newsletter.
246	2		Association for Library Collections & Technical Services newsletter
260			Chicago, IL: ‡b Association for Library Collections & Technical Services, American Library Association, ‡c 1990-c1998.
300			9 v.; ‡c 28 cm.
310			Eight no. a year
362	0		Vol. 1, no. 1-v. 9, no. 4-6 (1998).
500			Title from caption.
580			Continued online by: ALCTS newsletter online.
610	2	0	Association for Library Collections & Technical Services ‡v Periodicals.
650		0	Technical services (Libraries) ‡v Periodicals.
710	2		Association for Library Collections & Technical Services.
780	0	0	American Library Association. Resources and Technical Services Division. ‡t RTSD newsletter ‡x 0360-5906 ‡w (DLC) 78648097 ‡w (OCoLC)1978665
785	1	0	‡t ALCTS newsletter online ‡x 1523-018X ‡w (DLC)sn 98005101 ‡w (OCoLC)40507269

OCLC #1978665 (Earlier title in print)

Type a	ELvl	Srce c	GPub	Ctrl	Lang eng
BLvl s	Form	Conf 0	Freq q	MRec	Ctry ilu
S/L 0	Orig	EntW	Regl r	Alph a	
Desc	SrTp p	Cont	DtSt d	Dates 1976	, 1989

010			78648097 ‡z sc 76000295
022	0		0360-5906 ‡l 0360-5906 ‡2 1
042			nsdp ‡a pcc
043			n-us—
110	2		American Library Association. ‡b Resources and Technical Services Division.
245	1	0	RTSD newsletter.
246	3		Resources and Technical Services Division newsletter
260			[Chicago] ‡b Resources and Technical Services Division, American Library Association.
300			14 v. ‡c 28 cm.
310			Quarterly, ‡b winter 1987-1989
321			Six no. a year, ‡b <1980- >
321			8 no. a year, ‡b 1984-1986
362	0		v. 1-14, no. 6; Jan. 1976-1989.
500			"Official organ of the Resources and Technical Services Division."
610	2	0	American Library Association. ‡b Resources and Technical Services Division ‡v Periodicals.
650		0	Technical services (Libraries) ‡v Periodicals.
710	2		American Library Association. ‡b Resources and Technical Services Division. ‡t Newsletter.
785	0	0	‡t ALCTS newsletter ‡x 1047-949X ‡w (DLC) 91649699 ‡w (OCoLC)20820888

OCLC #40507269 (Later title online)

Type: a	ELvl:	Srce: d	GPub:	Ctrl:	Lang: eng
BLvl: s	Form: s	Conf: 0	Freq: q	MRec:	Ctry: ilu
S/L: 0	Orig:	EntW:	Regl: x	Alph: a	
Desc: a	SrTp: p	Cont:	DtSt: c	Dates: 1998	, 9999

006		[m d]
007		c ‡b r ‡d c ‡e n ‡f u
010		sn 98005101
022	0	1523-018X ‡y 1047-949X
042		nsdp ‡a lcd
043		n-us—
245	0 0	ALCTS newsletter online ‡h [electronic resource]
246	3	ALCTS online newsletter
260		Chicago, IL: ‡b Association for Library Collections & Technical Services, American Library Association, ‡c c1998-
310		4 no. a year, ‡b Spring 2000-
321		Six no. a year, ‡b Dec. 1998-Dec. 1999
362	0	Vol. 10, no. 1 (Dec. 1998)-
500		Title from journal homepage.
538		Mode of access: Internet via World Wide Web.
610	2 0	Association for Library Collections & Technical Services ‡v Periodicals.
710	2	Association for Library Collections & Technical Services.
780	0 0	‡t ALCTS newsletter ‡x 1047-949X ‡w (DLC) 91649699 ‡w (OCoLC)20820888
856	4 0	‡u http://bibpurl.oclc.org/web/25 ‡u http://www.ala.org/alcts/alctsnews/
936		Vol. 12, no. 4 (winter 2001) LIC

The advantages and disadvantages of these three methods have been the subject of much discussion in the literature and are addressed by such authors as Cole, Zajanc, Mueller, Case & Randall, and Lim.[22] Many have pointed out that successive entry cataloging was invented in the manual card catalog environment to deal with the increasingly heavy workload of recataloging serials because of the need for constant revision and refiling of card sets. It enables materials to be processed and made available to users more quickly and economically. While easier to maintain in a card catalog, successive entry cataloging has led to a proliferation of records—some of which appear to be for meaningless title changes. Furthermore, as Mueller points out,

> it has the disadvantages of fragmentation of description and access (the bibliographic history of the serial is not available in one record and multiple searches are required to retrieve information relating to earlier or later titles) and loss of continuity if a library has broken runs of the serial (only immediately adjacent titles are linked together).[23]

In the automated environment, it is easy to provide as many access points as needed. Consequently, by providing "one-stop shopping"—or a single bibliographic record with a history of the title variations of the serial—latest and earliest entry cataloging can achieve a high degree of success in terms of access by users and comprehensive bibliographic description representing the entire serial. Users do not have to conduct multiple searches when title changes have occurred. However, one disadvantage is that the master bibliographic record containing all title changes sometimes becomes too large and complicated for ordinary use.

Between earliest and latest entry cataloging, it seems that earliest entry cataloging is more efficient. It saves the cataloger's time and effort, as the descriptive paragraph is almost static, and all changes are recorded in the note area. However, taking into consideration other aspects of serials processing, such as serials check-in and binding as well as users who want the most current issue, latest entry cataloging is preferable.

IV. CONSER STANDARD RECORD (CSR)

In 2007, the CONSER Standard Record (CSR) was implemented with the goal of better meeting user needs while reducing serials cataloging costs in the digital environment. CSR identifies and requires in serials records only those data elements "as having the highest value in supporting users' efforts to find, identify, select, and obtain the resources they need, as well as navigate the relationships among titles."[24] Specified in the Metadata Application Profile (MAP), the mandatory data elements for CSR are main entry, title proper, edition statement, place of publication, publisher, current frequency, unformatted numbering statement, subject headings, most added entries, and most linking fields. Data elements to be simplified include the limited use of uniform titles, statement of responsibility, and many notes, such as those recorded in 321, 362, 530, 580, 550, and 787 fields. For example, when recording a numbering statement, the serials cataloger no longer has to indicate whether he or she has the first issue in hand (362 0_) or not in hand (362 1_). To streamline the process, the cataloger will always record the numbering statement in note format (362 1_), together with these notes: "Description based on," "Title from . . . " (even if title page), and "Latest issue consulted" (even if first issue). For recording enumeration and chronology, a serials cataloger is instructed to either transcribe what is found or use standard abbreviations, whichever is easier.[25] By simplifying serials records this way, a user will find consistency and clarity in the record.

The CSR "is intended to be a 'floor,' to which additional elements can be added if such elements are essential to meeting FRBR user tasks for a specific resource or to meet the needs of a particular institution."[26] For more information on CSR Documentation and Library of Congress Rule Interpretations (LCRI), Metadata Application Profile (MAP), Cataloger's Cheat Sheet, and background documents, see http://www.loc.gov/acq/conser/CSR.html.

V. SINGLE VS. SEPARATE RECORD APPROACH

CONSER gives two options for cataloging online resources: the single record option or the separate record option.[27] With the single record option, one bibliographic record is used to represent the print and online versions of a resource. The primary description, including fixed field coding, is for the print version, and additional information is added to the record to represent the online version. The single record approach is also called the "non-cataloging approach" because a new catalog record is not created to represent the online version. The greatest benefit of this approach is that both versions are represented in one place, making it easier for the user to identify and access the resource.

In the separate record approach, a different record is created for each format (i.e., print records describe only print versions and online records describe only online versions). Linking fields are used to show the relationship between the different formats. The MARC field 776, "other format available," would be used to represent a horizontal relationship because CONSER guidelines consider a resource available in multiple formats to be published simultaneously. Previously, separate records were often created for each version of an online resource. CONSER instructs catalogers choosing the separate record option to create only one: a "provider-neutral record" for resources whose content is essentially the same, even though it is available from more than one source. More information about the provider-neutral record follows in the next section of this introduction.

The advantages of the separate record approach are that it is easier to discern from the description which format is being described and to maintain records and corresponding links in the catalog, especially following the dramatically increased use of automated maintenance and bulk record loads. Although the choice of the single-record or the separate-record approach should be made based on the needs of the local catalog, CONSER gives a few guidelines for determining the best approach. The separate record approach is preferred when the access points in the print record are not sufficient to represent the online version or when the content of the online version is either equivalent to or significantly greater than the print. The single record approach is usually preferable when the access points in the print record are sufficient to represent the online version and when the online version contains less full text than the print version.

VI. PROVIDER-NEUTRAL RECORDS FOR ELECTRONIC SERIALS

The provider-neutral record, originally called aggregator-neutral record, was introduced by CONSER in 2003 to address the large number of records needed for each version of an online resource, including those necessitated by existing cataloging rules requiring a new record with changes in publishers, providers, and corporate bodies. As a result of the proliferation of records, Shadle notes, "CONSER reexamined its guidelines, concluding that the differences between versions supplied by different providers did not reflect bibliographic differences in the item, but rather different licensing arrangements and access."[28] In order to provide a solution, the provider-neutral record was conceived. Under this approach, a single record is used to describe all equivalent online versions of a serial, regardless of the provider of the serial.

The bibliographic description is applicable to all online versions, and provider-specific information should be excluded, with only a few exceptions. The provider used as the basis for description is specified. An added entry for a variant title found on a publisher's website can be supplied with the note "Issues from some providers have title:" in the 246 field. A separate 856 field is given to record the link for each provider. All other provider-specific information is omitted, including provider names used to qualify uniform titles, series statements that record provider names, and added entries for the name of the aggregator or provider.

CCM Module 31 provides a preferred list in the choice of the provider to be used as the basis of description:[29]

- Publisher's site when it contains the full text
- Host or archiving site. Prefer this site over the publisher's site when it contains the first issue and the publisher's site does not
- In choosing between sites that present titles involved in a title change and those that don't, prefer the site that presents both titles
- Record for the print version
- Aggregations and databases that are article based and do not maintain issue integrity

For additional information on provider-neutral records, see: http://www.loc.gov/acq/conser/pdf/agg-rec-guidelines.pdf. Similar guidelines have subsequently been created for both e-integrating resources and e-monographs. More information is available from the following websites: http://www.loc.gov/acq/conser/ProvNeutforE-IRs-Sept-21-2007.pdf and http://www.loc.gov/catdir/pcc/bibco/PN-Final-Report.pdf.

VII. LOOKING TO THE FUTURE: FRBR AND RESOURCE DESCRIPTION AND ACCESS (RDA)

Released on June 23, 2010, RDA is the new standard for resource description and access designed for the digital world. It is built on the foundation established by AACR2, and it is intended to provide a comprehensive set of guidelines and instructions on resource description and access for all types of content and media.[30] It is based on FRBR, which provides a conceptual entity-relationship model for describing entities, attributes, and relationship between entities. It shows the functions that bibliographic records perform in relation to library resources, to user tasks, and to catalogs. RDA is based on the user tasks identified by FRBR: finding, identifying, selecting, and obtaining information. According to the Report and Recommendations of the U.S. RDA Test Coordinating Committee, "The underlying principles of RDA include not just FRBR concepts, but the idea that bibliographic description should be regarded as a set of reusable relationship information packets, rather than a monolithic set of individual and indivisible records."[31]

The primary entities in FRBR, called Group 1 entities, are:

- Work (distinct intellectual or artistic creation)
- Expression (intellectual or artistic realization of a work)
- Manifestation (the embodiment of an expression of a work)
- Item (a single exemplar of a manifestation)[32]

These Group 1 entities are also known as "WEMI." At the 2011 ALA/ALCTS pre-conference on RDA, Kuhagen explains that serials are cataloged at the manifestation level, but the MARC bibliographic record also includes information about work and expression (and sometimes item).[33] She provides a list of the various entities represented in a bibliographic record:

MARC Bibliographic Record & FRBR WEMI
1XX/240 = work, expression
245–260, 490 = manifestation
300 = expression, manifestation
other 3XX = work, expression, manifestation
5XX = work, expression, manifestation
700–730 = related work, related expression
760–787 = related work, related expression, related manifestation
8XX = work, expression [& manifestation][34]

With FRBR, more emphasis is given to the clustering of related records and to specifying how serials are related. The concept of multilevel cataloging (work, expression, manifestation, and item) helps connect the related resources. The FRBR model goes beyond distinct records indexed by access points—to overarching structures bringing records together. Examples of relationships include work relationships (supplements, chronological relationships, such as earlier or later titles) and manifestation relationships (reprints or other formats).

A library user looking for an entire run of a journal may have difficulty seeing the entire title history because of the way a single bibliographic record links only to the immediately preceding and succeeding titles. A potential answer to this problem is the serial "superwork record"—a concept introduced in Melissa Bernhardt's article "Dealing With Serial Title Changes: Some Theoretical and Practical Considerations."[35] The term *super record* comes from the publications of Rahmatollah

Fattahi.[36] The concept involves creating work-level and expression-level citations and collocating variants of those titles—either in the form of chronological relationship (title changes) or in the form of horizontal relationship (multiple formats).

Standard identifiers that are found in bibliographic records already provide some linkage. FRBR's collocations will depend on machine links between records similar to those already provided by serial linking fields with embedded control numbers, such as the ISSN, LCCN, and OCLC numbers. A work-/expression-level record could use a linking title to bring together successive-entry records in the same way that the linking ISSN (ISSN-L) collocates the different formats of a serial title. To further support linking capabilities, work is under way to assign missing e-ISSNs to approximately 1,200 online serials. The goal is that there will be an ISSN for a print serial and a separate ISSN for the equivalent online serial (whether born digital or reproduced from the print).[37]

There has been evolution toward a solution based in the CONSER or OCLC database that relies on programming rather than on a MARC-based solution, in accordance with Bernhardt's solution noted earlier. Chains of successive entry and multiple version records are brought together by means of cascading searches of 780/785 and 776 control numbers embedded in linking fields. When the cluster is assembled, the super record displays links to the component records, and is itself linked to the collocated "universal holdings" or publication history as contained in the serial holding records according to each format, with all successive titles combined into one record. It is the product of the research of the CONSER Publication Patterns Initiative (Publication History Task Force).[38] The super record displays the earliest title or another agreed-upon super title, plus links to component titles, editions, and formats. Codes in the component records help programmers set the links and labels for linking field displays. Publication history and holdings records for each format are collocated for all titles.

According to the report of the U.S. RDA Test Coordinating Committee issued in June 2011, CONSER is working to resolve conflicts between standard CONSER practice and certain RDA rules, including the aggregator/provider neutral approach, the "single-record approach," and some aspects of the CONSER Standard Record.[39]

VIII. ORGANIZATION OF THE BOOK

This book is filled with examples illustrating important concepts for serials cataloging covering such topics as title as main entry, title changes, corporate body as main entry, changes in publisher or place of publication, changes in enumeration and chronology, serials published in different formats, serial supplements, serial uniform titles, notes, and standard numbers and control numbers. Each chapter starts with the introduction of the topic to be covered, followed by the application of the cataloging rules, and the explanation and illustration through various examples. To reinforce the concepts and rules learned in each chapter, practice exercises are included at the end of each chapter. Sources consulted include RDA, AACR2, *CONSER Cataloging Manual* (CCM), *CONSER Editing Guide* (CEG), LCRI, and OCLC *Bibliographic Formats and Standards*.

Titles are the most important attribute for the identification and access of serials. That is why two chapters are devoted to serial titles: Chapter 1 and Chapter 2, with the latter expanding on the differences between major and minor title changes in serials. Chapter 3 explains when a corporate body should be used as main entry and how to deal with changes in corporate body when the corporate body is the main entry. Chapter 4 explores what a publisher or place of publication change is in serials and how to use the new mechanism (i.e., repeatable 260 MARC fields to record the changes). Chapter 5 provides information on how to catalog serials with changes in enumeration and chronology. Chapter 6 discusses how to catalog serials that are available in print and online formats, using the single-record approach and the separate-record approach. It also covers how to catalog serials as they change formats. Chapter 7 explains what serial supplements are and expands on the relationship between the parent publication and the supplement. Chapter 8 focuses on what uniform titles are in serials and how to create them to distinguish different serial titles with the same name. Chapter 9 shows common notes used in serials, when they are used, and why some notes are required and some are optional. Chapter 10 deals with what standard numbers and control numbers are and how to record them correctly for serials identification and retrieval. Answers to practice exercises can be found in the appendix.

It is our hope that this book will help demystify serials cataloging through examples and help people working with serials find enjoyment and satisfaction in their work. As shown throughout the book, serials are entities with their own special bibliographic characteristics. They are dynamic, organic, and unpredictable. They can provide catalogers with hours of frustration, hours of enjoyment, and anything in between. Serials also present mystery, as we do not know what to expect from them. Will they live a calm life or a turbulent one, filled with remarriages (mergers) and offspring (splits)? Only time will tell, and this is why serials cataloging remains so fascinating.

A few final notes:

There are differences in practice when creating an original record as opposed to maintaining an existing record. As with previous implementations of new cataloging rules and guidelines, the usual practice is to not change existing bibliographic records to conform to the new standard.

In the cataloging examples used in this book, certain MARC fields have been deleted due to space limitations. However, the MARC fields needed to highlight a particular point have been retained.

NOTES

1. IFLA Study Group on the Functional Requirements for Bibliographic Records. *Functional Requirements for Bibliographic Records: The Final Report* (München: K.G. Saur, 1998).
2. International Federation of Library Associations and Institutions. *IFLA Cataloguing Principles: The Statement of International Cataloguing Principles (ICP) and Its Glossary: In 20 Languages*, ed. Barbara B. Tillett and Ana Lupe Cristán. (München: K.G. Saur, 2009). http://www.ifla.org/files/cataloguing/icp/icp_2009-en.pdf.
3. S.R. Ranganathan. *The Five Laws of Library Science* (Madras: Madras Library Association, 1931).
4. *Anglo-American Cataloguing Rules, North American Text* (Chicago: American Library Association, 1967).
5. American Library Association, the British Library, the Canadian Committee on Cataloging, the Library Association, the Library of Congress. *Anglo-American Cataloguing Rules*, 2nd ed. Michael Gorman and Paul W. Winkler, eds. (Chicago: ALA, 1978).
6. Jean Hirons, with Regina Reynolds and Judy Kuhagen. *Revising AACR2 to Accommodate Seriality: Report to the Joint Steering Committee on the Revision of AACR*, April 1999. http://www.rda-jsc.org/docs/ser-rep.pdf.
7. Ibid.

8. AACR2.

9. Kathryn Luther Henderson. "Personalities of Their Own: Some Informal Thoughts on Serials and Teaching About How to Catalog Them," in *Serials Cataloging: Modern Perspective and International Developments*, ed. Jim E. Cole and James W. Williams (Binghamton, NY: Haworth Press, 1992).

10. American Library Association. *A.L.A. Cataloging Rules for Author and Title Entries*, 2nd ed. (Chicago, American Library Association, 1949); AACR; AACR2; *Anglo-American Cataloguing Rules*, 2nd ed., 2002 revision. Joint Steering Committee for Revision of AACR, a committee of the American Library Association . . . [et al.] (Ottawa: Canadian Library Association; Chicago: American Library Association, 2002–).

11. *A.L.A Cataloging Rules.*

12. AACR.

13. Dorothy J. Glasby. "The Descriptive Cataloging of Serials: Library of Congress' Application of AACR," In *Serials Cataloging: The State of the Art*, ed. Jim E. Cole and Jackie Zajanc (New York: Haworth Press, 1987). Published simultaneously as *Serials Librarian*, v.12 no. 1/2, 1987.

14. Robert L. Maxwell. *Maxwell's Handbook for AACR2: Explaining and Illustrating the Anglo-American Cataloguing Rules Through the 2003 Update*, 4th ed. (Chicago: American Library Association, 2004). The reasons cited by Maxwell for the nonacceptance of the change include the wish to conform to the International Standards for Bibliographic Description for Serials, or ISBD(S), published in 1977, and the adherence of the 2nd edition of AACR to the guidelines of the Paris Principles.

15. AACR2 Chapter 25.

16. AACR2 25.5B1

17. LCRI 25.5B

18. *CONSER Standard Record Documentation*, July 22, 2010, http://www.loc.gov/catdir/cpso/conserdoc.pdf.

19. *RDA: Resource Description & Access*, developed by the Joint Steering Committee for Development of RDA (JSC), representing the American Library Association . . . [et al.]. (Chicago: American Library Association, 2010, c2011).

20. AACR.

21. Charles A. Cutter. *Rules for a Dictionary Catalog*, 4th ed., rewritten. (Washington, DC: Government Printing Office, 1904).

22. Jim E. Cole, "The First Shall Be Last: Earliest Entry Cataloging," *The Serials Librarian*, 11, no. 1 (Sept. 1986): 5–14; Jackie Zajanc, "Title Changes in an Automated Environment: The Last Shall Be First," *The Serials Librarian*, 11, no. 1 (Sept. 1986): 15–21; Carolyn J. Mueller, "AACR2 and Serials Management," *Advances in Serials Management*, 2(1988): 47–61; Mary M. Case and Kevin M. Randall, " Latest Entry Cataloging Locally and Nationwide: Some Observations," *The Serials Librarian*, 22, no. 3/4 (1992): 335–345; Sue C. Lim, "Successive Entry Serials Cataloging: An Evaluation," *Serials Librarian*, 14, no. 1/2 (1988): 59–69.

23. Mueller.

24. *CONSER Standard Record Documentation.*

25. Ibid.

26. Ibid.

27. *CCM Module 31: Remote Access Electronic Serials (Online Serials)*, www.loc.gov/acq/conser/Module31.pdf.

28. Steve Shadle and Holley R. Lange. "Case Studies in Electronic Serials Cataloging, or What Am I Supposed to Do with This?" *The Serials Librarian*, 46, no. 3 (2004): 202–208. http://www.tandfonline.com/doi/pdf/10.1300/J123v46n03_01.

29. *CCM Module 31.*

30. *RDA: Resource Description & Access.*

31. U.S. RDA Test Coordinating Committee. *Report and Recommendations of the U.S. RDA Test Coordinating Committee: 9 May 2011*, rev. June 2011 (Washington, DC: Library of Congress, 2011). http://www.loc.gov/bibliographic-future/rda/source/rdatesting-finalreport-20june 2011.pdf.

32. *Functional Requirements for Bibliographic Records.*

33. Judith A. Kuhagen. "Cataloging Serials With RDA." Presentation at ALCTS Preconference: *RDA 201* (New Orleans, June 23–24, 2011).

34. Ibid.

35. Melissa Bernhardt. "Dealing With Serial Title Changes: Some Theoretical and Practical Considerations," *Cataloging & Classification Quarterly*, 9, no. 2 (1988): 25–39.

36. Rahmatollah Fattahi, "International Conference on the Principles and Future Development of AACR" (Toronto, 1997); Rahmatollah Fattahi, "The Serial Super-Record," presentation at American Library Association Conference, 2005.

37. Rebecca Kemp. "Catalog/Cataloging Changes and Web 2.0 Functionality," *The Serials Librarian*, 53, no. 4, (2008). http://dx.doi.org/10.1300/J123v53n04_07.

38. Continuing Resources Cataloging Committee. Report at ALA Conference, 2011.

39. *Report and Recommendations of the U.S. RDA Test Coordinating Committee.*

CHAPTER 1

Source of Title and Recording the Title

A title is one of the most important access points for retrieving a serial publication. In this chapter, we will discuss where to get title information and how to record it—whether as title proper, other title information, or variant title. When cataloging serials, you should begin with a clear understanding of the basis of the description and the chief source of information.

According to *Anglo-American Cataloguing Rules* (2nd edition) (AACR2), catalogers should base the bibliographic description on the first issue published or the first available issue. The chief source of information is the title page or the title page substitute. As most serials tend to not have a title page, the title page substitute is usually used. The substitute is chosen in this order of preference:

1. The analytical title page
2. Cover
3. Caption
4. Masthead
5. Editorial pages
6. Colophon
7. Other pages

The source used as the title page substitute is specified in a note. *Resource Description and Access* (RDA) provides the same instruction but uses the term *preferred source of information* for *chief source of information*. According to RDA 2.2.2.2, for resources consisting of one or more pages, leaves, sheets, or cards (or images of one or more pages, leaves, sheets, or cards), use the title page, title sheet, or title card (or image thereof) as the preferred source of information.

If the resource lacks a title page, title sheet, or title card (or image thereof), use as the preferred source of information the first of the following sources that bears a title:

(a) a cover (or an image of a cover)
(b) a caption (or an image of a caption)
(c) a masthead (or an image of a masthead)
(d) a colophon (or an image of a colophon).

If none of the sources listed above bears a title, use as the preferred source of information another source within the resource that bears a title, giving preference to a source in which the information is formally presented.

Once the title information is obtained from the title page or the title page substitute, a cataloger must decide what the title proper is, whether other title(s) should be recorded, whether there are parallel titles involved, and whether variant titles need to be recorded in order to provide access. In most situations, titles will be recorded as main entry or, in RDA terminology, preferred title plus authorized access point for creator if appropriate. In this chapter, examples are provided to show how to record title proper, other title information, parallel title, and other variant titles to ensure the retrieval of a serial resource.

AACR2 defines the title proper as the chief name of an item, including any alternative title but excluding parallel titles and other title information. In RDA, the title proper is the chief name of a resource (that is, the title normally used when citing the resource), excluding any parallel titles proper, other title information, and parallel other title information. An alternative title is treated as part of the title proper. The title proper should be transcribed exactly as it appears on the chief source of information as to wording, order, and spelling but not necessarily as to punctuation and capitalization. However, information that varies from issue to issue, such as numbers, names, and dates, should be omitted from the title and be replaced by the mark of omission unless the variant information occurs at the beginning of the title, in which case no mark of omission is given.

In this chapter, examples are provided to show how to deal with:

- Titles that consist of a common title and a section title
- Titles that appear in full form as well as initialism form
- Titles that contain an ampersand
- Titles that have a title proper and a subtitle
- Titles that include a parallel title
- Varying titles that appear elsewhere in a serial other than the title page

When appropriate, relevant rules are cited from AACR2, RDA, *Library of Congress Rule Interpretations* (LCRI), and *CONSER Cataloging Manual* (CCM).

RESOURCES CONSULTED

AACR2

1.1B Title Proper
12.0B Sources of Information
12.1B7 Title Proper
21.1C1 Entry Under Title

LCRI

1.1B Title Proper

RDA

1.7 Transcription
2.2.2 Preferred source of information
2.3 Title
2.3.2 Title proper

CCM

4.7 When to Enter Under Title

6 Title Statement

MARC 21

MARC 21 Format for Bibliographic Data: http://www.loc.gov/marc/bibliographic

OCLC

Bibliographic Formats and Standards: http://www.oclc.org/bibformats

Title as Main Entry

Title: Well-being and social policy

Cover

Title Page

The bibliographic description of the serial *Well-being and Social Policy* is based on the first issue, published in 2005. The title information is taken from the title page. Like most serials, this serial publication is entered under title (i.e., it has a title main entry). This is because no corporate body (excluding commercial publishers) or individual is responsible for the whole run of the serial.

The title *Well-being and Social Policy* is transcribed as it appears on the title page, but in the bibliographic record, only the first word of the title is capitalized, according to AACR2 Appendix A.4A1. When coded in Machine-Readable Cataloging (MARC), this title is transcribed in the 245 field, with 00 as indicator values. The first 0 means the title is the main entry, not an added entry, and the second 0 means there are no definite or indefinite articles as nonfiling characters at the beginning of a title to be disregarded in sorting and filing processes.

This record was created before the implementation of the CONSER Standard Record (CSR) in 2007. In a CSR, information regarding the first and/or last issue of a serial is always entered in a 362 unformatted note, with first indicator 1, rather than a formatted 362 field, with first indicator 0, which indicates that a cataloger had the first/last issue in hand when creating the record. It is no longer necessary to make such a distinction.

Furthermore, the source of a title note is always required in a CSR, even if the title is taken from a title page. Both "description based on" and "latest issue consulted" notes are always required too. For more information on notes, see Chapter 9.

OCLC #73839540

	Type a	ELvl	Srce d	GPub	Ctrl		Lang eng
	BLvl s	Form	Conf 0	Freq u	MRec		Ctry mx
	S/L 0	Orig	EntW	Regl u	Alph		
	Desc a	SrTp p	Cont	DtSt c	Dates 2005	, 9999	

	022		1870-2961	
	043		cl-----	

CCM 4.7 6.1.3	245	0	0	Well-being and social policy.	AACR2 1.1B1 21.1C1

260			Mexico, D.F. : ‡b CISS : ‡b Universidad Iberoamericana, ‡c c2005-
300			v. ; ‡c 22 cm.
362	0		Vol. 1, num. 1 (2nd semester 2005)-
580			Also issued in Spanish ed.
650		0	Public welfare ‡z Latin America ‡v Periodicals.
650		0	Social service ‡z Latin America ‡v Periodicals.
650		0	Social security ‡z Latin America ‡v Periodicals.
711	2		Inter-American Conference on Social Security.
710	2		Universidad Iberoamericana (Mexico City, Mexico)

AACR2

1.1B1 - Transcribe the title proper exactly as to wording, order, and spelling, but not necessarily as to punctuation and capitalization

12.1B7 - For serials, if the title includes a date, name, number, etc., that varies from issue to issue, omit this date, name, number, etc., and replace it by the mark of omission, unless it occurs at the beginning of the title, in which case do not give the mark of omission

21.1C1 - Enter a work under its title proper or uniform title if:

 (a) the personal authorship is unknown, and it does not emanate from a corporate body; or

 (b) it is a collection of works by different persons or bodies; or

 (c) it emanates from a corporate body but does not fall into any of the categories given in 21.1B2 and is not of personal authorship; or

 (d) it is accepted as sacred scripture by a religious group

Appendix A Capitalization A.4A1 - In general, capitalize the first word of a title

RDA

1.7.1 - General guidelines on transcription: when the instructions in chapters 2–4 specify transcription of an element as it appears on the source of information, apply the general guidelines on capitalization, punctuation, symbols, abbreviations, etc., given under 1.7.2–1.7.9. When the guidelines given under 1.7.2–1.7.9 refer to an appendix, apply the additional instructions given in that appendix as applicable to the element being transcribed

2.3.1 - Basic instructions on recording titles

(Continued on next page)

2.3.1.4 - Recording titles: transcribe a title as it appears on the source of information. Apply the general guidelines on transcription given under 1.7

2.3.2.7 - Record the title proper applying the basic instructions on recording titles given under 2.3.1

CCM

4.7 - Enter a serial under title when:

- there is no responsible corporate body; or

- the serial does not emanate from the corporate body; or

- the serial does not fall into one of the categories under AACR2 21.1B2; and there is no person that is solely responsible for the entire run of the serial

6.1.3 - Transcribe the title as it appears on the chief source of information

6.1.3.e - Capitalization: capitalize words in the title according to AACR2 Appendix A. Always capitalize the first word in the title

Title Proper Consisting of a Common Title and a Section Title

Title: Journal of neurosurgery: Pediatrics

Cover

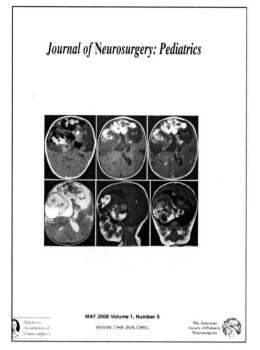

Cover

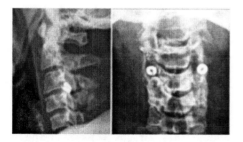

June 2011 Volume 14, Number 6

The title proper can sometimes consist of more than a single statement. It can have a common title and a section title, as in this example: *Journal of Neurosurgery: Pediatrics*. CCM defines a common title as a title that is common to two or more works—one or more of which also carries the title and/or designation of a section. The section title is defined in AACR2 as a separately published part of a bibliographic resource—usually representing a particular subject category within the larger resource and identified by a designation that may be a topic, an alphabetic or numeric designation, or a combination of these.

This publication—*Journal of Neurosurgery: Pediatrics*—is related to another resource: *Journal of Neurosurgery: Spine*. Both journals carry the common title as well as the unique title of the section.

According to AACR2 12.1B4, if the common title and the section title are grammatically independent of each other, give the common title and then the section title, preceded by a full stop. RDA 2.3.1.7 gives the same instructions as AACR2.

LCRI 12.1B4 further explains that if AACR2 12.1B4 is applied, the source containing the common title and the section title is the chief source of information for the item. For printed resources, the chief source of information is the title page or the title page substitute, which includes (in this order of preference) the analytical title page, cover, caption, masthead, editorial pages, colophon, or other pages. The source used as the title page substitute is given in a note (AACR2 12.0B2). In our example, the title information is taken from the cover because the journal does not have a title page and a note specifying the source—"Title from cover"—is provided.

When transcribing the title proper in MARC, the common title *Journal of Neurosurgery* is input in subfield ‡a of the 245 field and the section title *Pediatrics* is input in subfield ‡p, preceded by a full stop. An added entry is made for the section title for access (AACR2 21.30J2). The first indicator in this 246 field is 3 so the section title is accessible, but no note or print constant is generated. The second indicator 0 is used because the variant title is a portion of the title proper.

OCLC #54981900

	Type a	ELvl	Srce d	GPub	Ctrl	Lang eng
	BLvl s	Form	Conf 0	Freq m	MRec	Ctry vau
	S/L 0	Orig	EntW	Regl r	Alph a	
	Desc a	SrTp p	Cont	DtSt c	Dates 2004	, 9999

	022	0		1933-0707 ‡2 1	
	042			lcd ‡a nsdp	
CCM 6.2	245	0	0	Journal of neurosurgery. ‡p Pediatrics.	AACR2 12.1B4
7.2.1c	246	3	0	Pediatrics	21.30J2
	260			Charlottesville, VA : ‡b American Association of Neurological Surgeons, ‡c 2004-	
	300			v. : ‡b ill. ; ‡c 28 cm.	
	310			Monthly, ‡b 2008-	
	362	0		Vol. 100, no. 1 (Feb. 2004)-	
	500			Title from cover.	
	500			Latest issue consulted: Vol. 1, no. 5 (May 2008) (surrogate).	
	550			"Official journal of American Association of Neurological Surgeons, American Society of Pediatric Neurosurgeons, American Academy of Pediatrics Section on Neurological Surgery."	
	580			Formerly published as a supplement to: Journal of neurosurgery.	
	650		0	Spine ‡x Surgery ‡v Periodicals.	
	650		0	Children ‡x Surgery ‡v Periodicals.	
	650		0	Pediatric neurology ‡v Periodicals.	
	710	2		American Association of Neurological Surgeons.	
	710	2		American Society of Pediatric Neurosurgeons.	
	710	2		American Academy of Pediatrics. ‡b Section on Neurological Surgery.	
	780	1	1	‡t Journal of neurosurgery ‡x 0022-3085 ‡w (DLC)med47001541 ‡w (OCoLC)1800316	

AACR2

12.1B4 - If a resource is a separately published section of, or supplement to, another resource and its title proper as presented in the chief source of information consists of a) the title common to all sections (or the title of the main resource), and b) the title of the section or supplement, and if these two parts are grammatically independent of each other, give the common title followed by the section or supplement title preceded by a full stop

21.30J2 - If considered necessary for access, make an added entry for any version of the title (e.g., cover title, caption title, running title, panel title, title on container, title bar title) that is significantly different from the title proper

LCRI

12.1B4 - In applying rule 12.1B4, consider all presentations of the common title and section title within the item.... If rule 12.1B4 is to be applied, the source containing both titles is the chief source of information for the item. For printed resources, the source should be one of the preliminaries, the publisher's listing, or the colophon

RDA

2.3.1.7 - If the resource is a separately issued part or section of, or supplement to, another resource and its title as presented on the source of information consists of: a) the title common to all parts or sections (or the title of the larger resource) and b) the title of the part, section, or supplement and if these two titles are grammatically independent of each other, record the common title, followed by the title of the part, section, or supplement.... Use a full stop to separate the common title from the title of the part, section, or supplement

CCM

6.2 - When a publisher issues a group of serials under the same "common" title and gives each serial in the group a "section" title, both titles are given as part of the title proper, provided that both titles appear on the same source

7.2.1 - Give access to a portion of the title when a user might consider this portion to be the title proper or when access to the portion will improve the overall retrievability of the record. This category includes variant titles given for: portions of the title proper, alternative titles, section titles, parallel titles, other title information

7.2.1c - When the title proper consists of a common title and section title, give the section title in a 246 field when the title is distinctive and will provide useful access

Title in Full and Initialism Form

Title: Journal of Iberian and Latin American research

Cover

For the *Journal of Iberian and Latin American Research*, the cover serves as the chief source of information. On the cover, the title appears in full as well as in initialism form. According to AACR2 12.1B2 and 12.1E1a, the full form should be chosen as the title proper and the acronym or initialism transcribed as other title information.

In this example, the full form *Journal of Iberian and Latin American Research* is the title proper, even though the initialism JILAR is typographically prominent.

This method is a change from an earlier practice. Prior to the 2002 revision of AACR, when the full form and initialism appeared on the chief source—with the initialism being the only form appearing elsewhere in the resource—the initialism was chosen as the title proper and the full title was recorded as other title information. According to CONSER practice, no change is made to existing records where the acronym or initialism is the title proper, even when doing so might avoid a major change (CCM 6.1.4d).

For serials and integrating resources, RDA 2.3.2.5 also instructs to choose the full form as the title proper and record the acronym or initialism as other title information.

In MARC, the full form of the title is input in field 245:

245 00 Journal of Iberian and Latin American research : ǂb JILAR.

Field 246 is used for recording the initialism:

246 30 JILAR

Cover verso

JILAR – Journal of Iberian and Latin American Research

Volume 14, Number 1, July 2008

A refereed journal of the Association of Iberian and Latin American Studies of Australasia (AILASA)

OCLC #263029453

	Type a	ELvl	Srce c	GPub	Ctrl	Lang eng
	BLvl s	Form	Conf 0	Freq f	MRec	Ctry at
	S/L 0	Orig	EntW	Regl r	Alph	
	Desc a	SrTp p	Cont	DtSt c	Dates 2008	, 9999

	022		ǂy 1326-0219	
	041	0	eng ǂa spa	
	042		pcc	
	043		cl—— ǂa e-sp— ǂa e-po—	
CCM 6.1.4d 6.3.3a	245	0 0	Journal of Iberian and Latin American research : ǂb JILAR.	AACR2 12.1B2 12.1E1a
7.2.1f	246	3 0	JILAR	21.30j2
	260		[Australia] : ǂb Association of Iberian and Latin American Studies of Australasia	
	300		v. ; ǂc 26 cm.	
	310		Semiannual	
	362	1	Began publication with Vol. 14, no. 1 (July 2008).	
	500		Description based on: Vol. 14, no. 1 (July 2008); title from cover.	
	500		"Journal of the Association of Iberian and Latin American Studies of Australasia (AILASA)."	
	500		Latest issue consulted: Vol. 14, no. 2 (Dec. 2008).	
	546		Chiefly in English, with some articles in Spanish.	
	651	0	Latin America ǂv Periodicals.	
	710	2	Association of Iberian and Latin American Studies of Australasia.	
	780	0 0	ǂt Journal of Iberian and Latin American Studies ǂx 1326-0219 ǂw (DLC) 97657615 ǂw (OCoLC)36708990	

AACR2

12.1B2 - When the title appears both in full and in the form of an acronym or initialism in the chief source of information, choose the full form as the title proper

12.1E1a - If an acronym or initialism of the title appears in the chief source of information with the full form of the title, transcribe the acronym or initialism as other title information

21.30J2 - If considered necessary for access, make an added entry for any version of the title (e.g., cover title, caption title, running title, panel title, title on container, title bar title) that is significantly different from the title proper

LCRI

12.1B2 - LC/PCC practice: Prior to Dec. 1, 2002, this rule called for the selection of the acronym or initialism as the title proper if it was the only form of title presented in other locations. Do not change any existing bibliographic or series authority records created before Dec. 1, 2002

RDA

2.3.2.5 - If the source of information for the title proper bears a title in more than one form, and if both or all of the titles are in the same language and script, choose the title proper on the basis of the

(Continued on next page)

sequence, layout, or typography of the titles on the source of information. If the sequence, layout, and typography do not provide the basis for a clear choice, choose the most comprehensive title

Exception for serials and integrating resources: If the title of a serial or integrating resource appears on the source of information for the title proper in full as well as in the form of an acronym or initialism, choose the full form as the title proper. Record the acronym or initialism as other title information

CCM

6.1.4d - When an acronym or initialism appears on the chief source in addition to the spelled out or "full form" of the title, use the full form as the title proper and record the acronym or initialism as other title information

6.3.3a - When an acronym or initialism appears on the chief source with the full form, the full form is transcribed as the title proper and the acronym or initialism is given as other title information

7.2.1 - Give access to a portion of the title when a user might consider this portion to be the title proper or when access to the portion will improve the overall retrievability of the record. This category includes variant titles given for: portions of the title proper, alternative titles, section titles, parallel titles, other title information

7.2.1f - In most cases, do not give a 246 field variant title for other title information. When the title, as given on the piece, consists of an acronym or initialism and the full form, however, give an added entry for the acronym or initialism recorded in field 245 ǂb

Title Proper Consisting of Numbers

Title: 306090

Cover

Title Page

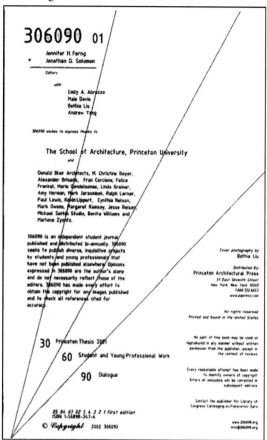

Some titles may consist of numbers, as with the journal *306090*. If it is reasonably expected that the catalog user may search the title under the spelled-out form, a title added entry is made for that form to improve access. After all, cataloging is done to help users find, identify, select, and obtain resources. The LCRI to AACR2 21.30J and the Library of Congress Policy Statements (LCPS) to RDA 2.3.6.3 provide the same guidelines for making title added entries for alternate forms, such as the spelled-out form of an abbreviation or a number as a word. Therefore, an added entry is made in the 246 field:

246 3_ Thirty sixty ninety

The first indicator value is 3 because a note for the added entry is not necessary. The second indicator value is blank because a display constant for the type of title is not needed in this case. *Thirty sixty ninety* is simply the spelled-out form of *306090*, and it does not belong to other types of titles, such as running title, caption title, or parallel title, etc.

Although the addition of other title information in the title and statement of responsibility area is not required, the other title information may be recorded in subfield ‡b of the 245 field if it explains the title proper. In this example, *A Journal of Emergent Architecture and Design* clarifies and provides important information about the title proper *306090*, and it is therefore recorded as other title information in subfield ‡b of the 245 field and in the 246 field for improved access.

OCLC #47413894

Type a	ELvl	Srce c	GPub	Ctrl	Lang eng	
BLvl s	Form	Conf 0	Freq a	MRec	Ctry nju	
S/L 0	Orig	EntW	Regl r	Alph a		
Desc a	SrTp p	Cont	DtSt c	Dates 2001	, 9999	

	022	0	1536-1519 ǂ2 1	
	042		lcd ǂa nsdp	
	222	0	306090	
CCM 6.1.3	245	0 0	306090 : ǂb a journal of emergent architecture and design.	AACR2 12.1B1
7.2.3e	246	3	Thirty sixty ninety	21.30J2
7.2.1	246	3 0	Journal of emergent architecture and design	12.1E1
	260		Princeton, NJ : ǂb 306090, School of Architecture, Princeton University ; ǂa New York : ǂb Distributed by Princeton Architectural Press, ǂc c2002-	
	300		v. : ǂb ill. ; ǂc 26 cm.	
	310		Annual, ǂb 2006-	
	321		Semiannual, ǂb 2001-2005	
	362	0	01 (09 2001)-	
	500		Issues 04 (03 2003)-have also a distinctive title.	
	500		Subtitle varies.	
	500		Latest issue consulted: v.12 published in 2008.	
	515		Issues for 09 2001-called also: Fall 2001-	
	515		Vol. 10-lack chronological designations.	
	650	0	Architecture, Modern ǂy 21st century ǂv Periodicals.	
	650	0	Architectural design ǂv Periodicals.	
	710	2	Princeton University. ǂb School of Architecture.	

AACR2

12.1B1 - Transcribe the title proper as instructed in 1.1B

1.1B1 - Transcribe the title proper exactly as to wording, order, and spelling, but not necessarily as to punctuation and capitalization . . . Capitalize according to appendix A

12.1E1 - Transcribe other title information as instructed in 1.1E if considered to be important

21.30J2 - If considered necessary for access, make an added entry for any version of the title (e.g., cover title, caption title, running title, panel title, title on container, title bar title) that is significantly different from the title proper

LCRI

12.1E - CONSER standard record practice: It is not required to record, in the title and statement of responsibility area, other title information appearing on the serial issue used as the basis of the description. Always record an acronym or initialism of the title proper in a 246 field. Other title information which is not an acronym or initialism may be recorded in the 246 field if considered important for access

21.30J - For Arabic numbers (excluding dates), when a number occurs as one of the first five words filed on in a title proper, make a 246-derived title added entry substituting the corresponding spelled-out form of the number in the language of the title proper if it is thought that some users of the catalog might reasonably expect that the form was spelled out in words in the source. In spelling out numbers in English, follow the style indicated in The Chicago Manual of Style

RDA

2.3.6.3 - Record variant titles that are considered to be important for identification or access applying the basic instructions on recording titles given under 2.3.1

6.2.1.5 - When recording a title for a work, record numbers expressed as numerals or as words in the form in which they appear on the source of information

CCM

6.1.3 - Transcribe the title as it appears on the chief source of information

7.2.1 - Give access to a portion of the title when a user might consider this portion to be the title proper or when access to the portion will improve the overall retrievability of the record

7.2.3e - In cases where a number has been given as part of the title proper, give an added entry for the spelled-out form

Title Proper Containing Ampersand "&"

Title: Journal of gay & lesbian mental health

Screenshot - Issues List

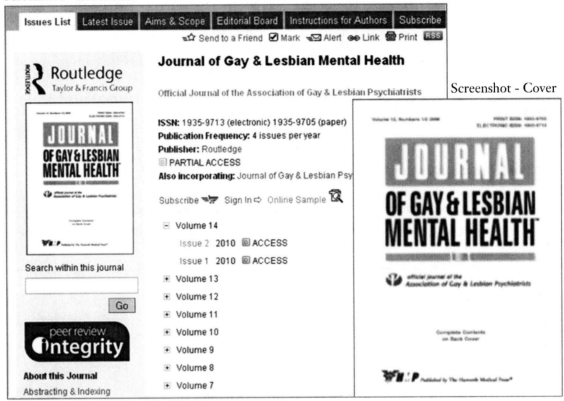

In this example, *Journal of Gay & Lesbian Mental Health* contains an ampersand (&) in the title. LCRI 21.30J offers guidelines for making title added entries for permutations related to titles proper. Specifically, when an ampersand (or other symbol [e.g., +] representing the word *and*) occurs as one of the first five words in a title proper, make a 246-derived title added entry, substituting the word *and* in the language of the title. The same guidelines have been included in LCPS 2.3.6.3, with the only change in wording from "make a 246-derived title added entry substituting the word 'and' " in LCRI to "make a variant title substituting the word 'and' " in LCPS.

Therefore, the title *Journal of Gay & Lesbian Mental Health* is transcribed as it appears and a title added entry is made, replacing the "&" with "and." The added entry is coded in field 246, with the first indicator 3 and the second indicator blank. The 3 means to make the variant title an added entry—so it can be searchable and accessible—without giving a note. The second indicator is blank because the variant title does not belong to the type of titles coded in MARC (e.g., 4 for cover title, 7 for running title, and 8 for spine title, etc.) because this form of the title (i.e., the title with the word *and*) does not appear elsewhere in the resource.

Because this is an electronic journal, the appropriate general material designation (GMD) "electronic resource" is added immediately following the title proper (AACR2 1.1C; 9.1C1). In RDA, the GMD is replaced by Media type (3.2), Carrier type (3.3), and Content type (6.9). For more information about cataloging electronic serials, please see Chapter 6.

A uniform title is created in this record and input in the 130 field, with the qualifier "online" added to distinguish the two formats because the titles for the online and the print versions are identical. However, since the implementation of CSR in 2007, a uniform title is no longer created except for generic titles and monographic series. To find out more about uniform titles, please see Chapter 8.

OCLC #83832445

Type a	ELvl	Srce c	GPub	Ctrl		Lang eng
BLvl s	Form s	Conf 0	Freq q	MRec		Ctry nyu
S/L 0	Orig s	EntW	Regl r	Alph a		
Desc a	SrTp p	Cont	DtSt c	Dates 2008	, 9999	

	022	0		1935-9713 ‡2 1	
	042			lcd ‡a nsdp	
	130	0		Journal of gay & lesbian mental health (Online)	
CCM 6.1.3 31.6.2	245	1	0	Journal of gay & lesbian mental health ‡h [electronic resource].	AACR2 9.1B1 9.1C1
7.2.3	246	3		Journal of gay and lesbian mental health	LCRI 21.30J
	260			New York, N.Y. : ‡b Haworth Medical Press	
	310			Quarterly	
	362	1		Began with vol. 12, no. 1/2 (2008).	
31.3.4	500			Description based on first issue; title from publisher's homepage (viewed June 5, 2008).	9.1B2 9.7B22
	530			Also issued in print.	
	538			Mode of access: World Wide Web.	
	650		0	Gays ‡x Mental health ‡v Periodicals.	
	650		0	Lesbians ‡x Mental health ‡v Periodicals.	
	710	2		Association of Gay & Lesbian Psychiatrists.	
	776	1		‡t Journal of gay & lesbian mental health ‡x 1935-9705 ‡w (DLC) 2007214197 ‡w (OCoLC)83831862	
	780	0	0	‡t Journal of gay & lesbian psychotherapy (Online) ‡x 1540-7128 ‡w (DLC) 2002214457 ‡w (OCoLC)50103807	
	856	4	0	‡u http://www.haworthpress.com/store/product.asp?sku=J529	

AACR2

9.1B1 - Transcribe the title proper as described in 1.1B1

9.1B2 - Always give the source of the title proper in a note (see 9.7B3)

9.1C1 - Give immediately following the title proper the appropriate general material designation as instructed in 1.1C

9.7B3 - Always give the source of the title proper

9.7B22 - For remote access resources, always give the date on which the resource was viewed for description

LCRI

21.30J - When an ampersand (or other symbol, e.g., +, representing the word "and") occurs as one of the first five words filed on in a title proper, make a 246-derived title added entry substituting the word "and" in the language of the title

(Continued on next page)

RDA

2.3.6.3 - Record variant titles that are considered to be important for identification or access applying the basic instructions on recording titles given under 2.3.1
The GMD has been replaced in RDA by media type (3.2), Carrier type (3.3), and Content type (6.9)

6.9 - Content type is a categorization reflecting the fundamental form of communication in which the content is expressed and the human sense through which it is intended to be perceived

3.2 - Media type is a categorization reflecting the general type of intermediation device required to view, play, run, etc., the content of a resource

3.3 - Carrier type is a categorization reflecting the format of the storage medium and housing of a carrier in combination with the type of intermediation device required to view, play, run, etc., the content of a resource

CCM

6.1.3 - Transcribe the title as it appears on the chief source of information

7.2.3 - If the title proper or a variant title contains words that the user might search in a different form, give a 246 field using the variant form. Such access may be given for compound words, spelled out forms of symbols, such as "and" for "&", and spelled out numbers, etc.

31.6.2 - Include the GMD "electronic resource" in brackets in subfield ‡h following the title proper

31.3.4 - Always give in a note the source of title for an online serial, according to AACR2 9.7B3. Give also, in new records, the date viewed in parentheses following the source of title per AACR2 9.7B22

Title Proper Containing Initialism and Subtitle

Title: BSAVA news

Cover

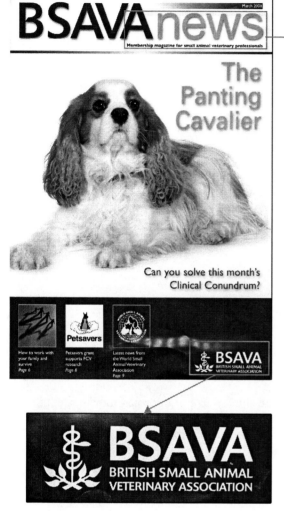

When an initialism or acronym is part of the title proper, an added entry is made to spell out the initialism. In this example, the title *BSAVA News* comes from the cover, which serves as the chief source of information. BSAVA stands for British Small Animal Veterinary Association. Because the catalog user may search this publication under the full form, *British Small Animal Veterinary Association News* is given as a variant title in field 246, with the first indicator value 3, indicating no note is needed for the added entry, and the second indicator value blank, indicating no display constant needs to be generated to specify the type of title recorded in the field 246.

If the initialism in the title proper does not contain spacing or separating punctuation, as in this example, a 246-derived title added entry with spacing or separating punctuation is normally not necessary. However, if an initialism occurs as one of the first five words in the title proper, with spacing or separating punctuation, it is a good idea to make a 246-derived title added entry without spacing or any separating punctuation if it is thought that some catalog users might expect that the letters would be recorded in that form in the source (LCRI 21.30J).

On the cover, the subtitle Membership *Magazine for Small Animal Veterinary Professionals* also appears under the title proper *BSAVA News*. It can either be ignored or be recorded in the 500 field if considered important. It is not transcribed as other title information in the 245 field. This is because the serials subtitle is usually unstable and tends to change.

AACR2 12.1E1 limits the use of other title information recorded in the title and statement of responsibility area to three situations, one of which is when an acronym or initialism of the title appears on the chief source of information with the full form of the title. In CSR practice, it is not required to record in the title and statement of responsibility area other title information appearing on the serial issue used as the basis of the description. However, an acronym or initialism of the title proper should always be recorded in a 246 field.

OCLC #227147847

Type a	ELvl I	Srce d	GPub	Ctrl	Lang eng
BLvl s	Form	Conf 0	Freq u	MRec	Ctry enk
S/L 0	Orig	EntW	Regl u	Alph a	
Desc a	SrTp	Cont	DtSt d	Dates 200u	, 2008

CCM 6.1.3	245	0 0	BSAVA news.	AACR2 12.1B1
7.2.3	246	3	British Small Animal Veterinary Association news	LCRI 21.30J
	260		Gloucester, England : ‡b British Small Animal Veterinary Association	
	300		v. : ‡b ill. ; ‡c 30 cm.	
	500		Description based on: March 2008; title from cover.	
6.3.4	500		"Membership magazine for Small Animal Veterinary professionals."	12.7B6.1
	610	2 0	British Small Animal Veterinary Association ‡v Periodicals.	
	650	0	Veterinary medicine ‡z Great Britain ‡v Periodicals.	
	710	2	British Small Animal Veterinary Association.	
	785	0 0	‡t Companion ‡w (DLC) 2008222326 ‡w (OCoLC)226297491	
	856	4 1	‡u http://www.blackwell-synergy.com/loi/jsap	

AACR2

12.1B1 - Transcribe the title proper as instructed in 1.1B

1.1B1 - Transcribe the title proper exactly as to wording, order, and spelling, but not necessarily as to punctuation and capitalization . . . Capitalize according to appendix A

12.1E1 - Always transcribe or supply other title information if it falls within one of the categories below:
   a. If an acronym or initialism of the title appears in the chief source of information with the full form of the title, transcribe the acronym or initialism as other title information
   b. If a statement of responsibility or the name of a publisher, distributor, etc., is an integral part of the other title information, transcribe it as such
   c. If the title proper consists solely of the name of a corporate body, conference, etc., supply a brief addition in the language of the title proper as other title information to explain the title.

If other title information has not been transcribed in the title and statement of responsibility area, give it in a note (see 12.7B6.1) or ignore it

12.7B6.1 - Make notes on other title information not recorded in the title and statement of responsibility area if considered to be important

LCRI

21.30J - When a series of letters or an initialism occurs as one of the first five words filed on in a title proper, apply the following: (1) With separating punctuation. If the transcription shows separating punctuation, make a 246-derived title added entry in the form without any separating punctuation if it is thought that some catalog users might expect that the letters would be recorded in that form in the source. (2) Without spacing or separating punctuation. If the transcription does not show spacing or separating punctuation, normally do not make a 246-derived title added entry with spacing or separating punctuation

RDA

2.3.1.4 -Transcribe a title as it appears on the source of information. Apply the general guidelines on transcription given under 1.7

2.3.6.3 - Record variant titles that are considered to be important for identification or access applying the basic instructions on recording titles given under 2.3.1

CCM

6.1.3 - Transcribe the title as it appears on the chief source of information

6.3.4 - Other title information that may be transcribed in the title statement, given as a note, or omitted

7.2.3 - If the title proper or a variant title contains words that the user might search in a different form, give a 246 field using the variant form

Omission in Title Proper and Running Title as Variant Title

Title: Variety international film guide

Cover   Title Page   Running Title

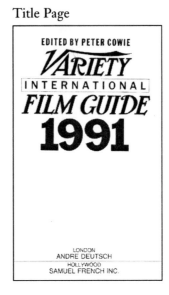

Although the title proper should be transcribed exactly as it appears on the chief source of information, some exceptions do exist. Such information as numbers or dates that vary from issue to issue should be omitted from the title statement, and be replaced with an ellipsis depending on where the omission occurs (AACR2 12.1B7). If the omission occurs at the beginning of a title, do not use an ellipsis; likewise, if it occurs at the end, do not use an ellipsis unless the date or number omitted was grammatically linked to the rest of the title (CCM 6.1.7a). If numbering occurs at the end of the title proper without a linking word, it is not considered as part of the title proper (LCRI 12.1B7); therefore, a mark of omission is not necessary. In this example, *Variety International Film Guide* is the title proper, while 1991 constitutes the issue's designation and is omitted from the title statement.

Sometimes, a serial publication may have titles elsewhere on the piece that are different from the title appearing on the chief source of information. Variant titles may include cover title, caption title, spine title, running title, parallel title, etc. If it is possible that the serial might be known and searched by the variant form, a note and an added entry should be generally given (AACR2 21.30J2).

In this example, the serial has the running title *International Film Guide*. A running title is a title or an abbreviated title that is repeated at the head or foot of each page or leaf in a publication (AACR2). Making the running title an added entry is important. For example, a user might have a copy of an article in PDF format in which the title of the serial occurs only at the foot of the page and might search for the serial using this title.

When coding variant titles in the 246 field, a cataloger should code the indicators correctly. The first indicator 1 used here means that a note and an added entry are made for the variant title, and the second indicator specifies the type of the variant title: 7 for running title; blank for no type specified; 0 for portion of title; 1 for parallel title; 2 for distinctive title; 3 for other title; 4 for cover title; 5 for added title page title; 6 for caption title; and 8 for spine title.

OCLC #20871480

Type a	ELvl	Srce d	GPub	Ctrl	Lang eng
BLvl s	Form	Conf 0	Freq a	MRec	Ctry enk
S/L 0	Orig	EntW	Regl r	Alph	
Desc a	SrTp	Cont	DtSt d	Dates 1990	, 2006

	022	0		0963-5769 ‡2 2	
	042			lc	
	210	0		Var. int. film guide	
	222		0	Variety international film guide	
CCM 6.1.7	245	0	0	Variety international film guide.	AACR2 LCRI 12.1B7
7.2.2d	246	1	7	International film guide	21.30J2
	260			London : ‡b Andre Deutsch ; ‡a Hollywood : ‡b Samuel French, ‡c c1989-c2006.	
	300			17 v. : ‡b ill. (some col.) ; ‡c 21-25 cm.	
	310			Annual	
	362	0		1990-2006.	
	500			Imprint varies.	
	580			Another ed. is published 2005-2006 in London by Button under title: The Guardian international film guide.	
	650		0	Motion pictures ‡v Periodicals.	
	730	0		Guardian international film guide.	
	775	1		‡t Guardian international film guide ‡w (DLC) 2005248120 ‡w (OCoLC)60692540	
	780	0	0	‡t International film guide ‡x 0074-6053 ‡w (DLC) 64001076 ‡w (OCoLC)1586325	
	785	0	0	‡t International film guide ‡w (DLC) 2008242081 ‡w (OCoLC) 219623127	

AACR2

12.1B1 - Transcribe the title proper as instructed in 1.1B

1.1B1 - Transcribe the title proper exactly as to wording, order, and spelling, but not necessarily as to punctuation and capitalization . . . Capitalize according to appendix A

12.1B7 - For serials, if the title includes a date, name, number, etc., that varies from issue to issue, omit this date, name, number, etc., and replace it by the mark of omission, unless it occurs at the beginning of the title, in which case do not give the mark of omission

21.30J2 - If considered necessary for access, make an added entry for any version of the title (e.g., cover title, caption title, running title, panel title, title on container, title bar title) that is significantly different from the title proper

LCRI

12.1B7 - If numbering occurs at the end of the title proper without a linking word, do not consider it as part of the title proper

(Continued on next page)

RDA

2.3.1.4 - If a title of a serial includes a date, name, number, etc., that varies from issue to issue, omit this date, name, number, etc.

2.3.6.3 - Record variant titles that are considered to be important for identification or access applying the basic instructions on recording titles given under 2.3.1

CCM

6.1.3 - Transcribe the title as it appears on the chief source of information

6.1.7 - Omit information that is specific to one or several issues. Such information includes designations (i.e., numbers or dates) that vary from issue to issue and names of persons that are likely to change on a frequent basis

7.2.2d - Make an added entry for a running title (i.e., one that appears at the head or foot of each page) if it differs from the title proper as it may be an important access point. The second indicator "7" identifies the variant as a running title

Creative Presentation of Title Proper

Title: T/here

Cover   Title Page

   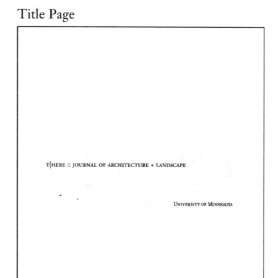

The presentation of this journal title is very interesting, in that the single word in the title—
T|here—is the combination of two words: there and here. As the title proper, *T|here* is transcribed exactly
as it appears in the 245 field based on the information from the title page.

However, because of the layout and the typography of the title *T|here* on the title page and on the cover, it
is possible that a user might search the title in a different form—either as *There* or *Here*. To provide access to
these variant forms, it is necessary to make added entries for these forms in the 246 fields, just like such access
is given for spelled-out forms of abbreviations, initialisms, or acronyms, as discussed in earlier examples.

Publishers can sometimes be very creative with titles, and LCRI 21.30J lists the situations in which added
entries may be given. But if you come across a situation not listed, the LCRI says, "When in doubt, be liberal
in making additional title added entries." So, keep the user in mind when cataloging serials publications. The
rules may not cover every situation, but as long as our goal is to provide and improves access for the user, that
should serve as our guide. The transcription of the subtitle *Journal of Architecture + Landscape* is another
example of this. Although it is not required to record, in the title and statement of responsibility area, other
title information appearing on the serial issue used as the basis of the description—in this example, the subtitle *Journal of Architecture + Landscape*—is transcribed as other title information because it provides important information about the title proper.

OCLC #66527461

	Type a	ELvl I	Srce d	GPub	Ctrl	Lang eng
	BLvl s	Form	Conf 0	Freq a	MRec	Ctry mnu
	S/L 0	Orig	EntW	Regl r	Alph	
	Desc a	SrTp	Cont	DtSt c	Dates 2005	, 9999

CCM 6.1.3	245	0	0	T/here : ‡b journal of architecture + landscape.	AACR2 12.1B1 12.1E1
7.2.2	246	1	4	There : ‡b journal of architecture and landscape	21.30J2
7.2.1	246	3	0	There	LCRI 21.30J
7.2.1	246	1	3	Here	LCRI 21.30J
	260			Minneapolis, Minn. : ‡b College of Architecture and Landscape	
	300			v. : ‡b ill. (some col.), plans ; ‡c 26 cm.	
	310			Annual	
	362	0		-2005	
	650		0	Architecture ‡v Periodicals.	
	650		0	Landscape architecture ‡v Periodicals.	
	650		0	Landscape architecture ‡z Minnesota ‡v Periodicals.	
	710	2		University of Minnesota. ‡b College of Architecture and Lands.	

AACR2

12.1B1 - Transcribe the title proper as instructed in 1.1B

1.1B1 - Transcribe the title proper exactly as to wording, order, and spelling, but not necessarily as to punctuation and capitalization ... Capitalize according to appendix A

12.1E1 - Transcribe other title information as instructed in 1.1E if considered to be important

21.30J2 - If considered necessary for access, make an added entry for any version of the title (e.g., cover title, caption title, running title, panel title, title on container, title bar title) that is significantly different from the title proper

LCRI

12.1E - CONSER standard record practice: It is not required to record, in the title and statement of responsibility area, other title information appearing on the serial issue used as the basis of the description. Always record an acronym or initialism of the title proper in a 246 field. Other title information which is not an acronym or initialism may be recorded in the 246 field if considered important for access

21.30J - If a title proper contains data within the first five words filed on for which there could be an alternate form that would be filed differently, make a 246-derived title added entry under that form if it is thought that some users of the catalog might reasonably expect that form to be given in the source

RDA

2.3.1.4 - Transcribe a title as it appears on the source of information. Apply the general guidelines on transcription given under 1.7

2.3.6.3 - Record variant titles that are considered to be important for identification or access applying the basic instructions on recording titles given under 2.3.1

CCM

6.1.3 - Transcribe the title as it appears on the chief source of information

7.2.1 - Give access to a portion of the title when a user might consider this portion to be the title proper or when access to the portion will improve the overall retrievability of the record

7.2.2 - Make added entries for cover titles, parallel titles, and added title page titles when they are significantly different from the title proper

Parallel Title

Title: Canadian university music review = ‡b Revue de musique des universités canadiennes

Cover

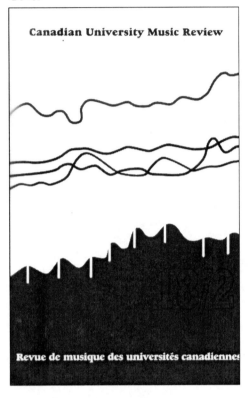

A parallel title is the title proper in another language and/or script (AACR2 Appendix D [Glossary]). When transcribing parallel titles, transcribe them in the order indicated by their sequence on or by the layout of the chief source of information (AACR2 1.1D1).

In this example, the cover, which serves as the chief source of information, has two titles—one in English and one in French: *Canadian University Music Review* and *Revue de musique des universités canadiennes*. Because it appears first and on the top of the cover, the English title is recorded as the title proper, and the French title is recorded as the parallel title, for which an added entry is made to provide access.

When a cataloger codes in MARC, the English title is recorded in the 245 field subfield ‡a and the French title in subfield ‡b, preceded by a space, an equal sign (=), and another space. The French title is also input in the 246 field as the parallel title added entry, with indicators 11. The first indicator 1 generates the display of a note and provides an added entry, while the second indicator 1 is used to show that the added entry is for the parallel title.

If following the CSR approach, a cataloger is not required to transcribe parallel titles in 245 subfield ‡b. Parallel titles not chosen as the title proper are only to be recorded in field 246.

In this record, there are two fields showing that this serial publication is in English and French. The codes in the 041 field designate the languages of the content, and the first indictor 0 means that the work is not a translation. The 546 field provides a textual note about the languages of the described work.

OCLC #7936807

	Type a	ELvl	Srce d	GPub	Ctrl	Lang eng
	BLvl s	Form	Conf 0	Freq f	MRec	Ctry onc
	S/L 0	Orig	EntW	Regl x	Alph a	
	Desc a	SrTp	Cont o	DtSt d	Dates 1980	, 2004

022	0	0710-0353 ‡2 4	
041	0	eng ‡a fre	
042		lc ‡a nst ‡a nlc ‡a isds/c	
210	0	Can. univ. music rev.	
222		0	Canadian university music review

CCM						AACR2
6.4 6.1.4c	245	0	0	Canadian university music review = ‡b Revue de musique des universités canadiennes.		1.1B8 12.1D1
7.2.1e	246	1	1	Revue de musique des universités canadiennes		21.30J2

260		Ottawa : ‡b Canadian University Music Society = Société de musique des universités canadiennes, ‡c c1980-	
300		v. : ‡b ill., music ; ‡c 23 cm.	
310		2 no. a year, ‡b -2004	
362	0	1 (1980)-	
362	1	Ceased with no. 24/2 (2004).	
500		Title from cover.	
546		Text in English and French.	
650		0	Music ‡v Periodicals.
710	2	Canadian University Music Society.	
780	0	0	‡t Journal (Canadian Association of University Schools of Music) ‡x 0315-3541 ‡w (DLC) 72649890 ‡w (CaOONL) 82311149
785	0	0	‡t Intersections (Canadian University Music Society) ‡x 1911-0146 ‡w (DLC)ce2006301345 ‡w (OCoLC)71208123

AACR2

1.1B8 - If the chief source of information bears titles in two or more languages or scripts, transcribe as the title proper the one in the language or script of the main written, spoken, or sung content of the item. If this criterion is not applicable, choose the title proper by reference to the order of titles on, or the layout of, the chief source of information. Record the other titles as parallel titles (see 1.1D)

1.1D1 - Transcribe parallel titles in the order indicated by their sequence on, or by the layout of, the chief source of information

12.1D1 - Transcribe parallel titles as instructed in 1.1D

21.30J2 - If considered necessary for access, make an added entry for any version of the title (e.g., cover title, caption title, running title, panel title, title on container, title bar title) that is significantly different from the title proper

LCRI

21.30J - If a title in another language appears prominently on the publication, make a 246-derived title added entry for it

(Continued on next page)

RDA

2.3.3.3 - Record a parallel title proper applying the basic instructions on recording titles given under 2.3.1. If there is more than one parallel title proper, record the titles in the order indicated by the sequence, layout, or typography of the titles on the source or sources of information

CCM

6.1.4c - If a title is given on the chief source in more than one language, select as the title proper the title in the language that comprises the main portion of the serial (AACR2 1.1B8). If the text is equally divided or it is difficult to determine, choose the first title that appears on the piece. CONSER catalogers will most often apply the latter provision of the rule (i.e., choosing the title from the order given). However, in cases where the first title given is in a language not represented in the text (e.g., Latin or Greek), it is best to choose another title

6.4 - When the title on the chief source appears in two or more languages, one is chosen as the title proper (AACR2 1.1B8; see CCM 6.1.4.c); the remaining titles are parallel titles (AACR2 1.1D1)

7.2.1e - Give an added entry for parallel titles appearing in the title statement or in a note, supplying a separate 246 field for each with second indicator value set to "1"

Parallel Title With Parallel Section Title

Title: FAO yearbook. ‡p Fishery and aquaculture statistics = ‡b FAO annuaire. Statistiques des peches et de l'aquaculture = FAO anuario. Estadísticas de pesca y acuicultura

Title Page

This serial publication is more complicated than the previous example because it has not only more than one parallel title, but it also has a parallel common title and a parallel section title.

The text of this serial is in English, French, and Spanish. Based on the layout of the title page, the English title *FAO Yearbook* is chosen as the title proper, as it appears first on the chief source (AACR2 1.1B8). It is followed by the section title *Fishery and Aquaculture Statistics*, preceded by a period. The full title proper is then followed by an equal sign and the parallel common title in French—*FAO Annuaire*—with its corresponding section title: *Statistiques des pêches et de l'aquaculture*. This, in turn, is followed by another equal sign and the parallel common title in Spanish—*FAO anuario*—with its own section title: *Estadísticas de pesca y acuicultura.*

Added entries for the parallel French and Spanish common titles and their respective section titles are made, and they are recorded in separate 246 fields, with the first indicator 3 to suppress the display of the note but generate an added entry and with the second indicator 1 for parallel titles:

246 31   FAO annuaire. ‡p Statistiques des pêches et de l'aquaculture

246 31   FAO anuario. ‡p Estadísticas de pesca y acuicultura

If considered important for access, added entries can also be made for the section title and the parallel section title. The first indicator is set to 3 so no note is generated; the second indicator is set to 0 to indicate that access is for a portion of the title:

246 30   Fishery and aquaculture statistics

246 30   Statistiques des peches et de l'aquaculture

246 30   Estadísticas de pesca y acuicultura

Note that 246 fields do not end with a period. Moreover, in the 245 field, subfield ‡p is used for the section title, and it is preceded by a period when following the common title. However, subfield ‡p is not repeated for the parallel section title. All parallel common titles and parallel section titles are input in subfield ‡b as the other title information following the title proper, and subfield ‡b is not repeatable:

245 00   FAO yearbook. ‡p Fishery and aquaculture statistics = ‡b FAO annuaire. Statistiques des peches et de l'aquaculture = FAO anuario. Estadísticas de pesca y acuicultura.

OCLC #301810348

Type a	ELvl	Srce	GPub i	Ctrl	Lang eng	
BLvl s	Form	Conf 0	Freq a	MRec	Ctry it	
S/L 0	Orig	EntW s	Regl r	Alph		
Desc a	SrTp	Cont	DtSt c	Dates 2006	, 9999	

	022		2070-6057 ‡2 0	
	042		lcd	
	041	0	eng ‡a fre ‡a spa	
CCM 6.4 6.6.2c	245	0 0	FAO yearbook. ‡p Fishery and aquaculture statistics = ‡b FAO annuaire. Statistiques des peches et de l'aquaculture = FAO anuario. Estadísticas de pesca y acuicultura.	AACR2 1.1B8 12.1D2
7.2.1c	246	3 0	Fishery and aquaculture statistics	21.30J2
7.2.1c	246	3 0	Statistiques des peches et de l'aquaculture	21.30J2
7.2.1c	246	3 0	Estadísticas de pesca y acuicultura	21.30J2
7.2.1e	246	3 1	FAO annuaire. ‡p Statistiques des peches et de l'aquaculture	21.30J2
7.2.1e	246	3 1	FAO anuario. ‡p Estadísticas de pesca y acuicultura	21.30J2
	260		Rome : ‡b FAO, ‡c 2008-	
	300		v. : ‡b maps (some fold.) ; ‡c 30 cm.	
	362	0	2006-	
	546		English, French, and Spanish.	
	588		Description based on: 2006; title from title page.	
	588		Latest issue consulted: 2008.	
	650	0	Fisheries ‡v Statistics ‡v Periodicals.	
	710	2	FAO Fisheries and Aquaculture Dept. ‡b Fishery and Aquaculture Information and Statistics Service.	
	780	0 0	‡t FAO yearbook. Fishery statistics ‡w (DLC) 89648510 ‡w (OCoLC) 20000254	

AACR2

1.1B8 - If the chief source of information bears titles in two or more languages or scripts, transcribe as the title proper the one in the language or script of the main written, spoken, or sung content of the item. If this criterion is not applicable, choose the title proper by reference to the order of titles on, or the layout of, the chief source of information. Record the other titles as parallel titles (see 1.1D)

1.1D1 - Transcribe parallel titles in the order indicated by their sequence on, or by the layout of, the chief source of information

12.1D1 - Transcribe parallel titles as instructed in 1.1D

12.1D2 - If, in the case of a resource with a title proper made up of a title common to a number of sections and a section title, the common title has a parallel title and the section title has a parallel title, give the common title and the section title that make up the title proper followed by the parallel common title and the parallel section title (see 12.1B4)

21.30J2 - If considered necessary for access, make an added entry for any version of the title (e.g., cover title, caption title, running title, panel title, title on container, title bar title) that is significantly different from the title proper

RDA

2.3.3.3 - Record a parallel title proper applying the basic instructions on recording titles given under 2.3.1. If there is more than one parallel title proper, record the titles in the order indicated by the sequence, layout, or typography of the titles on the source or sources of information

CCM

6.4 - When the title on the chief source appears in two or more languages, one is chosen as the title proper (AACR2 1.1B8; see CCM 6.1.4.c); the remaining titles are parallel titles (AACR2 1.1D1)

6.6.2c - Transcribe the common title and section title that constitute the title proper followed by the parallel common titles and section titles, based on the guidelines in AACR2 1.1D2

7.2.1c - When the title proper consists of a common title and section title, give the section title in a 246 field when the title is distinctive and will provide useful access

7.2.1e - Give an added entry for parallel titles appearing in the title statement or in a note, supplying a separate 246 field for each with second indicator value set to "1"

Title Added Entry Derived From 246 Field With Subfield ‡i

Title: Intersections

Title Page

For various reasons, a serial publication may contain additional titles that differ from the title on the chief source of information. These include cover titles, running titles, spine titles, caption titles, etc. Because it is possible that a user will search the serial under those variant names, added entries should be made for them to provide access.

In MARC, 246 fields with appropriate indicators are used to record variant titles, (e.g., 246 with 14 as indicators). The first indicator 1 serves two functions: First, it means that the system can generate a note, with the content of the note based on the second indicator; second, it means that the title is searchable as an access point. The second indicator determines the content of the display note— in this case. with a value of 4 for cover title.

In MARC, only the following indicator values have been defined for the second indicator: blank for no type specified; 0 for portion of title; 1 for parallel title; 2 for distinctive title; 3 for other title; 4 for cover title; 5 for added title page title; 6 for caption title; 7 for running title; and 8 for spine title.

If a situation arises that a print constant is needed but is not defined as above, a cataloger can construct a special note in subfield ‡i of the 246 field in the form of:

246 1 ‡i Explanatory note provided by the cataloger:
        ‡a Title

When using subfield ‡i, the first indicator value 1 is always used to generate an added entry, and subfield ‡i is used for a cataloger-supplied text to specify the source or the type of the title. The second indicator value is blank.

In this example, the serial *Intersections* still carries its earlier English title—*Canadian University Music Review*—and its French title—*Revue de musique des universités canadiennes*—on the front cover, and a cataloger has provided notes about them and made added entries for them:

246 1 ‡i Title from verso of front cover: ‡a Canadian university music review
246 1 ‡i Parallel title from verso of front cover: ‡a Revue de musique des universités canadiennes

In this way, a cataloger has the flexibility to create a note that can be better understood by a user.

OCLC #71208123

Type a	ELvl	Srce d	GPub	Ctrl	Lang eng
BLvl s	Form	Conf 0	Freq f	MRec	Ctry onc
S/L 0	Orig	EntW	Regl x	Alph a	
Desc a	SrTp p	Cont o	DtSt c	Dates 2005	, 9999

	022	0		1911-0146 ‡y 0710-0353
	037			‡b Becker Associates, Box 507, Station Q, Toronto, ON M4T 2M5 ‡c Free to members (Membership $50.00, individuals; $25.00, students, independent scholars, retirees).
	041	0		eng ‡a fre
	042			nlc ‡a isds/c ‡a lc
	043			n-cn—
	130	0		Intersections (Canadian University Music Society)
	222		0	Intersections ‡b (Toronto. 2006)

CCM 6.3.4	245	1	0	Intersections : ‡b Canadian journal of music = Revue canadienne de musique.	AACR2 12.1E1
7.2.2	246	1		‡i Title from verso of front cover: ‡a Canadian university music review	12.7B4.1 21.30J2
7.2.2	246	1		‡i Parallel title from verso of front cover: ‡a Revue de musique des universités canadiennes	LCRI 21.30J

260		Toronto : ‡b Becker Associates [for the] Canadian University Music Society = Becker Associates [pour la] Société de musique des universités canadiennes, ‡c c2005-
300		v. : ‡b ill. ; music ; ‡c 23 cm.
310		Semiannual (irregular)
362	0	No. 25 1/2 (2005)-
500		Title from cover.
546		Text in English and French.
650	0	Music ‡v Periodicals.
650	0	Music ‡z Canada ‡v Periodicals.
710	2	Canadian University Music Society.
780	0 0	‡t Canadian university music review. ‡x 0710-0353 ‡w (DLC) 83642314 ‡w (CaOONL) 820390291 ‡w (OCoLC)7936807

AACR2

12.1E1 - Transcribe other title information as instructed in 1.1E if considered to be important

12.7B4.1 - Make notes on titles other than the title proper borne by the resource, and changes to such titles, if considered to be important

21.30J2 - If considered necessary for access, make an added entry for any version of the title (e.g., cover title, caption title, running title, panel title, title on container, title bar title) that is significantly different from the title proper

LCRI

21.30J - If the source of the varying title recorded in a 246 field is not one of those represented by values 4-8, the source may be explicitly recorded in an ‡i subfield that precedes the title data

(Continued on next page)

RDA

2.3.6.3 - Record variant titles that are considered to be important for identification or access applying the basic instructions on recording titles given under 2.3.1

CCM

6.3.4 - Use judgment when considering whether to include other title information in the record

7.2.2 - In general, give a variant title when:

    (a) it differs substantially from the title proper

    (b) it contributes to the identification of the serial

    (c) it provides meaningful access (e.g., it provides a useful search in the online database)

    (d) it is located prominently and likely to be searched as the title

Cover

EXERCISE 1

Transcribe the title as found on the cover and then create a variant title as appropriate. Make sure the indicators in the 245 and 246 fields are set correctly.

OCLC #214284010

Type a	ELvl	Srce d	GPub	Ctrl	Lang eng
BLvl s	Form	Conf 0	Freq q	MRec	Ctry nyu
S/L 0	Orig	EntW	Regl r	Alph a	
Desc a	SrTp p	Cont	DtSt c	Dates 2008	, 9999

022		1946-4606 ‡y 0199-8986 ‡2 1
042		lcd ‡a nsdp
245		
246		
260		New York : ‡b Human Resource Planning Society
300		v. : ‡b ill. ; ‡c 28 cm.
310		Quarterly
362	1	Began with Vol. 31, issue 1 (2008).
500		Description based on first issue; title from cover.
650	0	Manpower planning ‡v Periodicals.
650	0	Personnel management ‡v Periodicals.
710	2	Human Resource Planning Society.
780	0 0	‡t Human resource planning ‡x 0199-8986 ‡w (DLC)sn 80009179 ‡w (OCoLC) 6281631

Screenshot – Journal Homepage

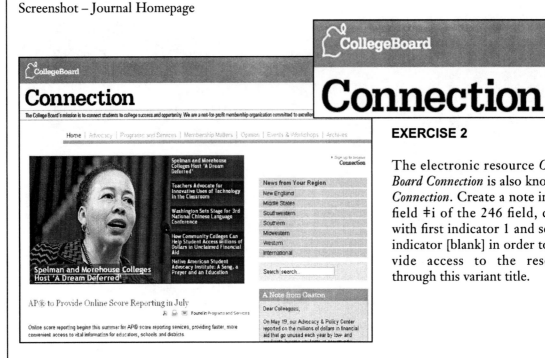

EXERCISE 2

The electronic resource *College Board Connection* is also known as *Connection*. Create a note in subfield ‡i of the 246 field, coded with first indicator 1 and second indicator [blank] in order to provide access to the resource through this variant title.

OCLC #190663506

Type a	ELvl	Srce c	GPub	Ctrl	Lang eng
BLvl s	Form s	Conf 0	Freq m	MRec	Ctry nyu
S/L 0	Orig s	EntW	Regl r	Alph a	
Desc a	SrTp p	Cont	DtSt c	Dates 2007	, 9999

042		lcd
245	0 0	College Board connection ‡h [electronic resource].
246		
260		New York, N.Y. : ‡b College Board, ‡c 2007-
310		Monthly
362	1	Began with Nov. 2007.
500		Description based on first issue; title from contents screen (CollegeBoard, viewed June 17, 2008).
500		Latest issue consulted: May 2008, viewed June 17, 2008. (CollegeBoard, viewed Jul. 10, 2008).
520		"Connection replaces our printed member newsletters and various online communications."
538		Mode of access: World Wide Web.
650	0	Universities and colleges ‡z United States ‡x Examinations ‡v Periodicals.
650	0	Universities and colleges ‡z United States ‡v Periodicals.
650	0	Universities and colleges ‡z United States ‡x Entrance requirements ‡v Periodicals.
710	2	College Entrance Examination Board.
780	0 0	‡t College Board review ‡x 0010-0951 ‡w (DLC) 56046771 ‡w (OCoLC)1564050
856	4 0	‡u http://www.connection-collegeboard.com

Screenshot – Journal Homepage

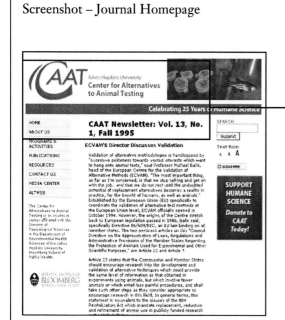

EXERCISE 3

There are two other ways the electronic publication *CAAT Newsletter* may be known or searched. Make added entries for the two variant titles to facilitate user access to the newsletter. Make sure to use the appropriate indicators.

OCLC #225581330

Type a	ELvl 4	Srce d	GPub	Ctrl	Lang eng
BLvl s	Form s	Conf 0	Freq t	MRec	Ctry mdu
S/L 0	Orig	EntW	Regl x	Alph a	
Desc a	SrTp p	Cont	DtSt c	Dates 1995	, 9999

245	0	0	CAAT newsletter ‡h [electronic resource].
246			
246			
260			[Baltimore, Md.] : ‡b Center for Alternatives to Animal Testing, ‡c 1995-
300			v. : ‡b ill. ; ‡c 28 cm.
310			Three times a year, ‡b <fall 1995–summer 1997>
362	0		Vol. 13, no. 1 (fall 1995)-
500			Only recent and archived issues (fall 1995-winter/spring 1998) available online.
500			Title from journal home page (The Center's Web site, viewed April 17, 2008)
538			System requirements: Internet connection ; Adobe Acrobat reader.
580			Beginning in 1998, CAAT newsletter is only available online.
650		0	Animal welfare ‡v Periodicals.
650		0	Vivisection ‡v Periodicals.
650		0	Toxicology, Experimental ‡v Periodicals.
650		0	Animal experimentation ‡v Periodicals.
650		2	Animal Testing Alternatives ‡v Periodicals.
710	2		Johns Hopkins Center for Alternatives to Animal Testing.
780	1	0	‡i Print version : ‡t Johns Hopkins Center for Alternatives to Animal Testing ‡x 1058-112X ‡w (OCoLC)11810216
856	4	0	‡3 Full text ‡u http://caat.jhsph.edu/publications/newsletter/index.htm
856	4	2	‡z Alternatives to Animal Testing Web site ‡u http:// altweb.jhsph.edu

Title Page

OCLC #77500752

EXERCISE 4

The title on this title page can be interpreted several ways. Think about the various options and then create alternate titles based on the information on the title page. Code the indicator values in the 246 field as appropriate.

Type a	ELvl	Srce c	GPub	Ctrl	Lang eng
BLvl s	Form	Conf 0	Freq f	MRec	Ctry ilu
S/L 0	Orig	EntW	Regl r	Alph a	
Desc a	SrTp p	Cont	DtSt c	Dates 2007	, 9999

022	0	1935-2743 ‡2 1
037		‡b University of Illinois Press, 1325 S. Oak St., Champaign IL 61820
042		nsdp ‡a lc
245	0 0	Black women, gender + families.
246		
246		
246		
260		Champaign, IL : ‡b University of Illinois Press
310		Semiannual
362	1	Began with: Vol. 1, no. 1 (spring 2007).
500		Description based on first issue; title from cover.
650	0	African American women ‡v Periodicals.
650	0	African American women ‡x Social conditions ‡v Periodicals.
650	6	Noires américaines ‡v Périodiques.
650	6	Noires américaines ‡x Conditions sociales ‡v Périodiques.
710	2	National Council for Black Studies (U.S.)
710	2	University of Illinois at Urbana-Champaign. ‡b Afro-American Studies and Research Program.
776	0 8	‡i Online version: ‡t Black women, gender & families ‡x 1944-6462 ‡w (DLC) 2008216364 ‡w (OCoLC)277050143

Cover

Canadian Journal for Traditional Music
Revue de musique folklorique canadienne

Published by The Canadian Society for Traditional Music
Publiée par La Société canadienne pour les traditions musicales

Volume 29   2002

OCLC #37846813

EXERCISE 5

The publication Canadian Journal for Traditional Music also has a parallel title in French: Revue de musique folklorique canadienne. Create an added entry for the parallel title.

Type a	ELvl	Srce c	GPub	Ctrl	Lang eng
BLvl s	Form	Conf 0	Freq a	MRec	Ctry abc
S/L 0	Orig	EntW	Regl r	Alph a	
Desc a	SrTp	Cont	DtSt d	Dates 1996	, 2006

022	0		1485-4422 ‡l 1485-4422 ‡y 0318-2568 ‡2 4
041	0		eng ‡b fre
042			pcc ‡a nlc ‡a isds/c
043			n-cn—
245	0	0	Canadian journal for traditional music = ‡b Revue de musique folklorique canadienne.
246			
260			Calgary : ‡b Canadian Society for Musical Traditions, ‡c 1996-2006.
300			10 v. : ‡b ill., music ; ‡c 23 cm.
310			Annual
362	1		Began with Vol. 24 (1996); ceased with vol. 33 (2006).
546			Includes some text in French.
588			Description based on: Vol. 24 (1996); title from cover.
588			Latest issue consulted: Vol. 33 (2006).
650		0	Folk music ‡z Canada ‡v Periodicals.
650		6	Musique folklorique ‡z Canada ‡v Périodiques.
710	2		Canadian Society for Traditional Music.
776	0	8	‡i Online version: ‡t Canadian journal for traditional music (Online) ‡w (OCoLC)63109630
780	0	0	‡t Canadian folk music journal ‡x 0318-2568 ‡w (DLC) 75643795 ‡w (OCoLC)2241418
785	0	0	‡t MUSICultures ‡x 1920-4213 ‡w (OCoLC)458291425 ‡w (DLC) 2009236585
776	0	8	‡i Online version: ‡t Canadian journal for traditional music ‡w (OCoLC)619573260
856	4	1	‡u http://cjtm.icaap.org/

Notes

CHAPTER 2

Title Changes

Because serials are issued on a continuing basis, it is not surprising that they tend to undergo changes in titles, issuing body/publisher, publication frequency, numbering designation, and, more frequently, format. Among these changes, title changes are the most important because the treatment of a title change determines whether a new description is needed. In this chapter, we will explain the differences between major and minor title changes for serials, and we will discuss how to catalog them. Examples with explanations will be included as well as practice exercises. Other changes in serials will be discussed in different chapters throughout this book.

In the serials world, change is the norm. Although some serials live "an orderly life," others go through such changes as mergers and splits. This contributes to the never-ending nature of serials cataloging. Not only do new serials in print or online formats continuously arrive and need to be cataloged, existing titles return to a cataloger's desk for additional work. When a title change occurs, the first thing a serial cataloger must do is to determine whether the title change is major or minor. But what constitutes a major change or a minor change in the title proper of a serial?

AACR2 21.2C provides definitions of major and minor title changes for serials and gives guidance on what to do when there is a major change in the serial title proper. 21.2C2a says:

> In general, consider as a major change in a title proper of a serial the addition, deletion, change, or reordering of any of the first five words (the first six words if the title begins with an article) unless the change belongs to one or more of the categories listed in 21.2C2b. Consider also as a major change the addition, deletion, or change of any word after the first five words (the first six words if the title begins with an article) that changes the meaning of the title or indicates a different subject matter. Also consider as a major change in title proper a change in a corporate body name given anywhere in the title if it is a different corporate body.

According to AACR2 21.2C1: "If a major change occurs in the title proper of a serial, make a new entry." Similarly, RDA 1.6.2.3 states: "Create a new description if there is a major change in the title proper of a serial (see 2.3.2.12.2)."

For minor changes, a new description is not made. Instead, a note is given, and added entries are made for the later titles if considered important for access, such as the note:

245 00 ‡a Chronic disease notes & reports ‡h [electronic resource].
246 1# ‡i Some issues have title: ‡a Chronic diseases notes & reports

AACR2 21.2C2b (CCM 16.2.4) lists nine categories of minor changes—the first two categories of which are:

  i) a difference in the representation of a word or words anywhere in the title (e.g., one spelling vs. another; abbreviated word or sign or symbol vs. spelled-out form; etc.)

  ii) the addition, deletion, or change of articles, prepositions, or conjunctions anywhere in the title

RDA provides the same categories of minor changes, as listed in 2.3.2.13.2. In addition, RDA 2.3.8.1 introduces a new element—"later title proper"—which is defined as "a title proper appearing on a later issue or part of a multipart monograph or serial that differs from that on the first or earliest issue or part." For recording later titles proper, RDA 2.3.8.3 says: "Record a change in the title proper of a multipart monograph or a minor change in the title proper of a serial appearing on a later issue or part if it is considered to be important for identification or access. Apply the basic instructions on recording titles given under 2.3.1."

Once it has been determined that the situation does not belong to any of the exceptions listed in the nine categories and a major change has occurred, a new description is made. This practice, that a new entry record is to be made for each title change, is called the successive entry cataloging convention. It was adopted in AACR, has been continued in AACR2, and will be carried on in RDA, although in AACR, the description was based on the latest issue.

In many library catalogs and bibliographic utilities, such as the Online Computer Library Center (OCLC), pre-AACR records still exist for serials because in the history of serials cataloging, different cataloging conventions have been followed. For example, the American Library Association (ALA) rules called for latest entry cataloging (i.e., a serial record is cataloged under its latest title or issuing body). All earlier titles and/or issuing bodies are given in notes (fields 247, 547, and 550). The latest entry cataloging for serials was practiced until the publication of AACR cataloging rules in 1967, when successive entry convention was introduced (CCM 22.2).

Because catalogers today are working in a hybrid environment, where records they come across could have been created under earlier cataloging rules, it is helpful for them to be able to recognize those records when they see them. However they usually do not need to upgrade the records created under the earlier cataloging rules because it is not cost effective to do so.

In this chapter, examples are provided to illustrate what major and minor changes are and how these changes are treated. For major changes where a new description is made, examples are used to show how to create 780 and 785 linking fields with correct indicators and subfields. When appropriate, relevant rules are cited from AACR2, LCRI, RDA, and CCM.

RESOURCES CONSULTED

AACR2

12.1 Title and Statement of Responsibility Area

12.7B8 Bibliographic History and Relationships With Other Resources

21.2 Changes in Titles Proper

LCRI

21.3B Serials

RDA

1.6 Changes requiring a new description

2.3.2.12 Recording changes in the title proper

2.3.2.13 Major and minor changes in the title proper of serials

2.3.8 Later title proper

CCM

6 Title Statement (Field 245)

14 Linking Relationships (Fields 765–787, 580)

16.2 Title Changes

22 Interpreting pre-AACR2 Serial Cataloging Records

OCLC

Bibliographic Format and Standards: http://www.oclc.org/bibformats

Pre-AACR Record with Latest Entry Cataloging

Title: Tax facts & figures

Cover

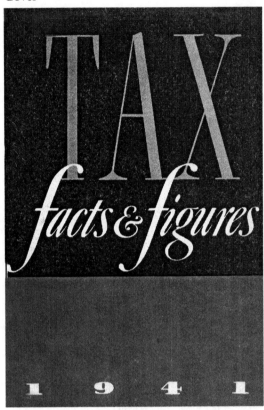

Title Page

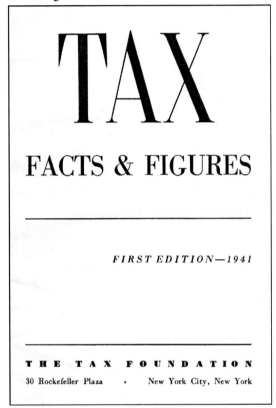

This serial publication has undergone three title changes: from *Tax Facts & Figures*, to *Facts and Figures on War Finance*, to *Facts and Figures on Government Finance*.

In the pre-AACR2 record created for this publication, the following points should be noted. First, Leader/18 Desc is coded blank, meaning the serial has not been cataloged according to International Standard Bibliographic Description (ISBD). Second, S/L entry convention in 008/34 is coded 1, meaning the record follows the practice of latest entry cataloging for serials under ALA rules. Third, the most current title is placed in the 245 field, and all the former titles are arranged in chronological order, with the earliest given at the top and later titles added beneath in separate 247 fields. Fourth, apart from the lack of ISBD punctuation, this record also shows the lack of a date in the 260 field and a different format of the designation in the 362 field.

When new cataloging rules are implemented, the standard practice is to not go back and update existing bibliographic records to conform to the new cataloging codes. Therefore, records created prior to AACR2 can be found in the OCLC database. Because serials catalogers are working in such a hybrid environment, it is beneficial to know what a pre-AACR2 record looks like. Catalogers performing record maintenance should continue with the existing practice.

OCLC #2144390

Type a	ELvl	Srce	GPub	Ctrl	Lang eng
BLvl s	Form	Conf 0	Freq a	MRec	Ctry dcu
S/L 1	Orig	EntW	Regl r	Alph a	
Desc	SrTp	Cont	DtSt d	Dates 1941	, 2004

022			0071-3678
043			n-us---
110	2		Tax Foundation.
222		0	Facts and figures on government finance
245	1	0	Facts and figures on government finance.
247	1	0	Tax facts & figures ǂf 1941
247	1	0	Facts and figures on war finance ǂf 1942
260			New York, ǂb Tax Foundation.
300			v. ǂb diagrs., tables. ǂc 23 cm.
310			Annual, ǂb <1992>-2004
321			Frequency varies, ǂb 1941-
362	0		[1st]-38th ed.; 1941-2004.
530			Also issued online.
650		0	World War, 1939-1945 ǂx Finance ǂz United States.
650		0	Finance, Public ǂz United States ǂx History ǂy 1933-
650		6	Finances publiques ǂz États-Unis.
710	2		Tax Foundation.
936			For CONSER successive entry record, see OCLC #04052798

Title Change: Continued by Later Title

Title: Harvard international journal of press/politics

Cover

Cover Verso

The **Harvard International Journal of Press/Politics** (ISSN 1081-180X) (J520) is published quarterly—Winter, Spring, Summer, and Fall—by Sage Publications, Thousand Oaks, CA 91320, USA. Copyright © 2007 by the President and the Fellows of Harvard College. All rights reserved. No portion of the contents may be reproduced in any form without written permission of the publisher. Periodicals postage is paid at Thousand Oaks, California, and at additional mailing offices.

The journal *The Harvard International Journal of Press/Politics* changed its name to *The International Journal of Press/Politics* in the fall of 2007. According to AACR2 and CCM guidelines, a change in the first five words of a serial's title is considered a major change; thus, a new record must be created for the new title. This is the successive entry cataloging convention.

While publishers often provide a library with advance notice that a title change is coming, there will no doubt be instances where a cataloger or library staff member will notice that an unanticipated change has occurred. If the change is major, a new record is created. The existing record should be updated and closed off, with the 785 field providing a link to the new record.

This example illustrates the changes made when closing the existing record. The example immediately following this one provides instructions for creating the new record. When closing the record, the following changes are made:

First, in the fixed fields, MARC 21 element type/position 008/06 DtSt, or publication status, is changed from "c" to "d," meaning the publication has ceased or has been continued by a different title. Date 1/Date 2 in 008/07-14 positions show the beginning and ending dates of the serial, and they should match the coverage dates recorded in the 362 fields, which are 1996 and 2007 in this example, rather than the publication dates from the 260 field subfield ‡c, which are 1995 and 2007.

Second, in the 260 field, which contains the place of publication, publisher and/or distributor, and date of publication, subfield ‡c should be updated with the complete beginning and ending dates of publications: 1995–2007. If following CSR practice, a cataloger is not required to supply dates in 260 subfield ‡c.

Third, the 362 field, which contains the beginning and/or ending issue number and/or dates, should also be updated—either in a formatted style note or in an unformatted style note. In CSR, an unformatted 362 field with the first indicator 1 is always used, regardless of whether the first/last issue(s) is in hand. Because this record was created before the implementation of CSR guidelines, the formatted note with first indicator 0 appears in the record.

Fourth, because the serial *The Harvard International Journal of Press/Politics* is continued by *The International Journal of Press/Politics*, the name of the succeeding serial is recorded in the 785 succeeding entry field. The first indicator controls whether notes should be generated and displayed, while the second indicator defines the type of relationship between the two titles. Here, the first indicator 0 means the display constant is to be generated, and the second indicator 0 means the relationship of the two titles is of continuation (i.e., one title is continued by the succeeding title). The linking field should include the title, International Standard Serial Number (ISSN), Library of Congress Control Number (LCCN), and OCLC number of the succeeding title.

OCLC #31995961

Type a	ELvl	Srce d	GPub	Ctrl	Lang eng
BLvl s	Form	Conf 0	Freq q	MRec	Ctry cau
S/L 0	Orig	EntW	Regl r	Alph a	
Desc a	SrTp p	Cont	DtSt d	Dates 1996	, 2007

	022	0		1081-180X ǂ2 1	
	042			nsdp ǂa lc	
CCM 6.1.3	245	0	0	Harvard international journal of press/politics.	AACR2 12.1B1
	246	3		Press politics	
	260			Cambridge, MA : ǂb MIT Press, ǂc 1995-2007.	
	300			v. : ǂb ill. ; ǂc 23 cm.	
	310			Quarterly	
	362	0		Vol. 1, no. 1 (winter 1996)-v. 12, no. 4 (fall 2007).	
	500			Title from cover.	
	500			Final issue consulted.	
	530			Also issued online.	
	550			Published by: MIT Press, 1996-2000; Sage Publications, 2001-	
	650		0	Press and politics ǂv Periodicals.	
	710	2		Joan Shorenstein Center on the Press, Politics, and Public Policy.	
	776	1		ǂt Harvard international journal of press/politics (Online) ǂx 1531-328X ǂw (DLC)sn 99023448 ǂw (OCoLC)42899908	
14.2.1 16.2.3	785	0	0	ǂt International journal of press/politics ǂx 1940-1612 ǂw (DLC) 2007213329 ǂw (OCoLC)173275455	12.7B8a

AACR2

12.1B1 - Transcribe the title proper as instructed in 1.1B

1.1B1 - Transcribe the title proper exactly as to wording, order, and spelling, but not necessarily as to punctuation and capitalization . . . Capitalize according to appendix A

12.7B8a - Continuation. If a resource continues a previously published resource, give the name of the preceding resource. If a resource is continued by a subsequently published resource, give the name of the succeeding resource

RDA

2.3.2.7 - Record the title proper applying the basic instructions on recording titles given under 2.3.1

2.3.1.4 - Transcribe a title as it appears on the source of information. Apply the general guidelines on transcription given under 1.7

2.3.8.3 - For changes in the title proper, apply the instructions given under 2.3.2.12.1 for multipart monographs and 2.3.2.12.2 for serials

(Continued on next page)

CCM

6.1.3 - Transcribe the title as it appears on the chief source of information

14.2.1 - Continues/Continued by (Fields 780 X0/785 X0): serial A changes to serial B; serial A ceases to exist;
Numbering may continue or start over again (Note: The AACR2 optional provision to add the date to a continued by note is not used in CONSER records.)
Linking entry fields: Serial A: one 785 X0 field; Serial B: one 780 X0 field

16.2.3 - Major changes in title proper: a) the addition, deletion, change or reordering of any of the first five words (six if there is an initial article), unless the change belongs to one of the categories in AACR2 21.2C2b; b) Words are added, dropped or changed anywhere in the title that change the meaning of the title or indicate different subject matter; c) A major change occurs in the name of a corporate body recorded as part of the title proper (i.e., the change requires a new established name heading)

Title Change: Continues Earlier Title

Title: The international journal of press/politics

Cover

Cover Verso

The International Journal of Press/Politics (ISSN 1081-180X) (J520) is published quarterly—in January, April, July, and October—by Sage Publications, Thousand Oaks, CA 91320, USA. Copyright © 2008 Sage Publications. All rights reserved. No portion of the contents may be reproduced in any form without written permission of the publisher. Periodicals postage is paid at Thousand Oaks, California, and at additional mailing offices. POSTMASTER: Send address changes to The International Journal of Press/Politics, c/o Sage Publications, 2455 Teller Road, Thousand Oaks, CA 91320.

With its January 2008 issue, *The Harvard International Journal of Press/Politics* changed its title to *The International Journal of Press/Politics*, dropping "Harvard" from its original title. Because the deletion of "Harvard" occurred within the first five words of the title proper, this is a major change and thus necessitates a new record.

When a new description is made, attention should be given to the following (the preceeding example shows how the existing record should be updated when the title has ceased):

First, for fixed fields, MARC 21 element type/position 008/06 DtSt is coded with "c" for publication status because the serial is currently being published. Date 1/Date 2 in 008/07–14 positions show the beginning and ending dates of the serial. In this example, Date 1 is coded "2008," which is based on the chronological designation from the 362 field. Because the serial is currently being published, Date 2 is coded as "9999."

Second, the 260 field contains the imprint information: the place of publication, publisher and/or distributor, and date of publication. In this example, subfield ‡c is not coded because in the CSR, a cataloger is not required to supply dates in 260 subfield ‡c.

Third, since the adoption of CSR guidelines, only the unformatted 362 field with the first indicator 1 is used to record beginning and/or ending designations of a serial, regardless of whether the cataloger has the first/last issue(s) in hand.

Fourth, two 588 fields are used: one for the "description based on" (DBO) note and the other for the "latest issue consulted" (LIC) note. These notes are required in CSR. Moreover, the DBO note is usually combined with the source of title note in one 588 note. It should be pointed out that DBO and LIC notes were previously coded in 500 fields, and they can still be found in the OCLC database. For more information on notes, see Chapter 9.

Fifth, as the later title *The International Journal of Press/Politics* continues the former title *The Harvard International Journal of Press/Politics*, in the record for the new title, the 780 field is used to record the preceeding title, thus creating a link between the new title and the old title. The first indicator controls whether a display constant should be generated, while the second indicator defines the type of relationship between the two titles. Here, the first indicator 0 means the display constant is to be generated, and the second indicator 0 is used to show the relationship of the two titles is of continuation (i.e., the succeeding title continues the preceding title). The linking field should include the title, ISSN, LCCN, and OCLC number of the preceding title.

OCLC #173275455

Type a	ELvl	Srce c	GPub	Ctrl	Lang eng
BLvl s	Form	Conf 0	Freq q	MRec	Ctry cau
S/L 0	Orig	EntW	Regl r	Alph a	
Desc a	SrTp p	Cont	DtSt c	Dates 2008	, 9999

	022	0	1940-1612 ǂy 1081-180X ǂ2 1		
	042		lcd ǂa nsdp		
	210	0	Int. j. press/polit.		
	222	4	The international journal of press/politics		
CCM 16.2.3	245	0 4	The international journal of press/politics.		AACR2 12.1B8a 21.2C1 21.2C2a
	246	1 3	Press/politics		
	246	1 3	IJPP		
	260		Thousand Oaks, CA : ǂb Sage Publications		
	310		Quarterly		
	362	1	Began with Vol. 13, no. 1 (Jan. 2008).		
	588		Description based on first issue; title from cover.		
	588		Latest issue consulted: Vol. 13, no. 2 (Apr. 2008).		
	650	0	Press and politics ǂv Periodicals.		
	776	0 8	ǂi Also issued online: ǂt International journal of press/politics ǂx 1940-1620 ǂw (DLC) 2007213330 ǂw (OCoLC)173275503		
14.2.1	780	0 0	ǂt Harvard international journal of press/politics ǂx 1081-180X ǂw (DLC) 96656165 ǂw (OCoLC)31995961		12.7B8a

AACR2

21.2C1 - If a major change occurs in the title proper of a serial, make a new entry

21.2C2a - Major changes. In general, consider as a major change in a title proper of a serial the addition, deletion, change, or reordering of any of the first five words (the first six words if the title begins with an article) unless the change belongs to one or more of the categories listed in 21.2C2b. Consider also as a major change the addition, deletion, or change of any word after the first five words (the first six words if the title begins with an article) that changes the meaning of the title or indicates a different subject matter. Also consider as a major change in title proper a change in a corporate body name given anywhere in the title if it is a different corporate body

12.1B8a - Serials. If a major change in the title proper occurs, make a new description (see 21.2C). If a minor change occurs in the title proper on a subsequent issue or part, in general, give the later title in a note

12.7B8a - Continuation. If a resource continues a previously published resource, give the name of the preceding resource. If a resource is continued by a subsequently published resource, give the name of the succeeding resource

RDA

1.6.2.3 - Create a new description if there is a major change in the title proper of a serial (see 2.3.2.12.2)

2.3.2.12.2 - If there is major change (as defined under 2.3.2.13.1) in the title proper on a subsequent issue or part of a serial, make a new description for the issues or parts appearing under the new title and treat the two descriptions as descriptions for related works (see 25.1)

2.3.2.13 - Differentiate between major and minor changes in the title proper of a serial as instructed under 2.3.2.13.1 major changes) and 2.3.2.13.2 (minor changes)

CCM

14.2.1 - Continues/Continued by (Fields 780 X0/785 X0): serial A changes to serial B; serial A ceases to exist; Numbering may continue or start over again (Note: The AACR2 optional provision to add the date to a continued by note is not used in CONSER records.)
  Linking entry fields: Serial A: one 785 X0 field; Serial B: one 780 X0 field

16.2.3 - Major changes in title proper: a) the addition, deletion, change or reordering of any of the first five words (six if there is an initial article), unless the change belongs to one of the categories in AACR2 21.2C2b; b) Words are added, dropped or changed anywhere in the title that change the meaning of the title or indicate different subject matter; c) A major change occurs in the name of a corporate body recorded as part of the title proper (i.e., the change requires a new established name heading)

Treatment of Title Changes in Pre-AACR2 vs. AACR2 Records

Title: The journal of English and Germanic philology

Title Page (1ˢᵗ title)

Title Page (2ⁿᵈ title)

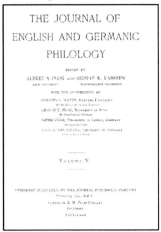

Title Page (3ʳᵈ title)

In this example, the serial has undergone two major title changes in its history: from the original title *The Journal of Germanic Philology* in 1897 to *The Journal of English and Germanic Philology* in 1903 and again to JEGP, *Journal of English and Germanic Philology*, in 1959. Because of its longevity, the descriptions for the first two titles were created based on AACR rather than AACR2.

The following elements indicate whether a record is a pre-AACR2 record. First, Leader/18 Desc (Descriptive cataloging form) is usually coded "a" for AACR2. In an AACR record, Leader/18 Desc is coded blank, meaning the serial has not been cataloged according to ISBD. Second, S/L entry convention in 008/34 is coded 0, meaning the record follows the successive entry convention, introduced by AACR to replace the practice of latest entry cataloging for serials under the ALA rules. The successive entry convention is also practiced under AACR2 and will remain in RDA. Third, apart from the lack of ISBD punctuation, the AACR records also show the lack of a date in the 260 field and a different format of the designation in the 362 field. Catalogers performing record maintenance should not modify pre-AACR2 entries to conform to current rules.

OCLC #2192721 (Initial Record; 1897 - 1902) (Pre-AACR2 record)

Type a	ELvl	Srce d	GPub	Ctrl	Lang eng
BLvl s	Form	Conf 0	Freq q	MRec	Ctry inu
S/L 0	Orig	EntW	Regl r	Alph a	
Desc	SrTp p	Cont	DtSt d	Dates 1897	, 1902

022	0	0364-2968 ‡2 1
042		nsdp ‡a lc
245	0 4	The Journal of Germanic philology.
260		Bloomington, Ind., ‡b Journal Pub. Co.
300		4 v. ‡b ports. ‡c 24 cm.
310		Quarterly
362	0	v. 1-4; 1897-1902.
555		Vols. 1-4, 1897-1902 (included in index for Journal of English and Germanic philology, v. 5-50, 1903-61).
650	0	Germanic philology ‡v Periodicals.
785	0 0	‡t Journal of English and Germanic philology ‡x 0363-6941 ‡w (DLC)sc 78000473 ‡w (OCoLC)1754568

AACR2

21.2C1 - If a major change occurs in the title proper of a serial, make a new entry

21.2C2a - Major changes. In general, consider as a major change in a title proper of a serial the addition, deletion, change, or reordering of any of the first five words

12.7B8a - Continuation. If a resource continues a previously published resource, give the name of the preceding resource. If a resource is continued by a subsequently published resource, give the name of the succeeding resource

RDA

1.6.2.3 - Create a new description if there is a major change in the title proper of a serial (see 2.3.2.12.2)

2.3.2.12.2 - If there is major change (as defined under 2.3.2.13.1) in the title proper on a subsequent issue or part of a serial, make a new description for the issues or parts appearing under the new title and treat the two descriptions as descriptions for related works (see 25.1)

CCM

14.2.1 - Continues/Continued by (Fields 780 X0/785 X0): serial A changes to serial B; serial A ceases to exist
     Linking entry fields: Serial A: one 785 X0 field; Serial B: one 780 X0 field

16.2.3 - Major changes in title proper: a) the addition, deletion, change or reordering of any of the first five words (six if there is an initial article), unless the change belongs to one of the categories in AACR2 21.2C2b

OCLC #1754568 (Interim title; 1903 - 1958) (pre-AACR2 record)

Type a	ELvl	Srce d	GPub	Ctrl	Lang eng
BLvl s	Form	Conf 0	Freq q	MRec	Ctry ilu
S/L 0	Orig	EntW	Regl r	Alph a	
Desc	SrTp p	Cont	DtSt d	Dates 1903	, 1958

210	0		J. Engl. Ger. philol.
222		4	The Journal of English and Germanic philology
245	0	4	The Journal of English and Germanic philology.
260			Urbana, Ill. [etc.] ‡b University of Illinois [etc.]
362	0		v. 5-57; 1903-58.
710	2		University of Illinois (Urbana-Champaign campus)
776	1		‡t Journal of English and Germanic philology ‡x 1945-662X
780	0	0	‡t Journal of Germanic philology ‡x 0364-2968 ‡w (DLC)sc 77000122 ‡w (OCoLC)2192721
785	0	0	‡t JEGP, Journal of English and Germanic philology ‡x 0363-6941 ‡w (DLC)sc 78000997 ‡w (OCoLC)2192801

(Continued on next page)

OCLC #2192801 (Latest/Current Title) (AACR2 record)

Type a	ELvl	Srce d	GPub	Ctrl	Lang eng
BLvl s	Form	Conf 0	Freq q	MRec	Ctry ilu
S/L 0	Orig	EntW	Regl r	Alph a	
Desc a	SrTp p	Cont	DtSt c	Dates 1959	, 9999

	022	0		0363-6941 ǂz 0022-0868 ǂ2 1
	042			nsdp ǂa lc
	210	0		J. Engl. Ger. philol.
	222		4	The Journal of English and Germanic philology
CCM 16.2.3a	245	0	0	JEGP, Journal of English and Germanic philology.
	246	3	0	Journal of English and Germanic philology
	260			Urbana, ǂb University of Illinois Press.
	300			v. ǂb ports. ǂc 24 cm.
	310			Quarterly
	362	0		v. 58- Jan. 1959-
	530			Some issues also available to subscribers via the World Wide Web.
14.2.1	780	0	0	ǂt Journal of English and Germanic philology ǂx 0363-6941 ǂw (DLC)sc 78000473 ǂw (OCoLC)1754568

Annotations in right margin: AACR2 21.2C1 21.2C2a (for 245); 12.7B8a (for 780)

Major Change: Print Ceased and Is Continued Online

Title: Harvard Middle Eastern and Islamic review

Cover

Cover Verso

Screenshot
Table of Contents

Here is another situation where a new entry for the serial is required. In 2009, *Harvard Middle Eastern and Islamic Review* ceased publication in print and continued online only, but its title has remained the same. LCRI 21.3B provides specific guidance for this situation: a new record is required when the physical medium in which the serial is issued changes.

Again, 780 and 785 linking fields are used to record the earlier print title and the later online title in the two records. It should be noted that because the online version continues the print journal with the same title, a uniform title is used in the record for the online version, although in a CSR record, the uniform title would not be needed in this situation. When the uniform title is present, the uniform title—rather than the title proper from the 245 field—will be used in subfield ǂt in the 780 or 785 linking fields. For more information on uniform titles, see Chapter 8.

OCLC #456291295

Type a	ELvl I	Srce d	GPub	Ctrl	Lang eng
BLvl s	Form s	Conf 0	Freq a	MRec	Ctry mau
S/L 0	Orig s	EntW b	Regl r	Alph a	
Desc a	SrTp p	Cont	DtSt c	Dates 2009	, 9999

	130	0	Harvard Middle Eastern and Islamic review (Online)	
CCM 16.4.1	245	1 0	Harvard Middle Eastern and Islamic review ǂh [electronic resource].	LCRI 21.3B
	260		Cambridge, MA : ǂb Center for Middle Eastern Studies, Harvard University, ǂc 2009-	
	310		Annual	
	362	1	Began with Vol. 8 (2009).	
	500		Description based on first issue; title from journal home page (publisher's Web site, viewed Oct. 12, 2009).	
	650	0	Islam ǂv Periodicals.	
	650	0	Islamic civilization ǂv Periodicals.	
	710	2	Harvard University. ǂb Center for Middle Eastern Studies.	
14.2.1	780	0 0	ǂt Harvard Middle Eastern and Islamic review ǂw (DLC) 94648524 ǂw (OCoLC)29742116	12.7B8a
	856	4 0	ǂu http://cmes.hmdc.harvard.edu/publications/hmeir/	

AACR2

12.1B1 - Transcribe the title proper as instructed in 1.1B

12.7B8a - Continuation. If a resource continues a previously published resource, give the name of the preceding resource. If a resource is continued by a subsequently published resource, give the name of the succeeding resource

LCRI

21.3B - One of the conditions for making a new entry for a serial: the physical medium in which the serial is issued changes as expressed in the specific material designation in the physical description area (not a reproduction or the same serial in another manifestation, e.g., a braille edition). Such a change could be from paper to microfiche, from paper to online, etc.

RDA

1.6.2.2 - Create a new description if there is a change in the media type (see 3.2) of a serial

1.6.2.3 - Create a new description if there is a major change in the title proper of a serial (see 2.3.2.12.2)

3.1.6.1 - For multipart monographs and serials, if there is a change in the media type in a subsequent issue or part, create a new description (see 1.6)

2.3.2.12.2 - If there is major change (as defined under 2.3.2.13.1) in the title proper on a subsequent issue or part of a serial, make a new description for the issues or parts appearing under the new title and treat the two descriptions as descriptions for related works (see 25.1)

2.3.2.13 - Differentiate between major and minor changes in the title proper of a serial as instructed under 2.3.2.13.1 (major changes) and 2.3.2.13.2 (minor changes)

CCM

6.1.3 - Transcribe the title as it appears on the chief source of information

14.2.1 - Continues/Continued by (Fields 780 X0/785 X0): serial A changes to serial B; serial A ceases to exist; Numbering may continue or start over again (note: the AACR2 optional provision to add the date to a continued by note is not used in CONSER records.)
    Linking entry fields: Serial A: one 785 X0 field; Serial B: one 780 X0 field

16.4.1 - In general, a change in the physical medium of the serial is a major change when the change would result in a change at the level of the GMD (e.g., print, electronic resource) or SMD (e.g., paper, microfiche, microfilm, CD-ROM, online). The new record is necessary because of differences in the fixed fields and description (particularly the physical description, field 300)

OCLC #29742116

Type a	ELvl	Srce d		GPub	Ctrl		Lang eng
BLvl s	Form	Conf 0		Freq a	MRec		Ctry mau
S/L 0	Orig	EntW		Regl r	Alph a		
Desc a	SrTp p	Cont		DtSt d	Dates 1994	, 2006	

	022	0		1074-5408 ǂ2 1	
	042			nsdp ǂa lc	
	043			aw——- ǂa ff——-	
CCM 6.1.3	245	0	0	Harvard Middle Eastern and Islamic review.	AACR2 12.1B1
	260			Cambridge, MA : ǂb Center for Middle Eastern Studies, Harvard University, ǂc c1994-2006.	
	300			v. ; ǂc 23 cm.	
	310			Annual, ǂb 1997-	
	321			Semiannual, ǂb 1994-1996	
	362	0		Vol. 1, no. 1 (Feb. 1994)-v.7 (2006).	
	500			Title from cover.	
	650		0	Islam ǂv Periodicals.	
	650		0	Islamic civilization ǂv Periodicals.	
	651		0	Middle East ǂv Periodicals.	
	651		0	Africa, North ǂv Periodicals.	
	710	2		Harvard University. ǂb Center for Middle Eastern Studies.	
14.2.1	785	0	0	ǂt Harvard Middle Eastern and Islamic review (Online) ǂw (OCoLC) 456291295	12.7B8a

Major Change: Title Change Involving Uniform Title

Title: AAA going places

In the early 2000s, the American Automotive Association changed the name of its regionally produced publications from *AAA Today* to *AAA Going Places*. To distinguish the various regional titles from each other, uniform titles qualified by place of publication were created. A title change therefore necessitates not only the creation of a new record and the closing out of the old record but also the creation of a new uniform title in the record, as seen in this example.

When a uniform title is present in the record, the uniform title from the 130 field—rather than the title proper from the 245 field—is used in subfield ‡t in the 780 or 785 linking fields. These linking fields connect the two publications together and reflect the consecutive nature of the serials. For more information on uniform titles, see Chapter 8.

The first indicator in the the 780 and 785 fields determines whether a display constant is to be generated, with the content of the display constant determined by the second indicator. The first indicator value 0 means the display constant will be generated, and it is used in most situations unless there is a 580 linking entry complexity note present in the record. In that case, the first indicator value will be set to 1. The second indicator value 0 allows the system to generate the display constant "continues" in the 780 field and "continues by" in the 785 field.

Other information can be recorded in the 780/785 linking fields: ISSN in subfield ‡x, LCCN in subfield ‡w, and OCLC control number in subfield ‡w.

Cover

Masthead

Cover

Masthead

OCLC #220900688

Type a	ELvl I	Srce d	GPub	Ctrl		Lang eng
BLvl s	Form	Conf 0	Freq b	MRec		Ctry pau
S/L 0	Orig	EntW	Regl r	Alph a		
Desc a	SrTp p	Cont	DtSt c	Dates 200u		, 9999

	022		‡y 0899-4986	
CCM 5.2	130	0	AAA going places (Easton, Pa.)	AACR2 25.5B1
16.2.3a	245	1 0	AAA going places.	21.2C1 21.2C2a
	246	3	American Automobile Association going places	
	246	3 0	Going places	
	260		Easton, Pa. : ‡b AAA Northampton County	
	300		v. : ‡b ill. ; ‡c 27 cm .	
	310		Bimonthly	
	500		Title from cover.	
	500		"The magazine for today's traveler."	
	650	0	Travel ‡v Periodicals.	
	710	2	Northampton County Motor Club (Easton, Pa.)	
14.2.1	780	0 0	‡t AAA today (Easton, Pa.) ‡x 0899-4986 ‡w (DLC)sn 88001825 ‡w (OCoLC)18116018	12.7B8a

AACR2

21.2C1 - If a major change occurs in the title proper of a serial, make a new entry

21.2C2a - Major changes. In general, consider as a major change in a title proper of a serial the addition, deletion, change, or reordering of any of the first five words

12.7B8a - Continuation. If a resource continues a previously published resource, give the name of the preceding resource. If a resource is continued by a subsequently published resource, give the name of the succeeding resource

25.5B1 - Add in parentheses an appropriate explanatory word, brief phrase, or other designation to distinguish a uniform title used as a heading from an identical or similar heading for a person or corporate body, or from an identical or similar uniform title used as a heading or reference

12.1B1 - Transcribe the title proper as instructed in 1.1B

RDA

1.6.2.3 - Create a new description if there is a major change in the title proper of a serial (see 2.3.2.12.2)

2.3.2.12.2 - If there is major change (as defined under 2.3.2.13.1) in the title proper on a subsequent issue or part of a serial, make a new description for the issues or parts appearing under the new title and treat the two descriptions as descriptions for related works (see 25.1)

2.3.2.7 - Record the title proper applying the basic instructions on recording titles given under 2.3.1

2.3.1.4 - Transcribe a title as it appears on the source of information. Apply the general guidelines on transcription given under 1.7

2.3.8.3 - For changes in the title proper, apply the instructions given under 2.3.2.12.1 for multipart monographs and 2.3.2.12.2 for serials

CCM

5.2 - Create a uniform title when the title proper of a serial entered under title is identical to the title proper of another serial. (The other serial may or may not be entered under title)

6.1.3 - Transcribe the title as it appears on the chief source of information

14.2.1 - Continues/Continued by (Fields 780 X0/785 X0): serial A changes to serial B; serial A ceases to exist
    Linking entry fields: Serial A: one 785 X0 field; Serial B: one 780 X0 field

16.2.3 - Major changes in title proper: a) the addition, deletion, change or reordering of any of the first five words (six if there is an initial article), unless the change belongs to one of the categories in AACR2 21.2C2b

(Continued on next page)

OCLC #18116018

Type a	ELvl 7	Srce d	GPub	Ctrl	Lang eng
BLvl s	Form	Conf 0	Freq q	MRec	Ctry pau
S/L 0	Orig	EntW	Regl x	Alph a	
Desc a	SrTp p	Cont	DtSt d	Dates 1988	, 200u

	022	1		0899-4986 ‡2 1	
	042			nsdp	
CCM 5.2	130	0		AAA today (Easton, Pa.)	AACR2 25.5B1
	222		0	AAA today ‡b (Easton, Pa.)	
6.1.3	245	0	0	AAA today : ‡b publication of Northampton County Motor Club.	12.1B1
	246	3		American Automobile Association today	
	246	1	0	Today	
	260			[Easton, PA] : ‡b The Club, ‡c 1988-	
	265			Northampton County Motor Club, Hecktown and Country Club Rd., Easton, PA 18042	
	300			v. : ‡b ill. ; ‡c 28 cm.	
	310			Four no. a year	
	362	0		[Vol. 1, no. 1] (Mar./Apr. 1988)-	
	500			Title from cover.	
	650		0	Travel ‡v Periodicals.	
	710	2		Northampton County Motor Club (Easton, Pa.)	
14.2.1	785	0	0	‡t AAA going places (Easton, Pa.) ‡w (OCoLC)220900688	12.7B8a

Major Change: Title Changes With the Corporate Body Name as the Main Entry

Title: Programs & Events by the Arnold Arboretum of Harvard University

Cover

Cover

Cover

This serial publication emanates from the corporate body the Arnold Arboretum of Harvard University and deals with its own news, events, and programs. Therefore, it falls under AACR2 21.1B2a and is entered under the corporate body heading Arnold Arboretum. (For more information on work entered under a corporate body, refer to Chapter 3.)

While the name of the corporate body has remained stable, the title of its publication has undergone some changes. First, the original title *Program & Events* merged with *News* to form *News, Programs & Events* in 2003. Then, the title was renamed *Silva: News, Classes & Visitor Guide* in 2005. This is still a major change, and a separate record is required for each change even though the name of the corporate body remains the same.

Major changes in records where the corporate body is the main entry are handled in much the same way as changes seen in other examples, where the title is the main entry; the existing records are closed out, and the 780 and 785 linking fields are used to link the preceding and succeeding titles. One difference to note is that when the corporate body is the main entry, the 780 and 785 fields will include the corporate body in subfield ‡a preceding subfield ‡t. The name of the body should be recorded as it appears in the 110 field of the record from which the title is taken.

Whenever separate descriptions are made for title changes, 780 and 785 fields are created in the records to provide links to the immediately preceding and/or succeeding titles, not links to all earlier or later titles. Therefore, in the record for *Program & Events*, the 785 fields only link to *News* and *News, Programs & Events* but not to *Silva: News, Classes & Visitor Guide*. In the same way, in the record for *Silva: News, Classes & Visitor Guide*, the 780 field only links to its immediate preceding title *News, Programs & Events*, not to *News* or *News, Programs & Events*.

The type of relationship is denoted by the second indicator of the 780 and 785 fields. In the record for *Program & Events*, the second indicator value 7 in the two 785 fields shows that the relationship between *Program & Events* and its succeeding titles are that of a merger. In the record for *News, Programs & Events*, the second indicator value 4 in the 780 fields identifies the relationship as that of the union of two serials. In both records, the first indicator value in 780 and 785 fields is set to 1 to suppress display constant generation because of the presence of the linking entry complexity note in the 580 field. In the record for *Silva: News, Classes & Visitor Guide*, the second indicator value 0 in the 780 field shows its relationship with the preceding title is that of continuation. The first indicator value 0 will generate the display constant "Continues:."

OCLC #40650663

	Type a	ELvl	Srce d	GPub	Ctrl	Lang eng
	BLvl s	Form	Conf 0	Freq f	MRec	Ctry mau
	S/L 0	Orig	EntW	Regl r	Alph	
	Desc a	SrTp p	Cont	DtSt d	Dates 1980	, 2003

	042		lcd	
	043		n-us-ma	
	110	2	Arnold Arboretum.	
CCM 6.1.3	245	1 0	Programs & events / ‡c The Arnold Arboretum of Harvard University.	AACR2 12.1B1
	246	3	Programs and events	
	260		[Jamaica Plain, Mass.] : ‡b The Arnold Arboretum of Harvard University, ‡c -2003.	
	300		v. : ‡b ill. ; ‡c 28 cm.	
	310		Semiannual	
	362	1	Began in 1980.	
	362	0	-spring/summer 2003.	
	500		Description based on: 1998/1999 (fall/winter); title from cover.	
14.2.6	580		Merged with: Arnold Arboretum. News, to become: Arnold Arboretum. News, programs & events.	12.7B8b
	610	2 0	Arnold Arboretum ‡v Periodicals.	
14.2.6	785	1 7	Arnold Arboretum. ‡t News ‡w (DLC) 2004235708 ‡w (OCoLC) 55520644	12.7B8b
14.2.6	785	1 7	Arnold Arboretum. ‡t News, programs & events ‡w (DLC) 2004235716 ‡w (OCoLC)55483705	12.7B8b

AACR2

12.1B1 - Transcribe the title proper as instructed in 1.1B

21.2C1 - If a major change occurs in the title proper of a serial, make a new entry

21.2C2a - Major changes. In general, consider as a major change in a title proper of a serial the addition, deletion, change, or reordering of any of the first five words

12.7B8a - Continuation. If a resource continues a previously published resource, give the name of the preceding resource. If a resource is continued by a subsequently published resource, give the name of the succeeding resource

12.7B8b - Merger. If a resource is the result of the merger of two or more other resources, give the names of the resources that were merged. If a resource is merged with one or more other resources to form a resource with a new title, give the name(s) of the resource(s) with which it has merged and the name of the new resource

RDA

1.6.2.3 - Create a new description if there is a major change in the title proper of a serial (see 2.3.2.12.2)

2.3.2.12.2 - If there is major change (as defined under 2.3.2.13.1) in the title proper on a subsequent issue or part of a serial, make a new description for the issues or parts appearing under the new title and treat the two descriptions as descriptions for related works (see 25.1)

2.3.2.13 - Differentiate between major and minor changes in the title proper of a serial as instructed under 2.3.2.13.1 major changes) and 2.3.2.13.2 (minor changes)

24.5.1.3 - Recording relationship designators : record an appropriate term from the list in appendix J to indicate the nature of the relationship more specifically than is indicated by the defined scope of the relationship element itself

CCM

6.1.3 - Transcribe the title as it appears on the chief source of information

14.2.1 - Continues/Continued by (Fields 780 X0/785 X0): serial A changes to serial B; serial A ceases to exist
Linking entry fields: Serial A: one 785 X0 field; Serial B: one 780 X0 field

14.2.6 - Merged with:. . . to form:. . . /Merger of: . . .; and:. . . (Fields 780 X4/785 X7) (AACR2 12.7B8b)
Aspects of the relationship: Serials A and B merge to form serial C which has a new title
Linking entry fields: Serial A: 580 field and two or more linking fields (785 17) for the title(s) it merged with and the new title; serial B: same; serial C: 580 and two or more linking fields (780 14) for the earlier titles

16.2.3a - Major changes in title proper: the addition, deletion, change or reordering of any of the first five words (six if there is an initial article), unless the change belongs to one of the categories in AACR2 21.2C2b

OCLC #55483705

Type a	ELvl	Srce d	GPub	Ctrl	Lang eng
BLvl s	Form	Conf 0	Freq f	MRec	Ctry mau
S/L 0	Orig	EntW	Regl r	Alph	
Desc a	SrTp p	Cont	DtSt d	Dates 2003	, 200u

	042		lcd	
	043		n-us-ma	
	110	2	Arnold Arboretum.	
CCM 16.2.3a	245	1 0	News, programs & events / ‡c Arnold Arboretum of Harvard University.	AACR2 21.2C2a
	246	3	News, programs and events	
	260		Jamaica Plain, Mass. : ‡b Arnold Arboretum of Harvard University, ‡c 2003-	
	300		v. : ‡b ill. ; ‡c 28 cm.	
	362	0	Fall/winter 2003/2004-	
	500		Title from cover.	
14.2.6	580		Merger of: Arnold Arboretum. Programs & events, and: Arnold Arboretum. News.	
	610	2 0	Arnold Arboretum ‡v Periodicals.	
	610	2 0	Arnold Arboretum ‡x Curricula ‡v Catalogs ‡v Periodicals.	
	610	2 0	Arnold Arboretum ‡v Calendars.	
14.2.6	780	1 4	Arnold Arboretum. ‡t Programs & events ‡w (DLC) 2004235711 ‡w (OCoLC)40650663	12.7B8b
14.2.6	780	1 4	Arnold Arboretum. ‡t News ‡w (DLC) 2004235708 ‡w (OCoLC) 55520644	12.7B8b
14.2.1	785	0 0	Arnold Arboretum. ‡t Silva ‡w (OCoLC)173983388	12.7B8a

(Continued on next page)

OCLC #173983388

Type a	ELvl I	Srce d	GPub	Ctrl	Lang eng
BLvl s	Form	Conf 0	Freq f	MRec	Ctry mau
S/L 0	Orig	EntW	Regl r	Alph	
Desc a	SrTp p	Cont	DtSt c	Dates 2005	, 9999

	110	2	Arnold Arboretum.	
CCM 16.2.3a	245	1 0	Silva : ‡b news, classes & visitor guide / ‡c The Arnold Arboretum of Harvard University.	AACR2 21.2C2a 21.2C1
	246	3	News, classes and visitor guide	
	260		Boston, Mass. : ‡b The Arnold Arboretum of Harvard University, ‡c 2005-	
	300		v. : ‡b ill. ; ‡c 28 cm.	
	310		Semiannual	
	362	1	Began publication with spring/summer 2005 issue.	
	500		Title from cover.	
	530		Also available online.	
	610	2 0	Arnold Arboretum ‡v Periodicals.	
	610	2 0	Arnold Arboretum ‡x Curricula ‡v Catalogs ‡v Periodicals.	
	610	2 0	Arnold Arboretum ‡v Calendars.	
14.2.1	780	0 0	Arnold Arboretum. ‡t News, programs & events ‡w (DLC) 2004235716 ‡w (OCoLC)55483705	12.7B8a
	856	4 1	‡u http://arboretum.harvard.edu/aboutus/silva/current.html	

Major Change: Merge With: . . . To Form . . .

Title: PIMA's . . . papermaker

Cover

Cover

Cover

A title change may occur when two titles merge to form a new title. As with all major title changes, a new record is created for the current title and the records for the two preceding titles are closed out.

In this example, two publications—*PIMA's . . . Papermaker* and *Tappi Journal*, each with its own unique history of title changes and mergers—merged in 2001 to form the new serial *Solutions!*

The two records for the merged titles are closed out, and two 785 linking fields are provided in each record: one linking to the other merged title and another linking to the new serial. Due to the complex nature of relationships among these three titles, the 580 linking entry complexity note is used in all three records to express the merger relationship between the serial *Solutions!* and the two preceding titles:

580 _ _ Merged with: Tappi journal, to form: Solutions! (Norcross, Ga.).
580 _ _ Merged with: PIMA's . . . papermaker, to form: Solutions! (Norcross, Ga.).
580 _ _ Formed by the union of: TAPPI journal; and: PIMA's papermaker.

Because of the presence of the 580 note field, the first indictor value in the 780 and 785 fields is set to 1 to suppress the display constant. The second indicator in the 785 field in the records for *PIMA's . . . Papermaker* and *Tappi Journal* shows the type of relationship between serials, and the indicator value 7 means the serial is "merged with x to form y."

The record for the later title *Solutions!* reflects the union of the two serials with two 780 linking felds. The second indicator is set to 4, meaning the serial is formed by the union of x and y. Again, because a 580 note is provided in the record to explicitly state how the new publication was formed (i.e., by the union of *PIMA's . . . Papermaker* and *TAPPI Journal*), the first indicator value is set to 1 to suppress the display constant.

OCLC #36353452

	Type a	ELvl	Srce d	GPub	Ctrl	Lang eng
	BLvl s	Form	Conf 0	Freq b	MRec	Ctry ilu
	S/L 0	Orig	EntW	Regl x	Alph a	
	Desc a	SrTp p	Cont	DtSt d	Dates 1997	, 2001

	022	0	1093-670X ‡y 1046-4352 ‡2 1
	042		lc ‡a nsdp
	043		n———
	210	0	PIMA's papermaker
	222	0	PIMA's . . . papermaker
CCM 6.1.3	245	0 0	PIMA's . . . papermaker.	AACR2 12.1B1
	246	1	‡i Four issues a year have title: ‡a PIMA's international papermaker
	246	1	‡i Four issues a year have title: ‡a PIMA's North American papermaker
	246	3 0	Papermaker
	260		Mount Prospect, IL : ‡b Paper Industry Management Association, ‡c c1996-2001.
	300		5 v. : ‡b ill. ; ‡c 28 cm.
	310		Eight no. a year
	362	0	Vol. 79, no. 1 (Jan. 1997)-v. 83, no. 8 (Aug. 2001).
	500		Title from cover.
	515		Issue for Jan. 1997 called Jan. 1996 in the masthead in error.
	515		Continues the numbering of PIMA magazine.
	530		Issued also on microfilm by University Microfilms International; also available online.
14.2.6	580		Merged with: Tappi journal, to form: Solutions! (Norcross, Ga.).	12.7B8b
	580		Formed by the merger of: PIMA magazine, American papermaker, and Canadian papermaker.
	580		Issues called PIMA's international papermaker includes contents for the Feb., May, Aug. and Nov. issues of Asia Pacific papermaker.
	650	0	Paper industry ‡v Periodicals.
	650	0	Wood-pulp industry ‡v Periodicals.
	710	2	Paper Industry Management Association.
	780	1 4	‡t PIMA magazine ‡x 1046-4352 ‡w (DLC) 88654850 ‡w (OCoLC) 17350292
	780	1 4	‡t American papermaker (Atlanta, Ga. : 1991) ‡x 1056-4772 ‡w (DLC) 96643231 ‡w (OCoLC)23722397
	780	1 4	‡t Canadian papermaker ‡x 1191-887X ‡w (DLC) 93658538 ‡w (OCoLC)26926275
14.2.6	785	1 7	‡t Tappi journal ‡x 0734-1415 ‡w (DLC) 83642134 ‡w (OCoLC) 8693713	12.7B8b
14.2.6	785	1 7	‡t Solutions! (Norcross, Ga.) ‡x 1537-0275 ‡w (DLC) 2001215218 ‡w (OCoLC)47914483	12.7B8b
	787	1	‡t Asia Pacific papermaker ‡x 1320-9787 ‡w (DLC)sn 97048674 ‡w (OCoLC)28480608
	856	4 1	TAPPI home page: ‡u http://www.tappi.org/

OCLC #8693713

	Type a	ELvl	Srce d	GPub	Ctrl	Lang eng
	BLvl s	Form	Conf 0	Freq m	MRec	Ctry gau
	S/L 0	Orig	EntW	Regl r	Alph a	
	Desc a	SrTp p	Cont	DtSt d	Dates 1982	, 2001

	022	0	0734-1415 ‡2 1
	042		lc ‡a nsdp
	210	0	Tappi j.
	222		0 Tappi journal

CCM 6.1.3 | 245 | 0 | 0 | Tappi journal. | AACR2 12.1B1

	246	3	Technical Association of the Pulp and Paper Industry journal
	260		Atlanta, Ga. : ‡b Technical Association of the Pulp and Paper Industry, ‡c c1982-c2001.
	300		20 v. : ‡b ill. ; ‡c 28 cm.
	310		Monthly, ‡b <Nov. 1991>-2001
	321		13 no. a year, ‡b <Apr. 1984->
	362	0	Vol. 65, no. 9 (Sept. 1982)-v. 84, no. 8 (Aug. 2001).
	500		Imprint varies: Norcross, Ga., <Apr. 1984->
	510	2	Chemical abstracts ‡x 0009-2258
	525		Supplements accompany some issues.
	525		Issues for <Apr. 2000>-Aug. 2001 have supplements containing the full-text of peer-reviewed articles that were only published as summaries in the original issues.
	530		Also issued in microform by Princeton Microfilm Corp.; also issued online.
	530		Also issued online.

14.2.6 | 580 | Merged with: PIMA's . . . papermaker, to form: Solutions!(Norcross, Ga.). | 12.7B8b

	580		Vols. for Sept. 1985- have separately numbered insert called: Advancing converting & packaging technologies.
	650		0 Paper industry ‡v Periodicals.
	710	2	Technical Association of the Pulp and Paper Industry.
	770	0	Technical Association of the Pulp and Paper Industry. ‡t Directory of members, products, and services ‡w (DLC)sn 88015936 ‡w (OCoLC) 12965287
	770	0	Technical Association of the Pulp and Paper Industry. ‡t TAPPI membership directory and company guide ‡w (DLC)sn 89012161 ‡w (OCoLC)14882334
	777	1	‡t Advancing converting & packaging technologies ‡x 0882-5777 ‡w (OCoLC)11893924
	780	0	0 ‡t Tappi ‡x 0039-8241 ‡w (DLC) 19005316 ‡w (OCoLC)6457012

14.2.6 | 785 | 1 | 7 | ‡t PIMA's . . . papermaker ‡x 1093-670X ‡w (DLC) 97646623 ‡w (OCoLC)36353452 | 12.7B8b

14.2.6 | 785 | 1 | 7 | ‡t Solutions! (Norcross, Ga.) ‡x 1537-0275 ‡w (DLC) 2001215218 ‡w (OCoLC)47914483 | 12.7B8b

	856	4	1 ‡z TAPPI home page: ‡u http://www.tappi.org/

(Continued on next page)

OCLC #47914483

Type a	ELvl	Srce c	GPub	Ctrl	Lang eng
BLvl s	Form	Conf 0	Freq m	MRec	Ctry gau
S/L 0	Orig	EntW	Regl r	Alph a	
Desc a	SrTp p	Cont	DtSt d	Dates 2001	, 2006

	022	0	1537-0275 ‡y 0734-1415 ‡2 1	
	042		nsdp ‡a lc	
	130	0	Solutions! (Norcross, Ga.)	
CCM 16.2.3a	245	0 0	Solutions! : ‡b for people, processes and paper.	AACR2 21.2C1 21.2C2a
	260		Norcross, GA : ‡b TAPPI, ‡c c2001-c2006.	
	300		v. : ‡b ill. ; ‡c 28 cm.	
	362	0	Vol. 01, no. 01 (Sept. 2001); Vol. 84, no. 10 (Oct. 2001)-v. 89, no. 07 (July 2006).	
	500		"The official publication of TAPPI & PIMA."	
	500		Title from cover.	
14.2.6	580		Formed by the union of: TAPPI journal; and: PIMA's papermaker.	12.7B8b
	650	0	Paper industry ‡v Periodicals.	
	710	2	Technical Association of the Pulp and Paper Industry.	
	710	2	Paper Industry Management Association.	
	776	0 8	‡i Also issued online: ‡t Solutions! (Norcross, Ga. : Online) ‡w (OCoLC)60639400	
14.2.6	780	1 4	‡t Tappi journal ‡x 0734-1415 ‡w (DLC) 83642134 ‡w (OCoLC) 8693713	12.7B8b
14.2.6	780	1 4	‡t PIMA's … papermaker ‡x 1093-670X ‡w (DLC) 97646623 ‡w (OCoLC)36353452	12.7B8b
	785	0 0	‡t Paper 360° ‡x 1933-3684 ‡w (DLC) 2006214968 ‡w (OCoLC) 71016973	

AACR2

12.1B1 - Transcribe the title proper as instructed in 1.1B

21.2C1 - If a major change occurs in the title proper of a serial, make a new entry

21.2C2a - Major changes. In general, consider as a major change in a title proper of a serial the addition, deletion, change, or reordering of any of the first five words

12.7B8b - Merger. If a resource is the result of the merger of two or more other resources, give the names of the resources that were merged. If a resource is merged with one or more other resources to form a resource with a new title, give the name(s) of the resource(s) with which it has merged and the name of the new resource

RDA

1.6.2.3 - Create a new description if there is a major change in the title proper of a serial (see 2.3.2.12.2)

2.3.2.12.2 - If there is major change (as defined under 2.3.2.13.1) in the title proper on a subsequent issue or part of a serial, make a new description for the issues or parts appearing under the new title and treat the two descriptions as descriptions for related works (see 25.1)

2.3.2.13 - Differentiate between major and minor changes in the title proper of a serial as instructed under 2.3.2.13.1 major changes) and 2.3.2.13.2 (minor changes)

24.5.1.3 - Recording relationship designators: record an appropriate term from the list in appendix J to indicate the nature of the relationship more specifically than is indicated by the defined scope of the relationship element itself

25.1.1.3 - Reference a related work applying the general guidelines on referencing related works, expressions, manifestations, and items given under 24.4

24.4 - Record the relationship between a work, expression, manifestation, or item and a related work, expression, manifestation, or item using one or more of the conventions described under 24.4.1 (identifier), 24.4.2 (authorized access point), or 24.4.3 (description), as applicable

CCM

6.1.3 - Transcribe the title as it appears on the chief source of information

14.2.6 - Merged with:...to form:.../Merger of: ...; and:...(Fields 780 X4/785 X7) (AACR2 12.7B8b)

> Aspects of the relationship: Serials A and B merge to form serial C which has a new title
> Linking entry fields: Serial A: 580 field and two or more linking fields (785 17) for the title(s) it merged with and the new title; serial B: same; serial C: 580 and two or more linking fields (780 14) for the earlier titles

16.2.3a - Major changes in title proper: the addition, deletion, change or reordering of any of the first five words (six if there is an initial article), unless the change belongs to one of the categories in AACR2 21.2C2b

Major Change: One Title Absorbs Another

Title: Mathematics teaching

Cover    Cover

When one serial absorbs another, the absorbing serial maintains its original title (this is in contrast to merging serials where a new serial/title is formed) and the record for the resource being absorbed is closed out.

In this example, the bimonthly publication *Mathematics Teaching* absorbed the serial *Micromath* in 2006. The record for the absorbed publication *Micromath* is closed out and a 785 linking field is provided in the record, linking it to the absorbing serial *Mathematics Teaching*. This relationship is indicated by the second indicator value 4, identifying the existing title as being absorbed by *Mathematics Teaching*. The display constant "Absorbed by:" will be generated because the first indicator value is set to 0.

The record for the absorbing resource—*Mathematics Teaching*, which has been published since 1955—reflects the absorbtion of *Micromath* with the 780 linking field, as indicated by the second indicator value 5. The display constant "Absorbed:" will be generated, as the first indicator value is set to 0. Subfield ‡g Jan. 2006 is given to show that the absorption of *Micromath* by *Mathmatics Teaching* occurred with the January 2006 issue.

OCLC #1756880

Type a	ELvl	Srce d	GPub	Ctrl	Lang eng
BLvl s	Form	Conf 0	Freq b	MRec	Ctry enk
S/L 0	Orig	EntW	Regl r	Alph a	
Desc	SrTp p	Cont	DtSt c	Dates 1955	, 9999

	022		0025-5785 ‡2 z		
	042		lcd ‡a nsdp		
	210	0	Math. teach.		
	222		0 Mathematics teaching		
CCM 6.1.3	245	0 0	Mathematics teaching.		AACR2 12.1B1
	246	1	‡i Issues for Jan. 2006- have additional title: ‡a MT incorporating Micromath		
	246	1 3	MT		
	246	1 7	Mathematics teaching incorporating Micromath ‡f Jan. 2006-		
	260		Derby [England, etc.] ‡b Association of Teachers of Mathematics.		
	300		v. ‡b ill. ‡c 29 cm.		
	310		Bimonthly, ‡b 2006-		
	321		Quarterly, ‡b 1955-2005		
	362	0	no. 1- 1955-		
	650	0	Mathematics ‡x Study and teaching ‡v Periodicals.		
	650	6	Mathématiques ‡x Étude et enseignement (Secondaire) ‡v Périodiques.		
	650	6	Mathématiques ‡v Périodiques.		
	710	2	Association of Teachers of Mathematics.		
CCM 14.2.4	780	0 5	‡t Micromath ‡g Jan. 2006 ‡x 0267-5501 ‡w (DLC)sf 93093991 ‡w (OCoLC)14437719		AACR2 12.7B8d

AACR2

12.1B1 - Transcribe the title proper as instructed in 1.1B

12.7B8d - If a resource absorbs another resource, give the name of the resource absorbed, and optionally the date of absorption. If a resource is absorbed by another resource, give the name of the absorbing resource

RDA

2.3.2.12.2 - If there is major change (as defined under 2.3.2.13.1) in the title proper on a subsequent issue or part of a serial, make a new description for the issues or parts appearing under the new title and treat the two descriptions as descriptions for related works (see 25.1)

2.3.2.13 - Differentiate between major and minor changes in the title proper of a serial as instructed under 2.3.2.13.1 (major changes) and 2.3.2.13.2 (minor changes)

24.5.1.3 - Recording relationship designators: record an appropriate term from the list in appendix J to indicate the nature of the relationship more specifically than is indicated by the defined scope of the relationship element itself

25.1.1.3 - Reference a related work applying the general guidelines on referencing related works, expressions, manifestations, and items given under 24.4

24.4 - Record the relationship between a work, expression, manifestation, or item and a related work, expression, manifestation, or item using one or more of the conventions described under 24.4.1 (identifier), 24.4.2 (authorized access point), or 24.4.3 (description), as applicable

CCM

6.1.3 - Transcribe the title as it appears on the chief source of information

14.2.4 - Absorbed/Absorbed by (Fields 780 X5/785 X4) (AACR2 12.7B8d)

Aspects of the relationship: Serials A and B begin as two separate publications; serial B becomes part of serial A; serial A retains the same title (if the title changes consider the relationship to be a merger rather than an absorption)

Linking entry fields: Serial A: one field tagged 780 X5; the date of the issue of title A that was the first to include title B may be given in subfield ‡g (LC/CONSER practice is to apply the option decision in the rule)

Serial B: one field tagged 785 X4; ‡g is given for date of issue absorbed

(Continued on next page)

OCLC #14437719

Type a	ELvl	Srce d	GPub	Ctrl	Lang eng
BLvl s	Form	Conf 0	Freq t	MRec	Ctry enk
S/L 0	Orig	EntW	Regl r	Alph	
Desc a	SrTp p	Cont	DtSt d	Dates 1985	, 2005

	022		0267-5501	
	042		lcd	
CCM 6.1.3	245	0 0	Micromath : ǂb a journal of the Association of Teachers of Mathematics.	AACR2 12.1B1
	246	3	Micro math	
	260		Oxford [England : ǂb Basil Blackwell Ltd.]	
	300		v. : ǂb ill. ; ǂc 30 cm.	
	310		Three no. a year	
	362	1	Began with: Vol. 1, no. 1, published 1985; ceased with: Vol. 21, no. 3 (autumn 2005).	
	500		Description based on: Vol. 3, no. 1 (spring 1987); title from cover.	
	500		Some issues accompanied by CD-ROMs.	
	500		Latest issue consulted: Vol. 19, no. 3 (autumn 2003).	
	650	0	Mathematics ǂx Data processing ǂv Periodicals.	
	650	0	Mathematics ǂx Computer-assisted instruction ǂv Periodicals.	
	710	2	Association of Teachers of Mathematics.	
CCM 14.2.4	785	0 4	ǂt Mathematics teaching ǂx 0025-5785 ǂw (DLC)sn 85012704 ǂw (OCoLC)1756880	AACR2 12.7B8d
	856	4	ǂ3 Selected articles ǂu http://www.atm.org.uk/mt/micromath.html	

Major Change vs. Minor Change

Title: Technology & learning

Cover

Cover

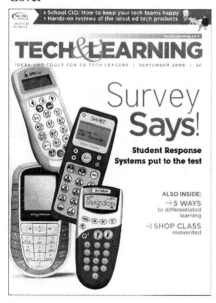

Some title changes may not require a new description. Instead, the existing serial bibliographic record should be updated. AACR2 21.2C2b lists nine categories when a variation/change in the title of a serial is considered a minor change and no new record needs to be created:

i)   a difference in the representation of a word or words anywhere in the title (e.g., one spelling vs. another; abbreviated word or sign or symbol vs. spelled-out form; arabic numeral(s) vs. roman numeral(s); numbers or dates vs. spelled-out form; hyphenated words vs. unhyphenated words; one-word compounds vs. two-word compounds, whether hyphenated or not; an acronym or initialism vs. full form; or a change in grammatical form (e.g., singular vs. plural))

ii)   the addition, deletion, or change of articles, prepositions, or conjunctions anywhere in the title

iii)   a difference involving the name of the same corporate body and elements of its hierarchy or their grammatical connection anywhere in the title (e.g., the addition, deletion, or rearrangement of the name of the same corporate body or the substitution of a variant form)

iv)   the addition, deletion, or change of punctuation, including initialisms and letters with separating punctuation vs. those without separating punctuation, anywhere in the title

v)   a different order of titles when the title is given in more than one language in the chief source of information, provided that the title chosen as title proper still appears as a parallel title

vi)   the addition, deletion, or change of words anywhere in the title that link the title to the numbering

vii)   two or more titles proper used on different issues of a serial according to a regular pattern

viii)   the addition to, deletion from, or change in the order of words in a list anywhere in the title, provided that there is no significant change in the subject matter

ix)   the addition, deletion, or rearrangement anywhere in the title of words that indicate the type of resource such as "magazine," "journal," or "newsletter" or their equivalent in other languages.

In this example, the serial *Technology & Learning* became *Tech & Learning* with the June 2008 issue. This is a minor change, as identified by AACR2 21.2C2bi, so no new record is created. The existing record has been updated with a specific introductory note in subfield ‡i followed by a colon in the 246 field: 246 1# ‡i Issues for June 2008- called: ‡a Tech & learning. The first indicator value is set to 1, and the second indicator value set to # (blank). When comparing titles, be sure to compare the title in hand to the title proper in the 245 field, not the 246 field in the serial bibliographic record. Also, remember that multiple minor changes do not constitute a major change.

OCLC #22361990

Type a	ELvl	Srce d	GPub	Ctrl	Lang eng
BLvl s	Form	Conf 0	Freq m	MRec	Ctry cau
S/L 0	Orig	EntW	Regl r	Alph a	
Desc a	SrTp p	Cont	DtSt c	Dates 1990	, 9999

022	0		1053-6728 ǂy 0746-4223 ǂ2 1
042			lc ǂa nsdp
245	0	0	Technology & learning.
246	1	0	Technology and learning

CCM 16.2.4i

				AACR2
246	1		ǂi Issues for June 2008- called: ǂa Tech & learning	21.2C2bi 21.30J1c

260		Dayton, OH : ǂb Peter Li, Inc., ǂc c1990-
300		v. : ǂb ill. ; ǂc 28 cm.
310		Monthly, ǂb 2006-
362	0	Vol. 11, no. 1 (Sept. 1990)-
500		Imprint varies: San Francisco, CA : Miller Freeman, Inc., <Nov./Dec. 1998->
500		Title from cover.
500		Latest issue consulted: Vol. 28, no. 11 (June 2008).
650	0	Computer-assisted instruction ǂv Periodicals.
780	0 0	ǂt Classroom computer learning ǂx 0746-4223 ǂw (DLC) 83647973 ǂw (OCoLC)10008037

AACR2

21.2C2bi - Consider a title change to be minor when there is a difference in the representation of a word or words anywhere in the title (e.g., one spelling vs. another; abbreviated word or sign or symbol vs. spelled-out form; arabic numeral(s) vs. roman numeral(s); numbers or dates vs. spelled-out form; hyphenated words vs. unhyphenated words; one-word compounds vs. two-word compounds, whether hyphenated or not; an acronym or initialism vs. full form; or a change in grammatical form (e.g., singular vs. plural)) . . . As appropriate, give, in the note area (see 12.7B4.2), those changes not considered to constitute a major change in the title proper. Make added entries as instructed in 21.30J1

21.30J1c - If considered necessary for access, make an added entry in the following situation: the changed title proper of a serial that is not a major change (see 21.2C2)

12.1B8a - Serials. If a major change in the title proper occurs, make a new description (see 21.2C). If a minor change occurs in the title proper on a subsequent issue or part, in general, give the later title in a note (see 12.7B4.2)

12.7B4.2a - Serials. Make notes on minor changes in title proper that occur after the first/earliest issue or part (see 12.1B8)

RDA

2.3.8.3 - Recording later titles proper: for changes in the title proper, apply the instructions given under 2.3.2.12.1 for multipart monographs and 2.3.2.12.2 for serials. Record a change in the title proper of a multipart monograph or a minor change in the title proper of a serial appearing on a later issue or part if it is considered to be important for identification or access. Apply the basic instructions on recording titles given under 2.3.1

2.3.2.12.2 - If there is major change (as defined under 2.3.2.13.1) in the title proper on a subsequent issue or part of a serial, make a new description for the issues or parts appearing under the new title and treat the two descriptions as descriptions for related works (see 25.1). If the change is a minor change (as defined in 2.3.2.13.2) but is considered to be important for identification or access, record the later title as a later title proper (see 2.3.8)

2.3.2.13.2 - Minor Changes. In general, consider the following to be minor changes in a title proper:
  i) a difference in the representation of a word or words anywhere in the title (e.g., one spelling vs. another; abbreviated word or sign or symbol vs. spelled-out form; arabic numeral vs. roman numeral; number or date vs. spelled-out form; hyphenated word vs. unhyphenated word; one-word compound vs. two-word compound, whether hyphenated or not; an acronym or initialism vs. full form; or a change in grammatical form (e.g., singular vs. plural))

CCM

16.2.4i - Minor changes in title proper: Category i. the only change is in the representation of a word or words (AACR2 21.2C2bi)

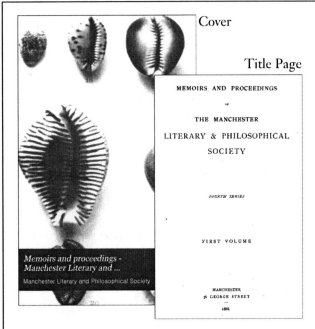

Cover

Title Page

MEMOIRS AND PROCEEDINGS

OF

THE MANCHESTER

LITERARY & PHILOSOPHICAL

SOCIETY

FOURTH SERIES

FIRST VOLUME

MANCHESTER
36 GEORGE STREET
--
1888.

EXERCISE 1   Pre-AACR2 Record or AACR2 Record?

Catalogers should be able to identify whether a record has been created according to pre-AACR2 standards or AACR2 standards. Examine the following cataloging record to determine whether it was created according to AACR2 standards. How do you know? How are title changes treated and recorded in this record?

OCLC #1756598

Type a	ELvl I	Srce	GPub	Ctrl	Lang eng
BLvl s	Form	Conf 0	Freq a	MRec	Ctry enk
S/L 1	Orig	EntW	Regl r	Alph a	
Desc	SrTp	Cont	DtSt c	Dates 1785	, 9999

022		0076-3721
110	2	Manchester Literary and Philosophical Society.
222	0	Memoirs and proceedings - Manchester Literary and Philosophical Society
245	1 0	Memoirs and proceedings - Manchester Literary and Philosophical Society.
247	0 0	Memoirs of the Literary and Philosophical Society of Manchester ‡f 1785-1879
247	0 0	Memoirs of the Manchester Literary and Philosophical Society ‡f 1882-87
247	0 0	Memoirs and proceedings of the Manchester Literary & Philosophical Society ‡f 1888-96
247	0 0	Memoirs and proceedings of the Manchester Literary & Philosophical Society. (Manchester memoirs) ‡f 1896/97-
260		Manchester [etc.]
310		Annual, ‡b 1887/88-
321		Irregular, ‡b v. 1-[30], 1789-1887.
362	0	v. 1- [1785]-
500		2d series, v. 13, 1856, has added t.-p.: Memoir of John Dalton . . . and history of the atomic theory up to his time. By Robt. Angus Smith.
500		3d series, v. 9, 1883, has title: For the hundredth year of the Literary and philosophical society of Manchester. (1881) A centenary of science in Manchester . . . by R. Angus Smith.
500		4th series, v. 6, 1892, has title: Memoir of James Prescott Joule . . . by Osborne Reynolds.

515			Vols. 1-40 are not consecutively numbered, but are divided into series as follows: v. 1-5, 1785-1802; 2d ser. v. 1-15, 1805-60; 3d ser., v. 1-10, 1862-87; 4th ser., v. 1-10, 1888-96. With v. 41 the numbering by series is discontinued.
515			Beginning with v. 41, each memoir is separately paged.
530			Also issued online.
555			"Index to the seventeen volumes of the memoirs of the Manchester literary and philosophical society, vol. 1 (old series) to vol. 12 (new series) inclusive," included in 2d ser., v. 12, p. [285]-318.
580			The Memoirs and Proceedings were published separately until 1888.
650		0	Science ‡x Societies, etc.
710	2		Manchester Literary and Philosophical Society. ‡t Memoirs.
780	1	5	Manchester Literary and Philosophical Society, Manchester, Eng. ‡t Proceedings ‡g 1888

Cover  Cover

EXERCISE 2   Major or Minor Change?

The journal *Genetical Research* changed its name to *Genetic Research* in 2008. Is this a major change or a minor change? Why?

OCLC #2113809

Type a	ELvl	Srce	GPub	Ctrl	Lang eng
BLvl s	Form	Conf 0	Freq b	MRec	Ctry enk
S/L 0	Orig	EntW	Regl r	Alph a	
Desc a	SrTp p	Cont b	DtSt d	Dates 1960	, 2007

022		0016-6723 ‡z 0435-2823 ‡2 z
042		nsdp ‡a lc
210	0	Genet. res.
222		0 Genetical research
245	0	0 Genetical research.
260		London ; ‡a New York : ‡b Cambridge University Press, ‡c 1960-2007.
300		v. : ‡b ill. ; ‡c 26 cm.
310		Bimonthly, ‡b <Aug. 1974->
321		3 no. a year, ‡b 1960-
362	0	Vol. 1, no. 1 (Feb. 1960)-v. 89, no. 5/6 (Oct./Dec. 2007).
500		Title from cover.
500		Latest issue consulted: Vol. 89, no. 5/6 (Oct./Dec. 2007).
510	2	Chemical abstracts ‡x 0009-2258
650		0 Genetics ‡v Periodicals.
650		0 Heredity ‡v Periodicals.
650		2 Genetics ‡v Periodicals.
650		6 Génétique ‡v Périodiques.
650		6 Hérédité ‡v Périodiques.
776	0	8 ‡i Microfiche version: ‡t Genetical research ‡w (OCoLC)6747622
776	0	8 ‡i Microfilm version: ‡t Genetical research ‡x 0016-6723 ‡w (OCoLC)56565304
776	0	8 ‡i Online version: ‡t Genetical research (Online) ‡x 1469-5073 ‡w (DLC) 2007233680 ‡w (OCoLC)43802193
785	0	0 ‡t Genetics research ‡w (DLC) 2009254003 ‡w (OCoLC)239614039
856	4	1 ‡u http://www.journals.cambridge.org/jid%5FGRH

EXERCISE 3 Recording Title Changes in Linking Fields

With its January 2009 issue, the serial *Perception & Psychophysics* changed its name to *Attention, Perception, & Psychophysics*. Based on the information provided in the two records here, create the 780 and 785 linking fields for the ceased title and the new title, respectively. Make sure to use the appropriate indicators and subfields in the linking fields.

For assistance with MARC coding, consult the *OCLC Bibliographic Formats and Standards* website at http://www.oclc.org/bibformats/en.

OCLC #1762090

Type a	ELvl	Srce	GPub	Ctrl	Lang eng
BLvl s	Form	Conf 0	Freq m	MRec	Ctry txu
S/L 0	Orig	EntW	Regl x	Alph a	
Desc	SrTp p	Cont	DtSt d	Dates 1966	, 2008

010		74201512 ǂz sn 78005032
022		0031-5117 ǂ2 1
042		nsdp ǂa lc
210	0	Percept. psychophys.
222	0	Perception & psychophysics
245	0 0	Perception & psychophysics.
246	3	Perception and psychophysics
260		[Austin, Tex., etc., ǂb Psychonomic Society, etc.]
300		70 v. ǂb ill. ǂc 27-29 cm.
310		8 no. a year, ǂb 1995-2008
321		Monthly
362	0	v. 1-70 ; Jan. 1966-Nov. 2008.
500		Latest issue consulted: Vol. 70, no. 8 (Nov. 2008).
515		Issues for Dec. 1967- published in 2 consecutively paged parts, A and B.
530		Also issued online.
550		"A journal of the Psychonomic Society, inc."
650	0	Senses and sensation ǂv Periodicals.
650	0	Perception ǂv Periodicals.
650	2	Perception ǂv Periodicals.
650	2	Psychophysiology ǂv Periodicals.
650	6	Sens et sensations ǂv Périodiques.
650	6	Perception ǂv Périodiques.
710	2	Psychonomic Society.
776	1	ǂt Perception & psychophysics (Online) ǂx 1532-5962 ǂw (DLC) 00215938 ǂw (OCoLC)45405246

856	4 1	ǂu http://app.psychonomic-journals.org/ ǂ3 v.63 (2007)-v.70 (2008)

Cover

Cover

OCLC #235533099

Type a	ELvl	Srce c	GPub	Ctrl	Lang eng
BLvl s	Form	Conf 0	Freq b	MRec	Ctry txu
S/L 0	Orig	EntW	Regl x	Alph a	
Desc a	SrTp p	Cont	DtSt c	Dates 2009	, 9999

010		2008212295
022	0	1943-3921 ‡2 1
037		‡b Psychonomic Society, 1710 Fortview Rd., Austin, TX 78704
042		lcd ‡a nsdp
130	0	Attention, perception & psychophysics (Print)
210	0	Atten. percept. psychophys. ‡b (Print)
210	1 0	Atten Percept Psychophys ‡2 dnlm
222	0	Attention, perception & psychophysics ‡b (Print)
245	1 0	Attention, perception & psychophysics.
246	3	Attention, perception and psychophysics
246	1 3	AP & P
260		Austin, Tex. : ‡b Psychonomic Society
310		Eight no. a year
362	1	Began with v. 71, no. 1 (Jan. 2009).
500		Description based on: Vol. 71, no. 1 (Jan. 2009); title from cover.
500		Latest issue consulted: Vol. 71, no. 1 (Jan. 2009).
530		Also issued online.
650	0	Senses and sensation ‡v Periodicals.
650	0	Perception ‡v Periodicals.
650	0	Attention ‡v Periodicals.
650	0	Psychophysics ‡v Periodicals.
650	1 2	Attention ‡v Periodicals.
650	2 2	Perception ‡v Periodicals.
710	2	Psychonomic Society.
776	0 8	‡i Also issued online: ‡t Attention, perception & psychophysics (Online) ‡x 1943-393X ‡w (DLC) 2008212296 ‡w (OCoLC)235533691
856	4	‡u www.psychonomic.org/PP
856	4 1	‡u http://app.psychonomic-journals.org/ ‡3 v.71 (2009)-

EXERCISE 4   Recording Serial Mergers

Cover

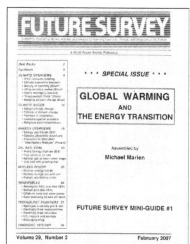

Cover

Cover

In 2009, the two serials *Future Survey* and *Future Research Quarterly* were merged into the new serial: *World Future Review*. Based on the information provided in the three records here, give 780 and 785 fields for the new title. You can also provide the linking entry complexity note in the 580 field to express the merger relationship. Make sure to use the appropriate indicators and subfields in the linking fields.

For assistance with MARC coding, consult the OCLC *Bibliographic Formats and Standards* website at http://www.oclc.org/bibformats/en.

OCLC #301795864

Type a	ELvl	Srce c	GPub	Ctrl	Lang eng
BLvl s	Form	Conf 0	Freq b	MRec	Ctry mdu
S/L 0	Orig	EntW	Regl r	Alph a	
Desc a	SrTp p	Cont	DtSt c	Dates 2009	, 9999

010			2009207441
022	0		1946-7567 ‡2 1
042			nsdp ‡a lcd
245	0	0	World future review.
260			Bethesda, MD : ‡b World Future Society
310			Bimonthly
362	1		Began with: Vol. 1, no. 1 (Feb.-Mar. 2009).
500			Description based on 1st issue; title from title page.
500			Latest issue consulted: Vol. 1, no. 3 (June-July 2009).

650		0	Forecasting ‡v Periodicals.
650		0	Forecasting ‡x Study and teaching ‡v Periodicals.
710	2		World Future Society.

OCLC #4693322

Type a	ELvl	Srce d	GPub	Ctrl	Lang eng
BLvl s	Form	Conf 0	Freq m	MRec	Ctry dcu
S/L 0	Orig	EntW a	Regl r	Alph a	
Desc a	SrTp p	Cont	DtSt d	Dates 1979	, 2008

010			81649971 $z sn 79001912
022	0		0190-3241 ǂ2 1
042			lc ǂa nsdp
245	0	0	Future survey.
260			Washington, D.C. : ǂb World Future Society, ǂc c1979-c2008.
300			v. ; ǂc 28 cm.
310			Monthly
362	0		Vol. 1, no. 1 (Jan. 1979)-v. 30, no. 12 (Dec 2008).
500			Title from cover.
650		0	Social prediction ǂv Abstracts ǂv Periodicals.
710	2		World Future Society.
776	0	8	ǂt Future survey (Online) ǂw (OCoLC)60626134
780	0	0	ǂt Public policy book forecast ǂx 0197-9035 ǂw (DLC)sc 79004758

OCLC #11276457

Type a	ELvl	Srce d	GPub	Ctrl	Lang eng
BLvl s	Form	Conf 0	Freq q	MRec	Ctry mdu
S/L 0	Orig	EntW	Regl r	Alph a	
Desc a	SrTp p	Cont o	DtSt d	Dates 1985	, 2008

010			87644223 $z sn 84002336
022	0		8755-3317 ǂy 0049-8092 ǂ2 1
042			nsdp ǂa lc
222		0	Futures research quarterly
245	0	0	Futures research quarterly.
260			Bethesda, MD : ǂb World Future Society, ǂc c1985-
300			v. : ǂb ill. ; ǂc 24 cm.
310			Quarterly
362	0		Vol. 1, no. 1 (spring 1985)-
362	1		Ceased in 2008.
500			Title from cover.
500			Latest issue consulted: vol. 24, no. 1 (spring 2008).
650		0	Forecasting ǂv Periodicals.
710	2		World Future Society.
780	0	0	ǂt World Future Society bulletin ǂx 0049-8092 ǂw (DLC) 87644228 ǂw (OCoLC)3302525

EXERCISE 5   Recording Title Absorption in Linking Fields

In 2006, the quarterly journal *Genetic, Social, and General Psychology Monographs* ceased and was absorbed by *The Journal of Social Psychology*. Based on the information provided in the two records here, create the 780 and 785 linking fields for the ceased title and absorbing title, respectively. Make sure to use the appropriate indicators and subfields in the linking fields.

For assistance with MARC coding, consult the OCLC *Bibliographic Formats and Standards* website at http://www.oclc.org/bibformats/en.

OCLC #11659641

Type a	ELvl	Srce d	GPub	Ctrl	Lang eng
BLvl s	Form	Conf 0	Freq q	MRec	Ctry dcu
S/L 0	Orig	EntW	Regl r	Alph a	
Desc a	SrTp p	Cont	DtSt d	Dates 1985	, 2006

010			85647127 $z sn 85000493
022	0		8756-7547 ‡2 1
037			‡b Heldref Publications, 4000 Albemarle St., N.W., Washington, DC 20016
042			nsdp ‡a lc
210	0		Genet. soc. gen. psychol. monogr.
222		0	Genetic, social, and general psychology monographs
245	0	0	Genetic, social, and general psychology monographs.
260			Washington, DC : ‡b Heldref Publications, ‡c c1985-
300			v. : ‡b ill. ; ‡c 23 cm.
310			Quarterly
362	0		Vol. 111, no. 1 (Feb. 1985)-
362	1		Ceased with vol. 132, no. 4 (Nov. 2006).
500			Final issue consulted.
530			Issued also in microform and online.
650		0	Psychology ‡v Periodicals.
650		0	Genetic psychology ‡v Periodicals.
650		0	Social psychology ‡v Periodicals.
650		2	Genetics ‡v Periodicals.
650		2	Psychology ‡v Periodicals.
650		2	Psychology, Social ‡v Periodicals.
650		6	Enfants ‡x Développement ‡v Périodiques.
776	1		‡t Genetic, social, and general psychology monographs (Online) ‡x 1940-5286 ‡w (DLC) 2007215294 ‡w (OCoLC)42815946
780	0	0	‡t Genetic psychology monographs ‡x 0016-6677 ‡w (DLC) 54004353 ‡w (OCoLC)1440765
856	4	1	‡u http://www.heldref.org

Cover   Cover

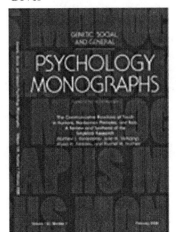 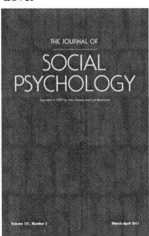

OCLC #1782304

Type a	ELvl	Srce	GPub	Ctrl	Lang eng
BLvl s	Form	Conf 0	Freq b	MRec	Ctry dcu
S/L 0	Orig	EntW	Regl r	Alph a	
Desc	SrTp p	Cont	DtSt c	Dates 1930	, 9999

010			33021284
022			0022-4545 ‡2 1
037			‡b Managing Editor, 2 Commercial St., Provincetown, MA 02657
041	0		eng ‡b freger
042			lc ‡a nsdp
210	0		J. soc. psychol.
222		4	The Journal of social psychology
245	0	4	The Journal of social psychology.
260			[Washington, D.C., etc. ‡b Helen Reid Educational Foundation, etc.]
300			v. ‡b ill., diagrs. ‡c 25 cm.
310			Bimonthly ‡b <, Apr. 1974- >
321			Quarterly, ‡b 1930-<Nov. 1932>
362	0		v. 1- Feb. 1930-
500			Includes section "Books."
530			Also issued online.
546			Each article is followed by résumés in French and German.
500			Editors: 1930-<32> John Dewey, Carl Murchison, and others.
650		0	Social psychology ‡v Periodicals.
650		2	Psychology, Social ‡v Periodicals.
650	1	7	Sociale psychologie. ‡2 gtt
700	1		Dewey, John, ‡d 1859-1952, ‡e ed.
700	1		Murchison, Carl Allanmore, ‡d 1887- ‡e ed.
710	2		Helen Dwight Reid Educational Foundation.
776	1		‡t Journal of social psychology (Online) ‡x 1940-1183 ‡w (DLC) 2007215267 ‡w (OCoLC)39109336

856	4	1	‡u http://heldref.metapress.com/openurl.asp? genre=journal&issn=0022-4545

CHAPTER 3

Corporate Body as Main Entry and Changes in Corporate Body

Under AACR2, most serials are entered under title main entry. Unlike monographs, where personal names are usually chosen as the main entry, serials are rarely cataloged with personal names as the main entry unless the serial publication would not have existed without the person and that person is responsible for the entire run of the serial. However, it is not unusual for the serial to be entered under corporate body main entry, following the instructions under AACR2 21.1B2.

According to AACR2 21.1B1, "a corporate body is an organization or a group of persons that is identified by a particular name and that acts, or may act, as an entity." Some examples of corporate bodies are associations, institutions, business firms, government agencies, and conferences. AACR2 21.1B2 lists several categories under which a publication, including a serial, will be entered under corporate body:

(a) those of an **administrative nature** dealing with the corporate body itself or

- its internal policies, procedures, finances, and/or operations or

- its officers, staff, and/or membership (e.g., directories) or

- its resources (e.g., catalogues, inventories)

(b) some **legal, governmental, and religious works** of the following types:

- laws (see 21.31)

- decrees of the chief executive that have the force of law (see 21.31)

- administrative regulations (see 21.32), etc.

(c) those that record the **collective thought of the body** (e.g., reports of commissions, committees, etc.; official statements of position on external policies)

(d) those that report the **collective activity of a conference** (e.g., proceedings, collected papers), **of an expedition** (e.g., results of exploration, investigation), **or of an event** (e.g., an exhibition, fair, festival) falling within the definition of a corporate body (see 21.1B1), provided that the conference, expedition, or event is named in the item being catalogued

(e) those that result from the **collective activity of a performing group** as a whole where the responsibility of the group goes beyond that of mere performance, execution, etc. Publications resulting from such activity include sound recordings, films, videorecordings, and written records of performances. (For corporate bodies that function solely as performers on sound recordings, see 21.23.)

(f) **cartographic materials** emanating from a corporate body other than a body that is merely responsible for their publication or distribution

Sometimes, it is hard to tell whether a serial falls under any of those categories. Rule 21.1B2 concludes that if in doubt about whether a work falls into one or more of these categories, treat it as if it does not.

In RDA, general rules and guidelines with regard to corporate bodies being responsible for a work remain the same. The same six categories under which a work will be entered under corporate body appear in RDA as well as AACR2, although the order of these categories have changed. RDA Rule 19.2.1.1.1 states that corporate bodies are considered to be creators when they are responsible for originating, issuing, or causing to be issued works that fall into one or more of the following categories:

(a) works of an **administrative nature** dealing with any of the following aspects of the body itself:
   i)   its internal policies, procedures, finances, and/or operations or
   ii) its officers, staff, and/or membership (e.g., directories) or
   iii) its resources (e.g., catalogues, inventories)
(b) works that record the **collective thought of the body** (e.g., reports of commissions, committees; official statements of position on external policies, standards)
(c) works that report the **collective activity** of
   i)   **a conference** (e.g., proceedings, collected papers) or
   ii) **an expedition** (e.g., results of exploration, investigation)
   iii) **an event** (e.g., an exhibition, fair, festival) falling within the definition of a corporate body (see RDA 18.1.2) provided that the conference, expedition, or event is named in the resource being described
(d) works that result from the **collective activity of a performing group** as a whole where the responsibility of the group goes beyond that of mere performance, execution, etc.
(e) **cartographic works** originating with a corporate body other than a body that is merely responsible for their publication or distribution.
(f) **legal works** of the following types:
   i)   laws of a political jurisdiction
   ii) decrees of a head of state, chief executive, or ruling executive body
   iii) bills and drafts of legislation, etc.

In this chapter, several serial publications are used as examples to show the decision process in determining whether a serial emanates from the corporate body and whether it falls under one of the categories of AACR2 21.1B2 or RDA 19.2.1.1.1. If a serial does fall under any of the categories, it is entered under the corporate body. Otherwise, it is most likely to be entered under the title.

RESOURCES CONSULTED

AACR2

21.1B2 General Rule

LCRI

21.1B2 General Rule

RDA

19.2.1.1.1 Corporate bodies considered to be creators

19.2.1.3 Recording creators

19.3.1.3 Recording other persons, families, and corporate bodies associated with a work

18.4 Recording relationships to persons, families, and corporate bodies associated with a resource

CCM

Module 4 Main and added entries (Fields 100–111 and 700–711)

Corporate Body Main Entry: About the Body Itself

Title: Membership directory

Cover

Membership directories like this one, published by the American Association of Bovine Practitioners (AABP), belong to Category A of AACR2 21.1B2: works of an administrative nature dealing with the officers, staff, and/or membership of the issuing corporate body. The main entry for these publications will be the name of the corporate body, as established in the authority file, available from http://authorities.loc.gov.

110   2_   ‡a American Association of Bovine Practitioners.

Table of Contents

American Association of Bovine Practitioners

MEMBERSHIP DIRECTORY 2008

P.O. Box 3610
Auburn, Alabama 36831-3610
phone: 1-800-COW-AABP (269-2227)
fax: (334) 821-9532
email: aabphq@aabp.org

TABLE OF CONTENTS

AABP Mission Statement

The American Association of Bovine Practitioners is an international association of veterinarians organized to enhance the professional lives of its members through relevant continuing education that will improve the well-being of cattle and the economic success of their owners, increase awareness and promote leadership for issues critical to cattle industries, and improve opportunities for careers in bovine medicine.

Note that because the name of the association is entered in direct order, the first indicator in the 110 field is coded 2. In this example, the name of the corporate body as well as the title proper is found on the publication's cover. Confirmation of the administrative function of this publication can be found in the table of contents.

OCLC #33600264

	Type: a	ELvl: l	Srce: d	GPub:	Ctrl:	Lang: eng
	BLvl: s	Form:	Conf: 0	Freq: u	MRec:	Ctry: inu
	S/L: 0	Orig:	EntW:	Regl: u	Alph:	
	Desc: a	SrTp:	Cont:	DtSt: c	Dates: 19uu,	9999

	043		n-us—	
CCM 4.4.1	110	2	American Association of Bovine Practitioners.	AACR2 21.1B2A
	245	1 0	Membership directory / ‡c American Association of Bovine Practitioners.	21.30J1
	246	1 7	AABP membership directory	21.30J2
	260		[West Layfayette, Ind.?] : ‡b The Association,	
	300		v. ; ‡c 28 cm.	
	500		Description based on: 1995; title from cover.	
	610	2 0	American Association of Bovine Practitioners ‡v Directories.	
	650	0	Cattle ‡x Diseases ‡v Directories.	
	650	0	Veterinarians ‡z United States ‡v Directories.	

AACR2

21.1B2A - Works of an administrative nature dealing with the officers, staff, and/or membership of the issuing corporate body

21.30J1 - Added entry for title proper

21.30J2 - Added entry for variant of title proper

LCRI

21.1B2 - Category A: to belong to this category the work must deal with the body itself

RDA

19.2.1.1.1 a) - Works of an administrative nature dealing with the body itself

CCM

4.1.4 - Considerations regarding main entry and choice of corporate body

4.4.1 - Category A: "Those of an administrative nature dealing with the corporate body itself"

Corporate Body Main Entry: About the Body Itself

Title: Biennial report of the Board of State Commissioners of Public Charities of the State of Illinois

Title Page

FIRST BIENNIAL REPORT

OF THE

BOARD OF STATE COMMISSIONERS

OF

PUBLIC CHARITIES

OF THE

STATE OF ILLINOIS.

———

PRESENTED TO THE GOVERNOR,

DECEMBER, 1870.

— — — — — — —

SPRINGFIELD:
ILLINOIS JOURNAL PRINTING OFFICE.
1871.

The Board of State Commissioners of Public Charities of the State of Illinois issued this biennual report. Its contents deal with the administrative activities of the board for the years 1870-1909.

In this example, the biennial report emanates from the corporate body because it is issued by the Board of State Commissioners of Public Charities of the State of Illinois. The body is named and formally presented on the title page.

The serial meets the criteria of category A of AACR2 21.1B2, which states that works emanating from a single corporate body that are of an administrative nature dealing with the body itself are to be entered under the name of the corporate body.

When chosen as main entry, the corporate body is entered as established in the authority file, available from http://authorities.loc.gov.

110 1_ Illinois. ǂb Board of State Commissioners of Public Charities.

Website screenshot

The Library of Congress >> Go to Library of Congress Online Catalog

LIBRARY OF CONGRESS AUTHORITIES

Help ⓘ | New Search | Search History | Headings List | Start Over

◀ Previous   Next ▶

MARC Display | Labelled Display

LC Control Number: no2007101751

HEADING: Illinois. Board of State Commissioners of Public Charities

000 00584nz a2200133n 450
001 7283148
005 20070901071053.0
008 070821n| acannaabn |a ana c
010 __ |a no2007101751
035 __ |a (OCoLC)oca07510762
040 __ |a MoSW |b eng |c MoSW
110 1_ |a Illinois. |b Board of State Commissioners of Public Charities
410 1_ |a Illinois. |b State Commissioners of Public Charities, Board of
670 __ |a Biennial report of the Board of State Commissioners of Public Charities of the State of Illinois, Nov. 1878: |b t.p. (Board of State Commissioners of Public Charities of the State of Illinois)

OCLC #1771401

Type: a	ELvl:	Srce: d	GPub: s	Ctrl:	Lang: eng
BLvl: s	Form:	Conf: 0	Freq: g	MRec:	Ctry: ilu
S/L: 0	Orig:	EntW:	Regl: r	Alph: a	
Desc: a	SrTp:	Cont:	DtSt: d	Dates: 1870,	1909

	042		msc	
CCM 4.4.1	110	1	Illinois. ‡b Board of State Commissioners of Public Charities.	AACR2 21.1B2A
	245	1 0	Biennial report of the Board of State Commissioners of Public Charities of the State of Illinois.	21.30J1
	246	3 0	Fractional biennial report of the Board of State Commissioners of Public Charities of the State of Illinois	21.30J2

260		Springfield, Ill. : ‡b The Board, ‡c 1871-1911.
300		21 v. ; ‡c 22 cm.
310		Biennial
362	0	1st (Dec. 1870)-21st (July 1, 1908/Dec. 31, 1909).
500		Vol. for 1908/1909 has title: Fractional biennial report of the Board of State Commissioners of Public Charities of the State of Illinois.
515		Report year irregular.
650	0	Public welfare ‡z Illinois ‡v Periodicals.
785	0 0	Illinois. State Charities Commission. ‡t Annual report of the State Charities Commission ‡w (OCoLC)1752571

AACR2

21.1B2A - Works emanating from a single corporate body that are of an administrative nature dealing with the corporate body itself

21.30J1 - Added entry for title proper

21.30J2 - Added entries for variants of title proper

LCRI

21.1B2 - Category A: to belong to this category the work must deal with the body itself

RDA

19.2.1.1.1 a) - Works of an administrative nature dealing with the body itself

CCM

4.1.4 - Considerations regarding main entry and choice of corporate body

4.4.1 - Category A: "Those of an administrative nature dealing with the corporate body itself"

Corporate Body Main Entry With Title Change

Title: Annual report of the State Charities Commission

Title Page

FIRST ANNUAL REPORT

OF THE

State Charities Commission

TO THE

Honorable CHARLES S. DENEEN

Governor of Illinois

SPRINGFIELD, ILLINOIS

December 31, 1910

SPRINGFIELD, ILL.:
ILLINOIS STATE JOURNAL CO., STATE PRINTERS
1911

This title is related to the earlier example. The change of the commission's name (from "the Board of State Commissioners of Public Charities of the State of Illinois" in the earlier title to "the State Charities Commission") necessitated a new record and a new corporate body main entry. For more discussion on the situations requiring the creation of a new record for a serial, see Chapter 2. Because the serial continues to fall under AACR2 21.1B2A, it is entered under the name of the commission.

The name of the body—"the State Charities Commission"—is entered as established in the authority file, available from http://authorities .loc.gov.

110 1_ ‡a Illinois. ‡b State Charities Commission.

Website screenshot

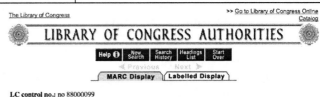

LIBRARY OF CONGRESS AUTHORITIES

LC control no.: no 88000099
LCCN permalink: http://lccn.loc.gov/no88000099
HEADING: Illinois. State Charities Commission

000 00481cz a2200157n 450
001 1597253
005 20080315071703.0
008 880314n| acannaabn |a ana c
010 __ |a no 88000099
035 __ |a (OCoLC)oca02246832
040 __ |a InU |b eng |c InU |d OCoLC
110 1_ |a Illinois. |b State Charities Commission
410 1_ |a Illinois. |b Charities Commission, State
670 __ |a Institution quarterly, Mar. 31, 1912: |b t.p. (State Charities Commission; Ill.)
953 __ |a xx00
985 __ |c OCLC |e LSPC

OCLC #1752571

Type: a	ELvl: l	Srce: d	GPub:	Ctrl:		Lang: eng
BLvl: s	Form:	Conf: 0	Freq: a	MRec:		Ctry: ilu
S/L: 0	Orig:	EntW:	Regl: r	Alph: a		
Desc: a	SrTp:	Cont:	DtSt: d	Dates: 1910,	191u	

	043		n-us-il	
CCM 4.4.1	110	1	Illinois. ‡b State Charities Commission.	**AACR2 21.1B2A 21.3B1**
	245	1 0	Annual report of the State Charities Commission.	**21.30J1**
	260		Springfield : ‡b The Commission, ‡c 1911-	
	300		v. ; ‡c 22 cm.	
	310		Annual	
	362	0	1st-	
	500		Report made to the Governor of Illinois.	
	500		Title varies slightly: Annual report of the State Charities Commission of Illinois.	
	650	0	Charities ‡z Illinois ‡v Periodicals.	
	780	0 0	Illinois. Board of State Commissioners of Public Charities. ‡t Biennial report of the Board of State Commissioners of Public Charities of the State of Illinois ‡w (DLC)sn 91034120 ‡w(OCoLC)1771401	
	785	0 0	Illinois. State Charities Commission. ‡t Annual report ‡w (OCoLC) 1642716	

AACR2

21.1B2A - Works emanating from a single corporate body that are of an administrative nature dealing with the corporate body itself

21.3B1 - Make a new entry for a serial when the heading for a corporate body under which the serial is entered changes

21.30J1 - Added entry for title proper

LCRI

21.1B2 - Category A: to belong to this category the work must deal with the body itself

RDA

19.2.1.1.1 a) - Works of an administrative nature dealing with the body itself

1.6.2.4 - Change in responsibility for a serial: create a new description if there is a change in responsibility that requires a change in the identification of the serial as a work

6.1.3.2.1 - When there is a change affecting the authorized access point representing a person, family, or corporate body that is used in constructing the work, that is a change in responsibility for the work. Construct the authorized access point representing the work to reflect responsibility for the work as represented in the issue or part used as the basis for the new description

(Continued on next page)

CCM

4.1.4 - Considerations regarding main entry and choice of corporate body

4.4.1 - Category A: "Those of an administrative nature dealing with the corporate body itself"

Corporate Body Main Entry: Collective Activity of a Conference

Title: Proceedings of the Grand Lodge of the State of Illinois Ancient Free and Accepted Masons

Title Page

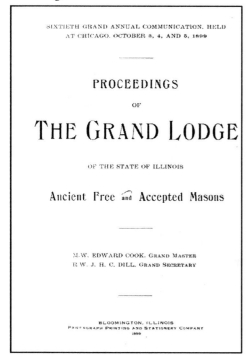

Until 1900, the "Grand Lodge of the State of Illinois"—the Illinois chapter of the Freemasons—published the proceedings of their annual meetings under the title proper *Proceedings of the Grand Lodge of the State of Illinois Ancient Free and Accepted Masons*.

The serial falls under the category of AACR2 21.1B2D, which states that works reporting the collective activity of a conference, of an expedition, or of an event falling within the definition of a corporate body are to be recorded with the corporate body as the main entry.

Because the Grand Lodge of the State of Illinois is a local chapter to the larger Freemason organization, it is entered as established in the authority file, available from http://authorities.loc.gov.

110 2_ ‡a Freemasons. ‡b Grand Lodge of Illinois.

Library of Congress practice changed effective December 2001 regarding the source of information for corporate bodies. Under the revised practice, a work covered by Category D is entered under the heading for the name of a conference, expedition, or event if the name appears anywhere in the item being cataloged.

Under the previous practice, from January 1981 to July 1991, the Library of Congress entered a Category D work under the heading for the name of the conference, etc., when the name appeared prominently on the item. For the period from August 1991 to November 2001, the Library of Congress entered a Category D work under the heading for the name of the conference, etc., when the name appeared on the chief source. Existing records are generally not updated to reflect the current policy.

OCLC #9493499

Type: a	ELvl: l	Srce: d	GPub:	Ctrl:		Lang: eng
BLvl: s	Form:	Conf: 1	Freq: a	MRec:		Ctry: ilu
S/L: 0	Orig:	EntW:	Regl: r	Alph: a		
Desc: a	SrTp:	Cont:	DtSt: d	Dates: 18uu,	1900	

	043		n-us-il	
CCM 4.4.3	110	2	Freemasons. ‡b Grand Lodge of Illinois.	AACR2 21.1B2D
	245	1 0	Proceedings of the Grand Lodge of the State of Illinois Ancient Free and Accepted Masons.	21.30J1
	246	1	‡i Some issues have title: ‡a Proceedings of the Grand Lodge of Illinois, of Ancient Free and Accepted Masons	21.30J2
	260		[S.l. : ‡b s.n.], ‡e (Bloomington, Ill. : ‡f Pantagraph Print. and Stationery Co.)	
	300		v. ; ‡c 22 cm.	
	310		Annual	
	500		Description based on: 60th (1899).	
	610	2 0	Freemasons. ‡b Grand Lodge of Illinois ‡v Congresses.	
	610	2 0	Freemasons ‡z Illinois ‡v Congresses	
	650	0	Secret societies ‡z Illinois ‡v Congresses.	
	785	0 0	Freemasons. Grand Lodge of Illinois. ‡t Proceedings of the Most Worshipful Grand Lodge of Ancient Free and Accepted Masons of the State of Illinois ‡w (OCoLC)9493378	

AACR2

21.1B2D - Works reporting the collective activity of a conference, of an expedition, or of an event falling within the definition of a corporate body

21.30J1 - Added entry for title proper

21.30J2 - Added entry for variant of title proper

LCRI

21.1B2 - Category D: it must deal with the activities of many persons involved in a corporate body covered by the category, not with the activities of a single person

- Amendments 2001 to AACR2 revised Category D of rule 21.1B2 to provide main entry for a Category D work under the heading for the name of a conference, expedition, or event if the name appears anywhere on the item being cataloged. Previously, main entry for a Category D work was under the heading for the name of the conference, expedition, or event when the name appeared prominently on the item

RDA

19.2.1.1.1 c) - Works that report the collective activity of a conference, an expedition, an event

CCM

4.1.4 - Considerations regarding main entry and choice of corporate body

4.4.3 - Category D: Conferences, exhibitions, and ad hoc events

Same Corporate Body Main Entry Change With Title Changes: Collective Activity of a Conference
First Title Change: Proceedings of the Most Worshipful Grand Lodge of Ancient Free and Accepted Masons of the State of Illinois
Second Title Change: Proceedings of the ... annual meeting of the Most Worshipful Grand Lodge, Ancient Free and Accepted Masons of the State of Illinois

Title Page

Title Page

SIXTY-SECOND GRAND ANNUAL COMMUNICATION, HELD
AT CHICAGO, OCTOBER 1, 2 AND 3, 1901

PROCEEDINGS

OF

THE MOST WORSHIPFUL
GRAND LODGE

OF ANCIENT FREE AND ACCEPTED MASONS

OF THE STATE OF ILLINOIS

GEORGE M. MOULTON, M.W. GRAND MASTER
J. H. C. DILL, R.W. GRAND SECRETARY

BLOOMINGTON, ILLINOIS
Pantagraph Printing and Stationery Co.
1901

In 1901 and again in 1933, a major change was made to the title proper of the Grand Lodge of Illinois's annual proceedings. New records were created to accurately reflect these changes, following AACR2 21.2c, which states that if a major change occurs in the title proper of a serial (i.e., a change of wording within the first five words), a new entry is made.

In both instances, the serial continues to fall under the category of AACR2 21.1B2D, which states that works reporting the collective activity of a conference, of an expedition, or of an event falling within the definition of a corporate body are to be recorded with the corporate body as the main entry.

Because the Grand Lodge of the State of Illinois is a local chapter of the larger Freemasons organization, it is entered as established in the authority file, available from http://authorities.loc.gov.

OCLC #9493378

Type: a	ELvl: l	Srce: d	GPub:	Ctrl:	Lang: eng
BLvl: s	Form:	Conf: 1	Freq: a	MRec:	Ctry: ilu
S/L: 0	Orig:	EntW:	Regl: r	Alph: a	
Desc: a	SrTp:	Cont:	DtSt: d	Dates: 1901,	1932

CCM 4.4.3					AACR2
	110	2		Freemasons. ǂb Grand Lodge of Illinois.	21.1B2D
	245	1	0	Proceedings of the Most Worshipful Grand Lodge of Ancient Free and Accepted Masons of the State of Illinois.	21.30J1
	246	1	8	Grand Lodge of Illinois	21.30J2
	246	1		ǂi Some issues have title: ǂa Proceedings of the Most Worshipful Grand Lodge, Ancient Free and Accepted Masons, State of Illinois	21.30J2
	260			S.l. : ǂb s.n., ǂe (Bloomington, Ill. : ǂf Pantagraph Printing and Stationery Co.)	
	362	1		Began with 62nd (1901), and ceased with 93rd (1932).	
	780	0	0	Freemasons. Grand Lodge of Illinois. ǂt Proceedings of the Grand Lodge of the State of Illinois Ancient Free and Accepted Masons ǂw (OCoLC)9493499	
	785	0	0	Freemasons. Grand Lodge of Illinois. ǂt Proceedings of the . . . annual meeting of the Most Worshipful Grand Lodge, Ancient Free and Accepted Masons of the State of Illinois ǂw(OCoLC)4945363	

OCLC #4945363

Type: a	ELvl: l	Srce: d	GPub:	Ctrl:	Lang: eng
BLvl: s	Form:	Conf: 1	Freq: a	MRec:	Ctry: ilu
S/L: 0	Orig:	EntW:	Regl: r	Alph: a	
Desc: a	SrTp:	Cont:	DtSt: u	Dates: 1933,	uuuu

CCM 4.4.3					AACR2
	110	2		Freemasons. ǂb Grand Lodge of Illinois.	21.1B2D
	245	1	0	Proceedings of the . . . annual meeting of the Most Worshipful Grand Lodge, Ancient Free and Accepted Masons of the State of Illinois.	21.30J1
	246	1	8	Grand Lodge of Illinois	21.30J2
	246	1		ǂi Some issues have title on cover: ǂa Grand Lodge, A. F. & A. M. of Illinois	21.30J2
	260			[S.l. : ǂb s.n.]	
	362	1		Began publication with 94th (1933).	
	780	0	0	Freemasons. Grand Lodge of Illinois. ǂt Proceedings of the Most Worshipful Grand Lodge of Ancient Free and Accepted Masons of the State of Illinois ǂw (OCoLC)9493378	

AACR2

21.1B2D - Works reporting the collective activity of a conference, of an expedition, or of an event falling within the definition of a corporate body

21.30J1 - Added entry for title proper

21.30J2 - Added entry for variant of title proper

LCRI

21.1B2 - Category D: it must deal with the activities of many persons involved in a corporate body covered by the category, not with the activities of a single person

RDA

19.2.1.1.1 c) - Works that report the collective activity of a conference, an expedition, an event

CCM

4.1.4 - Considerations regarding main entry and choice of corporate body

4.4.3 - Category D: Conferences, exhibitions, and ad hoc events

Corporate Body as Main Entry or Added Entry?

Title: Statistical abstract

Cover   Title Page

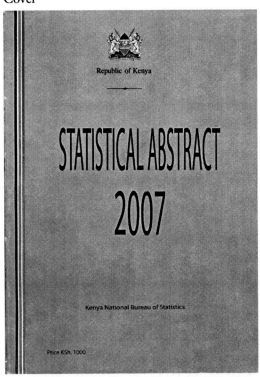

STATISTICAL ABSTRACT

2007

The Statistical Abstract is published annually by the **Kenya National Bureau of Statistics, Nairobi.** Any enquiries relating to this publication should be addressed to the Director General, Herufi House (situated between the Treasury Building and the Central Bank of Kenya). Subscription correspondence may be addressed directly to the Head Librarian in the same building.

Copyright © Kenya National Bureau of Statistics (KNBS)
All rights reserved

(Printed by Government Printer, Nairobi)

Extracts may be used or published if the source is duly acknowledged.

ISBN: 9966-767-10-X

This example requires a bit of thought. The serial seems to fit the categories given in AACR2 21.1B2, for publications recording the collective thought of the body, so it appears likely that it will be entered under the body "Kenya National Bureau of Statistics."

However, "the collective thought of the body" really refers to the opinions and/or recommendations of the body. CCM 4.4 makes it clear that when applying AACR2 21.1B2, the emphasis or purpose of the serial should be considered. "In general, if the serial is issued to present the activities, resources, or opinions of the body, enter it under the body; if the serial is issued to present current information, findings, results of research, etc. about a topic, enter it under the title." CCM 4.4.1 further elaborates that the following does not fit AACR2 21.1B2: "reports on matters external to the corporate body, particularly statistical publications that are not about the corporate body itself; reports of research done by the corporate body that are issued primarily to present the results of the research. . . ."

In this case, the Kenya National Bureau of Statistics primarily produces and presents statistical reports on Kenya rather than giving opinions on Kenya, so the serial should be entered under the title.

AACR2 21.30E1 gives instructions to make an added entry under the heading for a prominently named corporate body. Because the body "Kenya National Bureau of Statistics" is prominently named on the title page, an added entry is created.

Note: The generic nature of the title "Statistical abstract" necessitates this being entered with a uniform title as the main entry (CONSER5.3.2)

OCLC #220911142

	Type: a	ELvl:	Srce: d	GPub: f	Ctrl:		Lang: eng
	BLvl: s	Form:	Conf: 0	Freq: a	MRec:		Ctry: ke
	S/L: 0	Orig:	EntW: s	Regl: r	Alph:		
	Desc: a	SrTp:	Cont:	DtSt: c	Dates: 2007,		9999

	042		lcd	
	043		f-ke—	
CCM 5.3.2	130	0	Statistical abstract (Kenya National Bureau of Statistics)	AACR2 25.1A
	245	1 0	Statistical abstract.	21.30J1
	260		Nairobi : ǂb Kenya National Bureau of Statistics	
	300		v. ; ǂc 29 cm.	
	310		Annual	
	362	1	Began with 2007.	
	500		Description based on: 2007; title from title page.	
	500		Latest issue consulted: 2008.	
	650	0	Kenya ǂv Statistics ǂv Periodicals.	
4.8.3	710	2	Kenya National Bureau of Statistics.	21.1B3 21.30E
	780	0 0	ǂt Statistical abstract (Kenya. Central Bureau of Statistics) ǂx 1726-9938 ǂw (DLC) 73646387 ǂw (OCoLC)1788774	

AACR2

21.1B3 - If a work emanates from one or more corporate bodies and falls outside the categories given in 21.1B2, treat it as if no corporate body were involved. Make added entries under the headings for prominently named corporate bodies as instructed in 21.30E

21.30E1 - Added entry for prominently named corporate body

25.1A - Creation of a uniform title to distinguish from other works published under an identical title proper

21.30J1 - Added entry for title proper

LCRI

21.1B2 - The words "administrative nature" indicate works dealing with the management or conduct of the affairs of the body itself, including works that describe the activities of the body either in general terms or for a particular period of time, e.g., minutes of meetings, reports of activities for a particular period

RDA

19.3.1.3 - Record other persons, families, and corporate bodies associated with the work, if considered important for access, in accordance with the general guidelines on recording relationships to persons, families, and corporate bodies associated with a resource given under 18.4

(Continued on next page)

CCM

4.4.1 - To be considered for Category A, the publication must be of an "administrative nature" and include information that is about the activities of the corporate body or internal to its operations. Examples of serials that do not fit this category are: reports on matters external to the corporate body, particularly statistical publications that are not about the corporate body itself; reports of research done by the corporate body that are issued primarily to present the results of the research

4.8.1 - Corporate bodies not selected as the main entry may be given an added entry

4.8.3 - Corporate bodies as added entries, including most prominently named corporate bodies

5.3. 2 - Use a corporate body as a qualifier when the title proper consists solely of very general words that indicate the type of publication and/or periodicity

Corporate Body Main Entry: Collective Activity of a Conference

Title: Wildlife rehabilitation: a publication of the proceedings of the National Wildlife Rehabilitation Symposium

Cover

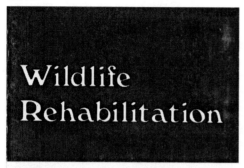

Title Page

Because this serial covers conference proceedings, it falls under AACR2 21.1B2D and should be entered under the heading for the conference. A search in the authority file (http://authorities.loc.gov) retrieves the established heading as:

> 111 2_ ‡a National Wildlife Rehabilitation
> Symposium.

Because the body is a named conference, a 111 field is used instead of a 110 field, which is used for corporate body names. The title proper *Wildlife Rehabilitation* is entered as an added entry.

Cover Verso

OCLC #9235390

	Type: a	ELvl:	Srce: d	GPub:	Ctrl:	Lang: eng
	BLvl: s	Form:	Conf: 1	Freq: a	MRec:	Ctry: ilu
	S/L: 0	Orig:	EntW:	Regl: r	Alph: a	
	Desc: a	SrTp:	Cont:	DtSt: d	Dates: 1982,	1983

	022	0	0737-1829 ǂ2 1	
	037		ǂb 525 S. Park Blvd., Glen Ellyn, IL 60137	
	042		lc ǂa nsdp	
CCM 4.4.3	111	2	National Wildlife Rehabilitation Symposium.	AACR2 21.1B2D
	245	1 0	Wildlife rehabilitation : ǂb a publication of the proceedings of the National Wildlife Rehabilitation Symposium.	21.30J1
	260		Glen Ellyn, Ill. : ǂb Friends of the Furred and Feathered of DuPage County, ǂc 1982-c1984.	
	300		2 v. ; ǂc 23 cm.	
	310		Annual	
	362	0	Vol. 1 (1982)-v. 2 (1983).	
	650	0	Wildlife rehabilitation ǂv Congresses.	
	650	0	Wildlife diseases ǂv Congresses.	
	650	0	Captive wild animals ǂv Congresses.	
	785	0 0	National Wildlife Rehabilitators' Association (U.S.). Symposium. ǂt Wildlife rehabilitation ǂx 0737-1829 ǂw (DLC)sn 90021193 ǂw (OCoLC)22523006	

AACR2

21.1B2D - Works reporting the collective activity of a conference, of an expedition, or of an event falling within the definition of a corporate body

21.30J1 - Added entry for title proper

LCRI

21.1B2 - Category D: it must deal with the activities of many persons involved in a corporate body covered by the category, not with the activities of a single person

RDA

19.2.1.1.1 c) - Works that report the collective activity of a conference, an expedition, an event

CCM

4.1.4 - Considerations regarding main entry and choice of corporate body

4.4.3 - Category D: Conferences, exhibitions, and ad hoc events

Corporate Body Main Entry Change: The Collective Activity of a Conference

Title: Wildlife rehabilitation: a publication of the proceedings of the ... symposium of the National Wildlife Rehabilitators' Association

Cover

Website screenshot

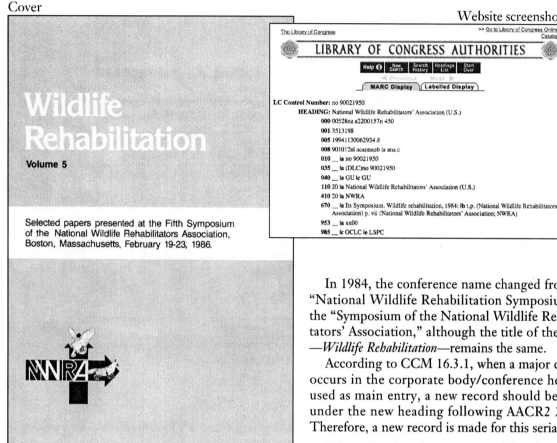

LIBRARY OF CONGRESS AUTHORITIES

LC Control Number: no 90021950

HEADING: National Wildlife Rehabilitators' Association (U.S.)

000 00528nz a2200157n 450
001 3513198
005 19941130062934.8
008 901012nl acannaab la ana c
010 __ la no 90021950
035 __ la (DLC)no 90021950
040 __ la GU lc GU
110 20 la National Wildlife Rehabilitators' Association (U.S.)
410 20 la NWRA
670 __ la Its Symposium. Wildlife rehabilitation, 1984: lb t.p. (National Wildlife Rehabilitators' Association) p. vii (National Wildlife Rehabilitators' Association; NWRA)
953 __ la xx00
985 __ lc OCLC le LSPC

(Cover: Wildlife Rehabilitation, Volume 5. Selected papers presented at the Fifth Symposium of the National Wildlife Rehabilitators Association, Boston, Massachusetts, February 19-23, 1986.)

In 1984, the conference name changed from the "National Wildlife Rehabilitation Symposium" to the "Symposium of the National Wildlife Rehabilitators' Association," although the title of the serial —*Wildlife Rehabilitation*—remains the same.

According to CCM 16.3.1, when a major change occurs in the corporate body/conference heading used as main entry, a new record should be made under the new heading following AACR2 21.3B. Therefore, a new record is made for this serial.

When creating the new record for this serial, AACR2 21.1B2D still applies (i.e., this is a publication of conference proceedings), so the serial is entered under the conference heading. As established in the authority record (http://authorities.loc.gov), the heading should be entered as:

110 2_ ‡a National Wildlife Rehabilitators' Association (U.S.). ‡b Symposium.

The title proper is given as an added entry (AACR2 21.30J1), and the corporate body "National Wildlife Rehabilitators' Association" is also given as an added entry (AACR2 21.30E) in the form established in the authority file:

110 2_ ‡a National Wildlife Rehabilitators' Association (U.S.)

OCLC #22523006

Type: a	ELvl:	Srce:	GPub:	Ctrl:	Lang: eng
BLvl: s	Form:	Conf: 1	Freq: a	MRec:	Ctry: ilu
S/L: 0	Orig:	EntW:	Regl: r	Alph:	
Desc: a	SrTp:	Cont:	DtSt: c	Dates: 1984,	9999

	022	0	0737-1829 ‡2 1	
	037		‡b NWRA, 14 North 7th Avenue, St. Cloud, Minnesota 56303-4766	
	042		lc ‡a nsdp	
CCM 4.4.3	110	2	National Wildlife Rehabilitators' Association (U.S.). ‡b Symposium.	AACR2 21.1B2D
	245	1 0	Wildlife rehabilitation : ‡b a publication of the proceedings of the . . . symposium of the National Wildlife Rehabilitators' Association.	21.30J1
	260		[Brighton, Ill.?] : ‡b National Wildlife Rehabilitators' Association, ‡c c1985-	
	300		v. ; ‡c 24 cm.	
	310		Annual	
	362	0	Vol. 3 (1984)-	
	500		Published: St. Cloud, Mn., <2000->	
	500		Latest issue consulted: Vol. 23 (2005).	
	650	0	Wildlife rehabilitation ‡v Congresses.	
	650	0	Wildlife rescue ‡v Congresses.	
4.8.3	710	2	National Wildlife Rehabilitators' Association (U.S.)	21.30E
	780	0 0	National Wildlife Rehabilitation Symposium. ‡t Wildlife rehabilitation ‡x 0737-1829 ‡w (DLC) 83641801 ‡w (OCoLC)9235390	

AACR2

21.3B1 - Make a new entry for a serial when the heading for a corporate body under which a serial is entered changes, even if the title proper remains the same

21.1B2D - Works reporting the collective activity of a conference, of an expedition, or of an event falling within the definition of a corporate body

21.30E - Added entry for prominently named corporate body

21.30J1 - Added entry for title proper

LCRI

21.1B2 - Category D: it must deal with the activities of many persons involved in a corporate body covered by the category, not with the activities of a single person

RDA

19.2.1.1.1 c) - Works that report the collective activity of a conference, an expedition, an event

1.6.2.4 - Change in responsibility for a serial: create a new description if there is a change in esponsibility that requires a change in the identification of the serial as a work

6.1.3.2.1 - When there is a change affecting the authorized access point representing a person, family, or corporate body that is used in constructing the work, that is a change in responsibility

(Continued on next page)

for the work. Construct the authorized access point representing the work to reflect responsibility for the work as represented in the issue or part used as the basis for the new description

19.3.1.3 - Record other persons, families, and corporate bodies associated with the work, if considered important for access, in accordance with the general guidelines on recording relationships to persons, families, and corporate bodies associated with a resource given under 18.4

CCM

16.3.1 - Changes to main entry name headings: when a major change in the corporate body/ conference heading used as main entry occurs, make a new record under the new heading

4.1.4 - Considerations regarding main entry and choice of corporate body

4.4.3 - Category D: Conferences, exhibitions, and ad hoc events

4.8.1 - Corporate bodies or persons that are not selected as the main entry may be given an added entry

4.8.3 - Corporate bodies as added entries, including most prominently named corporate bodies . . .

Title Page

YEARBOOK

OF THE

SOCIETY OF THE FRIENDLY SONS

OF

SAINT PATRICK

IN THE

CITY OF NEW-YORK

2001

New York, N.Y.

EXERCISE 1 Corporate Body as Main Entry or Added Entry?

The Society of the Friendly Sons of St. Patrick publishes a yearbook that documents the society's happenings for the previous year as well as any annual administrative reporting necessary for their membership. Determine the main entry for this record.

If entering under the corporate body, practice searching the authority file for established headings, available from the Library of Congress website at http://authorities.loc.gov.

Code the corporate body and the title in the appropriate MARC fields with correct indicators.

OCLC #5307017

Type: a	ELvl:	Srce: d	GPub:	Ctrl:	Lang: eng
BLvl: s	Form:	Conf: 0	Freq: a	MRec:	Ctry: nyu
S/L: 0	Orig:	EntW:	Regl: r	Alph: a	
Desc: a	SrTp:	Cont:	DtSt: c	Dates: 1966,	9999

042		lcd
043		n-us-ny
110		
245		
260		New York, NY : ‡b Society of the Friendly Sons of Saint Patrick in the City of New York
300		v. : ‡b ill. ; ‡c 24 cm.
310		Annual
362	0	1966-
500		Description based on: 2001
610	2	0	Society of the Friendly Sons of Saint Patrick in the City of New York ‡v Periodicals.
650		0	Irish periodicals ‡z United States.
650		0	Irish Americans ‡z New York (State) ‡z New York ‡x Societies, etc.
780	0	0	Society of the Friendly Sons of St. Patrick in the City of New York. ‡t Anniversary dinner ‡w (OCoLC)5313636

Cover

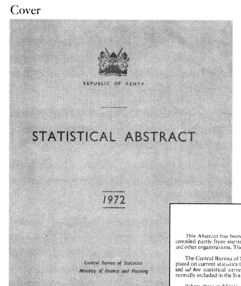

EXERCISE 2   Corporate Body as Main Entry or Added Entry?

Determine whether the corporate body should be entered as the main entry or as an added entry.

Code the corporate body and the title in the appropriate MARC fields with correct indicators.

Title Page Verso

vii

INTRODUCTION

This Abstract has been prepared by the Central Bureau of Statistics of the Ministry of Finance and Planning. The tables have been compiled partly from statistics collected directly by the Bureau and partly from statistics compiled by other Government Departments and other organizations. The source of the statistics is shown under each table.

The Central Bureau of Statistics is also responsible for the preparation of the quarterly Kenya Statistical Digest in which emphasis is placed on current statistics for which monthly and quarterly series are available. In addition, reports are published on the various regular and ad hoc statistical surveys undertaken by the Bureau. A quarterly Economic Report reviewing the current economic situation is normally included in the Statistical Digest.

Where these publications aim at providing statistical coverage of the important fields of economic, financial and social activity in Kenya, the published material may not meet detailed requirements of all users. Additional information, whenever available, will be supplied by the Bureau on request, although in certain circumstances, depending on the amount of work involved in extracting the required particulars, it may be necessary to make a charge. All enquiries relating to the Statistical Abstract and the Kenya Statistical Digest and on statistical matters generally should be addressed to:—

THE DIRECTOR OF STATISTICS,
MINISTRY OF FINANCE AND PLANNING,
P.O. BOX 30266,
NAIROBI, KENYA.

OCLC #1788774

Type: a	ELvl:	Srce:	GPub: f	Ctrl:	Lang: eng
BLvl: s	Form:	Conf: 0	Freq: a	MRec:	Ctry: ke
S/L: 0	Orig:	EntW: s	Regl: r	Alph:	
Desc: a	SrTp:	Cont:	DtSt:d	Dates: 1972,	2006

022		1726-9938
042		lc
043		f-ke—
130		
245		
260		[Nairobi] : ‡b Central Bureau of Statistics
300		v. ; ‡c 29 cm.
310		Annual
362	0	1972-2006.
530		Also available on microfiche from Greenwood Press and Chadwyck-Healey.
651	0	Kenya ‡v Statistics ‡v Periodicals.
710		
776	1	‡t Statistical abstract (Kenya. Central Bureau of Statistics) ‡c Microfiche ‡d Greenwood Press ‡w (DLC)sn 92037345 ‡w (OCoLC) 25738851
780	0 0	Kenya. Ministry of Finance and Planning. Statistics Division. ‡t Statistical abstract - [Statistics Division, Ministry of Finance and Planning] ‡w (DLC) 78648724 ‡w (OCoLC)4960424
785	0 0	‡t Statistical abstract (Kenya National Bureau of Statistics) ‡w (DLC) 2008238469 ‡w (OCoLC)220911142

Title from caption

EXERCISE 3   Corporate Body as Main Entry or Added Entry?

Determining the entry for newsletters can be a challenge. When making a decision as to whether the serial should be entered under the title proper or the corporate body, consider the following:

• Are there any statements of intent published with the newsletter? What is the purpose and main audience of the newsletter?

• Is the intent of the newsletter to disseminate information about the association/organization as a corporate body?

In this example, the newsletter published by the Michigan Entomological Society not only informs its members about the administrative happenings and activities of the society, but it also serves as a membership list. What should the main entry be for this newsletter?

Code the corporate body and the title in the appropriate MARC fields with correct indicators.

OCLC #8004048

Type: a	ELvl: 7	Srce: d	GPub:	Ctrl:	Lang: eng
BLvl: s	Form:	Conf: 0	Freq: q	MRec:	Ctry: miu
S/L: 0	Orig:	EntW:	Regl: x	Alph: a	
Desc: a	SrTp:	Cont:	DtSt: c	Dates: 1956,	9999

022	0	1554-2092 ‡2 1
037		‡b Michigan Entomological Society, c/o Dept. of Entomology, Michigan State University, East Lansing, Michigan 48824
042		nsdp ‡a lcd
043		n-us-mi
110		
245		
246		
260		[East Lansing?] : ‡b Michigan Entomological Society
300		v. : ‡b ill. ; ‡c 23-28 cm.
310		Four no. a year
362	1	Began in 1956.
500		Includes Membership list.
500		Description based on: Vol. 5, no. 1 (Mar. 1961).
500		Latest issue consulted: Vol. 49, nos. 1 & 2 (May 2004).
650	0	Entomology ‡v Periodicals.
650	0	Entomology ‡z Michigan ‡x Societies, etc.
655	0	Newsletters.
856	4	0 ‡u http://insects.ummz.lsa.umich.edu/MES/mesnewsl.html

CHAPTER 4

Publication Statement and Changes in Publisher and Place of Publication

Many changes can occur during the life span of a serial publication. These include changes in the title proper or corporate body. There can also be changes in place of publication, publisher, frequency, or chronological designation. All these changes have the potential to affect the bibliographic record one way or another; some require that new catalog records be created, while others require that existing records be updated. This chapter will show examples of changes in the place of publication and publisher, comparing past and present practices for dealing with these changes.

A new bibliographic record is not required when changes occur in place of publication or publisher for a serial publication. Under the old practice, if the information was important, it was given as a note in field 500 or 550, with no change made to the publication and distribution information in the 260 field. The new practice began when MARC 21 was revised to make the 260 field repeatable, making it possible to account for publisher changes over time. This means that newer information is more prominent and therefore easier for a user to match with more recent citations. The Library of Congress (LC) and the Program for Cooperative Cataloging (PCC) decided to implement the repeatability of the MARC 21 260 field on Sept. 1, 2009.

In accordance with standard practice, when rules change, existing serials bibliographic records will not be updated to reflect the new treatment. It is therefore important for catalogers to be familiar with the historical treatment of changes in place of publication and publisher. For that reason, the examples presented here show the old and new ways of recording changes in publisher and place of publication.

Under the old way (i.e., before the implementation of the repeatable 260 field), the earliest publisher and place of publication were recorded in the 260 field and any subsequent changes recorded in notes in either the 500 or 550 field.

Under the new practice, serials catalogers can use the repeatable 260 fields to clearly record the original publisher, intervening publisher, and current/latest publisher. This will help library users and reference librarians by making it easier to match recent citations with catalog records and will help acquisitions staff with ordering and subscription maintenance.

Multiple 260 fields appear in chronological order—from earliest to most recent:

260 _ _ ‡3 span for first publication statement: ‡a Earliest Place : ‡b Earliest Publisher, ‡c Beginning date-
260 2 _ ‡3 span2: ‡a Intervening Place : ‡b Intervening Publisher
260 3 _ ‡3 span3- : ‡a Latest Place : ‡b Latest Publisher

The first indicator in the 260 field is defined for the sequence of publication statements, while the second indicator remains undefined. According to current LC/PCC guidelines for the MARC 21 repeatable 260 field, the indicator values are:

blank   Not applicable/no information provided/earliest available publisher
2   Intervening publisher
3   Current/latest publisher

A new subfield ǂ3 has been created for "Materials Specified," where numbering or dates can be added to differentiate multiple 260 fields. Angle brackets are used when the data might not represent the first or last issue in the span. To clarify the record display in the catalog, a colon should be placed at the end of the subfield 3. If the range is open, the punctuation would be hyphen-space-colon (e.g., ǂ3 2010- : ǂa).

Only one 260 field may have the subfield ǂc (date of publication, distribution, etc.). This subfield is used to record beginning date of publication, distribution, etc., as well as an ending date for a resource that has ceased or completed publication.

For serials, subfield ǂc should appear in the first 260 field (with blank indicators). However, it may not be present in that field when:

1. The description is based on an issue other than the first or earliest issue.
2. The cataloger is following CSR guidelines and chooses the option of not providing it.

RDA, Section 1, Chapter 2, provides instructions on recording the attributes of manifestations and items most used for identifying a resource. Rules for publication information are listed under Rule 2.8 "Publication Statement," which is defined as a statement identifying the place or places of publication, publisher or publishers, and date or dates of publication of a resource. The subrules under Rule 2.8 cover scope and source of information for publication statement and provide instructions on recording the publication statement and changes in publication statement.

As changes in publication information can occur multiple times in a serial's life span, it is left to the cataloger's discretion to determine whether these changes should be recorded in a note. If information about changes is needed for identification or access, it should be added. LCRI 12.7B11.2 limits the number of notes by considering important only those situations involving a change in the place or country of publication that has been used as a qualifier in a uniform title.

RESOURCES CONSULTED

AACR2

12.4 Publication, Distribution, Etc., Area

LCRI

1.4 Publication, Distribution, Etc., Area. Appendix, for LC/PCC guidelines for MARC 21 repeatable 260 field

RDA

2.8 Publication statement

CCM

Module 10 Publication, distribution, etc. area (Field 260)

Guidelines developed by the Library of Congress and the PCC for implementing MARC 21 repeatable 260 field are available at http://www.loc.gov/catdir/cpso/260field.pdf.

MARC 21

MARC 21 Format for Bibliographic Data, 1999 Edition, Update No. 1 (October 2001) through Update No. 11 (February 2010), Library of Congress Network development and MARC Standards Office. Available at http://www.loc.gov/marc/bibliographic/bd260.html.

Recording Place of Publication and Publisher Information

Title: Human resource planning: HR

Cover

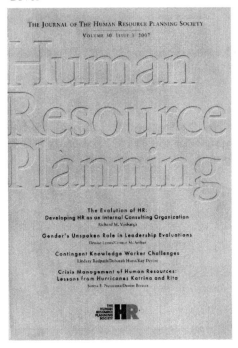

Masthead

Human Resource Planning
VOLUME 30, ISSUE 3

Human Resource Planning is published by:

The Human Resource Planning Society
317 Madison Avenue, Suite 1509
New York, NY 10017
Telephone: (212) 490-6387
Fax: (212) 682-6851
ISSN: 0199-8986

© Copyright 2007 by The Human Resource Planning Society. All rights reserved. Permission must be obtained from the editors to reproduce any article in any form by any means, electronic or mechanical, including photocopy, recording, or any information storage and retrieval system.

According to AACR2 Rule 12.0B3, the prescribed source for publication information is the entire resource. CCM 10.1.1 states that when information can be found in more than one place within the resource, preference should be given to the chief source or other prescribed sources (i.e., verso of the title page, cover, colophon, etc.).

Under both the previous and current treatments, the name of the earliest publisher and place of publication are recorded in the 260 field, with the initial place of publication recorded in the ‡a subfield; the name of the initial publisher in the ‡b subfield; and the date range of publication recorded in the ‡c subfield:

260 _ _ ‡a Tempe, Ariz. : ‡b Human Resource Planning Society, ‡c 1978-2007.

Before September 1, 2009, the first and second indicators for the 260 field were undefined and thus remained blank. Any changes to the publisher or place of publication were recorded in a 500 note field:

500 _ _ Published: New York, NY, <Mar. 1987>-2007.

In this example, the Human Resource Planning Society began publishing the journal *Human Resource Planning* from Tempe, Arizona, in 1978. However, from March 1987 to 2007, the serial was published in New York City, New York. Because this record was created in 1980, it followed the practice that was in place before the implementation of new procedures and new MARC coding for repeatable 260 fields. The initial publisher and the place of publication are recorded in the 260 field and the changes are documented in the 500 field as a note. The angle brackets around the first date indicate that March 1987 may not be the first issue in which the place of publication changed, but it was the earliest issue available to the cataloger at the time the note was made.

OCLC #6281631

Type a	ELvl	Srce d	GPub	Ctrl	Lang eng
BLvl s	Form	Conf 0	Freq q	MRec	Ctry nyu
S/L 0	Orig	EntW	Regl r	Alph a	
Desc a	SrTp p	Cont	DtSt d	Dates 1978	, 2007

022	0		0199-8986 ‡2 1
037			‡b Human Resource Planning Society, 41 E. 42nd St., New York, N.Y. 10017
042			nsdp ‡a lcd
245	0	0	Human resource planning : ‡b HR.
246	3	0	HR

CCM 10.2.1 10.3.3 10.4.2 | 260 | Tempe, Ariz. : ‡b Human Resource Planning Society, ‡c 1978-2007. | AACR2 12.4B1 12.4F

300		30 v. ; ‡c 28 cm.
310		Quarterly
362	0	Vol. 1, no. 1 (spring 1978)-
362	1	Ceased with v. 30, issue 4 (2007).

10.6 | 500 | Published: New York, NY, <Mar. 1987>-2007. | 12.4C2

500		Final issue consulted.
555		Vols. 1 (1978)-12 (1989). 1 v.
650	0	Manpower planning ‡v Periodicals.
650	0	Personnel management ‡v Periodicals.
710	2	Human Resource Planning Society.
785	0	0	‡t People & strategy ‡x 1946-4606 ‡w (DLC) 2008242000 ‡w (OCoLC)214284010

AACR2

12.4B1 - Record information about the place, name, and date of all types of publishing, distributing, etc., activities as instructed in 1.4B

12.4C2 - Record changes to the place of publication in a note

12.4F - Record the beginning and, if appropriate, end date(s) of publication

RDA

2.8.1 - Publication statement has place of publication, publisher's name, and date of publication as core elements for published resources; see 2.8.2 for place of publication, 2.8.4 for publisher's name, and 2.8.6 for date of publication

2.8.1.4 - Recording Publication Statements: transcribe places of publication and publishers' names in the form in which they appear on the source of information. Apply the general guidelines on transcription given under 1.7

2.8.1.5.2 - If the place of publication changes on a later issue or part of a serial, make a note on the change if considered to be important

2.20.7.5.2 - Makes notes on changes in place of publication and/or publishers' names that occur after the first/earliest issue or part of a serial if they are considered to be important for identification or access

(Continued on next page)

CCM

10.2.1 - Corporate body as publisher; capitalize the name as found in AACR2 A.7A1 and omit preceding words as defined within AACR2 1.4D3

10.3.3 - Record the place of publication as it appears; if the higher jurisdiction is found on the piece in an abbreviated form, use this form in the place of publication. When it appears in the full form, use the abbreviations found in AACR2 Appendix B (per rule 1.4B4)

10.4.2 - When the first and/or last issues are in hand, provide the dates of publication. Do not provide dates when the first and/or last issues are not in hand

10.6 - With the exception of the final date of publication, significant changes in place of publication, publisher and date, appearing on later issues, are recorded in a 500 note field

Place of Publication and Publisher Unknown

Title: Regional science review

Cover

REGIONAL SCIENCE REVIEW
Vol. 14 May 1984

When the place of publication and publisher are unknown, AACR2 Rule 12.4C1 refers catalogers to instructions in 1.4C. This rule—specifically 1.4C6—stipulates that if no place or probable place can be given, give s.l. (sine loco) (e.g., [S.l.]). Rule 1.4D6 similarly instructs that if the name of the publisher is unknown, give s.n. (sine nomine) (e.g., Paris : [s.n.]).

According to CCM 10.1.2, brackets are used only when supplying information not found on the piece or when using the Latin abbreviations "s.l." or "s.n." Closed brackets are used whether or not the field is complete. This is a change in practice as of 2002.

In order to put the convenience of the user first, with the understanding that library users do not usually understand what "s.l" and " s.n." represent, RDA has replaced "s.l." with "Place of publication not identified" (RDA 2.8.2.6) and "s.n." with "publisher not identified" (RDA 2.8.4.7).

In this example, because no information about place of publication and publisher is found in the journal, two cataloging records have been created based on AACR2 and RDA, respectively.

OCLC #13429020 (AACR2 record)

Type a	ELvl I	Srce d	GPub	Ctrl		Lang eng
BLvl s	Form	Conf 0	Freq u	MRec		Ctry nyu
S/L 0	Orig	EntW	Regl u	Alph		
Desc a	SrTp	Cont	DtSt c	Dates 1984	, 9999	

	245	0 0	Regional science review.	
CCM 10.1.2	260		[S.l : ‡b s.n.] ; ‡c 1984-	AACR2 1.4C6 1.4D6 12.4Ba
	300		v. ; ‡c 28 cm.	
	362	0	Vol. 14 (May 1984)-	
	500		Title from cover.	
	500		"Contains some of the selected papers presented at the . . . Annual Conference of the Northeast Regional Science Association."	
	520		Consists of papers presented at the Annual Conference of the Northeast Regional Science Association.	
	650	0	Regional planning ‡v Periodicals.	
	650	0	City planning ‡v Periodicals.	
	710	2	Northeast Regional Science Association.	
	780	0 0	‡t Northeast regional science review ‡w (OCoLC) 6466400	

(Continued on next page)

OCLC #13429020 (RDA record)

Type a	ELvl I	Srce d	GPub	Ctrl	Lang eng
BLvl s	Form	Conf 0	Freq u	MRec	Ctry nyu
S/L 0	Orig	EntW	Regl u	Alph	
Desc i	SrTp	Cont	DtSt c	Dates 1984	, 9999

	040		EEM ‡c EEM ‡d OCL ‡d ZYU ‡e rda
	245	0 0	Regional science review.
RDA 2.8.1 2.8.2.6 2.8.4.7	260		[Place of publication not identified] : ‡b [publisher not identified], ‡c 1984-
	300		v. ; ‡c 28 cm.
	336		text ‡b txt ‡2 rdacontent
	337		unmediated ‡b n ‡2 rdamedia
	338		volume ‡b nc ‡2 rdacarrier
	362	0	Vol. 14 (May 1984)-
	500		Title from cover.
	500		"Contains some of the selected papers presented at the . . . Annual Conference of the Northeast Regional Science Association."
	520		Consists of papers presented at the Annual Conference of the Northeast Regional Science Association.
	650	0	Regional planning ‡v Periodicals.
	650	0	City planning ‡v Periodicals.
	710	2	Northeast Regional Science Association.
	780	0 0	‡t Northeast regional science review ‡w (OCoLC) 6466400

AACR2

12.4B1- Record information about the place, name, and date of all types of publishing, distributing, etc., activities as instructed in 1.4B

1.4C6 - If no place or probable place can be given, give s.l. (sine loco), [S.l.]

1.4D6 - If the name of the publisher, distributor, etc., is unknown, give s.n. (sine nomine), Paris : [s.n.]

RDA

2.8.1 - Publication statement has place of publication, publisher's name, and date of publication as core elements for published resources; see 2.8.2 for place of publication, 2.8.4 for publisher's name, and 2.8.6 for date of publication

2.8.2.6 - Place of Publication Not Identified in the Resource: if neither a known nor a probable local place or country, state, province, etc., of publication can be determined, record Place of publication not identified

2.8.4.7 - For a resource in a published form, if no publisher is named within the resource itself, and the publisher cannot be identified from other sources as specified under 2.2.4, record publisher not identified

CCM

10.1.2 - Brackets are used only when supplying information not found on the piece or when using the abbreviations "s.l." or "s.n." Use closed brackets whether or not the field is complete. This is a change in practice as of 2002

Change in Publisher and Place of Publication

Title: Tech & learning

Cover

Masthead

The publisher of a serial can be a corporate body, an individual, or the name of the serial or it might be unknown from information in hand. In this example, the term *Inc.* has been retained in the corporate body names for "Peter Li, Inc." and "Miller Freeman, Inc." so it is clear that the publishers are corporations rather than individuals. CCM 10.4 defines the publication date as the year in which a work is made available to the public. It usually consists solely of the year and often appears with the place and name of the publisher. If no publication dates are present and only copyright dates are found, the copyright dates can be used as the publishing dates. In this example, the small "c" preceding 1990 indicates that it is a copyright date.

When the first issue is in hand, a cataloger should record the date of publication of the first issue, followed by a hyphen. If the serial is complete and the last issue is also in hand, the date of the last issue is added after the hyphen. In this example, the cataloger had access to the first issue, Vol. 11, no. 1 (Sept. 1990), when cataloging this publication under the present title: *Tech & Learning*. The copyright date c1990 is followed by a hyphen to show that the serial publication is still ongoing.

According to AACR2 1.4F8, if the first and/or last published issue is not available, a date of publication should not be given. When no date of publication is given, the comma that usually follows the publisher name should be omitted. The comma is meant to precede the publication date, so is not needed when there is no date. This is a change in practice as of 2002.

For the place of publication, generally record the local place or city in which the publisher is located. If the place and its higher jurisdiction appear in the same source on the piece, record both. AACR2 Rule 1.4B4 instructs that abbreviations from Appendix B should be used instead of the full form of the jurisdiction name. However, common practice is that if the jurisdiction name is abbreviated on the piece, this abbreviation is used without reference to Appendix B. This corresponds to the guidelines in LCRI B.14. Therefore, in this example, the U.S. postal code found on the piece—"CA"—is used rather than the abbreviation "Calif." given in Appendix B. Also, the U.S. postal code "OH" is taken from the piece rather than "Ohio." (In this case, Appendix B gives no abbreviation for Ohio, so the full form would be used if no abbreviation appeared on the piece.)

This catalog record shows the past practice of recording the original publication information in the 260 field and recording changes in publication information in the 500 field.

Under both current and previous practices, whenever there is a change in place of publication, the country of publication code in fixed field element 008/15–17 should be modified to reflect the latest place of publication. In this example, the country code has been changed from "ohu" to "cau."

OCLC #22361990

Type a	ELvl	Srce d	GPub	Ctrl	Lang eng
BLvl s	Form	Conf 0	Freq m	MRec	Ctry cau
S/L 0	Orig	EntW	Regl r	Alph a	
Desc a	SrTp p	Cont	DtSt c	Dates 1990	, 9999

022	0	1053-6728 ǂy 0746-4223 ǂ2 1
042		lc ǂa nsdp
245	0 0	Technology & learning.
246	1 0	Technology and learning
246	1	ǂi Issues for June 2008- called: ǂa Tech & learning

CCM
10.2.1
10.3.3
10.4.2

260	Dayton, OH : ǂb Peter Li, Inc., ǂc c1990-

AACR2
12.4B1
12.4F

300		v. : ǂb ill. ; ǂc 28 cm.
310		Monthly, ǂb 2006-
321		Monthly (except June, July, Aug., Dec.), ǂb 1990-May/June 1991
321		Monthly (except July, Dec.), ǂb <Nov./Dec. 1998->
321		Monthly (except July), ǂb <2003>-2005
362	0	Vol. 11, no. 1 (Sept. 1990)-

10.6

500	Imprint varies: San Francisco, CA : Miller Freeman, Inc., <Nov./Dec. 1998->

12.4C2
12.4D2

500		Title from cover.
500		Latest issue consulted: Vol. 28, no. 11 (June 2008).
650	0	Computer-assisted instruction ǂv Periodicals.
780	0 0	ǂt Classroom computer learning ǂx 0746-4223 ǂw (DLC) 83647973 ǂw (OCoLC)10008037

AACR2

12.4B1 - Record information about the place, name, and date of all types of publishing, distributing, etc., activities as instructed in 1.4B

12.4C2 - Record changes to the place of publication in a note

12.4D2 - Provide later name(s) of publishers if considered important

12.4F - Record the beginning and, if appropriate, end date(s) of publication

12.7B11.2.a - Makes notes on changes in the place and/or name of publisher that occur after the first/earliest issue or part if considered to be important

RDA

2.8.1 - Publication statement has place of publication, publisher's name, and date of publication as core elements for published resources; see 2.8.2 for place of publication, 2.8.4 for publisher's name, and 2.8.6 for date of publication

2.8.1.4 - Recording Publication Statements: transcribe places of publication and publishers' names in the form in which they appear on the source of information. Apply the general guidelines on transcription given under 1.7

(Continued on next page)

2.8.1.5.2 - If the place of publication changes on a later issue or part of a serial, make a note on the change if considered to be important

2.20.7.5.2 - Makes notes on changes in place of publication and/or publishers' names that occur after the first/earliest issue or part of a serial if they are considered to be important for identification or access

CCM

10.2.1 - Corporate body as publisher; capitalize the name as found in AACR2 A.7A1 and omit preceding words as defined within AACR2 1.4D3

10.3.3 - Record the place of publication as it appears; if the higher jurisdiction is found on the piece in an abbreviated form, use this form in the place of publication. When it appears in the full form, use the abbreviations found in AACR2 Appendix B (per rule 1.4B4)

10.4.2 - When the first and/or last issues are in hand, provide the dates of publication. Do not provide dates when the first and/or last issues are not in hand

10.4.3 - If there is no publication date, a copyright date may be used

10.6 - With the exception of the final date of publication, significant changes in place of publication, publisher and date, appearing on later issues, are recorded in a 500 notes field

Change in Publisher

Title: Boston

Cover

Masthead

This bibliographic record illustrates a couple of things. First, although the publication date is not available and therefore is not recorded in subfield ‡c of the 260 field, a comma follows the publisher name. This is because the record was created before 2002, following the practice in use at the time.

Generally, catalogers do not modify records cataloged according to earlier conventions. Since the 2002 revision of AACR2, if no date is recorded, a comma is not input after the publisher name.

Second, the name of the serial has been recorded as the publisher. The original publisher was a corporate body: the Greater Boston Chamber of Commerce.

The publishing statement now gives only the name of the serial that is being cataloged, and in accordance with CCM, the name of the serial is recorded as the publisher. Each word in the title is capitalized according to the rules for corporate bodies.

The records below demonstrate the old and new ways of recording a change in publisher. In the first record, the original publisher is entered in the 260 field and the later publisher is noted in a 500 field. In the second record, another 260 field is entered with the first indicator 3 for current publisher.

OCLC #4300100 (Past Practice)

Type a	ELvl	Srce d	GPub	Ctrl	Lang eng
BLvl s	Form	Conf 0	Freq m	MRec	Ctry mau
S/L 0	Orig	EntW	Regl r	Alph a	
Desc a	SrTp p	Cont	DtSt c	Dates 1962	, 9999

	022	0	0006-7989 ‡y 0006-4989 ‡2 1
	042		nsdp ‡a lc
	043		n-us-ma
	245	0 0	Boston.
	246	1 3	Boston magazine
CCM 10.2.1 10.3.3 10.4.2	260		Boston, Mass. : ‡b Greater Boston Chamber of Commerce,	AACR2 12.4B1 12.4F
	362	1	Began with Sept. 1962 issue.
	500		Some issues have title: Boston magazine.
10.2.3 10.6.	500		Published by: Boston Magazine, <July 1978-Nov. 1991>.	12.4D2
	500		Description based on: Vol. 63, no. 1 (Jan. 1971); title from cover.
	515		Beginning with <Aug. 2002-> the vol. number changed to <v. 40-> to reflect the number of years that the title Boston has been in existence.
	580		Has annual special issue <1993- > called: New England travel guide, which is internumbered.
	651	0	Boston (Mass.) ‡v Periodicals.
	710	2	Greater Boston Chamber of Commerce.
	770	1	‡t New England travel guide ‡x 1069-7861 ‡w (DLC)sn 93007476 ‡w (OCoLC)28153217
	780	0 0	‡t Greater Boston business ‡w (OCoLC)8232970

(Continued on next page)

AACR2

12.4B1 - Record information about the place, name, and date of all types of publishing, distributing, etc., activities as instructed in 1.4B

12.4D2 - Provide later name(s) of publishers if considered important

12.4F - Record the beginning and, if appropriate, end date(s) of publication

12.7B11.2.a - Makes notes on changes in the place and/or name of publisher that occur after the first/earliest issue or part if considered to be important

RDA

2.8.1 - Publication statement has place of publication, publisher's name, and date of publication as core elements for published resources; see 2.8.2 for place of publication, 2.8.4 for publisher's name, and 2.8.6 for date of publication

2.8.1.4 - Recording Publication Statements: transcribe places of publication and publishers' names in the form in which they appear on the source of information. Apply the general guidelines on transcription given under 1.7

2.8.1.5.2 - If the place of publication changes on a later issue or part of a serial, make a note on the change if considered to be important

2.20.7.5.2 - Makes notes on changes in place of publication and/or publishers' names that occur after the first/earliest issue or part of a serial if they are considered to be important for identification or access

CCM

10.2.1 - Corporate body as publisher: capitalize the name as found in AACR2 A.7A1 and omit preceding words as defined within AACR2 1.4D3

10.2.3 - Name of serial as publisher: capitalize each word in the title according to the rules for corporate bodies

10.3.3 - Record the place of publication as it appears; if the higher jurisdiction is found on the piece in an abbreviated form, use this form in the place of publication. When it appears in the full form, use the abbreviations found in AACR2 Appendix B (per rule 1.4B4)

10.4.2 - When the first and/or last issues are in hand, provide the dates of publication. Do not provide dates when the first and/or last issues are not in hand

10.6 - With the exception of the final date of publication, significant changes in place of publication, publisher and date, appearing on later issues, are recorded in a 500 notes field

OCLC #4300100 (Present Practice)

Type a	ELvl	Srce d	GPub	Ctrl	Lang eng
BLvl s	Form	Conf 0	Freq m	MRec	Ctry mau
S/L 0	Orig	EntW	Regl r	Alph a	
Desc a	SrTp p	Cont	DtSt c	Dates 1962	, 9999

022	0		0006-7989 ǂy 0006-4989 ǂ2 1
042			nsdp ǂa lc
043			n-us-ma
245	0	0	Boston.
246	1	3	Boston magazine

CCM
10.2.1
10.3.3
10.4.2

260			Boston, Mass. : ǂb Greater Boston Chamber of Commerce,

AACR2
12.4B1
12.4F

10.2.3
10.6.

260	3		ǂ3 <July 1978-Nov. 1991> : ǂa Boston, Mass. : ǂb Boston Magazine

12.4D2

362	1		Began with Sept. 1962 issue.
500			Some issues have title: Boston magazine.
500			Description based on: Vol. 63, no. 1 (Jan. 1971); title from cover.
515			Beginning with <Aug. 2002-> the vol. number changed to <v. 40-> to reflect the number of years that the title Boston has been in existence.
580			Has annual special issue <1993- > called: New England travel guide, which is internumbered.
651		0	Boston (Mass.) ǂv Periodicals.
710	2		Greater Boston Chamber of Commerce.
770	1		ǂt New England travel guide ǂx 1069-7861 ǂw (DLC)sn 93007476 ǂw (OCoLC)28153217
780	0	0	ǂt Greater Boston business ǂw (OCoLC)8232970

Change in Place of Publication and Publisher

Title: Child life

Cover

The journal *Child Life* was first published in 1921 and has lived a relatively stable life. Around 1984, the publisher and the place of publication changed from Rand McNally in Chicago, Illinois, to the Children's Better Health Institute, Benjamin Franklin Literary & Medical Society, in Indianapolis, Indiana.

While the old practice was to record changes in publisher and place of publication in a 500 field, a cataloger may now use multiple 260 fields to track changes and make current publishing information more prominent to users. The order of the repeatable 260 fields is determined by the first indicator, where # (blank) is used for the initial publication information, 2 is used for an intervening publisher, and 3 is used for the current/latest publisher information. In the two cataloging records presented here, the change in the publisher and the publication location is demonstrated by using the old and new practices.

Note that "Chicago, Ill." is enclosed in square brackets. This is because the information is taken from outside the prescribed source, which is "the whole resource" for the publication area of print serials (AACR2 12.0B3). This should not be confused with the angle brackets used around "1984-" in the 500 field. The angle brackets mean that "1984" is subject to change (i.e., it may or may not be the earliest date associated with the change).

Title Page / Table of Contents

CHILD LIFE (ISSN 0009-3971) is published monthly, except bimonthly February/March, April/May, June/July, and August/September by Children's Better Health Institute, Benjamin Franklin Literary & Medical Society, Inc. at 1100 Waterway Blvd., P.O. Box 567, Indianapolis, IN 46206. Copyright © 1983 by

It should also be pointed out that because the country of publication code in fixed field element 008/15–17 should be updated to reflect the latest place of publication, the country code in this example has been changed from "ilu" to "inu." However, the place name "Chicago, Ill." used as the qualifier in the uniform title in the130 field remains the same. More information about uniform titles can be found in Chapter 8.

OCLC #8726318 (Past Practice)

Type a	ELvl	Srce d	GPub	Ctrl	Lang eng
BLvl s	Form	Conf 0	Freq b	MRec	Ctry inu
S/L 0	Orig	EntW	Regl r	Alph a	
Desc a	SrTp p	Cont	DtSt c	Dates 1922	, 9999

	022	0	0009-3971 ǂz 0884-447X ǂ2 1
	037		ǂb Children's Better Health Institute, Benjamin Franklin Literary & Medical Society, 1100 Waterway Blvd., POB 567, Indianapolis, IN 46206
	042		nsdp ǂa lc
	130	0	Child life (Chicago, Ill.)
	245	0 0	Child life.
CCM 10.2.1 10.3.3 10.4.2	260		[Chicago, Ill.] : ǂb Rand McNally, ǂc c1921-
	300		v. : ǂb ill. ; ǂc 24-31 cm.
	310		Bimonthly, ǂb 2003-
	321		Monthly, ǂb 1922-
	321		Eight no. a year, ǂb <1984>- 2002
	362	0	[Vol. 1, no. 1] (Jan. 1922)-
10.6	500		Published: Indianapolis, by: Children's Better Health Institute, Benjamin Franklin Literary & Medical Society, <1984- >
	500		Title from cover.
	500		Latest issue consulted: Vol. 83, no. 6 (Nov./Dec. 2004).
	650	0	Children's periodicals.
	780	0 5	ǂt Children's playtime ǂg 1932

(Against the 260 row on the right: AACR2 12.4B1 12.4F)
(Against the 500 row on the right: 12.4C2 12.4D2)

AACR2

12.4B1 - Record information about the place, name, and date of all types of publishing, distributing, etc., activities as instructed in 1.4B

12.4C2 - Record changes to the place of publication in a note

12.4D2 - Provide later name(s) of publishers if considered important

12.4F - Record the beginning and, if appropriate, end date(s) of publication

12.7B11.2.a - Makes notes on changes in the place and/or name of publisher that occur after the first/earliest issue or part if considered to be important

RDA

2.8.1 - Publication statement has place of publication, publisher's name, and date of publication as core elements for published resources; see 2.8.2 for place of publication, 2.8.4 for publisher's name, and 2.8.6 for date of publication

2.8.1.4 - Recording Publication Statements: transcribe places of publication and publishers' names in the form in which they appear on the source of information. Apply the general guidelines on transcription given under 1.7

(Continued on next page)

2.8.1.5.2 - If the place of publication changes on a later issue or part of a serial, make a note on the change if considered to be important

2.20.7.5.2 - Makes notes on changes in place of publication and/or publishers' names that occur after the first/earliest issue or part of a serial if they are considered to be important for identification or access

CCM

10.2.1 - Corporate body as publisher; capitalize the name as found in AACR2 A.7A1 and omit preceding words as defined within AACR2 1.4D3

10.3.3 - Record the place of publication as it appears; if the higher jurisdiction is found on the piece in an abbreviated form, use this form in the place of publication. When it appears in the full form, use the abbreviations found in AACR2 Appendix B (per rule 1.4B4)

10.4.2 - When the first and/or last issues are in hand, provide the dates of publication. Do not provide dates when the first and/or last issues are not in hand

10.6 - With the exception of the final date of publication, significant changes in place of publication, publisher and date, appearing on later issues, are recorded in a 500 note field

OCLC #8726318 (Present Practice)

Type a	ELvl	Srce d	GPub	Ctrl	Lang eng
BLvl s	Form	Conf 0	Freq b	MRec	Ctry inu
S/L 0	Orig	EntW	Regl r	Alph a	
Desc a	SrTp p	Cont	DtSt c	Dates 1922	, 9999

022	0		0009-3971 ǂz 0884-447X ǂ2 1
037			ǂb Children's Better Health Institute, Benjamin Franklin Literary & Medical Society, 1100 Waterway Blvd., POB 567, Indianapolis, IN 46206
042			nsdp ǂa lc
130	0		Child life (Chicago, Ill.)
245	0	0	Child life.

CCM				AACR2
10.2.1 10.3.3 10.4.2	260		[Chicago, Ill.] : ǂb Rand McNally, ǂc c1921-	12.4B1 12.4F
10.6	260	3	ǂ3 <1984- > ǂa Indianapolis, IN : ǂb Children's Better Health Institute, Benjamin Franklin Literary & Medical Society	12.4C2 12.4D2

300			v. : ǂb ill. ; ǂc 24-31 cm.
310			Bimonthly, ǂb 2003-
321			Monthly, ǂb 1922-
321			Eight no. a year, ǂb <1984>- 2002
362	0		[Vol. 1, no. 1] (Jan. 1922)-
500			Title from cover.
500			Latest issue consulted: Vol. 83, no. 6 (Nov./Dec. 2004).
650		0	Children's periodicals.
780	0	5	ǂt Children's playtime ǂg 1932

EXERCISE 1

Basic Education Statistics in Tanzania was published between 1984 and 1994. It was originally published in Dar es Salaam, Tanzania, by the Ministry of Education, with issues from 1980/1984 to 1985/1989. Later issues, from 1986/1990 to 1990/1994, were published by the Ministry of Education and Culture. For the purposes of this exercise, assume that all issues have been received—from the first issue to the final issue.

Fill in the country of publication code in the fixed field "Ctry" by consulting MARC 21 Code List for Countries, which is available at http://www.loc.gov/marc/countries.

Using the old and the new practices, record the initial publication information and the change in publisher in the blank fields provided. Moreover, in the record created under the old practice, add a note to the 550 field. This field is designated to record the issuing body, so it is used instead of a 500 field note, which is used to record publication changes that relate to commercial publishers, distributors, or places of publication.

Note that for multiple 260 fields, the order of change is indicated by the first indicator, where [blank] is used for the initial publication information, 2 is used for an intervening change, and 3 is used for the current/latest publisher information.

Consult the OCLC *Bibliographic Formats and Standards* website at: ttp://www.oclc.org/bibformats for additional assistance.

OCLC #31854991 (Past Practice)

Type a	ELvl	Srce d	GPub f	Ctrl	Lang eng
BLvl s	Form	Conf 0	Freq a	MRec	Ctry
S/L 0	Orig	EntW s	Regl r	Alph	
Desc a	SrTp	Cont	DtSt d	Dates 1984	, 1994

042		lc	
043		f-tz—-	
245	0	0	Basic education statistics in Tanzania / ‡c the United Republic of Tanzania.
246	1	3	BEST
260			
300		v. ; ‡c 21 cm.	
310		Annual	
362	0	1980/1984-1990/1994.	
550			
580		Beginning in 1991, the Ministry began publishing: Basic education statistics in Tanzania. Regional data, and they subsequently changed the title of the national report to: Basic statistics in education. National data.	
650		0	School enrollment ‡z Tanzania ‡v Statistics ‡v Periodicals.
710	1	Tanzania. ‡b Wizara ya Elimu.	
710	1	Tanzania. ‡b Wizara ya Elimu na Utamaduni.	
785	1	0	‡t Basic statistics in education. National data ‡w (DLC) 00235640 ‡w (OCoLC)44854950
787	1	‡t Basic education statistics in Tanzania. Regional data ‡w (DLC) 96983482 ‡w (OCoLC)33145798	

(Continued on next page)

Title Page

Title Page

THE UNITED REPUBLIC OF TANZANIA

THE UNITED REPUBLIC OF TANZANIA

Basic
Education
Statistics in
Tanzania
(BEST)

Basic
Education
Statistics in
Tanzania
(BEST)

1980 - 1984

1986 - 1990

The Ministry of Education
Dar es Salaam
September, 1984

The Ministry of Education and Culture
Dar es Salaam
September, 1990

OCLC #31854991 (Present Practice)

Type a	ELvl	Srce d	GPub f	Ctrl	Lang eng
BLvl s	Form	Conf 0	Freq a	MRec	Ctry
S/L 0	Orig	EntW s	Regl r	Alph	
Desc a	SrTp	Cont	DtSt d	Dates 1984	, 1994

042		lc	
043		f-tz—	
245	0 0	Basic education statistics in Tanzania / ‡c the United Republic of Tanzania.	
246	1 3	BEST	
260			
260			
300		v. ; ‡c 21 cm.	
310		Annual	
362	0	1980/1984-1990/1994.	
580		Beginning in 1991, the Ministry began publishing: Basic education statistics in Tanzania. Regional data, and they subsequently changed the title of the national report to: Basic statistics in education. National data.	
650	0	School enrollment ‡z Tanzania ‡v Statistics ‡v Periodicals.	
710	1	Tanzania. ‡b Wizara ya Elimu.	
710	1	Tanzania. ‡b Wizara ya Elimu na Utamaduni.	
785	1 0	‡t Basic statistics in education. National data ‡w (DLC) 00235640 ‡w (OCoLC)44854950	
787	1	‡t Basic education statistics in Tanzania. Regional data ‡w (DLC) 96983482 ‡w (OCoLC)33145798	

EXERCISE 2

Since 1992, this serial has been published under the title *MultiCultural Review* by GP Subscription Publications of Westport, Connecticut. Beginning with the March 2003 edition, the publisher changed to the Goldman Group from Tampa, Florida. Assume that all issues of this serial have been received—from the first issue to the most recent.

Fill in the country of publication code in the fixed field by consulting the MARC 21 Code List for Countries, which is available at http://www.loc.gov/marc/countries.

Using the old and the new practices, record the initial publication information and the change in publisher in the blank fields provided. A note should be added to a 500 field rather than a 550 field because the information in this case refers to a commercial publisher instead of an issuing body.

Remember that for multiple 260 fields, the order of change is indicated by the first indicator, where [blank] is used for the initial publication information, 2 is used for intervening publisher, and 3 is used for the current/latest publisher information.

Consult the OCLC *Bibliographic Formats and Standards* website at http://www.oclc.org/bibformats for additional assistance.

OCLC #24433867 (Past Practice)

Type a	ELvl	Srce d	GPub	Ctrl	Lang eng
BLvl s	Form	Conf 0	Freq q	MRec	Ctry
S/L 0	Orig	EntW	Regl r	Alph a	
Desc a	SrTp p	Cont o	DtSt c	Dates 1992	, 9999

022	0	1058-9236 ‡2 1
037		‡b MultiCultural Review, 88 Post Road West, P.O. Box 5007, Westport, CT 06881
042		nsdp ‡a lc
210	0	MultiCult. rev.
222	0	MultiCultural review
245	0 0	MultiCultural review : ‡b dedicated to a better understanding of ethnic, racial, and religious diversity.
260		
300		v. : ‡b ill. ; ‡c 28 cm.
310		Quarterly
362	0	Vol. 1, no. 1 (Jan. 1992)-
500		Title from cover.
500		
500		Latest issue consulted: Vol. 12, no. 2 (June 2003).
580		With v. 14, no. 4 (winter 2005), absorbed: EMIE bulletin.
650	0	Multicultural education ‡v Periodicals.
650	0	Cultural pluralism ‡v Periodicals.
650	0	Ethnicity ‡v Periodicals.
780	0 5	‡t Journal of multicultural librarianship ‡x 0950-1649 ‡w (DLC) 87640645 ‡w (OCoLC)15088492
780	0 5	‡t EMIE bulletin ‡w (DLC)sn 83000624 ‡w (OCoLC)9477747

(Continued on next page)

Cover

Masthead

MultiCultural Review (ISSN 1058-9236) is published quarterly by GP Subscription Publications, an imprint of Greenwood Publishing Group, Inc., 88 Post Rd. W., P. O. Box 5007, Westport, CT 06881-5007. Subscription Rate is $59 per year in the U.S. and its possessions; $79 per year elsewhere. Single copies and back issues are $15 per copy in the U.S. and its possessions; $25 per copy elsewhere. Bulk rates quoted on request.

Cover

Masthead

Editor-in-Chief
Lyn Miller-Lachmann
mcreview@aol.com

Managing Editor
Valerie Shea

Layout and Design
Wendy Hummel

Advertising
The Goldman Group, Inc.
Deb Goldman
deb@ggpubs.com
(813) 264-2772

Publisher
The Goldman Group, Inc.
Todd Goldman
todd@ggpubs.com
14497 N. Dale Mabry, #205N
Tampa, FL 33618
(813) 264-2772

OCLC #24433867 (Present Practice)

Type a	ELvl	Srce d	GPub	Ctrl	Lang eng
BLvl s	Form	Conf 0	Freq q	MRec	Ctry
S/L 0	Orig	EntW	Regl r	Alph a	
Desc a	SrTp p	Cont o	DtSt c	Dates 1992	,9999

022	0	1058-9236 ‡2 1
037		‡b MultiCultural Review, 88 Post Road West, P.O. Box 5007, Westport, CT 06881
042		nsdp ‡a lc
210	0	MultiCult. rev.
222	0	MultiCultural review
245	0 0	MultiCultural review : ‡b dedicated to a better understanding of ethnic, racial, and religious diversity.
260		
260	3	
300		v. : ‡b ill. ; ‡c 28 cm.
310		Quarterly
362	0	Vol. 1, no. 1 (Jan. 1992)-
500		Title from cover.
500		Latest issue consulted: Vol. 12, no. 2 (June 2003).
580		With v. 14, no. 4 (winter 2005), absorbed: EMIE bulletin.
650	0	Multicultural education ‡v Periodicals.
650	0	Cultural pluralism ‡v Periodicals.
650	0	Ethnicity ‡v Periodicals.
780	0 5	‡t Journal of multicultural librarianship ‡x 0950-1649 ‡w (DLC) 87640645 ‡w (OCoLC)15088492
780	0 5	‡t EMIE bulletin ‡w (DLC)sn 83000624 ‡w (OCoLC)9477747

Cover

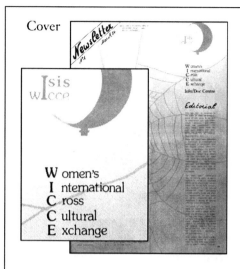

W omen's
I nternational
C ross
C ultural
E xchange

EXERCISE 3

The newsletter of the Isis-WICCE (Women's International Cross Cultural Exchange) was first published in 1984 from the organization's headquarters in Geneva, Switzerland. When the group relocated to Kampala, Uganda, the newsletter began to be published from the new location. Assume you have received issues published in Kampala from 1996 to 2001, but they may or may not be the first or last issue published in Kampala.

Using the old and the new practices, record the initial publication information and the change in publisher location in the blank fields provided. As a reminder, the order of change, when multiple 260 fields are used, is shown by the first indicator, where [blank] is used for the initial publication information, 2 indicates an intervening publisher, and 3 is used for the current/latest publisher information.

The country of publication code in the fixed field should be modified to reflect the latest place of publication, with the abbreviation from the MARC 21 Code List for Countries (available at http://www.loc.gov/marc/countries).

OCLC #11845413 (Past Practice)

Type a	ELvl	Srce d	GPub	Ctrl	Lang eng
BLvl s	Form	Conf 0	Freq a	MRec	Ctry
S/L 0	Orig	EntW	Regl r	Alph a	
Desc a	SrTp p	Cont	DtSt c	Dates 1984	, 9999

22		1019-1534 ‡2 0
37		‡b Women's World, Isis-WICCE, P.O. Box 4934, Kampala, Uganda
42		lc ‡a nsdp
43		d———
130	0	Women's world (Geneva, Switzerland)
222	0	Women's world
245	0 0	Women's world / ‡c Isis-WICCE.
246	3	Women's world (Kampala, Uganda)
260		
300		v. : ‡b ill. (some col.) ; ‡c 29-42 cm.
310		Annual, ‡b <1996-2001>
321		Quarterly, ‡b 1984-
321		2 times a year, ‡b <1989- >
362	0	No. 1 (Mar. 1984)-
500		Each issue called also newsletter, dossier, or report.
500		
500		Description based on surrogate; title from cover.
515		Some issues combined.
515		None published some years.
530		Also available by subscription via the World Wide Web.

(Continued on next page)

580			Issued also in Spanish and French, with French edition dated the year after the English ed. (e.g., no. 30 (1996) in English published as no 9 (1997) in French).
650		0	Feminism ǂv Periodicals.
650		0	Women ǂv Periodicals.
650		0	Women ǂz Developing countries ǂv Periodicals.
710	2		Isis-WICCE (Organization)
780	0	1	ǂt Women's international bulletin ǂw (DLC)sc 84007447 ǂw (OCoLC)9662823
856	4	1	ǂu http://www.softlineweb.com/softlineweb/genderw.htm

OCLC #11845413 (Present Practice)

Type a	ELvl	Srce d	GPub	Ctrl	Lang eng
BLvl s	Form	Conf 0	Freq a	MRec	Ctry
S/L 0	Orig	EntW	Regl r	Alph a	
Desc a	SrTp p	Cont	DtSt c	Dates 1984	, 9999

022			1019-1534 ǂ2 0
037			ǂb Women's World, Isis-WICCE, P.O. Box 4934, Kampala, Uganda
042			lc ǂa nsdp
043			d———
130	0		Women's world (Geneva, Switzerland)
222		0	Women's world
245	0	0	Women's world / ǂc Isis-WICCE.
246	3		Women's world (Kampala, Uganda)
260			
260			
300			v. : ǂb ill. (some col.) ; ǂc 29-42 cm.
310			Annual, ǂb <1996-2001>
321			Quarterly, ǂb 1984-
321			2 times a year, ǂb <1989- >
362	0		No. 1 (Mar. 1984)-
500			Each issue called also newsletter, dossier, or report.
500			Description based on surrogate; title from cover.
515			Some issues combined.
515			None published some years.
530			Also available by subscription via the World Wide Web.
580			Issued also in Spanish and French, with French edition dated the year after the English ed. (e.g., no. 30 (1996) in English published as no 9 (1997) in French).
650		0	Feminism ǂv Periodicals.
650		0	Women ǂv Periodicals.
650		0	Women ǂz Developing countries ǂv Periodicals.
710	2		Isis-WICCE (Organization)
780	0	1	ǂt Women's international bulletin ǂw (DLC)sc 84007447 ǂw (OCoLC) 9662823
856	4	1	ǂu http://www.softlineweb.com/softlineweb/genderw.htm

CHAPTER 5

Changes in Frequency and Numbering
(Enumeration and Chronology)

When a serial publication continues for some time, changes in frequency and numbering can occur quite often. Rather than creating a separate bibliographic record, the serials cataloger updates the existing record for these changes. In this chapter, we will talk about how to record frequency and numbering for serials publications and what to do when frequency and numbering change.

A. RECORDING FREQUENCY AND CHANGES IN FREQUENCY

According to AACR2 12.7B1, the frequency of the serial as well as changes in frequency are recorded in notes. The rules in RDA 2.14.1 provide more detailed instructions on making notes on frequency. RDA 2.14.1.1 defines frequency as the intervals at which the issues or parts of a serial or the updates to an integrating resource are issued. For sources of information, RDA 2.14.1.2 instructs the cataloger to take information on frequency from any source. In terms of recording frequency, RDA 2.14.1.3 provides a list of appropriate terms to use:

daily, three times a week, biweekly, weekly, semiweekly, three times a month, bimonthly, monthly, semimonthly, quarterly, three times a year, semiannual, annual, biennial, triennial, irregular.

If the frequency is irregular or if none of the terms from RDA 2.14.1.3 are appropriate or sufficiently specific, a note is made to give details of the frequency (see RDA 2.20.12.3). RDA 2.14.1.4 instructs the cataloger to make a note to record a change in frequency (see RDA 2.20.12.4).

Note that the guidelines for the CONSER Standard Record (CSR) only require that the current frequency be recorded in a 310 field—if known. Recording the former frequency in the 321 field is not required. However, when maintaining an existing record, a cataloger should follow the established practice of moving the former frequency to a 321 field and recording the current frequency in the 310 field. Former frequencies should not be deleted just to conform to the new standard. In order to meet the needs of the users, elements that are not required in the CSR can still be added based on the characteristics of the particular resource or the needs of the local institution.

B. RECORDING NUMBERING AND CHANGES IN NUMBERING

Numbering is one of the crucial elements used in identifying serial publications. A serial is defined as a continuing resource issued in a succession of discrete parts—usually bearing numbering—that has no predetermined conclusion (AACR2 Appendix D). Serials in general carry numeric and/or chronological designation, through which the user identifies a certain issue of a serial and gains access to the article in the issue. Under AACR2, numbering refers to the identification of each of the successive items of a publication. It can include a numeral, a letter, any other character, or the combination of these, with or without an accompanying word (volume, number, etc.) and/or a chronological designation.

Similarly, in RDA, the numbering of serials is defined as the identification of each of the issues or parts of a serial. The numbering may include a numeral, a letter, any other character, or the combination of these, with or without an accompanying caption (volume, number, etc.) and/or a chronological designation. Considered as core elements are the numeric and/or alphabetic designation of the first issue or part of the sequence, the chronological designation of the first issue or part of the sequence, the numeric and/or alphabetic designation of the last issue or part of the sequence, and the chronological designation of the last issue or part of the sequence.

The prescribed source of information for the numbering area is the whole resource (AACR2 12.0B3). In the second half of this chapter, we will cover how to record numeric, alphabetic, or chronological designations of the first and/or last issues of a serial, applying the formatted and unformatted styles of notes in the 362 field. Moreover, examples are used to illustrate what to do when there is no numbering on the first issue, how to determine whether the word "edition" is used as an edition statement or as the numbering, and how to record the successive designation when the numbering starts over with the same numbering system, with or without a "new series" designation.

The practice under CSR guidelines will also be discussed, as the numbering area under these guidelines represents significant changes from the existing practice under AACR2. CSR was implemented in 2007 in an effort to streamline the serials cataloging process by focusing on the core elements of a serial record and reducing the number of unnecessary or redundant elements. LCRI has been revised to support CSR guidelines that may differ from AACR2 rules. According to LCRI 12.3, it is not required to give numbering in a formatted note (the 362 field, with indicators 0[blank]), even if the description is based on the first and/or last issue(s).

RESOURCES CONSULTED

AACR2

12.3 Numbering Area
12.7B1 Frequency

LCRI

12.3 Numbering Area
12.7B1 LC/PCC practice: Noting Frequency

RDA

2.14.1 Basic instructions on recording frequency
2.6 Numbering of serials
2.6.1 Basic instructions on recording numbering of serials
2.20.12 Note on frequency

CCM

Module 8 Numbering (Fields 362/500)
13.3 Frequency notes (Fields 310/321)

Identifying and Recording the Frequency of a Serial

Title: African communication research

Cover

Title Page Verso

ISSN 1821-6544

African Communication Research

a peer-reviewed journal

Published by the Faculty of Social Sciences and

Communications at St. Augustine University of Tanzania,

Mwanza, Tanzania

as a service to communication research in Africa.

African Communication Research

is available on line

**Simply enter the title in any
search engine**

This issue dedicated to

Media and Democratisation in Africa

AFRICAN COMMUNICATION RESEARCH. VOL. 1. NO. 3 (2008)

African Communication Research (ISSN 1821-6544)
**is published three times a year, May, September and
December, as a service of the Faculty of Social Sciences and
Communications at St. Augustine University of Tanzania,
Mwanza, Tanzania for communication
researchers of Africa.**

All correspondence should be directed to:

Prof. Robert A. White,
Coordinating Editor
St. Augustine University of Tanzania, P.O. Box 307, Mwanza Tanzania

Email: whitesaut@yahoo.com Tel: +255786 777 972

Subscriptions and exchange of journals

Personal and Institutional Subscriptions are:
US$25.00 for addresses in Africa
US$35.00 for addresses in the Middle East, India and
South Asia
US$40.00 for addresses in Europe and Australia
US$45.00 for addresses in the USA, Latin America and
East Asia.

To obtain a subscription and arrange a suitable form of payment or
establish an exchange of journals, send an email to whitesaut@yahoo.com

Coordinating Editor
St. Augustine University of Tanzania,
P.O. Box 307, Mwanza – Tanzania
Email: whitesaut@yahoo.com Tel: +255786 777 972
Web: http://www.saut.ac.tz

Proposals for book reviews or requests to review books are welcome

---

To identify a serial's frequency, one can search through the issue in hand to find an explicit statement of publication frequency. This statement may be found on the title page verso or within a magazine's masthead. The current frequency is coded in two places: the variable field 310 and the fixed field 008/18 "Freq." In addition, the regularity of issuance is coded in the fixed field 008/19 "Regl." Because the Frequency and Regularity elements are coded based on information given in field 310, the current frequency in the 310 field should be determined first before these elements are coded. If the frequency of a publication cannot be identified, then no 310 field is provided and the "Freq" and "Regl" fixed fields are coded 'u,' indicating unknown.

In this example, a statement identifying the frequency of issuance ("Three times a year, May, September and December") is provided at the top of the title page verso. The cataloging record for this serial reflects this information in the fixed fields "Freq" and "Regl" as well as in the variable 310 field. The issuance "Three times a year" is represented in the "Freq" field as "t," while the "Regl" field is coded "r" because the serial is issued regularly.

As instructed in CCM 13.3.2, if the frequency requires further explanation to account for stated irregularities in the publishing pattern, it may be given in parentheses following the frequency. In this example, the serial is known to be issued in May, September, and December, so this information is noted after the frequency statement "Three times a year."

For more information on the appropriate codes for publication frequency, consult the CONSER *Editing Guide* (CEG) available by subscription from http://desktop.loc.gov, or the MARC record information found in either the *MARC 21 Format for Bibliographic Data* (available at http://www.loc.gov/marc/bibliographic) or the OCLC *Bibliographic Formats and Standards* (http://www.oclc.org/bibformats).

OCLC #402467346

Type a	ELvl	Srce c	GPub	Ctrl	Lang eng
BLvl s	Form	Conf 0	Freq t	MRec	Ctry tz
S/L 0	Orig	EntW	Regl r	Alph	
Desc a	SrTp p	Cont	DtSt c	Dates 2008	, 9999

	022	1821-6544
	042	pcc
	043	f———
	245 0 0	African communication research.
	260	Mwanza, Tanzania : ‡b Faculty of Social Sciences and Communications at St. Augustine University of Tanzania
CCM 13.3.1 13.3.2	310	Three times a year (May, Sept, and Dec.) *AACR2 12.7B1*
	362 1	Began with Vol. 1, no. 1 (May 2008).
	500	Description based on: Vol. 1, no. 1 (May 2008); title from title page.
	500	Issues have also thematic titles.
	500	Latest issue consulted: Vol. 1, no. 3 (Dec. 2008).
	650 0	Communication ‡x Research ‡z Africa ‡v Periodicals.

AACR2

12.7B1 - Note the frequency of the serial unless it is apparent from the title, the statement of responsibility, or is unknown

LCRI

12.7B1 - Make a note on the known frequency of a serial even if the frequency is apparent from the rest of the description

RDA

2.14.1.2 - Take information on frequency from any source

2.14.1.3 - Record the frequency of using an appropriate term from the list provided

2.20.12.3 - Make notes providing details on currency of the contents or frequency of updating

CCM

13.3.1 - The serial's current frequency is expressed in both variable field 310 and in fixed field 008/18 "Freq"
  – The regularity of issuance is expressed in fixed field 008/19 "Regl"

13.3.2 - The frequency is taken from information found in the piece or supplied by the publisher or from evidence of issues already published; if the frequency requires further explanation to account for stated irregularities in the publishing pattern, it may be given in parentheses following the frequency

Identifying and Recording Changes in Frequency in an Online Journal

Title: Economic bulletin

Caption from Page 1

> ## Economic Bulletin
> ## Change in Frequency
>
> Please note that effective 2009, the Economic Bulletin will be published twice yearly January and July. The first issue of this new publication will be July 2009.

Cover

Changes to a serial's frequency may be announced in the serial or on a publisher's website. Often, an e-mail with a link to additional information will be sent to subscribers informing them of the change in the frequency of the issuance.

In this example, the *Economic Bulletin* of the Central Bank of Trinidad and Tobago is reducing the frequency from three times yearly to twice a year. A notification of this change was posted at the head of the Vol. XI, no. 1 (July 2009) online issue and an e-mail message was sent to the subscribers.

The cataloging record has been updated to reflect this change: The fixed field "Freq" and the 310 frequency field have been updated to show the current frequency, while the 321 former publication frequency field has been added. The updated issuance "twice yearly" is represented in the "Freq" field as "f" for semiannual. Because the serial will continue to be issued regularly, the coding of the "Regl" field remains unchanged.

The 310 field should reflect the current frequency information and must match the designated code in the "Freq" fixed field. In this cataloging record, the 310 field has been updated to state the current frequency: "Twice yearly." The date when the current publication frequency takes effect ("July 2009") has been given in the 310 subfield ‡b because it is now different from the initial publication date and the former frequency is given in field 321.

The 321 field records the former frequency of issuance and can be repeated when additional changes to the frequency need to be noted. In this example, the previous frequency "Three times a year" has been recorded, and the date of the former publication frequency ("1999–") is given in subfield ‡b because this subfield is required in all 321 fields.

The subfield ‡b in the 310 and 321 fields should be preceded by a comma but should not end with a period. The date should be enclosed in angle brackets if it is not known whether it is the earliest or latest date.

OCLC #164437093

	Type a	ELvl I	Srce d	GPub	Ctrl	Lang eng
	BLvl s	Form s	Conf 0	Freq f	MRec	Ctry tr
	S/L 0	Orig s	EntW s	Regl r	Alph	
	Desc a	SrTp p	Cont	DtSt c	Dates 1999	, 9999

	022		1818-0027
	043		nwtr—
	130	0	Economic bulletin (Central Bank of Trinidad and Tobago : online)
	245	1 0	Economic bulletin ǂh [electronic resource] / ǂc Central Bank of Trinidad and Tobago.
	246	1 8	Central Bank economic bulletin
	260		Port of Spain : ǂb Central Bank of Trinidad and Tobago, ǂc [1999]-

CCM 13.3.1 13.3.2 13.3.4	310	Twice yearly (Jan. and July), ǂb July 2009-	AACR2 12.7B1
13.3.4	321	Three times a year, ǂb 1999-	12.7B1

	362	0	Vol. 1, no. 1 (May 1999)-
	500		Title from volume contents page (viewed on Aug. 14, 2007).
	500		Latest issue consulted: Vol. 11, no. 1 (July 2009).
	530		Also issued in print.
	651	0	Trinidad and Tobago ǂx Economic conditions ǂv Statistics ǂv Periodicals.
	710	2	Central Bank of Trinidad and Tobago.
	776	0	ǂt Economic bulletin (Central Bank of Trinidad and Tobago) ǂw (DLC) 2002229170 ǂw (OCoLC)45204505
	780	0 0	Central Bank of Trinidad and Tobago. ǂt Quarterly economic bulletin
	856	4 0	ǂu http://www.central-bank.org.tt/publications/index.php?pid=6002&pub=eb

AACR2

12.7B1 - Note the frequency of the serial unless it is apparent from the title, the statement of responsibility, or is unknown

LCRI

12.7B1 - Make a note on the known frequency of a serial even if the frequency is apparent from the rest of the description

RDA

2.14.1.2 - Take information on frequency from any source

2.14.1.3 - Record the frequency by using an appropriate term from the list provided

2.14.1.4 - Make a note on a change in frequency

2.20.12.3 - Make notes providing details on currency of the contents or frequency of updating

2.20.12.4 - Make notes on changes in frequency, stating the frequencies and their respective dates in chronological order

CCM

13.3.1 - The serial's current frequency is expressed in both variable field 310 and in fixed field 008/18 "Freq"

- The regularity of issuance is expressed in fixed field 008/19 "Regl"

13.3.2 - The frequency is taken from information found in the piece or supplied by the publisher or from evidence of issues already published; if the frequency requires further explanation to account for stated irregularities in the publishing pattern, it may be given in parentheses following the frequency

13.3.4 - Field 321 is used for former frequencies. When this field is given, a designation must be also included in all of the frequency fields (310 and 321)

Recording Irregular Frequency

Title: Fodor's essential Europe

Cover

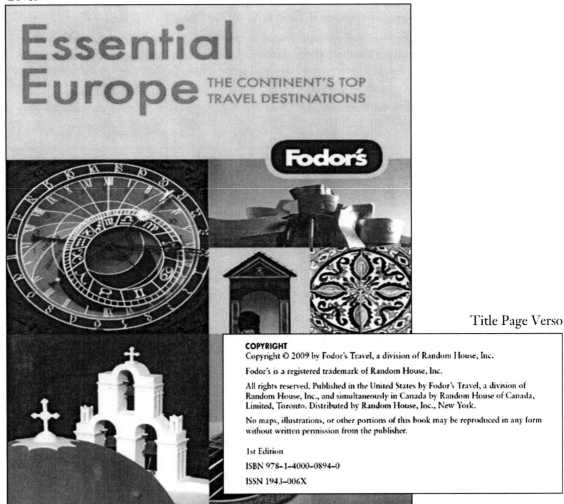

Title Page Verso

COPYRIGHT

Copyright © 2009 by Fodor's Travel, a division of Random House, Inc.

Fodor's is a registered trademark of Random House, Inc.

All rights reserved. Published in the United States by Fodor's Travel, a division of Random House, Inc., and simultaneously in Canada by Random House of Canada, Limited, Toronto. Distributed by Random House, Inc., New York.

No maps, illustrations, or other portions of this book may be reproduced in any form without written permission from the publisher.

1st Edition

ISBN 978-1-4000-0894-0

ISSN 1943-006X

When a serial is not issued on a regularly scheduled basis, the current frequency may be recorded in the 310 field as "Irregular" or, if the publisher's intent is known, the publisher's statement of future frequency may be recorded.

In this example, the publisher's intent is to issue an updated version every two to three years. This information has been used in the 310 field and the "Freq" fixed field—here coded as "g" for biennial (issued or updated every two years). The intended regularity is not known, so the "Regl" fixed field is coded "x" to indicate the irregularity of the issuance.

OCLC #232607742

Type a	ELvl	Srce c	GPub	Ctrl	Lang eng
BLvl s	Form	Conf 0	Freq g	MRec	Ctry nyu
S/L 0	Orig	EntW	Regl x	Alph a	
Desc a	SrTp	Cont	DtSt c	Dates 2009	, 9999

022	0		1943-006X ǂ2 1
037			ǂb Fodor's Travel, 1745 Broadway, Maildrop 6-2, New York, NY 10019 ǂc $24.95
042			nsdp ǂa lcd
043			e———
245	0	0	Fodor's essential Europe.
246	1	3	Essential Europe
260			New York : ǂb Fodor's Travel Publications
310			Every two to three years
362	1		Began with: 1st ed., copyrighted in 2009.
500			Description based on: First issue; title from title page.
651		0	Europe ǂv Guidebooks.

CCM 13.3.1 (for 310) — AACR2 12.7B1 (for 310)

AACR2

12.7B1 - Note the frequency of the serial unless it is apparent from the title, the statement of responsibility, or is unknown

LCRI

12.7B1 - Make a note on the known frequency of a serial even if the frequency is apparent from the rest of the description

RDA

2.14.1.2 - Take information on frequency from any source

2.14.1.3 - Record the frequency by using an appropriate term from the list provided

2.20.12.3 - Make notes providing details on currency of the contents or frequency of updating

CCM

13.3.1 - The serial's current frequency is expressed in both variable field 310 and in fixed field 008/18 "Freq"
   – The regularity of issuance is expressed in fixed field 008/19 "Regl"

Recording the History of Frequency Change

Title: Hotel & motel management

Cover

Screenshot of subscription page

Hotel & Motel Management supplies the credible news analysis and operating resources the lodging industry needs to prosper amid constant change.

Comprehensive reporting and research offer top-of-mind and quick-hitting insights while introducing the people driving the future of the hotel community.

Strategies about marketing, finance, technology, design, and product purchasing go beyond the bricks & mortar to bring readers closer to the fundamentals of operating in the lodging business.

Hotel & Motel Management appears once a month in January, February, March, April, May, July, August, September and December; twice a month in June, October and November.

Sometimes, changes to the frequency of publication occur multiple times. These changes can be recorded in the cataloging record for the serial publication. This is accomplished through updating existing MARC fields and adding new fields: updating the fixed fields "Freq" and "Regl" and the 310 field (where the current frequency of issuance is recorded) and adding 321 field(s) to record the history of former frequencies.

The serial *Hotel & Motel Management* is issued "once a month in January, February, March, April, May, July, August, September and December; twice a month in June, October and November." This information can be confirmed on the publisher's website.

Following *OCLC Bibliographic Formats and Standards*, the "Freq" fixed field is coded "m" to indicate that the serial is issued or updated on a monthly basis and the "Regl" fixed field is coded "n" for normalized irregular, meaning that the serial is irregular but that the pattern is predictable (e.g., once a month, except June, October, and November). When "Regl" is coded "n," the frequency should be input in the 310 field.

The current frequency is recorded in the 310 field, entered as: Monthly (except semimonthly in June, Oct., Nov.), and the date of current publication frequency (i.e., when the change to the new frequency began) is recorded in the subfield ǂb. Angle brackets are used with the date: Feb. 2009. This is to show that it is unknown whether the date available to the cataloger when the note was made is the earliest date that the frequency changed.

All former frequencies are recorded in the repeatable 321 fields—one frequency per field. When more than one 321 field is used, each is input in chronological order—from earliest to latest—after the 310 field. There is no period at the end of either the 310 field or the 321 field. The first word in each field is capitalized.

Alternatively, according to the *CONSER Editing Guide*, "Frequency varies" may be used in the 321 field when more than three past frequencies are known. When using the term, provide inclusive dates in subfield ǂb of field 321 and always provide the current frequency in field 310. If multiple 321 fields exist in the record, delete them at the time the "Frequency varies" note is added. For example:

310 _ _ Annual, ǂb 1985-

321 _ _ Frequency varies, ǂb 1948-1984

OCLC #1681167

Type a	ELvl	Srce d	GPub	Ctrl	Lang eng
BLvl s	Form	Conf 0	Freq m	MRec	Ctry mnu
S/L 0	Orig	EntW	Regl n	Alpha a	
Desc a	SrTp p	Cont	DtSt c	Dates 1967	, 9999

022	0		0018-6082 ǂ2 1
037			ǂb Hotel & Motel Management, P.O. Box 6195, Duluth, MN 55806-9895
042			nsdp
245	0	0	Hotel & motel management.
246	3		Hotel and motel management
246	1	7	H & MM ǂb <1983- >
260			[Duluth, Minn., etc. : ǂb Edgell Communications, etc.]
300			v. : ǂb ill. ; ǂc 28 cm.

CCM			
13.3.1 13.3.2 13.3.4	310	Monthly (except semimonthly in June, Oct., Nov.), ǂb <Feb. 2009->	AACR2 12.7B1
13.3.4	321	Monthly, ǂb 1967-1979	12.7B1
13.3.2 13.3.4	321	Monthly (except semimonthly in Apr.), ǂb 1980-1982	12.7B1
13.3.4	321	Monthly, ǂb 1983-	12.7B1
13.3.4	321	18 issues yearly, ǂb <Sept. 1989- >	12.7B1
13.3.2 13.3.4	321	Semimonthly (except monthly in Jan., Aug., Dec.), ǂb <Jan. 14, 1991- >	12.7B1
13.3.2 13.3.4	321	Semimonthly (except monthly in Jan., Aug.), ǂb <Dec. 27, 2007- >	12.7B1

362	0		Vol. 182, no. 5 (May 1967)-
500			Latest issue consulted: Vol. 224, no. 2 (Feb. 2009).
500			Published by: Duluth, MN : Questex, <2007- >
650		0	Hotel management ǂv Periodicals.
650		0	Motel management ǂv Periodicals.
780	0	0	ǂt Hotel management & innkeeping ǂw (OCoLC)1639129
780	0	5	ǂt Motor inn journal ǂw (DLC) 79642833 ǂg Oct. 1979 ǂw (OCoLC) 4545493

AACR2

12.7B1 - Note the frequency of the serial unless it is apparent from the title, the statement of responsibility, or is unknown

LCRI

12.7B1 - Make a note on the known frequency of a serial even if the frequency is apparent from the rest of the description

RDA

2.14.1.2 - Take information on frequency from any source

(Continued on next page)

2.14.1.3 - Record the frequency by using an appropriate term from the list provided

2.14.1.4 - Make a note on a change in frequency

2.20.12.3 - Make notes providing details on currency of the contents or frequency of updating

2.20.12.4 - Make notes on changes in frequency, stating the frequencies and their respective dates in chronological order

CCM

13.3.1 - The serial's current frequency is expressed in both variable field 310 and in fixed field 008/18 "Freq"
    – The regularity of issuance is expressed in fixed field 008/19 "Regl"

13.3.2 - The frequency is taken from information found in the piece or supplied by the publisher or from evidence of issues already published; if the frequency requires further explanation to account for stated irregularities in the publishing pattern, it may be given in parentheses following the frequency

13.3.4 - Field 321 is used for former frequencies. When this field is given, a designation must be also included in all of the frequency fields (310 and 321)

Numbering Following AACR2

Title: Women's world

Cover

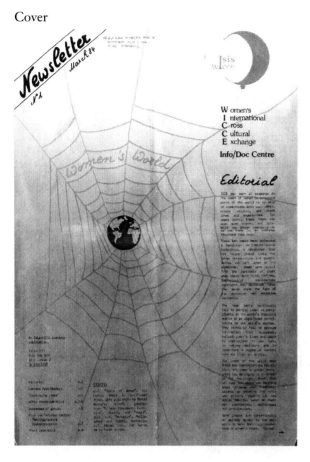

Serials usually bear numeric, alphabetic, and/or chronological designations. The first and last issues of a serial are recorded in the 362 field, with the same terms found on the issue but using abbreviations as instructed in Appendix B for numeric, alphabetic, and chronological designations and Appendix C for numerals.

In this example, *Women's World* began publication with No. 1 in March 1984, so the information is entered in the 362 field. The number and the date sufficiently and uniquely identify the issue.

Because the prescribed source of information for the numbering is the entire serial (AACR2 12.0B3), "No. 1, March1984," found on the cover, is recorded without the use of brackets. As AACR2 allows abbreviations to be used in numbering, the abbreviation Mar. for March is used (AACR2 Appendix B).

RDA is based on the principle of representation. This is commonly stated to as "Take what you see. Accept what you get." Abbreviations are therefore allowed in transcribed elements if the data already appears in an abbreviated form in the source.

In our example, "No. 1 (Mar. 1984)" is entered in the 362 field, with the first indicator value 0. This means the cataloger had the first issue—No. 1 (Mar. 1984)—in hand when the serial was cataloged.

As mentioned earlier, it is important to have information about the first and/or last issue of a serial when recording the 362 field. Whether or not the first or last issue is in hand is equally important, and it affects how the first indicator in the 362 field is coded. If the first or last issue is present, a formatted 362 field is used, with the first indicator 0. Numbering information that has been coded this way will appear following the title (or edition when present) in the cataloging record. If the first or last issue is not in hand but the beginning or ending date/number is known from other sources, an unformatted 362 field is used, with the first indicator set to 1. The numbering information recorded this way will display as a note. Whenever the first issue is not in hand, the numbering of the earliest available issue is given in the field 588 for Source of Description Note, preceded by the phrase "Description based on:" (AACR2 12.7B23). This is a change from the old practice of recording the "Description based on" note in a 500 field for General Note. For more information on notes, see Chapter 9.

OCLC #11845413

Type a	ELvl	Srce d	GPub	Ctrl	Lang eng
BLvl s	Form	Conf 0	Freq a	MRec	Ctry ug
S/L 0	Orig	EntW	Regl r	Alph a	
Desc a	SrTp p	Cont	DtSt c	Dates 1984	, 9999

022			1019-1534 ‡2 0
037			‡b Women's World, Isis-WICCE, P.O. Box 4934, Kampala, Uganda
042			lc ‡a nsdp
130	0		Women's world (Geneva, Switzerland)
245	0	0	Women's world / ‡c Isis-WICCE.
246	3		Women's world (Kampala, Uganda)
260			Geneva, Switzerland : ‡b Isis-WICCE, ‡c 1984-
300			v. : ‡b ill. (some col.) ; ‡c 29-42 cm.
310			Annual, ‡b <1996-2001>
321			Quarterly, ‡b 1984-
321			2 times a year, ‡b <1989- >

CCM				AACR2
8.1.1				12.3B1
8.4.1	362	0	No. 1 (Mar. 1984)-	12.3C1
8.4.2				12.3C4

500			Each issue called also newsletter, dossier, or report.
500			Place of publication varies: Kampala, Uganda, <1996-2001>
500			Title from cover.
515			Some issues combined.
515			None published some years.
530			Also available by subscription via the World Wide Web.
580			Issued also in Spanish and French, with French edition dated the year after the English ed. (e.g., no. 30 (1996) in English published as no 9 (1997) in French).
650		0	Feminism ‡v Periodicals.
650		0	Women ‡v Periodicals.
710	2		Isis-WICCE (Organization)
780	0	1	‡t Women's international bulletin ‡w (DLC)sc 84007447 ‡w (OCoLC)9662823
856	4	1	‡u http://www.softlineweb.com/softlineweb/genderw.htm

AACR2

12.3B1 - Record the numeric and/or alphabetic designation of the first and, if known, last issues of the serial. Use the abbreviations from AARC2 Appendix B and numerals from Appendix C

12.3C1 - If the first and/or last issue of a serial is identified by a chronological designation, give it in the same terms, but not necessarily with the same punctuation, used in that issue. Use abbreviations as instructed in appendix B and numerals as instructed in Appendix C

12.3C4 - If the first and/or last issue of a serial is identified by both a numeric and/or alphabetic designation and a chronological designation, give the numeric and/or alphabetic designation before the chronological designation

RDA

2.6.1 - Basic instructions on recording numbering of serials

2.6.1.4 - Record numbers expressed as numerals or as words applying the general guidelines given under 1.8 rda
  – Transcribe other words, characters, or groups of words and/or characters as they appear on the source of information. Apply the general guidelines on transcription given under 1.7 rda

2.6.2 - Numeric and/or alphabetic designation of first issue or part of sequence

2.6.3 - Chronological designation of first issue or part of sequence

CCM

8.1.1 - A formatted 362 field is given when the first and/or last issue is in hand

8.3.1 - The prescribed source of information for the numbering is the entire serial

8.4.1 - General rule: record the numbering as it appears on the piece, with some exceptions; when both a numeric and a chronological designation are present, give the chronological designation in parentheses following the numeric designation

8.4.2 - Modifying the numbering: e.g., use the abbreviations from AARC2 Appendix B

Numbering Following CONSER Standard Record (CSR) Guidelines

Title: Getty research journal

Cover

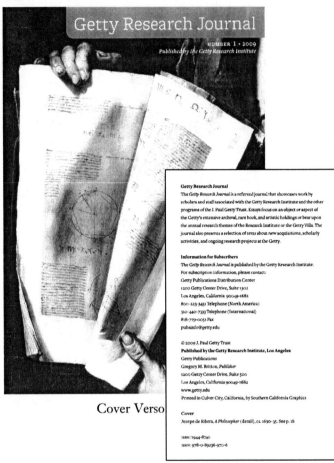

Cover Verso

This example shows how numeric/alphabetic and chronological designations and related notes are recorded following CSR guidelines. The practice under CSR guidelines is quite different from the previous practice under AACR2, and the LCRI has been revised to support the policy decision. The differences are shown below:

First, according to CSR guidelines, when creating an original cataloging record, the cataloger should always use an unformatted note in the 362 field, with the first indicator value 1, when the information is known, regardless of whether the first or last issue is actually in hand. Wordings like "Began . . ." and "Ceased . . ." can be used in the note.

Second, the "Description based on: "(DBO) note is provided on all records in the 588 field—used for source of description notes—to make clear which issue was used as the basis for description, even if it is the first issue. This note should be combined with the "Source of title" note, even if the title is taken from the title page. Also, the "Latest issue consulted" (LIC) note is always recorded, even if it is the issue cited in the DBO note or is the final issue.

Third, it is not required to use standard abbreviations and capitalization in designation and note fields, so the cataloger may transcribe data as found (including abbreviations and capitalization) or use AACR2 standard abbreviations.

In short, the unformatted 362 field is used to record numbering and dates of publication and the 588 field to record the DBO note and LIC note in the CSR.

    362 1 _ Began with . . .
    588 _ _ Description based on: . . . ; title from . . .
    588 _ _ Latest issue consulted: . . .

As far as our example is concerned, the first issue of *Getty Research Journal*, Number 1 (2009), is recorded as an unformatted note in the 362 field, with the first indicator value 1. Because the serial includes numbering and dates of publication, the existing convention is followed of placing the date in parentheses. The "Description based on: Number 1 (2009)" note is combined with the source of title note "title from cover" in the 588 field. Another 588 field records "Latest issue consulted: Number 2 (2010)." Note that the captions, numbers, and dates are transcribed as found on the issue, and no abbreviations have been used. This practice continues in RDA, under which the cataloger can generally transcribe data as they appear on the source of information (RDA 2.6.1.4).

OCLC #239617254

Type a	ELvl	Srce c	GPub	Ctrl	Lang eng
BLvl s	Form	Conf 0	Freq f	MRec	Ctry cau
S/L 0	Orig	EntW	Regl r	Alph a	
Desc a	SrTp p	Cont	DtSt c	Dates 2009	, 9999

022	0		1944-8740 ‡2 1
037			‡b Getty Publications Distribution Center, P.O. Box 49659, Los Angeles, CA 90049-0659
042			lcd ‡a nsdp
245	0	0	Getty research journal.
260			Los Angeles, Calif. : ‡b Getty Research Institute
300			v. : ‡b ill. ; ‡c 26 cm.
310			Semiannual
362	1		Began with: Number 1 (2009).
500			Description based on: Number 1 (2009); title from cover.
650		0	Art ‡x History ‡v Periodicals.
650		0	Art ‡x Archival resources ‡v Periodicals.
610	2	0	Getty Research Institute ‡v Periodicals.
610	2	0	J. Paul Getty Trust ‡v Periodicals.
710	2		Getty Research Institute.
710	2		J. Paul Getty Trust.

AACR2
12.3B1
12.3C1
12.3C4

AACR2

12.3B1 - Record the numeric and/or alphabetic designation of the first and, if known, last issues of the serial. Use the abbreviations from AARC2 Appendix B and numerals from Appendix C

12.3C1 - If the first and/or last issue of a serial is identified by a chronological designation, give it in the same terms, but not necessarily with the same punctuation, used in that issue. Use abbreviations as instructed in Appendix B and numerals as instructed in Appendix C

12.3C4 - If the first and/or last issue of a serial is identified by both a numeric and/or alphabetic designation and a chronological designation, give the numeric and/or alphabetic designation before the chronological designation

LCRI

12.3. Numbering area [replaces all existing 12.3 LCRIs.] CONSER standard and minimal record practice: It is not required to give numbering in a formatted note (362 field, with indicators 0#) if the description is based on the first and/or last issue(s)

RDA

2.6.1 - Basic instructions on recording numbering of serials

2.6.1.4 - Record numbers expressed as numerals or as words applying the general guidelines given under 1.8

(Continued on next page)

– Transcribe other words, characters, or groups of words and/or characters as they appear on the source of information. Apply the general guidelines on transcription given under 1.7

2.6.2 - Numeric and/or alphabetic designation of first issue or part of sequence

2.6.3 - Chronological designation of first issue or part of sequence

CSR

– An unformatted 362 field ("Began...") is created to record numeric/alphabetic and chronological designations when the information is available

– If numbering includes both numeric/alphabetic and a chronological designations, then place parenthesis around chronological designations

– Catalogers are required to provide the description based on (DBO) information and the source of title on all records. This information should be combined into one note. Always cite the source of title, even if it is the title page

– Latest issue consulted (LIC) note is required, even when cataloging based on only one issue

– Standard abbreviations and capitalization in notes are not required

Numbering With Beginning and Ending Designations

Title: University of Pennsylvania journal of labor and employment law

Cover

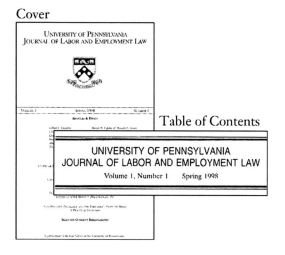

Cover

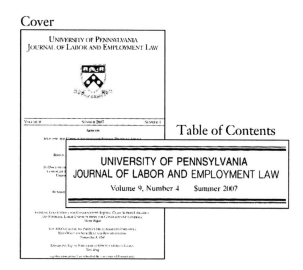

When the duration of a serial publication is known, the beginning and ending designations will be recorded in the 362 field, with a period at the end of the field. If both the numeric and the chronological designations are present, the chronological designation is enclosed in parentheses following the numeric designation.

If the first and the last issue of the serial are in hand, the numbering information will be recorded in one formatted 362 field, with the beginning designation followed by the ending designation.

In this example, the University of Pennsylvania Law School published the *University of Pennsylvania Journal of Labor and Employment Law* from Spring 1998 (vol. 1, no. 1) through Summer 2007 (vol. 9, no. 4). Because the cataloger had both issues in hand when recording the numbering information, the beginning and ending designations of the journal were input in 362 fields, with the first indicator value 0:

362 0 _   Vol. 1, no. 1 (spring 1998)-v. 9, no. 4 (summer 2007)

However, it should be pointed out that if CSR guidelines were followed, the cataloger would always use an unformatted note in the 362 field with first indicator value 1, regardless of whether the first/last issue(s) is in hand. It is also required that the description based on (DBO) information and the source of title be provided on all records, and this information should be combined in one note in the 588 field. The source of title should always be cited, even when it is the title page. A separate 588 field is required for a latest issue consulted (LIC) note, even if cataloging from the last issue in hand or when information about the last issue is known. For this example, the 362 field would be revised and 588 fields would be added if following CSR guidelines:

362 1 _   Began with: Vol. 1, no. 1 (spring 1998); ceased with Vol. 9, no. 4 (summer 2007).

588 _ _   Description based on: Vol. 1, no. 1 (spring 1998); title from title page.

588 _ _   Latest issue consulted: Vol. 9, no. 4 (summer 2007)

It is also important to point out that the "Dates" in fixed fields are based on the chronological designation from the 362 field (formatted or unformatted) or from the date of publication in the 260 field when no chronological designation is given in the 362 field.

OCLC #38164375

Type a	ELvl	Srce d	GPub	Ctrl	Lang eng
BLvl s	Form	Conf 0	Freq q	MRec	Ctry pau
S/L 0	Orig	EntW g	Regl x	Alph a	
Desc a	SrTp p	Cont	DtSt d	Dates 1998	, 2007

022	0		1097-4938 ǂ2 1
037			ǂb University of Pennsylvania Law School, 3400 Chestnut St., Philadelphia, PA 19104-6204 $45.00
042			nsdp ǂa lc
043			n-us—
245	0	0	University of Pennsylvania journal of labor and employment law.
246	3	0	Journal of labor and employment law
246	1		ǂi May be cited as: ǂa U. PA. J. LAB. & EMP. LAW
260			Philadelphia, PA : ǂb University of Pennsylvania Law School, ǂc c1998-c2007.
300			9 v. ; ǂc 26 cm.
310			Four times per year, ǂb <2007>
321			Three times per year, ǂb 1998-

CCM				AACR2
8.1.1	362	0	Vol. 1, no. 1 (spring 1998)-v. 9, no. 4 (summer 2007).	12.3B1
8.4.1				12.3C1
8.4.2				12.3C4

580			Issued also online through the Hein-On-Line project.
650		0	Labor laws and legislation ǂz United States ǂv Periodicals.
710	2		University of Pennsylvania. ǂb Law School.
776	1		ǂt University of Pennsylvania journal of labor and employment law (Online) ǂx 1942-9304 ǂw (DLC) 2008228567 ǂw (OCoLC)47015137
785	0	0	ǂt University of Pennsylvania journal of business and employment law ǂx 1940-8064 ǂw (DLC) 2007216438 ǂw (OCoLC)182574804
856	4	1	ǂu http://heinonline.org/HOL/Index?index=journals/upjlel&collection=journals

AACR2

12.3B1 - Record the numeric and/or alphabetic designation of the first and, if known, last issues of the serial. Use the abbreviations from AARC2 Appendix B and numerals from Appendix C

12.3C1 - If the first and/or last issue of a serial is identified by a chronological designation, give it in the same terms, but not necessarily with the same punctuation, used in that issue. Use abbreviations as instructed in Appendix B and numerals as instructed in Appendix C

12.3C4 - If the first and/or last issue of a serial is identified by both a numeric and/or alphabetic designation and a chronological designation, give the numeric and/or alphabetic designation before the chronological designation

RDA

2.6.1 - Basic instructions on recording numbering of serials

2.6.1.4 - Record numbers expressed as numerals or as words applying the general guidelines given under 1.8

   – Transcribe other words, characters, or groups of words and/or characters as they appear on the source of information. Apply the general guidelines on transcription given under 1.7

2.6.2 - Numeric and/or alphabetic designation of first issue or part of sequence

2.6.3 - Chronological designation of first issue or part of sequence

2.6.4 - Numeric and/or alphabetic designation of last issue or part of sequence

2.6.5 - Chronological designation of last issue or part of sequence

CCM

8.1.1 - A formatted 362 field is given when the first and/or last issue is in hand

8.3.1 - The prescribed source of information for the numbering is the entire serial

8.4.1 - General rule: record the numbering as it appears on the piece, with some exceptions; when both a numeric and a chronological designation are present, give the chronological designation in parentheses following the numeric designation

8.4.2 - Modifying the numbering: e.g., use the abbreviations from AARC2 Appendix B

No Volume Designation on First Issue

Title: Frontiers in neuroendocrinology

Title Page

Frontiers in
Neuroendocrinology, 1969

EDITED BY
WILLIAM F. GANONG
Department of Physiology
University of California School of Medicine
San Francisco Medical Center

AND
LUCIANO MARTINI
Istituto di Farmacologia e di Terapia
Università degli Studi, Milan

New York
OXFORD UNIVERSITY PRESS
London   Toronto   1969

Title Page

Frontiers in
Neuroendocrinology
Volume 4

Edited by

Luciano Martini, M.D.
Professor and Chairman
Institute of Endocrinology
University of Milan
Milan, Italy

William F. Ganong, M.D.
Professor of Physiology
Chairman, Department of Physiology
University of California
School of Medicine
San Francisco, California

Raven Press • New York

Title Page Verso

The journal *Frontiers in Neuroendocrinology* first came out in 1969 and was published on a biennial basis until 1989. The first issue did not carry any numbering. In fact, the volume numbering did not start until Vol. 4. When this happens, the cataloger should follow the instructions from AACR2 for recording numbering.

According to AACR2 12.3D1, when the first issue lacks any numbering but subsequent issues consistently carry a designation pattern, the numbering designation should be supplied in brackets for the first issue. In this example, the volume designation begins with v. 4 and appears in subsequent issues. This information is recorded in the 515 field for Numbering Peculiarities Note, and "Vol. 1," enclosed in brackets, is recorded in the 362 field.

RDA gives similar but more detailed instructions with regard to the lack of numbering designation on the first issue. For example, RDA 2.2.4 states that if information, such as numeric/alphabetic or chronological designation of the first or last issue, is taken from a source outside the resource itself, that fact should be indicated by means of a note or by some other means (e.g., through coding or the use of square brackets).

The instructions in RDA 2.6.2.3 and 2.6.3.3 correspond to those in RDA 2.2.4.

OCLC #1388525

Type a	ELvl	Srce d	GPub	Ctrl	Lang eng
BLvl s	Form	Conf 0	Freq q	MRec	Ctry nyu
S/L 0	Orig	EntW	Regl r	Alph a	
Desc	SrTp	Cont	DtSt c	Dates 1969	, 9999

022	0	0091-3022 ‡z 0532-7466 ‡2 1	
037		‡b Raven Press, 1185 Ave. of the Americas, New York NY 10036	
042		nsdp ‡a lc	
245	0 0	Frontiers in neuroendocrinology.	
260		New York, ‡b Raven Press [etc.]	
300		v. ‡b ill., ports. ‡c 24 cm.	
310		Quarterly, ‡b Jan. 1990-	
321		Biennial, ‡b 1969-1989	

CCM 8.5.1	362	0	[Vol. 1] (1969)-	AACR2 12.3D1

500		Editors: 1969- W.F. Ganong and L. Martini.

CCM 13.4.2	515	Volume numbering begins with v. 4.	AACR2 12.7B10.2

530		Also available to subscribers via the World Wide Web.	
650	0	Neuroendocrinology ‡v Periodicals.	
700	1	Ganong, William F.	
700	1	Martini, Luciano, ‡d 1927-	
776	1	‡t Frontiers in neuroendocrinology (Online) ‡x 1095-6808 ‡w (DLC)sn 97006905 ‡w (OCoLC)36980284	
856	4 1	‡u http://www.sciencedirect.com/science/journal/00913022	
856	4 1	‡u http://www.idealibrary.com/links/toc/frne	

AACR2

12.3D1 - If the first issue or part of a serial lacks any numbering, but subsequent issues or parts define a designation pattern, supply numbering for the first issue or part based on that pattern. If information about designations of subsequent issues or parts is not available, give [No. 1]- (or its equivalent in the language of the title proper) or a chronological designation for the first issue or part, as appropriate

12.7B10.2 - Make notes on complex or irregular numbering not already specified in the numbering area if considered to be important. Make notes on issuing peculiarities if considered to be important

RDA

2.2.4 - If information taken from a source outside the resource itself is supplied in the data elements, such as numeric and/or alphabetic designation of first/last issue, or chronological designation of first/last issue, indicate that fact either by means of a note or by some other means (e.g., through coding or the use of square brackets)

2.6.2.3 - Recording numeric and/or alphabetic designation of first issue: if the first issue lacks any numeric and/or alphabetic designation, but subsequent issues define a numeric and/or alphabetic

(Continued on next page)

designation pattern for the sequence, supply a numeric and/or alphabetic designation for the first issue or part of the sequence based on that pattern. Indicate that the information was taken from a source outside the resource itself as instructed under 2.2.4

2.6.3.3 - Recording chronological designation of first issue: if the first issue lacks any chronological designation, but subsequent issues define a chronological designation pattern for the sequence, supply a chronological designation for the first issue or part of the sequence based on that pattern. Indicate that the information was taken from a source outside the resource itself as instructed under 2.2.4

2.20.5.4 - Make notes on complex or irregular numbering of a serial, or numbering errors, not already specified in the numbering of serials element if they are considered to be important for identification

CCM

8.5.1 - When the first issue has no numbering, supply a designation following the form of numbering on subsequent issues when that is known; when only a single issue is in hand, give "[No. 1]-" or its equivalent, according to AACR2 12.3D1

13.4.2 - The numbering peculiarities note (Field 515) is used to explain a situation that cannot be fully expressed in fields 362 and/or the 500 "Description based on" note

Serials in Which the Word "Edition" Is Used as the Numbering

Title: AVMA report on veterinary compensation

Cover

AVMA
Report on
Veterinary
Compensation

In this example, different issues of the *AVMA Report on Veterinary Compensation* are identified by the dated edition. It is important not to confuse this with the edition statement.

With serials, when the word "edition" is accompanied by a number or date, it usually indicates a chronological progression of "editions" and the wording constitutes the numbering for the serial (CCM 9.1.1). Statements indicating numbering (e.g., 1st ed., 1916 ed.) should be in the numbering area (AACR2 12.2B2). RDA gives similar instructions, but no abbreviations are required when recording the numbering information; for serials, statements indicating numbering (e.g., First edition, 1916 edition) should be recorded as numbering (RDA 2.5.2.5).

CCM 9.1.2 defines a serial edition as a serial issued simultaneously with other editions of the serial, each of which has a core of the same, similar, or related contents, usually bearing the same title (or the same title in a different language). Each edition is intended for a specific audience, such as geographic editions (e.g., Midwest ed., California ed.), special format editions (e.g., Braille ed., Large print ed.), and language editions (French ed., English ed.). In such cases, the edition statement really applies to the whole serial rather than to only one issue, and the word "edition" and its accompanying words are recorded as the edition statement in the 250 field.

In this example, the numbered edition statement "2007 edition" is not a real serial edition statement because it applies only to one issue. The next issue could be the 2008 edition if the publication is issued annually or the 2009 edition if issued biennially. Because the 2007 edition is the first issue of *AVMA Report on Veterinary Compensation* after its title changed from the earlier title *Economic Report on Veterinarians & Veterinary Practices*, it is recorded as a formatted note in the 362 field, with the first indicator value 0, because the cataloger had the 2007 edition in hand when cataloging.

When information is recorded in the 362 field, the abbreviations from AARC2 Appendix B should be used (e.g., "edition" is recorded as "ed."). However, if following RDA, the cataloger should transcribe the numbering as it appears on the source of information (e.g., 2007 EDITION). If following CSR guidelines, the cataloger has the option of transcribing captions and dates as found (including abbreviations and capitalization) or using standard AACR2 abbreviations.

OCLC #166290984

Type a	ELvl	Srce	GPub	Ctrl	Lang eng
BLvl s	Form	Conf 0	Freq u	MRec	Ctry ilu
S/L 0	Orig	EntW s	Regl u	Alph a	
Desc a	SrTp	Cont	DtSt c	Dates 2007	, 9999

042		lcd	
043		n-us—	
245	0	0	AVMA report on veterinary compensation.
246	3		American Veterinary Medical Association report on veterinary compensation
246	3	0	Report on veterinary compensation
260			[Schaumburg, Ill.] : ‡b American Veterinary Medical Association, ‡c c2007-
300			v. : ‡b ill. ; ‡c 28 cm.

CCM				AACR2
8.1.1				12.2B2
8.3.2.e	362	0	2007 ed.-	12.3B1
8.4.1				12.3C1
8.4.2				

650		0	Veterinarians ‡z United States ‡x Economic conditions ‡v Statistics.
650	2	2	Veterinarians ‡x economics ‡z United States.
650	2	2	Veterinarians ‡x statistics & numerical data ‡z United States.
780	0	1	‡t Economic report on veterinarians & veterinary practices ‡x 1545-066X ‡w (DLC) 2003209207 ‡w (OCoLC)52335513
710	2		American Veterinary Medical Association.

AACR2

12.2B2 - For serials, give statements indicating numbering (e.g., 1st ed., 1916 ed.) in the numbering area

12.3B1 - Record the numeric and/or alphabetic designation of the first and, if known, last issues of the serial. Use the abbreviations from AARC2 Appendix B and numerals from Appendix C

12.3C1 - If the first and/or last issue of a serial is identified by a chronological designation, give it in the same terms, but not necessarily with the same punctuation, used in that issue. Use abbreviations as instructed in Appendix B and numerals as instructed in Appendix C

RDA

2.5.2.5 - For serials, record statements indicating numbering (e.g., First edition, 1916 edition) as numbering

2.6.1 - Basic instructions on recording numbering of serials

2.6.1.4 - Record numbers expressed as numerals or as words applying the general guidelines given under 1.8
- Transcribe other words, characters, or groups of words and/or characters as they appear on the source of information. Apply the general guidelines on transcription given under 1.7

2.6.2 - Numeric and/or alphabetic designation of first issue or part of sequence

2.6.3 - Chronological designation of first issue or part of sequence

CCM

9.1.1 - Uses of the word "edition" on serials: if the word "edition" is accompanied by a number or date, the result is a series of revisions of the same publication which may be treated as a monograph or a serial, depending on the frequency of the revisions. If treated as a serial, this wording constitutes the numbering for the serial (area 3, fields 362/500)

8.1.1 - A formatted 362 field is given when the first and/or last issue is in hand

8.3.1 - The prescribed source of information for the numbering is the entire serial

8.3.2e - Numbered editions almost never constitute an edition statement for a serial. They either constitute the numbering or, in some cases, are ignored. Many serials use the word "edition" (or its equivalent in other languages) in the numbering. If the publication is cataloged as a serial, the word "edition" is given as part of the numbering

8.4.1 - General rule: record the numbering as it appears on the piece, with some exceptions; when both a numeric and a chronological designation are present, give the chronological designation in parentheses following the numeric designation

8.4.2 - Modifying the numbering: e.g., use the abbreviations from AARC2 Appendix B

Numbering Restarts With a "New Series" Designation

Title: Gradhiva

Cover   Cover

Screenshot of Table
of Contents page

Sometimes, the title proper of a serial remains the same, but the numbering system restarts with the same numeric/alphabetic or chronological designation as found in the initial sequence. When this happens, the existing serial record is updated to reflect the new numbering sequence rather than a new record being created.

In this example, the journal *Gradhiva* was published for 34 issues from 1986 to 2003, numbered as 1–34. In 2005, the numbering system started over with "1," accompanied by the wording "nouvelle série" appearing on the cover. In accordance with AACR2 12.3G1, the existing record was revised to add the successive designations. The numbering designation of the first issue under the old system is followed by space-semicolon-space, while the new series ("nouv. sér.") is followed by the designation of the first issue under the new system. A Numbering Peculiarities Note in a 515 field is added to explain the change of the numbering system.

OCLC #17398464

Type a	ELvl	Srce	GPub l	Ctrl	Lang fre
BLvl s	Form	Conf 0	Freq f	MRec	Ctry fr
S/L 0	Orig	EntW	Regl r	Alph	
Desc a	SrTp p	Cont	DtSt c	Dates 1986	, 9999

	022		0764-8928
	037		‡b Editions Jean-Michel Place, 12, rue Pierre et Marie Curie, 75005 Paris
	042		lc
	245	0 0	Gradhiva.
	260		Paris : ‡b Département d'archives de l'ethnologie du Musée de l'homme, ‡c c1986-
	300		v. : ‡b ill. ; ‡c 27 cm.
	310		Semiannual
CCM 8.7.2	362	0	1 (automne 1986)- ; nouv. sér., 1 (2005)- · AACR2 12.3G1
13.4.2	515		Issues for 1986-2003 numbered 1-34; new series begins with nouv. sér., 1 (2005). · 12.7B10.2
	500		Title from cover.
	500		Last issue consulted: nouv. sér., 3 (2006).
	546		In French.
	500		On cover: "Revue d'histoire et d'archives de l'anthropologie", 1986-2003; "au Musée du quai Branly", 2005-
	550		Published by: Département d'archives de l'ethnologie du Musée de l'homme, 1986-2003; by: Musée du quai Branly, 2005-
	650	0	Anthropology ‡v Periodicals.
	650	0	Anthropology ‡x History ‡v Periodicals.
	710	2	Musée de l'homme (Muséum national d'histoire naturelle). ‡b Département d'archives de l'ethnologie.
	710	2	Musée du quai Branly.

AACR2

12.3G1 - If a new sequence is accompanied by wording to differentiate the sequence, such as new series, include this wording

12.7B10.2 - Make notes on complex or irregular numbering not already specified in the numbering area if considered to be important. Make notes on issuing peculiarities if considered to be important

RDA

2.6.2.3 - If a second or subsequent sequence of numbering with the same system as before is accompanied by wording such as new series, include this wording

(Continued on next page)

CCM

8.7.2 - A successive designation is a numeric designation that begins over again with no. 1 (or its equivalent) that may or may not be distinguishable from the first numbering scheme. When numbering systems are distinguishable, i.e., the new scheme must use different terminology (e.g., "v." rather than "no.") or include words such as "new series" (or their equivalent), give the latter system after the first preceded by a space-semicolon-space. Close off the old system if the last issue with that numbering is available

13.4.2 - The numbering peculiarities note (Field 515) is used to explain a situation that cannot be fully expressed in fields 362 and/or the 500 "Description based on" note

Numbering Restarts With [New Ser.] Supplied by Cataloger

Title: Illinois seed news

Front Page

Front Page

Like the previous journal *Gradhiva*, the title proper of *Illinois Seed News* remains the same, but the numbering systems started over with v. 1, no. 1, in 1992. However, unlike *Gradhiva*, *Illinois Seed News* does not carry such wordings as "new series" or "second series" with the new numbering system. Prior to the 2002 revision of AACR2, these changes would require the creation of a new record. In other words, a new record would be created for the title with the new numbering system if the new system adopts the same form of numeric and chronological designation of the earlier numbering system.

However, with the 2002 revision of AACR2, this practice has changed. Instead of creating a new record, the existing record should be revised and the new numbering system should be recorded with "new ser." in square brackets preceding the new numeric designation.

In this example, the publisher issued 23 volumes of *Illinois Seed News*, designated as v. 1 to v. 23, from 1970 to 1992. In the July/August 1992 issue, the numbering reverted back to v. 1, no. 1. In order to distinguish the new numbering scheme from the old numbering scheme, the existing record was revised. The designation of the first and last issues under the old system is followed by space-semicolon-space and "new ser." enclosed in square brackets is followed by the designation of the first issue under the new system. In addition, a 515 note field is given to clarify peculiarities in the numbering system.

OCLC #9810380

Type a	ELvl 7	Srce	GPub	Ctrl	Lang eng
BLvl s	Form	Conf 0	Freq m	MRec	Ctry ilu
S/L 0	Orig	EntW	Regl r	Alph a	
Desc a	SrTp p	Cont	DtSt c	Dates 1970	, 9999

	245	0	0	Illinois seed news.
	260			Urbana, Ill. : ǂb Illinois Crop Improvement Association : ǂb Illinois Seed Dealers Association
	300			v. : ǂb ill. ; ǂc 23-28 cm.
	310			Monthly
CCM 8.7.2	362	1		Began in 1970, and ended wtih v. 23, no. 3/4 (May-June, 1992) ; [new ser.] v. 1, no. 1 (July-Aug. 1992)- AACR2 12.3G1
	500			Description based on: Vol. 1, no. 4 (Sept. 1979); title from caption.
	500			Latest issue consulted: Vol. 5, no. 4 (Jan.-Feb. 1997).
13.4.2	515			[New series] began with v. 1, no. 1, published in July-August, 1992. 12.7B10.2
	650		3	Seeds ǂz Illinois ǂv Periodicals.
	650		3	Seed industry and trade ǂz Illinois ǂv Periodicals.
	710	2		Illinois Crop Improvement Association.
	710	2		Illinois Seed Dealers Association.

AACR2

12.3G1 - If a new sequence with the same system as before is not accompanied by wording such as new series, supply [new ser.] or another appropriate term (or its equivalent in the language of the title proper)

12.7B10.2 - Make notes on complex or irregular numbering not already specified in the numbering area if considered to be important. Make notes on issuing peculiarities if considered to be important

RDA

2.6.2.3 - If a new sequence with the same system as before is not accompanied by wording such as new series, supply new series or another appropriate term. Indicate that the information was taken from a source outside the resource itself as instructed under 2.2.4

2.2.4 - If information taken from a source outside the resource itself is supplied in the data elements, such as numeric and/or alphabetic designation of first/last issue, or chronological designation of first/last issue, indicate that fact either by means of a note or by some other means (e.g., through coding or the use of square brackets)

CCM

8.7.2 - A successive designation is a numeric designation that begins over again with no. 1 (or its equivalent) that may or may not be distinguishable from the first numbering scheme. When numbering systems are not distinguishable (i.e., when the numbering begins again with no. 1 or its equivalent using the same form of numeric and chronological designation without words, such as "new series") supply these words or their equivalent in the language of the serial

13.4.2 - The numbering peculiarities note (field 515) is used to explain a situation that cannot be fully expressed in fields 362 and/or the 500 "Description based on" note

Cover

Extension Bulletin 337

EXERCISE 1

Between 1925 and 1944, 126 issues of the *Extension Bulletin* were published by Michigan State College, Extension Service Division.

The issuance of the *Bulletin* was irregular (meaning there was no stated frequency of issuance from the publisher and no clear distribution pattern could be discerned based on the issues at hand).

Using the information provided, complete the 310 field, the "Freq" and "Regl" fixed fields, and the "Dates" fixed fields.

OCLC Bibliographic Formats and Standards is available at http://www.oclc.org/bibformats.

OCLC #23897773

Type a	ELvl	Srce d	GPub s	Ctrl	Lang eng
BLvl s	Form	Conf 0	Freq	MRec	Ctry miu
S/L 0	Orig	EntW	Regl	Alph a	
Desc a	SrTp m	Cont	DtSt d	Dates ,	

042		lcd	
043		n-us-mi	
130	0	Ext. bulletin (Michigan State College. Extension Division)	
245	1	0	Ext. bulletin.
246	1	3	Bulletin
246	1	3	Extension bulletin ‡f 1926-1944
246	1		‡i No. 44 (July 1925) has title: ‡a Extension series
260			East Lansing : ‡b Michigan State College, Extension Service Division, ‡c 1925-1944.
300			126 v. : ‡b ill. ; ‡c 24 cm.
310			
362	0		No. 41 (May 1925)-no. 255 (Feb. 1944).
500			Title from caption.
515			Some numbers issued in revised editions.
515			Some issues have earlier title: Bulletin.
650		0	Agriculture ‡z Michigan.
710	2		Michigan State College. ‡b Extension Division.
780	0	0	‡t Bulletin (Michigan Agricultural College. Extension Division) ‡w (OCoLC)9086024
785	0	0	‡t Extension bulletin (Michigan State College. Extension Service) ‡w (DLC)sn 92035528 ‡w (OCoLC)9086036

Cover

VOLUME 8 I NUMBER 1 I 2008

Studies in Ethnicity and Nationalism

Themed issue on Identity and Nationalism in Asia

SEN

AS EN
Association for the Study of Ethnicity and Nationalism

EXERCISE 2

The Association for the Study of Ethnicity and Nationalism publishes the journal *Studies in Ethnicity and Nationalism*. From 2002–2007, two issues of the journal were published per year. Since 2008, the journal has increased its issuance to three times a year. The issues of this journal have been published on a regular basis.

Suppose you have Vol. 1, no. 1 (2002) in hand. Use the information provided here to make a formatted note in the 362 field for volume designations and dates of publication. Record the journal's current frequency in the 310 field and the former frequency in the 321 field. Make sure the fixed fields for "Freq," "Regl," and "Dates" are also correctly coded.

OCLC Bibliographic Formats and Standards is available at http://www.oclc.org/bibformats.

OCLC #50525160

Type a	ELvl	Srce c	GPub	Ctrl	Lang eng
BLvl s	Form	Conf 0	Freq	MRec	Ctry enk
S/L 0	Orig	EntW	Regl	Alph	
Desc a	SrTp p	Cont	DtSt c	Dates ,	

022		1473-8481
042		lcd
245	0 0	Studies in ethnicity and nationalism / ‡c Association for the Study of Ethnicity and Nationalism.
260		London : ‡b Association for the Study of Ethnicity and Nationalism, ‡c 2001-
310		
321		
362		
550		Published jointly with the London School of Economics and Political Science.
500		Latest issue consulted: Vol. 8, no. 3 (2008).
650	0	Nationalism ‡v Periodicals.
650	0	Ethnicity ‡v Periodicals.
610	2 0	Association for the Study of Ethnicity and Nationalism ‡v Periodicals.
710	2	Association for the Study of Ethnicity and Nationalism.
710	2	London School of Economics and Political Science.
776	0 8	‡i Online version: ‡t Studies in ethnicity and nationalism ‡x 1754-9469 ‡w (DLC) 2008242151 ‡w (OCoLC)170924159
780	0 0	‡t ASEN bulletin ‡x 1353-8004 ‡w (DLC)sn 97032462 ‡w (OCoLC)36150091
856	4 1	‡u http://www.blackwell-synergy.com/loi/sena

Screenshot of Subscription Page

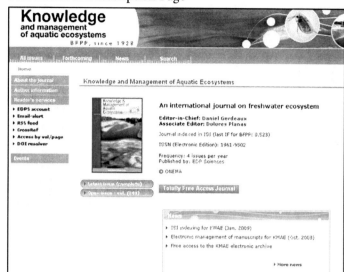

EXERCISE 3

The journal *Knowledge and Management of Aquatic Ecosystems* was first published in 1928 and has undergone several title changes since then: *Bulletin français de pisciculture* (1928–1984), *Bulletin français de la pêche et de la pisciculture* (1985–1996), and *BFPP* (1996–2007).

In 2008, the journal changed to its present title with no. 388. It publishes four issues per year regularly. Use the information provided to make an unformatted note in the 362 field for volume designations and dates of publication and record the journal's frequency in the 310 field. Make sure the fixed fields for "Freq," "Regl," and "Dates" are also correctly coded.

OCLC Bibliographic Formats and Standards is available at http://www.oclc.org/bibformats.

OCLC #236201500

Type a	ELvl	Srce d	GPub	Ctrl	Lang eng
BLvl s	Form s	Conf 0	Freq	MRec	Ctry fr
S/L 0	Orig s	EntW	Regl	Alph	
Desc a	SrTp p	Cont	DtSt c	Dates ,	

022		1961-9502
041	0	eng ‡b eng ‡b fre
042		lcd
245	0 0	Knowledge and management of aquatic ecosystems ‡h [electronic resource].
246	1 3	KMAE
260		Les Ulis, France : ‡b EDP Sciences, ‡c 2008-
310		
362		
500		Description based on: No. 388 (2008); title from table of contents (publisher's Web site, viewed Sep. 29, 2008).
500		Latest issue consulted: No. 388 (2008) (publisher's Web site, viewed Sep. 29, 2008).
500		"An international journal on freshwater ecosystem."
538		Mode of access: World Wide Web.
650	0	Aquatic ecology ‡v Periodicals.
650	0	Fishes ‡v Periodicals.
650	0	Fish culture ‡v Periodicals.
780	0 0	‡t BFPP ‡x 1297-6318 ‡w (DLC) 2005252230 ‡w (OCoLC)60554279
856	4 0	‡u http://www.kmae-journal.org/

Title Page

Title Page Verso

GAZETTE

of The Grolier Club

New Series

Number 1   June 1966

"*As long ago as 1885, the suggestion was made that a bulletin issued by the Club would serve as a*

EXERCISE 4

The *Gazette of the Grolier Club* has been published since May 1921, and its frequency varied from 1921 to 1979. However, since 1980, it has been published annually. Suppose you have the whole run of this serial publication and you have noticed that between May 1921 and May 1949, the issues are numbered No. 1–2. Starting in June 1966, the numbering restarts with New Series Number 1. Use the information provided here to make a formatted note in the 362 field for volume designations and dates of publication. Record the journal's current frequency in the 310 field and the former frequency in the 321 field. Make sure the fixed fields for "Freq," "Regl," and "Dates" are also correctly coded.

OCLC Bibliographic Formats and Standards is available at: http://www.oclc.org/bibformats/.

OCLC #1642923

Type a	ELvl	Srce	GPub	Ctrl	Lang eng
BLvl s	Form	Conf 0	Freq	MRec	Ctry nyu
S/L 0	Orig	EntW	Regl	Alph a	
Desc a	SrTp p	Cont	DtSt c	Dates ,	

022		0533-2990 ǂ2 1	
042		nsdp ǂa lcd ǂa premarc	
110	2	Grolier Club.	
245	1	0	Gazette of the Grolier Club.
260		[New York] : ǂb Grolier Club	
300		v. : ǂb ill. ; ǂc 18 cm.	
310			
321			
362			
610	2	0	Grolier Club ǂv Periodicals.
650		0	Bibliography ǂx Societies, etc. ǂv Periodicals.

Cover

Caption

Masthead

Masthead

EXERCISE 5

The Illinois Farm Bureau issues its publication *Illinois Farm Bureau Partners* four times yearly. The publication was started in the summer of 1995 with Vol. 1, no. 1, and the numbering system continued to the autumn of 2008 with vol. 14, no. 3. The publisher restarted its numbering at vol. 1, no. 1, with the winter 2008/2009 issue.

Use the information provided here to enter the dates of publication/sequential designations into the 362 field in the formatted style and record the journal's frequency in the 310 field. Make sure the fixed fields for "Freq," "Regl," and "Dates" are also correctly coded.

OCLC #33073503

Type a	ELvl	Srce d	GPub	Ctrl	Lang eng
BLvl s	Form	Conf 0	Freq	MRec	Ctry ilu
S/L 0	Orig	EntW	Regl	Alph a	
Desc a	SrTp p	Cont	DtSt c	Dates ,	

022		1092-6879 ǂy 0725-5380	
037		ǂb Illinois Farm Bureau Partners, P.O. Box 2901, Bloomington, Ill. 61701	
043		n-us-il	
210	0	Ill. Farm Bur. partn.	
222		0	Illinois Farm Bureau partners
245	0	0	Illinois Farm Bureau partners.
246	3	0	Partners
260		Bloomington, Ill. : ǂb Illinois Agricultural Association, ǂc 1995-	
300		v. : ǂb ill. ; ǂc 36 cm.	
310			
362			
500		Title from caption.	
500		Latest issue consulted: Vol. 1, no 1 (winter 2008/2009).	
650		0	Agriculture ǂz Illinois ǂv Periodicals.
650		0	Farm life ǂz Illinois ǂv Periodicals.
650		0	Farmers ǂz Illinois ǂv Periodicals.
710	2	Illinois Farm Bureau.	
780	0	0	ǂt Illinois Farm Bureau almanac ǂx 0744-4648 ǂw (OCoLC)18709610

Notes

CHAPTER 6

Serials Published in Different Formats

This chapter will discuss what an electronic serial is and how it relates to other formats as well as fields that are needed for electronic resources, specifically as applied to serials. It must first be determined what resource is being cataloged and how it is issued (see LCRI 1.0). For our purposes

(as with CONSER), the focus will be on electronic resources that are made available as discrete issues that continue to be available over time. This would therefore exclude integrating resources, such as integrating websites. One title that can help us to see the distinction is *Booklist Online. Booklist* is published in print and online formats. The online format is the equivalent of the print version and is available from multiple providers. *Booklist* is also available as *Booklist Online*, which is a website that provides free content and a database that requires a subscription. Although the website contains additional content as well as previously published reviews, it does not retain an archive of discrete volumes that correspond to either the print or aggregated online volumes.

Once it has been decided what is being cataloged, we also need to determine the relationship when there is a print counterpart. Online serials can be either "born digital" or online versions of print issues and can be issued simultaneously with print, after print, or more increasingly before print (with "preprints" of forthcoming articles sometimes available). There is not always a one-to-one correlation between the formats. For example, the online version of *Academic Library Trends and Statistics* incorporates the content of three print titles: *Academic Library Trends and Statistics for Carnegie Classification. Associate of Arts Colleges; Academic Library Trends and Statistics for Carnegie Classification. Master's Colleges and Universities, Baccalaureate Colleges;* and *Academic Library Trends and Statistics for Carnegie Classification. Doctoral-Granting Institutions.* It is also necessary to consider changes in format, title, or both, as these often require updates to the bibliographic records and may even be justification for the creation of a new record.

According to the rules in AACR2 0.24, which give instructions for cataloging multiple aspects of a resource, electronic journals are cataloged according to AACR2 Chapters 9 and 12. RDA should also be consulted when cataloging electronic journals. Instructions added in RDA address the long-standing issue of distinguishing between content and carrier by providing a separate and more specific description of each. This will help online catalogs take full advantage of the more specific description and additional indexing capabilities, which will greatly facilitate search and identification of the needed content and format. The replacement of the general material designation (GMD) (MARC field 245 subfield ǂh) with fields for specifying content, media, and carrier types

175

(MARC fields 336, 337 and 338) fulfill this function. These content designators are found in RDA as follows:

MARC field 336 Content type (RDA 6.9)
MARC field 337 Media type (RDA 3.2)
MARC field 338 Carrier type (RDA 3.3)

Electronic serials can be cataloged according to the "single record approach," in which one bibliographic record is used to represent the print and online versions of a serial, or the "separate record approach," in which each format is represented by its own record. The single record approach is also called the "non-cataloging approach" because a separate catalog record for the online version is not created. In this approach, the primary description, including the fixed field "Form," is for the print version, but additional fields are added to represent the online version. These fields include a 530 field to note the existence of the online version as well as an 856 field that gives the location of the online resource. If the title of the online version is different from the title of the print version, the online title is given in a 740 field. Optionally, a 007 physical description fixed field can be added to record the electronic aspects of the serial. Also, a 776 linking field can be added to record the ISSN for the electronic version if a separate one has been assigned.

As the name implies, a separate record is created for each format when the separate record approach is used. As described earlier, the record for the print version again includes a 530 "Additional format available" note and an 856 field that gives details about the online version's location. If the title of the online version is different, it is placed in a 730 field. The 776 field would be used to link to the record for the online version. The description in the record for the online version would include all fields, including the fixed field "Form" ("form of item"), to describe the electronic version of the serial. Because CONSER treats an online version as published simultaneously with the print version, the fixed field "Orig" ("form of original") would also be coded to describe the online. The 856 field would give information on which part of the resource is being described (subfield ǂ3, "material specified"), the address for the location of the resource, and notes (in subfield ǂz), such as restrictions on access. The 856 first indicator is usually coded 4 (for HTTP), and the second indicator would be coded 0 since the description is of the resource itself. This contrasts with the coding in the print record, where the second indicator is 1 to show that the description is for a version of the resource, even when cataloged according to the single record approach. Other fields used in cataloging electronic journals are shown in the first example of this chapter.

The separate record approach used by CONSER also incorporates the concept of **provider-neutral records**, originally called aggregator-neutral records. The bibliographic record for a serial cataloged with this treatment would contain no provider-specific information, with the following exceptions: The version of the resource used for the basis of description would be specified in the source of title note and a separate 856 linking field would be given for each provider. CONSER module 31 gives guidance on choosing which provider to select as the basis for description, including a list of preferred sources. Things to consider include whether full text is provided, whether the first issue is available from a provider, and whether title changes are represented.

The description of a serial, according to AACR2 12.0B1, is based on the first issue or part or, lacking this, on the earliest available issue or part. Formally presented bibliographic information is also considered, with preference given to the source with the most complete information when the completeness of sources varies. Because cataloging of electronic resources focuses more on content than carrier, the chief source of information is the resource itself. This is the prescribed source for the title, edition, numbering, and publication information. The prescribed source for all other areas is even more general, as information can come from "any source." If the first issue is not available at the time of cataloging but later becomes available, the description can be changed to reflect the data in that issue.

RESOURCES CONSULTED

AACR2

Chapters 9 Electronic Resources

Chapter 12 Continuing Resources

RDA

6.9 Content type

3.2 Media type

3.3 Carrier type

CCM

Module 31 Remote access electronic serials (Online serials)

CONSER

Editing Guide 76X-78X Linking Entries *ISBD(ER)*

International Standard Bibliographic Description for Electronic Resources (München : K.G. Saur, 1997): http://archive.ifla.org/VII/s13/pubs/isbd.htm

Library of Congress. *Draft Interim Guidelines for Cataloging Electronic Resources:* http://lcweb.loc.gov/catdir/cpso/dcmb19_4.html

Library of Congress. *Use of Fixed Fields 006/007/008 and Leader Codes in CONSER Records:* http://www.loc.gov/acq/conser/ffuse.html

MARC 21

MARC 21 Format for Bibliographic Data: http://www.loc.gov/marc/bibliographic

OCLC

Bibliographic Formats and Standards: http://www.oclc.org/bibformats

Online Audiovisual Catalogers

Source of Title Notes for Internet Resources: http://www.olacinc.org/drupal/?q=node/20

Jay Weitz. *Cataloging Electronic Resources: OCLC-MARC Coding Guidelines:* http://www.oclc.org/support/documentation/worldcat/cataloging/electronicresources

MARC Fields Needed for Online Serials

Title: Adaptive harvest management

Cover

PDF Cover

Adaptive Harvest Management is a journal that has been published since 1996. The following record shows data elements unique to electronic resources:

Form: "Form of item" is coded "o" for online. This code was added in Fall 2009 in preparation for RDA, along with "q" for direct electronic. Many records have been converted, but it is still possible to find records coded with the more general "s" for electronic. Because electronic serials are generally considered by CONSER to be published simultaneously with the print, "Orig" ("Form of original item") is also coded as an online resource but usually with the less specific "s."

006 Additional material characteristics: to record the electronic aspects of the resource. The "Type of material" is coded "m" for computer file, the "Type of file" is coded "d" for document, and for this record, "GPub" is coded "f" for "federal/national publication." Thus the entire field is: m d f.

007 Physical description fixed field: "category of material" is coded "c" for electronic resource; the "specific material designation" is "r" for remote; subfield ‡e ("dimensions") is coded "n" as it is "not applicable" for remote electronic resources. Other subfields, such as "color" and "sound," are coded as appropriate for the resource.

022: ISSN for the online version. An ISSN for the print version would be added to the subfield ‡y if coded.

130: Uniform title qualified with "Online" to differentiate from other formats of the journal. Under CSR guidelines, this is no longer required.

245 subfield ‡h: general material designation "[electronic resource]." In RDA, this subfield is replaced by fields 336, 337, and 338:

336 Content Type: the form of communication through which a work is expressed *[RDA 6.9]*.
337 Media Type: the general type of intermediation device required to view, play, run, etc., the content of a resource) *[RDA 3.2]*.
338 Carrier Type: the format of the storage medium and housing of a carrier in combination with the media type *[RDA 3.3]*.

500 Source of title note: (See chapter 9 for more information.)

530 Additional physical form available note: Add this for print and other formats.

538 System details: Include "Mode of access" (per AACR2 9.7B1c) but not "System requirements" unless unusual and applicable to all versions.

580 Linking complexity note: The 776 (subfield ‡i) is now the preferred field for recording information about linking complexity when it can adequately describe the linking relationship.

588 Source of description note: Use this for describing the source of description and the latest issue consulted.

776 Additional physical form entry: This is a linking field that describes other available formats, including print.

856 Electronic location and access: The first indicator is usually 4 (HTTP). The second indicator is 0 in the online record and 1 in the print record.

The following fields are omitted or in limited use in CONSER: 300 (Physical description); 256 (Computer File Characteristics); 506 (Restrictions on access; used only when it applies to all versions); 516 (Type of Computer File or Data; included only when the file type is unusual).

OCLC #57379502

Type a	ELvl	Srce c	GPub f	Ctrl	Lang eng
BLvl s	Form o	Conf 0	Freq a	MRec	Ctry mdu
S/L 0	Orig s	EntW	Regl r	Alph a	
Desc a	SrTp	Cont	DtSt c	Dates 1996	, 9999

006		m d f	
007		c ‡b r ‡d m ‡e n	
010		2009231074	
022	0	2152-3177 ‡2 1	
042		pcc ‡a nsdp	
043		n-us—	
130	0	Adaptive harvest management (Online)	
245	1	0	Adaptive harvest management ‡h [electronic resource] / ‡c Department of the Interior, U.S. Fish and Wildlife Service.
260		[Laurel, Md.] : ‡b U.S. Fish and Wildlife Service	
310		Annual	
362	1	Print began with 1996.	
500		Subtitle varies.	
588		Description based on: 1996; title from PDF caption (viewed Oct. 22, 2009).	
588		Latest issue consulted: 2009.	
538		Mode of access: World Wide Web.	
580		Issued in online format only, 2004-	
650		0	Waterfowl management ‡z United States ‡v Periodicals.
650		0	Waterfowl shooting ‡z United States ‡v Periodicals.
710	2	U.S. Fish and Wildlife Service.	
776	0	8	‡i Print version: ‡t Adaptive harvest management ‡w (DLC) 96646924 ‡w (OCoLC)35630108
780	0	0	‡t Adaptive harvest management ‡w (DLC) 96646924 ‡w (OCoLC) 35630108
856	4	0	‡ http://www.fws.gov/migratorybirds/CurrentBirdIssues/Management/ AHM/AHM-intro.htm ‡z Select report year under "AHM Working Group - Meeting Reports"

Single vs. Separate Record Approach for Print and Online Versions Published Simultaneously

Screenshot – Table of Contents

Title: Journal of pidgin and creole languages

Serials published in print and online formats can be cataloged following either the "single record approach" or "separate record approach." The single record approach is also called the "non-cataloging approach" because a new record is not created for the online version. Rather, one record represents both versions. The basic description is for the print, but additional fields are added to represent the online. The first record shown for this title illustrates this approach.

Specific fields added to the print record are the 530 note field (other physical medium), the 776 field (additional physical format entry), at least one 856 field (electronic location and access), and, optionally, a fixed field 007 to represent the online aspects of the journal. The separate record approach is prescribed by CONSER. In this approach, the first record shown would be edited as necessary (in this case, by removing the 007 field), and a separate record created to represent the online version. The 856 field in the online record would have the second indicator coded as 0 (for "resource") rather than a second indicator 1 (for a version of the resource) because the record represents the actual resource in its entirety. The single record approach is used primarily when the online version has less content than the print or when the content is equivalent. When there is more online content or it is significantly different, the separate record approach is preferable.

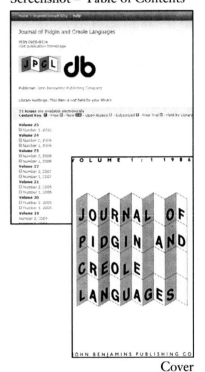

Cover

OCLC #14765516 (Single record approach)

Type a	ELvl	Srce c	GPub	Ctrl	Lang eng
BLvl s	Form	Conf 0	Freq f	MRec	Ctry ne
S/L 0	Orig	EntW	Regl x	Alph a	
Desc a	SrTp p	Cont o	DtSt c	Dates 1986	, 9999

CCM 31.2.4	007	c ‡b r ‡d u ‡e n ‡f u
	010	88659212 ‡z sn 87040088
	022	0920-9034 ‡1 0920-9034
	042	pcc
	245 0 0	Journal of pidgin and creole languages.
	246 1 3	JPCL ‡f <1998->
	260	[Amsterdam] ; ‡a Philadelphia/Pa. : ‡b John Benjamins, ‡c 1986-
	265	John Benjamins Pub. Co., One Buttonwood Square, Philadelphia, PA 19130
	300	v. : ‡b ill. ; ‡c 22 cm.
	310	Two no. a year
	362 0	Vol. 1 : 1-
31.14.7	530	Also issued online; available to subscribers via the World Wide Web.
	650 0	Creole dialects ‡v Periodicals.
	650 0	Pidgin languages ‡v Periodicals.
31.15.2	856 4 1	‡u http://openurl.ingenta.com/content?genre=journal&issn=0920-9034

AACR2 12.7B16

AACR2

12.7B16 - Give the details of other formats in which the content or partial content of the resource is, or has been, issued

RDA

27.1.1.3 - Reference a related manifestation applying the general guidelines on referencing related works, expressions, manifestations, and items given under 24.4 (Recording Relationships between Works, Expressions, Manifestations, and Items)

CCM

31.2.3 - Access to online versions: CONSER single record option vs. separate records

31.2.4 - MARC 21 format and fixed field coding

31.14.7 - Other physical medium

31.15.2 - Uses of field 856 in CONSER records

31.16 - Linking relationships

OCLC #47093342 (Separate record approach)

Type a	ELvl I	Srce d	GPub	Ctrl	Lang eng
BLvl s	Form o	Conf 0	Freq f	MRec	Ctry ne
S/L 0	Orig s	EntW	Regl x	Alph a	
Desc a	SrTp p	Cont	DtSt c	Dates 1986	, 9999

	006		m d
	007		c ǂb r ǂd c ǂe n ǂf u
	022		ǂy 0920-9034
	130	0	Journal of Pidgin and Creole languages (Online)
	245	1 0	Journal of pidgin and creole languages ǂh [electronic resource].
	246	1 3	JPCL ǂf <1998->
	260		[Amsterdam] ; ǂa Philadelphia/Pa. : ǂb John Benjamins
	310		Two no. a year
	362	1	Print began with vol. 1:1, published in 1986.
	500		Title from cover.
	588		Description based on: Vol. 25, no. 1 (July 2000); title from journal information screen (viewed June 6, 2001).
CCM 31.14.7	530		Also available in print. — AACR2 12.7B16
	538		Mode of access: World Wide Web.
	550		Internet access provided through Ingenta (Firm).
	650	0	Creole dialects ǂv Periodicals.
	650	0	Pidgin languages ǂv Periodicals.
31.16	776	1	ǂt Journal of pidgin and creole languages ǂx 0920-9034 ǂw (DLC) 88659212 ǂw (OCoLC)14765516
31.15.2	856	4 0	ǂu http://openurl.ingenta.com/content?genre=journal&issn=0920-9034

Provider-Neutral Records for Print and Online Formats Published Simultaneously

Title: Linguistics and philosophy

Cover

Screenshot - Table of Contents

Screenshot - Table of Contents

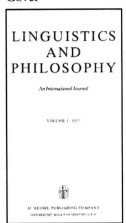

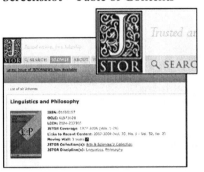

Linguistics and Philosophy is another serial published in print and online formats. Separate records have been created for each format. A 776 field has been added to each record representing the other available format. For example, the linking field in the print record includes the title and standard numbers associated with the online version and the linking field in the online record describes the print. Additionally, the 530 field noting the additional physical format has been replaced in these records by a note in the subfield ‡i of the 776 field (with a second indicator 8, "display note"), which is given as an option in CCM.

The online version has been cataloged with an "provider-neutral record" (CONSER prescribed). A provider-neutral record describes all available online versions. The only provider-specific information given is identification of the provider used as the basis for description as well as a separate 856 field for each provider.

OCLC #3127141 (Print version)

Type a	ELvl	Srce c	GPub	Ctrl	Lang eng
BLvl s	Form	Conf 0	Freq b	MRec	Ctry ne
S/L 0	Orig	EntW	Regl r	Alph a	
Desc	SrTp p	Cont bo	DtSt c	Dates 1977	, 9999

010		77641536
022	0	0165-0157 ‡l 0165-0157 ‡2 z
042		pcc ‡a nsdp
245	0 0	Linguistics and philosophy.
246	1 3	L & P ‡f <Feb. 1990->
260		Dordrecht, ‡b Kluwer Academic Publishers [etc.]
300		v. ‡c 24 cm.
310		Bimonthly, ‡b <Feb. 1990->
362	0	v. 1- Jan. 1977-
650	0	Linguistics ‡v Periodicals.
650	0	Language and languages ‡x Philosophy ‡v Periodicals.

CCM 31.14.7	776	0	8	‡i Also issued online: ‡t Linguistics and philosophy (Online) ‡w (DLC) 2004233305 ‡w (OCoLC)41973628	AACR2 12.7B16
31.15	856	4	1	‡u http://www.springerlink.com/openurl.asp?genre=journal&issn=0165-0157	
	856	4	1	‡u http://www.jstor.org/journals/01650157.html	
	856	4	1	‡u http://firstsearch.oclc.org/journal=0165-0157;screen=info;ECOIP ‡z Address for accessing the journal from an authorized IP address through OCLC FirstSearch Electronic Collections Online. Subscription to online journal required for access to abstracts and full text	

AACR2

9.7B3 - Always give the source of the title proper

9.7B22 - Item described. For remote access resources, always give the date on which the resource was viewed for description

12.7B16 - Give the details of other formats in which the content or partial content of the resource is, or has been issued

12.7B23 - Item described: If the description is not based on the first issue or part or on the first iteration, make a note

RDA

2.20.2.3 - Make a note on the source from which the title proper is taken if it is a source other than that specified in 2.2.2.2 - 2.2.2.3 (for example, other than title page)

2.20.13.5 - For online resources, make a note identifying the date on which the resource was viewed for description

27.1.1.3 - Reference a related manifestation applying the general guidelines on referencing related works, expressions, manifestations, and items given under 24.4 (Recording Relationships between Works, Expressions, Manifestations, and Items)

CCM

31.2.3B - Separate record approach–Provider-neutral option

31.3.4 - Citing the source of the title proper

31.9 - Latest issue consulted note

31.14.7 - Other physical medium: Make notes describing the existence of other medium (e.g., print) in which the serial is issued

31.15 - Electronic location and access

(Continued on next page)

OCLC #41973628 (Online version)

Type a	ELvl	Srce c	GPub	Ctrl	Lang eng
BLvl s	Form s	Conf 0	Freq b	MRec	Ctry ne
S/L 0	Orig s	EntW	Regl r	Alph	
Desc a	SrTp p	Cont o	DtSt c	Dates 1977	, 9999

	006		m d		
	007		c ǂb r ǂd m ǂe n ǂf u		
	010		2004233305		
	022	0	1573-0549 ǂl 0165-0157 ǂy 0165-0157 ǂ2 j		
	042		pcc		
	130	0	Linguistics and philosophy (Online)		
	245	1 0	Linguistics and philosophy ǂh [electronic resource].		
	260		Dordrecht, Holland ; ǂa Boston : ǂb D. Reidel Publishing Co., ǂc 1977-		
	310		Bimonthly, ǂb 1989-		
	362	0	Vol. 1, no. 1 (Jan. 1977)-		
CCM 31.3.4	500		Title from cover (JSTOR, viewed Jan. 22, 2009).		AACR2 9.7B3 9.7B22
	500		Published: Dordrecht, The Netherlands; Norwell, MA : Kluwer Academic Publishers, May 1988-2004; Dordrecht, The Netherlands; Hingham, MA : Springer, 2005-		
31.9	588		Latest issue consulted: Vol. 28, issue 6 (Dec. 2005) (JSTOR, viewed Jan. 22, 2009).		12.7B23
	538		Mode of access: World Wide Web.		
	650	0	Linguistics ǂv Periodicals.		
	650	0	Language and languages ǂx Philosophy ǂv Periodicals.		
	776	0 8	ǂi Also issued in print: ǂt Linguistics and philosophy ǂx 0165-0157 ǂw (DLC) 77641536 ǂw (OCoLC)3127141		
	780	0 1	ǂt Foundations of language ǂw (DLC) 2009235068 ǂw (OCoLC) 297262767		
31.15	856	4 0	ǂu http://www.jstor.org/journals/01650157.html		
	856	4 0	ǂu http://www.springerlink.com/openurl.asp? genre=journal&issn=0165-0157		
	856	4 0	ǂu http://firstsearch.oclc.org/journal=0165-0157;screen=info;ECOIP ǂz Address for accessing the journal from an authorized IP address through OCLC FirstSearch Electronic Collections Online		

Multiple Linking Fields for Different Formats and Title Changes

Titles: Journal of English & Germanic Philology; JEPG

Cover

Cover

In 2006, CONSER practice changed to allow multiple linking fields. Prior practice was to record only the primary relationship in a linking field and to describe other relationships in a 580 note. In current practice, linking fields are used to show other formats available as well as preceding or succeeding titles (horizontal and chronological relationships).

In 2007, CCM included this change, along with instructions to minimize use of the 580 field in order to more closely align the practice with Functional Requirements for Bibliographic Records (FRBR) principles. The 776 subfield ‡i should be used to replace the 580 field, except when the linking relationships are too complex to be described otherwise.

OCLC #1754568 (Print version: 1903–1958)					
	022	0	0363-6941 ‡l 0363-6941 ‡2 1		
	042		nsdp ‡a pcc		
	245	0	4	The Journal of English and Germanic philology.	
	260		Urbana, Ill. [etc.] ‡b University of Illinois [etc.]		
	362	0	v. 5-57; 1903-58.		
	650		0	English philology ‡v Periodicals.	
	650		0	Germanic philology ‡v Periodicals.	
	710	2	University of Illinois (Urbana-Champaign campus)		
CCM 31.14.7	776	0	8	‡i Also issued online: ‡t Journal of English and Germanic philology (Online) ‡x 1945-662X ‡w (DLC) 2008247631 ‡w (OCoLC) 60625079	AACR2 12.7B16
31.16	785	0	0	‡t JEGP, Journal of English and Germanic philology ‡x 0363-6941 ‡w (DLC)sc 78000997 ‡w (OCoLC)2192801	

(Continued on next page)

OCLC #60625079 (Online version: 1903–1958)

	006		m d
	007		c ‡b r ‡d u ‡e n
	010		2008247631
	022	0	1945-662X ‡l 0363-6941 ‡y 0363-6941 ‡2 1
	042		pcc ‡a nsdp
	130	0	Journal of English and Germanic philology (Online)
	245	1 4	The journal of English and Germanic philology ‡h [electronic resource].
	246	1 3	JEGP
	260		Bloomington, Ind. : ‡b Journal Publishing Company, ‡c 1903-
	362	0	Vol. 5, no. 1 (Sept. 1903)-v. 57 (1958).
	500		Title from title page (JSTOR, viewed Feb. 24, 2010).
	588		Latest issue consulted: Vol. 109, no. 1 (Jan. 2010) (Project Muse, viewed Feb. 3, 2010).
	650	0	English philology ‡v Periodicals.
31.14.7	776	0 8	‡i Print version: ‡t Journal of English and Germanic philology ‡g 1903-1958 ‡x 0363-6941 ‡w (DLC)sc 78000473 ‡w (OCoLC) 1754568	AACR2 12.7B16
31.16	785	0 0	‡t Journal of English and Germanic philology (Online) ‡x 1945-662X ‡w (DLC) 2008247631 ‡w (OCoLC)427666046	
	856	4 0	‡u http://www.press.uillinois.edu/journals/jegp.html
	856	4 0	‡u http://muse.jhu.edu/journals/egp
	856	4 0	‡u http://www.jstor.org/journals/03636941.html

AACR2

12.7B16 - Give the details of other formats in which the content or partial content of the resource is, or has been issued

RDA

27.1.1.3 - Reference a related manifestation applying the general guidelines on referencing related works, expressions, manifestations, and items given under 24.4 (Recording Relationships between Works, Expressions, Manifestations, and Items)

CCM

31.14.7 - Other physical medium: Make notes describing the existence of other medium (e.g., print) in which the serial is issued

31.16.1 - Multiple linking relationships allowed

OCLC #2192801 (Print version: 1959–)

	022	0		0363-6941 ‡l 0363-6941 ‡2 1
	042			nsdp ‡a pcc
	245	0	0	JEGP, Journal of English and Germanic philology.
	246	3	0	Journal of English and Germanic philology
	260			Urbana, ‡b University of Illinois Press.
	362	0		v. 58- Jan. 1959-
	650		0	English philology ‡v Periodicals.
	650		0	Germanic philology ‡v Periodicals.
CCM 31.14.7	776	0	8	‡i Also issued online: ‡t Journal of English and Germanic philology (Online) ‡x 1945-662X ‡w (DLC) 2008247631 ‡w (OCoLC) 427666046
31.16	780	0	0	‡t Journal of English and Germanic philology ‡x 0363-6941 ‡w (DLC)sc 78000473 ‡w (OCoLC)1754568
	856	4	1	‡u http://www.jstor.org/journals/03636941.html

The 776 and 780 fields box is labeled **AACR2 12.7B16** on the right.

OCLC #427666046 (Online version: 1959–)

	006			m d
	007			c ‡b r ‡d c ‡e n ‡f u
	022	0		1945-662X ‡y 0363-6941 ‡2 1
	130	0		JEGP, Journal of English and Germanic philology (Online)
	245	1	0	JEGP, Journal of English and Germanic philology ‡h [electronic resource].
	246	3	0	Journal of English and Germanic philology
	260			Urbana, ‡b University of Illinois Press.
	362	0		v. 58- Jan. 1959-
	538			Mode of access: World Wide Web.
	650		0	English philology ‡v Periodicals.
	650		0	Germanic philology ‡v Periodicals.
CCM 31.16	776	1		‡t Journal of English and Germanic philology ‡x 0363-6941 ‡w (OCoLC)2192801
31.14.7	780	0	0	‡t Journal of English and Germanic philology (Online) ‡x 1945-662X ‡w (DLC) 2008247631 ‡w (OCoLC)60625079
	856	4	0	‡u http://www.jstor.org/journals/03636941.html

The 776 and 780 fields box is labeled **AACR2 12.7B16** on the right.

Basis of Description for Different Manifestations of an Online Journal

Titles: Potato news bulletin et al.

PDF Caption

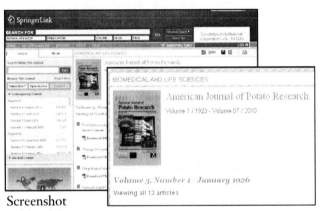

Screenshot
Table of Contents

The preferred basis of description for a provider-neutral record is the publisher's site if it provides full text. However, a host or archiving site is preferred if it contains full text and the publisher's site does not. A site that includes title changes is next in the order of preference, followed by the record for the print version. Finally, the description can be based on aggregations and databases, which are article based and do not maintain issue integrity.

In this example, the basis of description for this title is the publisher's website. However, it should be noted that the publisher includes all earlier titles under current title on its website. Therefore when citing the source of an earlier title, the serial cataloger has used the PDF running title rather than the current title from the publisher's site. This is because, according to CCM 31.3.2, "Where changes in a print title are not displayed prominently, a less prominent source may be selected as the source of title." On their websites, publishers of online journals frequently list older issues under the current title even though they were published in print under a previous title. The user should be made aware of this practice in order to search more effectively.

OCLC #302402183

Type a	ELvl M	Srce	GPub	Ctrl	Lang eng
BLvl s	Form s	Conf 0	Freq b	MRec	Ctry meu
S/L 0	Orig	EntW	Regl r	Alph a	
Desc a	SrTp p	Cont	DtSt d	Dates 1926	, 1997

	006		m d	
	007		c ‡b r ‡e n ‡f u	
	022		‡l 1874-9380	
	130	0	American potato journal (Online)	
	245	1	0	American potato journal ‡h [electronic resource].

CCM 31.7	246	1	‡i Some providers include under later title: ‡a American journal of potato research	AACR2 21.30J2

	260		Takoma Park, D.C. : ‡b Potato Association of America, ‡c 1926-[1997]	
	362	0	Vol. 3, no. 1 (Jan. 1926)-v. 74, no. 6 (Nov./Dec. 1997).	

31.3.2	588	Description based on: v.74, no.1 (Jan. 1997); title from PDF running title (SpringerLink, Jan. 7, 2010).	9.0B1 9.7B3
	588	Final issue consulted (SpringerLink, Jan. 7, 2010).	

	710	2	Potato Association of America.
	776	0	8	‡i Print version: ‡t American potato journal ‡x 0003-0589 ‡w (DLC) sn 91016058‡w (OCoLC)23195488
	780	0	0	‡t Potato news bulletin (Online) ‡w (OCoLC)271826222
	785	0	0	‡t American journal of potato research ‡x 1874-9380 ‡w (OCoLC)60626757
	856	4	0	‡u http://www.springerlink.com/content/120949/

AACR2

9.0B1 - The chief source of information for an electronic resource is the resource itself

9.7B3 - Always give the source of the title proper

21.30J2 - If considered necessary for access, make an added entry for any version of the title that is significantly different from the title proper

RDA

2.2.4 - If the resource does not contain a source of information falling into other categories specified in 2.2.2.2 -2.2.2.4, use as the preferred source of information another source forming part of the resource itself, giving preference to sources in which the information is formally presented

2.20.2.3 - Make a note on the source from which the title proper is taken if it is a source other than that specified in 2.2.2.2 - 2.2.2.3 (for example, other than title page)

24.4 - Record the relationship between a work, expression, manifestation, or item and a related work, expression, manifestation, or item using one or more of the conventions described under 24.4.1 (identifier), 24.2.2 (authorized access point), or 24.4.3 (description), as applicable

CCM

31.7 - Variant title and title added entries

31.3.2 - Determining the chief source

(Continued on next page)

OCLC #60626757

Type a	ELvl I	Srce d	GPub	Ctrl	Lang eng
BLvl s	Form s	Conf 0	Freq b	MRec	Ctry nyu
S/L 0	Orig s	EntW	Regl r	Alph	
Desc a	SrTp p	Cont	DtSt c	Dates 1998	, 9999

006		m d
007		c ǂb r ǂd u ǂe n
022		1874-9380 ǂl 1099-209X
130	0	American journal of potato research (Online)
245	0 0	American journal of potato research ǂh [electronic resource].
246	3 0	Potato research
260		Orono, Me. : ǂb Potato Association of America
260	3	ǂ3 <2008>- ǂa New York ǂb Springer
362	1	Began with: v. 75, no. 1 (Jan./Feb. 1998).
588		Description based on: v.75, no.1 (1998:Jan.); title from journal home page (SpringerLink, Jan. 7, 2009).
588		Latest issue consulted: v.86, no.6 (2009:Nov.) (SpringerLink, Jan. 7, 2009).
710	2	Potato Association of America.
776	0 8	ǂi Print version ǂt American journal of potato research ǂx 1099-209X ǂw (DLC)sn 98007420 ǂw (OCoLC)38759877
780	0 0	ǂt American potato journal
856	4 0	ǂu http://www.springerlink.com/content/120949/
856	4	ǂu http://gateway.proquest.com/openurl?ctx%5Fver=Z39.88-2003&res%5Fid=xri:ItemLocation:PMID=52780

AACR2
9.7B3
9.7B22

Multiple Linking Relationships for Title Changes and Formats

Title: Potato news bulletin

Title from Caption (1st title)   Title from Caption (2nd title)   Cover (3rd title)

The *Potato News Bulletin* has undergone two title changes, and all volumes are available in print and online. Because of the 2006 change in CONSER policy, multiple linking entry fields have been used to represent all the relationships.

The record for the second title includes links to the preceding and succeeding titles as well as a linking field for the other format.

OCLC #5587245 (Print version: 1923–1925)

245	0	0	Potato news bulletin.
260			East Lansing, Mich. : ‡b The Potato Association of America, ‡c 1923-1925.
362	0		Vol.1 (1923)-v.2 (1925).
776	0	8	‡i Online version: ‡t Potato news bulletin (Online) ‡w (OCoLC) 271826222
785	0	0	‡t American potato journal ‡x 0003-0589 ‡w (DLC)sn 91016058 ‡w (OCoLC)23195488 ‡g 1925-

OCLC #23195488 (Print version: 1926–1997)

Type a	ELvl	Srce	GPub	Ctrl	Lang eng
BLvl s	Form	Conf 0	Freq b	MRec	Ctry meu
S/L 0	Orig	EntW	Regl r	Alph a	
Desc a	SrTp p	Cont	DtSt d	Dates 1926	, 1997

010		sn 91016058
022	0	0003-0589 ‡l 0003-0589 ‡2 1
042		pcc ‡a nsdp
245	0 0	American potato journal.
260		Takoma Park, D.C. : ‡b Potato Association of America, ‡c 1926-[1997]
362	0	Vol. 3, no. 1 (Jan. 1926)-v. 74, no. 6 (Nov./Dec. 1997).
500		Title from caption.

CCM
31.14.7

776	0	8	‡i Online version: ‡t American potato journal (Online) ‡x 0003-0589 ‡w (OCoLC)302402183

31.16

780	0	0	‡t Potato news bulletin ‡w (OCoLC)5587245
785	0	0	‡t American journal of potato research ‡x 1099-209X ‡w (DLC)sn 98007420 ‡w (OCoLC)38759877

AACR2
12.7B8

(Continued on next page)

OCLC #38759877 (Print version: 1998-)

010			sn 98007420
022			1099-209X ‡l 1099-209X ‡y 0003-0589 ‡2 1
245	0	0	American journal of potato research : ‡b an official publication of the Potato Association of America.
260			Orono, Me. : ‡b The Association, ‡c 1998-
362	0		Vol. 75, no. 1 (Jan./Feb. 1998)-
776	0	8	‡i Online version: ‡t American journal of potato research (Online) ‡w (OCoLC)60626757
780	0	0	‡t American potato journal ‡x 0003-0589 ‡w (DLC)sn 91016058 ‡w (OCoLC)23195488

AACR2

12.7B8 - Make notes on the bibliographic history and on important relationships between the resource being described and the immediately preceding, immediately succeeding, or simultaneously issued resources

RDA

27.1.1.3 - Reference a related manifestation applying the general guidelines on referencing related works, expressions, manifestations, and items given under 24.4

CCM

31.14.7 - Make notes describing the existence of other medium in which the serial is issued

31.16.1 - Description of multiple linking relationships allowed

OCLC #271826222 (Online version: 1923–1925)

130	0		Potato news bulletin (Online)
245	1	0	Potato news bulletin ‡h [electronic resource].
260			East Lansing, Mich., : ‡b The Potato Association of America
362	1		Began with: v.1, no. 1 (Nov. 1923); ceased with: v. 2, no. 12 (Dec. 1925).
776	0	8	‡i Print version: ‡t Potato news bulletin ‡w (OCoLC)5587245
785	0	0	‡t American potato journal (Online) ‡w (OCoLC)302402183
856	4	0	‡u http://www.springerlink.com/content/120949

OCLC #302402183 (Online version: 1926–1997)

Type a	ELvl M	Srce	GPub	Ctrl		Lang eng
BLvl s	Form s	Conf 0	Freq b	MRec		Ctry meu
S/L 0	Orig	EntW	Regl r	Alph a		
Desc a	SrTp p	Cont	DtSt d	Dates 1926	, 1997	

006		m d	
007		c ‡b r ‡e n ‡f u	
022		‡l 1874-9380	
130	0	American potato journal (Online)	
245	1	0	American potato journal ‡h [electronic resource].
260		Takoma Park, D.C. : ‡b Potato Association of America, ‡c 1926-[1997]	
362	0	Vol. 3, no. 1 (Jan. 1926)-v. 74, no. 6 (Nov./Dec. 1997).	
588		Description based on: v.74:no.1 (Jan. 1997); title from PDF running title (SpringerLink, Jan. 7, 2010)	

CCM 31.14.7

776	0	8	‡i Print version ‡t American potato journal ‡x 0003-0589 ‡w (DLC) sn 91016058‡w (OCoLC)23195488
780	0	0	‡t Potato news bulletin (Online) ‡w (OCoLC)271826222
785	0	0	‡t American journal of potato research ‡x 1874-9380 ‡w (OCoLC) 60626757

31.16

AACR2 12.7B8

856	4	0	‡u http://www.springerlink.com/content/120949/

OCLC #60626757 (Online version: 1998–)

022			1874-9380 ‡l 1099-209X
130	0		American journal of potato research (Online)
245	1	0	American journal of potato research ‡h [electronic resource].
260			Orono, Me. : ‡b Potato Association of America
260	3		‡3 <2008>- ‡a New York ‡b Springer
362	1		Began with: v. 75, no. 1 (Jan./Feb. 1998).
776	0	8	‡i Print version ‡t American journal of potato research ‡x 1099-209X ‡w (DLC)sn 98007420 ‡w (OCoLC)38759877
780	0	0	‡t American potato journal
856	4	0	‡u http://www.springerlink.com/content/120949/

Journal Available in Print and Online Becomes Online Only

Titles: Un magazine

PDF Cover

Un Magazine was originally issued in print and online formats. After two years, the print ceased and the journal became online only. When the journal was published in both formats, each record had a 776 field linking to the other format. When the print ceased, the dates were closed on the print record. A 785 field was added to the print record and a 780 field added to the online record. Additionally, 580 note fields were added to both records to express the cessation of the print and the continuation of the online.

OCLC #225598063

Type a	ELvl I	Srce d	GPub	Ctrl	Lang eng
BLvl s	Form	Conf 0	Freq f	MRec	Ctry vra
S/L 0	Orig	EntW	Regl r	Alph a	
Desc a	SrTp p	Cont	DtSt d	Dates 2004 , 2005	

022			1449-6747 ǂl 1449-6747
245	0	0	Un magazine.
246	3		Art review magazine
260			North Melbourne, Vic. : ǂb Lily Hibberd, ǂc 2004-2005.
300			v. ; ǂc 30 cm.
310			Quarterly
362	0		Issue 1 (2004)- Issue 6 (2005).

CCM 31.16 | 580 | Ceased in print format 2005. Continued online. | AACR2 12.7B8

| 650 | | 0 | Art criticism ǂz Australia ǂv Periodicals. |

| 776 | 0 | 8 | ǂi Also issued online: ǂt Un magazine ǂx 1449-955X ǂw (DLC) 2009247563 ǂw (OCoLC)310356867 | 21.30G

31.16 | 785 | 1 | 0 | ǂt Un magazine ǂx 1449-955X ǂ w (DLC) 2009247563 ǂw (OCoLC) 310356867

AACR2

12.7B8 - Make notes on the bibliographic history and on important relationships between the resource being described and the immediately preceding, immediately succeeding, or simultaneously issued resources

21.30G - Make an added entry under the heading for a work to which the work being catalogued is closely related (see 21.8-21.28 for guidance in specific cases)

RDA

27.1.1.3 - Reference a related manifestation applying the general guidelines on referencing related works, expressions, manifestations, and items given under 24.4

24.4 - Record the relationship between a work, expression, manifestation, or item and a related work, expression, manifestation, or item using one or more of the conventions described under 24.4.1 (identifier), 24.2.2 (authorized access point), or 24.4.3 (description), as applicable

CCM

31.16.1 - Representation of multiple linking relationships is allowed. "CONSER's earlier policy of describing multiple relationships in a 580 note and only providing one linking entry field for the primary relationship was made optional in 2006." – CCM 2007 draft

OCLC #310356867

Type a	ELvl	Srce c	GPub	Ctrl	Lang eng
BLvl s	Form	Conf 0	Freq f	MRec	Ctry vra
S/L 0	Orig	EntW	Regl r	Alph	
Desc a	SrTp p	Cont	DtSt c	Dates 2004	, 9999

006		m u	
007		c ǂb r	
010		2009247563	
022		1449-955X ǂl 1449-6747 ǂy 1449-6747	
042		pcc	
245	0	0	Un magazine ǂh [electronic resource].
260		North Melbourne, Vic. : ǂb Un Projects Inc.	
310		Quarterly	
362	1		Began with Issue 1 (2004).
588		Description based on Issue 1 (2004); title from contents page (publisher's website, viewed January 28, 2009).	
588		Latest issue consulted: Issue 2.2 (November 2008) (viewed January 28, 2009).	

CCM 31.16 | 580 | Ceased in print format 2005. Continued online.

| 650 | | 0 | Art criticism ǂz Australia ǂv Periodicals. |

| 776 | 0 | 8 | ǂi Also issued in print through 2005: ǂt Un magazine ǂx 1449-6747 ǂw (OCoLC)225598063 |

31.16 | 780 | 1 | 0 | ǂt Un magazine ǂx 1449-6747 ǂw (OCoLC)225598063

| 856 | 4 | 0 | ǂu http://www.unmagazine.org/ |

Journal Available in Three Formats Becomes Online Only

Titles: PC magazine

Cover (Print)

Cover (Website)

August 1, 2000
Volume 19, Number 14

PC Magazine was issued in a print, an online, and a CD-ROM formats, with each format represented by its own record. The three formats are linked to each other by the linking fields 776 to show the horizontal relationship. In 2009, the journal became online only. The record for the print was closed, and linking fields were added to show the chronological relationship, with a "later title" linking field added to the print version record, ; and a "former title" linking field was added to the online version. Notes about the other formats, and the dates they are available, are included in the 776 subfield ǂi.

In addition to the format-specific fields, the formats are also distinguished by the qualifiers in the uniform titles in the records for the online and CD-ROM versions. The numbering for the online version is taken from the first print volume, but the description is based on the earliest available online volume, as described in CCM 31.9. If earlier volumes subsequently become available online, the description can be revised to include them. Also, the information in the 520 field describes features of the online version that confirm that the separate record approach is the best treatment for this title.

OCLC #13566002 (Print version)

Type a	ELvl	Srce	GPub	Ctrl	Lang eng
BLvl s	Form	Conf 0	Freq m	MRec	Ctry nyu
S/L 0	Orig	EntW	Regl r	Alph a	
Desc a	SrTp p	Cont	DtSt d	Dates 1986	, 2009

	010		86644488 ǂz sn 86029673
	022	0	0888-8507 ǂl 0888-8507 ǂy 0745-2500 ǂ2 1
	042		pcc ǂa nsdp
CCM 31.5	130	0	PC magazine (New York, N.Y.)	AACR2 25.5B1
	245	1 0	PC magazine : ǂb the independent guide to IBM-standard personal computing.
	260		[New York, N.Y. : ǂb PC Communications Corp., ǂc 1986-2009].
	310		Monthly, ǂb 2008-2009
	321		Biweekly (except July and Aug.)
	321		Biweekly (except one issue in Jan. and July, 3 issues in Oct.), ǂb <2003->
	321		Semimonthly (with occasional exceptions), ǂb <2005->2007
	362	0	Vol. 5, no. 2 (Jan. 28, 1986)-v. 28, no. 1 (Jan. 2009).
	500		Title from cover.
	500		Published: New York, N.Y. : Ziff Davis Media, Inc., <2008>-2009.
	515		Vols. for <2003-> have an extra issue in Oct., called special fall issue.

	650		0	IBM microcomputers ‡v Periodicals.
	775	0	8	‡i Also issued in Spanish: ‡t PC magazine en español ‡x 1069-9953 ‡w (DLC)sn 93002726 ‡w (OCoLC)28210102
31.14.7	776	0	8	‡i Also issued in CD-ROM format: ‡t PC magazine (New York, N.Y. : CD-ROM) ‡x 1078-8085 ‡w (DLC) 94646727 ‡w (OCoLC) 31201262
	776	0	8	‡i Also issued online; beginning Feb. 2009 published only in online format: ‡t PC magazine ‡w (DLC) 2009252661 ‡w (OCoLC) 34196174
31.16	780	0	0	‡t PC (San Francisco, Calif.) ‡x 0745-2500 ‡w (DLC) 84644391 ‡w (OCoLC)8853934
	785	0	0	‡t PC magazine (New York, N.Y. : Online) ‡w (DLC) 2009252661 ‡w (OCoLC)34196174

AACR2

12.3B1 - Record the numeric and/or alphabetic designation of the first and, if known, last issues of the serial

12.7B23 - Make a note if the description is not based on the first issue or part or on the first iteration. If more than one issue or part has been consulted, make a note of the latest issue or part consulted in making the description

25.5B1 Additions to uniform titles for the purposes of conflict resolution

RDA

2.6.2.3 - If the first issue or part of a sequence of a serial is identified by a numeric and/or alphabetic designation, record the designation applying the basic instructions on recording numbering given under 2.6.1

2.20.13.3.1 - If more than one issue or part has been consulted, make a separate note identifying the latest issue or part consulted in preparing the description

LCRI

25.5B - When creating a bibliographic record for a serial, construct a uniform title made up of the title proper plus a parenthetical qualifier to distinguish the serial from another with the same title proper in a bibliographic record

CCM

31.5 - Create uniform titles according to LCRI 25.5B

31.14.7 - Make notes describing the existence of other medium in which the serial is issued

31.16.1 - Description of multiple linking relationships is allowed

(Continued on next page)

OCLC #34196174 (Online version)

Type a	ELvl	Srce d	GPub	Ctrl	Lang eng
BLvl s	Form s	Conf 0	Freq m	MRec	Ctry nyu
S/L 0	Orig s	EntW	Regl r	Alph a	
Desc a	SrTp p	Cont	DtSt c	Dates 1986	, 9999

	006		m d	
	007		c ǂb r ǂd c ǂe n ǂf u	
	010		2009252661	
	042		lcd	
CCM 31.5	130	0	PC magazine (New York, N.Y. : Online)	AACR2 25.5B1
	245	0 0	PC magazine ǂh [electronic resource].	
	246	1 3	PC magazine online	
	260		[New York, N.Y.] : ǂb Ziff-Davis Pub.	
	310		Monthly, ǂb 2008-	
	321		Biweekly (except July and Aug.), ǂb 1986-	
	362	1	Print began with: Vol. 5, no. 2 (Jan. 28, 1986).	12.3B1
	500		News items are updated daily.	
	588		Description based on: Vol. 19, no. 14 (Aug. 1, 2000); title from table of contents HTML header (publisher's website, viewed Mar. 19, 2009).	12.7B23
	588		Latest issue consulted: Vol. 28, no. 2 (Feb. 1, 2009) (viewed Mar. 19, 2009).	
	520		Contains full text articles related to computers and computing found in the print version of PC magazine, as well as material issued exclusively for the online version.	
	538		Mode of access: World Wide Web.	
	650	0	IBM microcomputers ǂv Periodicals.	
31.14.7	776	0 8	ǂi Prior to Feb. 2009, also issued in print: ǂt PC magazine (New York, N.Y.) ǂx 0888-8507 ǂw (DLC) 86644488 ǂw (OCoLC)13566002	
	776	0 8	ǂi Also issued on CD-ROM: ǂt PC magazine (New York, N.Y. : CD-ROM)ǂx 1078-8085 ǂw (DLC) 94646727 ǂw (OCoLC)31201262	
31.16	780	0 0	ǂt PC magazine (New York, N.Y.) ǂx 0888-8507 ǂw (DLC) 86644488 ǂw (OCoLC)13566002	
	856	4 0	ǂu http://www.pcmag.com/	

OCLC #31201262 (CD-ROM version)

Type a	ELvl	Srce	GPub	Ctrl	Lang eng
BLvl s	Form s	Conf 0	Freq q	MRec	Ctry nyu
S/L 0	Orig	EntW	Regl x	Alph a	
Desc a	SrTp	Cont o	DtSt d	Dates 1993	, 200u

	006		m d	
	007		c ǂb o ǂd u ǂe g ǂf u	
	010		94646727	
	022	0	1078-8085 ǂl 0888-8507 ǂ2 1	
	042		pcc ǂa nsdp	
CCM 31.5	130	0	PC magazine (New York, N.Y. : CD-ROM)	AACR2 25.5B1
	245	0 0	PC magazine CD ǂh [electronic resource].	
	260		New York, NY : ǂb Ziff-Davis Pub. Co.	
	300		CD-ROMs ; ǂc 4 3/4 in.	
	310		Four no. a year	
	362	1	Began in 1993.	
	588		Description based on: Vol. 2, no. 2 (July 1994); title from disc label.	
	515		Issues for <July 1994-> cumulate articles and reviews published in the print version from <June 1993/June 1994->	
	650	0	IBM microcomputers ǂv Databases ǂv Periodicals.	
31.14.7	776	0 8	ǂi Also issued online: ǂt PC magazine ǂw (DLC) 2009252661 ǂw (OCoLC)34196174	
	776	0 8	ǂi CD-ROM version of: ǂt PC magazine (New York, N.Y.) ǂx 0888-8507 ǂw (DLC) 86644488 ǂw (OCoLC)13566002	
	785		ǂt PC magazine (New York, N.Y. : Online) ǂw (DLC) 2009252661 ǂw (OCoLC)34196174	

EXERCISE 1

Wasafiri is issued in print and online. For each record, **provide a linking field** to represent the other format. The title, LCCN, ISSN, and OCLC numbers needed for the linking fields can be found in the record for the other format.

OCLC #67618880

Type a	ELvl	Srce c	GPub	Ctrl	Lang eng
BLvl s	Form s	Conf 0	Freq q	MRec	Ctry enk
S/L 0	Orig s	EntW	Regl r	Alph	
Desc a	SrTp p	Cont	DtSt c	Dates 1984	, 9999

006		m d	
007		c ‡b r ‡d u ‡e n	
010		2010250523	
022		1747-1508 ‡y 0269-0055	
042		pcc	
130	0	Wasafiri (Online)	
245	1	0	Wasafiri ‡h [electronic resource].
260		London : ‡b Instructa	
310		Quarterly, ‡b 2008-	
362	1	Print began with v. 1, no. 1 (autumn 1984).	
500		Description based on print version record.	
538		Mode of access: World Wide Web.	
650		0	African literature (English) ‡x Black authors ‡x History and criticism ‡v Periodicals.
650		0	Caribbean literature (English) ‡x Black authors ‡x History and criticism ‡v Periodicals.
650		0	Oriental literature (English) ‡x History and criticism ‡v Periodicals.
650		0	English literature ‡v Periodicals.
710	2	Association for the Teaching of Caribbean, African, Asian and Associated Literatures.	
776	0	8	
856	4	0	‡u http://journalsonline.tandf.co.uk/openurl.asp?genre=journal&issn=0269-0055

Cover (Print)

Cover (Online)

OCLC #14929302

Type a	ELvl	Srce c	GPub	Ctrl	Lang eng
BLvl s	Form	Conf 0	Freq q	MRec	Ctry enk
S/L 0	Orig	EntW	Regl r	Alph a	
Desc a	SrTp p	Cont	DtSt c	Dates 1984	, 9999

010		sn 86023450	
022		0269-0055 ‡l 0269-0055	
042		pcc	
245	0	0	Wasafiri.
260		London : ‡b Instructa, ‡c 1984-	
300		v. : ‡b ill. ; ‡c 28 cm.	
310		Quarterly, ‡b 2008-	
362	0	Vol. 1, no. 1 (autumn 1984)-	
500		Published by: Routledge, 2006-	
500		Title from cover.	
500		Latest issue consulted: issue 53 (spring 2008).	
515		Volume designation discontinued after spring 1985; some issues published in combined form.	
650		0	African literature (English) ‡x Black authors ‡x History and criticism ‡v Periodicals
650		0	Caribbean literature (English) ‡x Black authors ‡x History and criticism ‡v Periodicals.
650		0	Oriental literature (English) ‡x History and criticism ‡v Periodicals.
650		0	English literature ‡v Periodicals.
710	2	Association for the Teaching of Caribbean, African, Asian and Associated Literatures.
776	0	8	

EXERCISE 2

The *ACM Journal of Data and Information Quality* is issued in print and online. Separate records are created following CSR guidelines. Add 776 linking fields to show the relationships between the two formats. Include subfields for standard numbers and other identifiers (found in the record for the other format).

OCLC #85776277

Type a	ELvl	Srce c	GPub	Ctrl	Lang eng
BLvl s	Form	Conf 0	Freq q	MRec	Ctry nyu
S/L 0	Orig	EntW	Regl r	Alph a	
Desc a	SrTp p	Cont	DtSt c	Dates 2009	, 9999

010			2007214262
022	0		1936-1955 ‡2 1
042			pcc
245	1	0	ACM journal of data and information quality.
246	1	3	JDIQ
260			New York, N.Y. : ‡b Association for Computing Machinery
300			v. : ‡b ill. ; ‡c 26 cm.
310			Quarterly
362	0		Vol. 1, no. 1 (June 2009)-
588			Description based on: Vol. 1, no. 1 (June 2009); title from cover.
588			Latest issue consulted: Vol. 1, no. 2 (2009).
650		0	Database management ‡x Quality control ‡v Periodicals.
650		0	Databases ‡x Quality control ‡v Periodicals.
650		0	Electronic data processing ‡x Quality control ‡v Periodicals.
710	2		Association for Computing Machinery.
776	0	8	

Cover (Print)

Screenshot - Table of Contents

OCLC #85776286

Type a	ELvl	Srce c	GPub	Ctrl	Lang eng
BLvl s	Form s	Conf 0	Freq q	MRec	Ctry nyu
S/L 0	Orig s	EntW	Regl r	Alph	
Desc a	SrTp p	Cont	DtSt c	Dates 2009	, 9999

006		m d	
007		c ‡b r ‡d c ‡e n ‡f u	
010		2007214263	
022	0	1936-1963 ‡y 1936-1955	
042		pcc	
130	0	AMC journal of data and information quality (Online)	
245	0	0	ACM journal of data and information quality ‡h [electronic resource].
246	1	3	JDIQ
260		New York, N.Y. : ‡b Association for Computing Machinery	
310		Quarterly	
362	1	Began with Vol. 1, no. 1 (June 2009).	
538		Mode of access: World Wide Web.	
588		Description based on: Vol. 1, no. 1 (June 2009); title from PDF of cover (viewed July 29, 2009).	
650		0	Database management ‡x Quality control ‡v Periodicals.
650		0	Databases ‡x Quality control ‡v Periodicals.
650		0	Electronic data processing ‡x Quality control ‡v Periodicals.
650		0	Management information systems ‡x Quality control ‡v Periodicals.
710	2	Association for Computing Machinery.	
776	0	8	
856	4	0	‡u http://portal.acm.org/jdiq

EXERCISE 3

Applied Stochastic Models and Data Analysis was issued in print and online. The title changed to *Applied Stochastic Models in Business and Industry* in 1999. After the title changed, it continued to be published in both formats under the new title. Add a 776 field in each of the four records. Also, add a "former title" (780) field to two of the records and a "later title" (785) field to the other two.

OCLC #11241541 (Print version 1985–1999)

007			c ‡b r ‡d u ‡e n ‡f u
010			86643430 ‡z sn 84002275
022	0		8755-0024 ‡l 1099-0747 ‡2 1
042			nsdp ‡a pcc
245	0	0	Applied stochastic models and data analysis.
260			Chichester ; ‡a New York, N.Y. : ‡b John Wiley & Sons, ‡c [c1985]-c1999.
362	0		Vol. 1, no. 1 (July 1985)-v. 15, no. 1 (Mar. 1999).
530			Issued also online.
650		0	Stochastic analysis ‡v Periodicals.
650		0	Probabilities ‡v Periodicals.
776	0		
785	0	0	
856	4	1	Wiley InterScience ‡u http://www3.interscience.wiley.com/cgi-bin/jhome/15783

OCLC #43969746 (Online version 1985–1999)

006			m d
007			c ‡b r ‡d m ‡e n ‡f u
010			2001212357
022	0		1099-0747 ‡l 1099-0747 ‡y 8755-0024 ‡2 1
042			nsdp ‡a pcc
130	0		Applied stochastic models and data analysis (Online)
245	1	0	Applied stochastic models and data analysis ‡h [electronic resource].
260			[Chichester ; ‡a New York, N.Y.] : ‡b John Wiley & Sons, Ltd., ‡c -c1999.
362	1		Print began with: Vol. 1, no. 1 (July 1985).
362	0		-v. 15, issue 1 (Mar. 1999).
650		0	Stochastic analysis ‡v Periodicals.
650		0	Probabilities ‡v Periodicals.
776	0	8	
785	0	0	
856	4	0	Wiley InterScience ‡u http://www3.interscience.wiley.com/cgi-bin/jhome/15783
856	4	0	‡u http://www3.interscience.wiley.com/journal/117943444/tocgroup

Cover (Print)   Screenshot - Table of Contents

   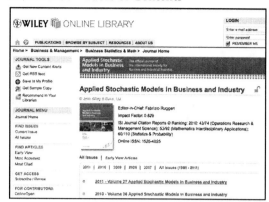

OCLC #40963631 (Print version 1999–)

010			sn 99008399
022	0		1524-1904 ‡l 1524-1904 ‡2 1
042			pcc ‡a nsdp
245	0	0	Applied stochastic models in business and industry.
260			Chichester : ‡b John Wiley & Sons, ‡c c1999-
362	0		Vol. 15, no. 2 (Apr.-June 1999)-
500			Latest issue consulted: Vol. 26, no. 1 (Jan./Feb. 2010).
650		0	Stochastic analysis ‡v Periodicals.
650		0	Business mathematics ‡v Periodicals.
776	0	8	
780	0	0	
856	4	1	Wiley InterScience ‡u http://www3.interscience.wiley.com/cgi-bin/jhome/66002616

OCLC #42212556 (Online version 1999–)

006			m d
007			c ‡b r ‡d c ‡e n ‡f u
010			sn 99009168
022	0		1526-4025 ‡l 1524-1904 ‡y 1524-1904 ‡2 1
042			nsdp ‡a pcc
130	0		Applied stochastic models in business and industry (Online)
245	1	0	Applied stochastic models in business and industry ‡h [electronic resource].
260			[Chichester] : ‡b John Wiley & Sons, Ltd., ‡c c1999-
362	0		Vol. 15 issue 2 (Apr./June 1999)-
650		0	Stochastic analysis ‡v Periodicals.
650		0	Business mathematics ‡v Periodicals.
776	0	8	
780	0	0	
856	4	0	Wiley InterScience ‡u http://www3.interscience.wiley.com/cgi-bin/jhome/66002616

EXERCISE 4

The bimonthly journal *CAA News* was published in print from 1990 to May 2009. Sometime in 2000, it began to also be published online, and with the July 2009 issue, it became online only. The archive of online issues, available at http://www.collegeart.org/news/archives, begins with March 2002. Close out the dates on the print record. Create 776 fields in both records to link to the other format. Include a note in subfield ‡i with information about the relationship to the other format. Also, add 780/785 fields to link earlier or later titles and add a 580 note field if necessary.

OCLC #21009074

Type a	ELvl	Srce c	GPub	Ctrl	Lang eng
BLvl s	Form	Conf 0	Freq b	MRec	Ctry nyu
S/L 0	Orig	EntW	Regl r	Alph a	
Desc a	SrTp p	Cont	DtSt d	Dates 1990	

010			sn 90033514
022	0		1557-511X ‡l 1557-511X ‡y 2100-9074 ‡2 1
042			pcc ‡a nsdp
245	0	0	CAA news : ‡b the newsletter of the College Art Association of America.
246	2		College Art Association news
246	2		College Art Association of America news
260			New York, N.Y. : ‡b College Art Association of America, ‡c 1990-2009.
362	0		Vol. 15, no. 1 (Jan./Feb. 1990)-v. 34, no. 3 (May 2009).
500			Title from caption.
515			Vol. 32, no. 4-v. 33, no. 4 (July 2007-July 2008) not published; issued online only.
580			
650		0	Art ‡x Study and teaching ‡v Periodicals.
650		0	Art in universities and colleges ‡v Periodicals.
610	2	0	College Art Association of America ‡v Periodicals.
710	2		College Art Association of America.
776	0	8	
780	0	0	‡t CAA newsletter ‡w (DLC)sn 83010620 ‡w (OCoLC)2946431
785	1	0	
856	4	1	‡u http://bibpurl.oclc.org/web/31344 ‡u http://www.collegeart.org/news/

Cover (Print)	Cover (Online)	Screenshot – Table of Contents
	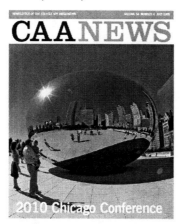	

OCLC #52717321

Type a	ELvl	Srce c	GPub	Ctrl	Lang eng
BLvl s	Form s	Conf 0	Freq b	MRec	Ctry nyu
S/L 0	Orig s	EntW	Regl r	Alph a	
Desc a	SrTp p	Cont	DtSt c	Dates 1990	, 9999

006			m d
007			c ‡b r ‡d m ‡e n ‡f u
010			2007236533
022	0		1942-4892 ‡l 1557-511X ‡2 1
042			pcc ‡a nsdp
130	0		CAA news (Online)
245	1	0	CAA news ‡h [electronic resource] : ‡b the newsletter of the College Art Association of America.
246	1	3	College Art Association of America news
246	3	0	Newsletter of the College Art Association of America
260			New York, N.Y. : ‡b College Art Association of America
362	1		Print began with vol. 15, no. 1 (Jan./Feb. 1990).
500			Description based on: 2000 (Sept.); title from journal information screen (viewed July 23, 2003).
500			Latest issue consulted: Vol. 34, no. 6 (Nov. 2009) (CAA website, viewed Dec. 11, 2009).
538			Mode of access: World Wide Web.
650		0	Art ‡x Study and teaching ‡v Periodicals.
650		0	Art in universities and colleges ‡v Periodicals.
610	2	0	College Art Association of America ‡v Periodicals.
710	2		College Art Association of America.
776	0	8	
780	0	0	
856	4	0	‡u http://www.collegeart.org/news

Notes

CHAPTER 7

Supplements and Special Issues

By nature, serial publications tend to be complex. One of the reasons for this complexity is the presence of relationships between a serial and other resources. The relationship can be chronological or horizontal. Chronological relationships for title changes were discussed earlier in Chapter 2. In Chapter 6, one type of horizontal relationship was discussed: the relationship between serials published in different formats. This chapter will discuss another type of horizontal relationship: that of accompanying relationship, as exemplified by supplements and special issues.

AACR2 defines a supplement as "an item, usually issued separately, that complements one already published by bringing up-to-date or otherwise continuing the original or by containing a special feature not included in the original. The supplement has a formal relationship with the original as expressed by common authorship, a common title or subtitle, and/or a stated intention to continue or supplement the original."

Rather than defining a supplement as an item, RDA uses "supplement" as one of the relationship designators that indicates the specific nature of relationships between works, expressions, manifestations, and items (RDA Appendix J). When used as a relationship designator for related works, "supplement" is defined as a work that updates or otherwise complements the predominant work, and it indicates the accompanying work relationship as supplement to (work) (RDA J.2.5). When used as a relationship designator for related expressions, a "supplement" is defined as an expression of a work that updates or otherwise complements the predominant entity, and it indicates the accompanying expression relationship as supplement to (expression) (RDA J.3.5).

When serial publications have supplements, a cataloger must first decide whether the supplement will be cataloged separately or be described in a note on the record for the parent publication. This decision is based on differences among supplements. Some supplements have distinctive titles, while others have the generic title "supplement." Some carry their own numbering, while others follow designations of the main work. It is important to treat supplements on a case-by-case basis, taking into account the nature of the supplement and its numbering.

If a supplement is of an updating nature (i.e., it updates information contained in the parent publication) and is to be used with the main work, it is not usually cataloged on a separate record. Instead information about the supplement will be added to the bibliographic record for the main work in the MARC field 525, used to record supplement notes.

If a supplement has its own title and numbering, it is usually cataloged on a separate record, and MARC fields 770 and 772 are used to provide links between the supplement and the parent publication. The first indicator in either of these fields determines whether a short predetermined note or "display constant" will be machine-generated to describe the specific relationship. The following examples show MARC fields followed by the display generated:

770 0_ Journal of the Royal Numismatic Society

Has supplement: Journal of the Royal Numismatic Society

772 0_   Philosophical magazine

Supplement to: Philosophical magazine

The first indicator value 0 in the 770 field generates the display constant "Has supplement," while the 0 in the 772 field generates the term "Supplement to." However, if these terms are insufficient to explain the relationship, the first indicator value will be set to 1 to suppress the display of a machine-generated note. In addition, a 580 field (linking entry complexity note) will be used to specify the relationship.

In this chapter, we will use examples to illustrate what serial supplements are and how to record the relationship between the parent publication and the supplement.

RESOURCES CONSULTED

AACR2

12.7B8 Bibliographic History and Relationships With Other Resources
21.28 Related work

LCRI

12.7B8 Bibliographic History and Relationships With Other Resource
21.28 Related work

RDA

24.4 Recording relationships between works, expressions, manifestations, and items

CCM

17.4 Serial supplement
14.3.4 Supplements (Fields 770/772)

Parent Serial With Supplement, With Linking Relationship Represented in 770 and 772 fields

Title: Union membership and earnings data book

Title Page

Union Membership and
Earnings Data Book
Compilations from the Current Population Survey
(2009 Edition)

Barry T. Hirsch
W.J. Usery Chair of the American Workplace
Andrew Young School of Policy Studies
Georgia State University
Atlanta, Georgia 30302
and

David A. Macpherson
Rod and Hope Brim Eminent Scholar
Department of Economics

Additional Earnings and
Union Membership Data
(2009)

Companion to
*Union Membership and Earnings Data Book:
Compilations from the Current Population Survey
(2009 Edition)*

Title Page

Since 1998, the serial *Union Membership and Earning Data* Book has been accompanied by the supplement *Additional Earnings and Union Membership Data*. Both are issued by the corporate body, the Bureau of National Affairs. Because of the regularity of issuance (i.e., as an ongoing supplement to the whole serial) and the uniqueness of content in the supplement, the supplemental serial has been cataloged in a separate record.

When the supplement is cataloged separately, linking fields 770 (Has supplement) and 772 (Supplement to) are used. The 770 field, which is added to the record for the parent serial, contains an entry for the supplement. The 772 field is added to the record for the supplement and contains the entry for the parent serial.

On the record for the parent serial, a 580 linking entry complexity note is created because the display constant generated from the 770 field cannot adequately express the relationship. When a 580 note field is used, the first indicator of the 770 field is set to 1 in order to suppress the display of the machine-generated note "Has supplement." Similarly, on the record for the supplement, a 580 linking note is used to explain the relationship to the parent publication. In the 772 field, the first indicator 1 will suppress the display constant "Supplement to."

Because the supplement has its own distinct title, different from that of the parent serial, an added entry with the title proper of the parent serial has been added to the record for the supplement. However, according to LCRI 21.28B, the cataloger should not generally give an added entry for the supplement on the record for the main work.

OCLC #31807865

Type a	ELvl	Srce d	GPub	Ctrl	Lang eng
BLvl s	Form	Conf 0	Freq a	MRec	Ctry dcu
S/L 0	Orig	EntW s	Regl r	Alph a	
Desc a	SrTp	Cont	DtSt c	Dates 1993	, 9999

022	0		1087-8629 ‡y 1088-7539 ‡2 1
042			lc ‡a nsdp
043			n-us—
245	0	0	Union membership and earnings data book : ‡b compilations from the Current population survey / ‡c the Bureau of National Affairs, Inc.
246	1	7	Union data book
260			Washington, D.C. : ‡b BNA PLUS, ‡c c1994-
300			v. ; ‡c 28 cm.
310			Annual
362	0		-1993
500			Latest issue consulted: 1998 ed.

CCM
17.4.4c
580	Accompanied 1998- by supplement called: Additional earnings and union membership data.	AACR2 12.7B8g

650		0	Labor unions ‡z United States ‡v Statistics ‡v Periodicals.
710	2		Bureau of National Affairs (Arlington, Va.)

14.3.4
17.4.4a
770	1	‡t Additional earnings and union membership data ‡x 1544-4732 ‡w (DLC) 2003212246 ‡w (OCoLC)38961459	12.7B8g

(Continued on next page)

AACR2

12.7B8g - If a resource is a supplement to another resource, give the name of the main resource. If a resource has supplement(s) that are described separately, make notes identifying the supplement(s). Make brief general notes on irregular, informal, numerous, or unimportant supplements that are not described separately

21.28B1 - Enter a related work under its own heading according to the appropriate rule in this chapter. Make an added entry (name-title or title, as appropriate) for the work to which it is related

LCRI

12.7B8 - In notes referring to another resource (i.e., linking notes), cite the entry under which the resource appears in the catalog against which the searching and cataloging is done

21.28B - Give an added entry for the main work on the record for the supplement, except when the title of the main work is the common title for the supplement. Do not generally give an added entry for the supplement on the record for the main work

21.28B1 - When cataloging serial supplements to other serials … make an added entry for the related work in addition to the appropriate reciprocal linking notes (12.7B8). Otherwise, make the reciprocal linking notes instead of an added entry for the related work

RDA

24.4 - Record relationships between works, expressions, manifestations, and items using one or more of the conventions described under 24.4.1 rda (identifier), 24.4.2 rda (authorized access point), or 24.4.3 rda (description)

24.5.1.3 - Record an appropriate term from the list in Appendix J rda to indicate the nature of the relationship more specifically than is indicated by the defined scope of the relationship element itself

CCM

14.3.4 - When a supplement is cataloged separately from its parent serial, link from the supplement to the parent serial, and vice versa. When cataloging the supplement, give an added entry for the parent serial, unless the supplement has a common title that is identical to the title proper of the related serial

17.4.3b2a - When a supplement is ongoing and has its own designation, a separate record is created

17.4.4a - Use linking entry fields 772 (Supplement to) and 770 (Has supplement) when the supplement is cataloged separately

17.4.4b1 - Give an added entry for the main work on the record for the supplement, except when the title of the main work is the common title for the supplement

17.4.4c - A note for a supplement is recorded in field 772 or 580 when the supplement is cataloged separately and in field 525 when the supplement is not cataloged separately

OCLC #38961459

Type a	ELvl	Srce d	GPub	Ctrl		Lang eng
BLvl s	Form	Conf 0	Freq a	MRec		Ctry dcu
S/L 0	Orig	EntW s	Regl r	Alph a		
Desc a	SrTp	Cont	DtSt c	Dates 1998	, 9999	

	022	0		1544-4732 ‡2 1	
	042			nsdp ‡a lcd	
	043			n-us—	
CCM 17.4.3b2a	245	0	0	Additional earnings and union membership data / ‡c Bureau of National Affairs, Inc.	AACR2 21.28B1
	260			Washington, D.C. : ‡b BNA PLUS, ‡c 1998-	
	300			v. : ‡b map ; ‡c 28 cm.	
	362	0		-1998	
	500			Title from cover.	
	500			Latest issued consulted: 2008.	
17.4.4c	580			"Companion to Union membership and earnings data book: compilations from the Current population survey."	12.7B8g
	650		0	Labor unions ‡z United States ‡v Statistics ‡v Periodicals.	
	710	2		Bureau of National Affairs (Arlington, Va.)	
17.4.4b1	730	0		Union membership and earnings data book.	21.28B1
14.3.4 17.4.4a	772	1		‡t Union membership and earnings data book ‡x 1087-8629 ‡w (DLC) 98642207 ‡w (OCoLC)31807865	12.7B8g

Related Title as Supplement in 770 Field, as Issued With Entry in 777 Field, and as Preceding Title in 780 Field

Title: First proof

Cover

Cover

First Proof is *BOMB* magazine's literary supplement, with its own distinctive title and its own numbering. As in the earlier example, the 770 and 772 fields seem to be sufficient to record the relationship between the related works in the bibliographic records for the main work and the supplement. However, the way *First Proof* has been issued makes the relationship to *BOMB* more complex.

This complexity in the issuance of *First Proof* is recorded in the 580 field for a Linking Entry Complexity Note in the record for the supplement. The 580 note indicates that there are three types of relationships between *BOMB* and *First Proof*; therefore, three linking fields are needed.

In addition to the "main work–supplement" relationship mentioned earlier, there are two additional relationships: the "main work–issued with" relationship and the "main work–separated from" relationship. From Fall 1995 to Winter 2007, *First Proof* was inserted into the main work *BOMB*—at first separately paginated and then later interpaged. This horizontal relationship has been recorded in the 777 field, used for "Issued with entry." From Spring 2008 to Winter 2008/2009, *First Proof* was published as a separate publication. The relationship has been recorded in the 780 field, with the second indicator value 7 (meaning "separated from"), to show the chronological relationship between *First Proof* and the immediately preceding title: *BOMB*.

The linking fields required by the complexity of the issuance are the fields 770/772, 777, and 780. Because a 580 note is needed, the first indicators in all the linking fields have been set to 1 in order to suppress the display of the notes generated automatically from the linking fields.

OCLC #10226319

Type a	ELvl	Srce c	GPub	Ctrl	Lang eng
BLvl s	Form	Conf 0	Freq q	MRec	Ctry nyu
S/L 0	Orig	EntW	Regl r	Alph a	
Desc a	SrTp p	Cont a	DtSt c	Dates 1981	, 9999

130	0		Bomb (New York, N.Y.)
245	0	0	Bomb.
260			New York : ‡b X Motion Picture and Center for New Art Activities, ‡c 1981-
300			v. : ‡b ill. (some col.) ; ‡c 28-38 cm.
310			Quarterly, ‡b <winter 1994/95->
321			Three issues a year, ‡b spring 1981-<spring 1986>
362	0		Vol. 1, issue 1 (spring 1981)-

CCM 14.3.4 17.4.4a

770	0	‡t Firstproof ‡x 2152-2502 ‡w (DLC) 2009254103 ‡w (OCoLC) 36654443

AACR2 12.7B8g

AACR2

12.7B8 - Make notes on the bibliographic history and relationships with other resources

12.7B8c - If a resource has separated from another resource, give the name of the resource of which it was once a part

12.7B8g - If a resource is a supplement to another resource, give the name of the main resource. If a resource has supplement(s) that are described separately, make notes identifying the supplement(s). Make brief general notes on irregular, informal, numerous, or unimportant supplements that are not described separately

12.7B22 - If the description is of a resource issued with one or more other resources, make a note beginning *Issued with*: and listing the other resource(s)

RDA

24.4 - Record relationships between works, expressions, manifestations, and items using one or more of the conventions described under 24.4.1 rda (identifier), 24.4.2 rda (authorized access point), or 24.4.3 rda (description)

24.5.1.3 - Record an appropriate term from the list in appendix J rda to indicate the nature of the relationship more specifically than is indicated by the defined scope of the relationship element itself

CCM

14.2.2 - Separated from/Continued in part by (Fields 780 07/785 X1)

14.3.6 - When a separately cataloged serial is "issued with" (i.e., included in) the serial being cataloged, use field 777 to link the two records. Due to the complexity of most "issued with" relationships, field 580 is usually input to provide the note

14.3.4 - When a supplement is cataloged separately from its parent serial, link from the supplement to the parent serial, and vice versa. When cataloging the supplement, give an added entry for the parent serial, unless the supplement has a common title that is identical to the title proper of the related serial

17.4.4a - Use linking entry fields 772 (Supplement to) and 770 (Has supplement) when the supplement is cataloged separately

17.4.4c - A note for a supplement is recorded in field 772 or 580 when the supplement is cataloged separately and in field 525 when the supplement is not cataloged separately

(Continued on next page)

OCLC #36654443

Type a	ELvl	Srce d	GPub	Ctrl	Lang eng
BLvl s	Form	Conf 0	Freq q	MRec	Ctry nyu
S/L 0	Orig	EntW	Regl r	Alph a	
Desc a	SrTp p	Cont	DtSt c	Dates 1995	, 9999

	022	0		2152-2502 ‡2 1
	042			lcd ‡a nsdp
	245	0	0	Firstproof.
	246	3		First proof
	246	1	5	Bomb literary supplement firstproof
	246	3	0	Bomb literary supplement
	260			[New York : ‡b New Art Publications], ‡c 1995-
	300			v. : ‡b ill. ; ‡c 23-38 cm.
	310			Quarterly
	362	0		#1 (fall 1995)-
	500			Title from cover; imprint from Bomb.
	500			Latest issue consulted: winter 2008.
	515			Numbering dropped after no. 16, fall 1998 issue.

CCM 17.4.4c	580	Issued as literary supplement to Bomb, fall 1995-winter 2008 (paged separately fall 1995-spring 1996; inter-paged with main title, summer 1996-winter 2007); thereafter as a separate publication, spring 2008-winter 2008/2009; again as a literary supplement to Bomb (paged separately), spring 2009-	AACR2 12.7B8

	650	0	American literature ‡y 20th century ‡v Periodicals.

14.2.2	780	1	7	‡t Bomb (New York, N.Y.) ‡g 2008- ‡x 0743-3204 ‡w (OCoLC) 10226319	12.7B8c

14.3.4 17.4.4a	772	1	‡t Bomb (New York, N.Y.) ‡x 0743-3204 ‡w (OCoLC)10226319	12.7B8g

14.3.6	777	1	‡t Bomb (New York, N.Y.) ‡g no. 53 (fall 1995)-2007 ‡x 0743-3204 ‡w (OCoLC)10226319	12.7B22

Multiple Supplements (720) and Multiple Nonspecific Relationship Entries (787)

Title: International residential code for one- and two-family dwellings

Cover

Sometimes, the main work has multiple related resources—some of which may be supplements or "issued with entries," as discussed earlier. Others may not have a clearly specified relationship with the main work, although they are somehow related.

In this example, the serial *International Residential Code for One- and Two-Family Dwellings* is supplemented by *Supplement to the International Codes* and *Accumulative Supplement to the International Codes*. Both have been cataloged separately as serials on their own records, as shown in the two 770 fields, as well as in the linking entry complexity note in the 580 field.

Two additional resources related to the main work are the *International Residential Code for One- and Two-Family Dwellings Commentary* and *Approved Code Changes Resulting in the . . . IRC*.

These have been recorded in separate 787 fields used to link titles that are related in a manner other than those defined in fields 760–785. The publications included in this category are companions, summaries, and other related resources.

A linking entry complexity note has been given in the 580 field for the complementary title *International Residential Code for One- and Two-Family Dwellings Commentary*. In order to specify the relationship, the note is preceded by the term "complemented by." The other related title—*Approved Code Changes Resulting in the . . . IRC*—only appears in the 787 field because its specific relationship with the main title is not known or easily identified.

Linking entry fields are important for users because they provide links among related records in the online catalog. The links enable a user to search a title in the OPAC and retrieve records for that title as well as for related titles. Linking entry fields include these common subfields (in input order): ‡a, ‡t, ‡x, and ‡w. The subfield ‡a is used to record the related title's main entry heading, if present. All the individual components of the name heading are included in a single subfield ‡a. Subfield ‡t contains the title—either from the 130 field (uniform title heading) or the 245 field, including subfields ‡a, ‡n, and ‡p. All individual components of the title are in a single subfield ‡t. Subfield ‡x is used to record the ISSN from field 022 of the related record, but the term "ISSN" is not included. Subfield ‡w is used for record control numbers, which are given only when the related record appears in OCLC. The only required numbers are the LCCN (preceded by DLC enclosed within parentheses) and the OCLC control number (preceded by OCoLC enclosed within parentheses). For more information on record control numbers, consult Chapter 10.

The indicators of the linking entry fields are used to generate a note—either a predefined display constant or a customized note. If the display constant can accurately define the relationship between the resources, the first indicator is set to 0 (to display a note) and the second indicator is coded to show the appropriate display constant. When the display constant does not adequately define the relationship, subfield "‡i" can be used to customize the display text. In this case, the second indicator value is set to 8 to suppress the display constant.

OCLC #44163922

	Type a	ELvl	Srce d	GPub	Ctrl	Lang eng
	BLvl s	Form	Conf 0	Freq u	MRec	Ctry vau
	S/L 0	Orig	EntW	Regl u	Alph	
	Desc a	SrTp	Cont	DtSt c	Dates 2000	, 9999

	029	1		AU@ ǂb 000021576699	
	042			lcd	
CCM 6.2.2c	245	0	0	International residential code for one- and two-family dwellings.	
	260			Falls Church, Va. : ǂb International Code Council, ǂc c2000-	
	300			v. : ǂb ill. ; ǂc 28 cm.	
	362	0		2000-	
	500			Latest issue consulted: 2006.	
17.4.4c	580			Has supplements: Supplement to the international codes, 2001; Accumulative supplement to the international codes, 2002.	AACR2 12.7B8g
17.4.4c	580			Complemented by: International residential code for one- and two family dwellings commentary.	12.7B8
	650		0	Housing ǂx Standards.	
	650		0	Building laws.	
	710	2		International Code Council.	
	730	0		International residential code for one- and two family dwellings commentary.	
14.3.4 17.4.4a	770	1		ǂt Supplement to the international codes ǂw (DLC) 2004208749 ǂw (OCoLC)47016159	12.7B8g
14.3.4 17.4.4a	770	1		ǂt Accumulative supplement to the international codes ǂx 1550-0675 ǂw (DLC) 2004208577 ǂw (OCoLC)50881101	12.7B8g
	780	0	0	ǂt International one- and two-family dwelling code ǂw (DLC)sn 99038367 ǂw (OCoLC)40743293	
14.3.7	787	1		ǂt International residential code for one- and two family dewellings commentary ǂw (DLC) 2006245510 ǂw (OCoLC)64573909	12.7B8
14.3.7	787	0		ǂt Approved code changes resulting in the ... IRC ǂx 1942-5392 ǂw (DLC) 2008209614 ǂw (OCoLC)225867326	12.7B8

AACR2

12.7B8 - Make notes on the bibliographic history and relationships with other resources

12.7B8g - If a resource is a supplement to another resource, give the name of the main resource. If a resource has supplement(s) that are described separately, make notes identifying the supplement(s). Make brief general notes on irregular, informal, numerous, or unimportant supplements that are not described separately

RDA

24.4 - Record relationships between works, expressions, manifestations, and items using one or more of the conventions described under 24.4.1 rda (identifier), 24.4.2 rda (authorized access point), or 24.4.3 rda (description)

24.5.1.3 - Record an appropriate term from the list in appendix J rda to indicate the nature of the relationship more specifically than is indicated by the defined scope of the relationship element itself

CCM

6.2.2c - The supplement to a serial is issued under the name of the parent serial plus the generic term "supplement" (or its equivalent). The two titles are not grammatically linked

17.4.4a - Use linking entry fields 772 (Supplement to) and 770 (Has supplement) when the supplement is cataloged separately

17.4.4c - A note for a supplement is recorded in field 772 or 580 when the supplement is cataloged separately and in field 525 when the supplement is not cataloged separately

14.3.4 - When a supplement is cataloged separately from its parent serial, link from the supplement to the parent serial, and vice versa. When cataloging the supplement, give an added entry for the parent serial, unless the supplement has a common title that is identical to the title proper of the related serial

14.3.7 - Companions, summaries, and other related resources (Field 787): a resource that is related to a serial in a manner that is not expressed by one of the other linking entry fields and that is separately cataloged falls into this category

Supplement Note (525) and Supplement Title Changes

Title: Tappi journal

Cover

The serial *Tappi Journal* (a publication of the Technical Association of the Pulp and Paper Industry) has many related resources, as shown in the various linking and notes fields. As discussed in earlier examples, the 770/772 and 777 fields are used to link the main work with supplements and "issued with" resources (separately numbered inserts).

There are two things worth noting about the record for *Tappi Journal*. First, the two supplements recorded in the 770 fields are the same member directory of the Technical Association of the Pulp and Paper Industry, but the title changed from *Directory of Members, Products, and Services* to *Tappi Membership Directory and Company Guide*. Both have been cataloged separately and are linked to the main work through the use of 770 fields. The first indicator is set to the value 0 to produce the display text "Has supplement." For this supplement, there is no need for an additional linking entry complexity note (580 field). Secondly, instead of a 580 field, the 525 supplement note field has been used to give information about an unnamed supplement. Unnamed supplements are not cataloged in separate records or recorded in linking entry 770 fields.

The presence of linking entry fields and notes makes it possible for users looking for resources related to *Tappi Journal* to easily identify and access these related materials.

OCLC #8693713

Type a	ELvl	Srce d	GPub	Ctrl	Lang eng
BLvl s	Form	Conf 0	Freq m	MRec	Ctry gau
S/L 0	Orig	EntW	Regl r	Alph a	
Desc a	SrTp p	Cont	DtSt d	Dates 1982	, 2001

	022	0	0734-1415 ‡2 1	
	042		lc ‡a nsdp	
	245	0 0	Tappi journal.	
	260		Atlanta, Ga. : ‡b Technical Association of the Pulp and Paper Industry, ‡c c1982-c2001.	
	362	0	Vol. 65, no. 9 (Sept. 1982)-v. 84, no. 8 (Aug. 2001).	
CCM 17.4.4c	525		Supplements accompany some issues.	AACR2 12.7B8g
17.4.4c	525		Issues for <Apr. 2000>-Aug. 2001 have supplements containing the full-text of peer-reviewed articles that were only published as summaries in the original issues.	12.7B8g
	580		Merged with: PIMA's . . . papermaker, to form: Solutions!(Norcross, Ga.).	
17.4.4c	580		Vols. for Sept. 1985- have separately numbered insert called: Advancing converting & packaging technologies.	

14.3.4 17.4.4a	770	0		Technical Association of the Pulp and Paper Industry. ‡t Directory of members, products, and services ‡w (DLC)sn 88015936 ‡w (OCoLC) 12965287	12.7B8g
14.3.4 17.4.4a	770	0		Technical Association of the Pulp and Paper Industry. ‡t TAPPI membership directory and company guide ‡w (DLC)sn 89012161 ‡w (OCoLC)14882334	12.7B8g
14.3.6	777	1		‡t Advancing converting & packaging technologies ‡x 0882-5777 ‡w (OCoLC)11893924	12.7B22
	780	0	0	‡t Tappi ‡x 0039-8241 ‡w (DLC) 19005316 ‡w (OCoLC)6457012	
	785	1	7	‡t PIMA's … papermaker ‡x 1093-670X ‡w (DLC) 97646623 ‡w (OCoLC)36353452	
	785	1	7	‡t Solutions! (Norcross, Ga.) ‡x 1537-0275 ‡w (DLC) 2001215218 ‡w (OCoLC)47914483	
	856	4	1	‡z TAPPI home page: ‡u http://www.tappi.org/	

AACR2

12.7B8g - If a resource is a supplement to another resource, give the name of the main resource. If a resource has supplement(s) that are described separately, make notes identifying the supplement(s). Make brief general notes on irregular, informal, numerous, or unimportant supplements that are not described separately

12.7B22 - If the description is of a resource issued with one or more other resources, make a note beginning Issued with: and listing the other resource(s)

RDA

24.4 - Record relationships between works, expressions, manifestations, and items using one or more of the conventions described under 24.4.1 rda (identifier), 24.4.2 rda (authorized access point), or 24.4.3 rda (description)

24.5.1.3 - Record an appropriate term from the list in appendix J rda to indicate the nature of the relationship more specifically than is indicated by the defined scope of the relationship element itself

CCM

14.3.6 - When a separately cataloged serial is "issued with" (i.e., included in) the serial being cataloged, use field 777 to link the two records. Due to the complexity of most "issued with" relationships, field 580 is usually input to provide the note

14.3.4 - When a supplement is cataloged separately from its parent serial, link from the supplement to the parent serial, and vice versa. When cataloging the supplement, give an added entry for the parent serial, unless the supplement has a common title that is identical to the title proper of the related serial

17.4.4a - Use linking entry fields 772 (Supplement to) and 770 (Has supplement) when the supplement is cataloged separately

17.4.4c - A note for a supplement is recorded in field 772 or 580 when the supplement is cataloged separately and in field 525 when the supplement is not cataloged separately

(Continued on next page)

OCLC #12965287

	245	1	0	Directory of members, products, and services.	
	260			[Norcross, Ga.] : ‡b TAPPI, ‡c c1985-	
	310			Annual	
CCM 17.4.4c	580			Published as a special numbered issue of: Tappi journal.	AACR2 12.7b8g
	730	0		Tappi journal.	
14.3.4 17.4.4a	772	0		‡t Tappi journal ‡x 0734-1415 ‡w (DLC) 83642134 ‡w (OCoLC) 8693713	12.7b8g

OCLC #14882334

	245	1	0	TAPPI membership directory and company guide.	
	260			[Norcross, Ga.] : ‡b TAPPI, ‡c c1986-c1991.	
	310			Annual	
CCM 17.4.4c	580			Published as an issue of: Tappi journal.	AACR2 12.7b8g
	730	0		Tappi journal.	
14.3.4 17.4.4a	772	1		‡t Tappi journal ‡x 0734-1415 ‡w (DLC) 83642134 ‡w (OCoLC) 8693713	12.7b8g

OCLC #11893924

	022	0		0882-5777 ‡2 1	
	245	0	0	Advancing converting & packaging technologies.	
	260			[Atlanta, GA] : ‡b TAPPI, ‡c 1985-	
	310			Quarterly	
CCM 17.4.4c	580			Issued as separately numbered insert to: Tappi journal.	12.7b8g
	710	2		Technical Association of the Pulp and Paper Industry.	
14.3.6	777	1		‡t Tappi journal ‡x 0734-1415 ‡w (DLC) 8362134	12.7B22

Supplements Not Cataloged on Separate Record

Title: Jane's international defense review

Cover

Table of Contents

Sometimes, a serial includes supplemental materials for which no separate records are created because the supplements are not independent publications. An example of this is *Jane's International Defense Review*, which, as noted in the 580 field of the record for the main work, "includes bound in supplement: Defense electronics & computing, <1996>-, as separately titled section every second month (later titled: Defense, Science & Technology, <2001->)."

To facilitate a user's search in the catalog and access to the supplements, the 740 added entry field is used to provide information about the related or analytical titles. In this record, a separate 740 field is created for each title:

Cover

740 02 Defense electronics & computing.
740 02 Defense science & technology.

The second indicator 2 is chosen to show that the main work contains the supplement represented by the added entry (that is, the supplement is an analytical entry).

There are additional resources related to the main work. Separate 525 fields are used in the record for the main work to note two unnamed supplements. Additionally, two named supplements—*Jane's IDR Extra* and *Jane's International Defense Review: Quarterly Report*—are input in 770 fields. Because the first indicator value is set to 0, the linking field will produce a display constant. Because the second indicator value is blank, the display constant "Has supplement:" will precede the data in the linking entry field. When a display constant is generated by the linking entry field, a 580 field (Linking Entry Complexity Note) should not be added.

However, 580 fields are needed to describe the relationship of other related resources to the main work. One 580 field expresses the relationship of the main work to Jane's Year of Defence on CD-ROM, coded in the 777 field (Issued With Entry). Another 580 field shows a different kind of relationship between the main work and *Jane's Year of Defence*, described in the 787 field (Nonspecific Relationship Entry) to show that selected articles from the main work are issued in or included in the CD-ROM. Because 580 fields have been used, the first indicator in field 777 and field 787 has been set to 1 in order to suppress the machine-generated display constant "Issued with" (for the 777 field) and "Related item" (for the 787 field).

OCLC #34306242

Type a	ELvl	Srce d	GPub	Ctrl	Lang eng
BLvl s	Form	Conf 0	Freq m	MRec	Ctry enk
S/L 0	Orig	EntW	Regl r	Alph	
Desc a	SrTp p	Cont	DtSt c	Dates 1996	, 9999

	022		1476-2129 ǂy 0020-6512	
	245	0 0	Jane's international defense review : ǂb IDR.	
	246	1	ǂi Issues for Nov. 2004- called: ǂa Jane's international defence review	
	260		Coulsdon, Surrey, U.K. : ǂb Jane's Information Group, ǂc c1996-	
	362	0	Vol. no. 29 (Jan. 1996)-	
	500		Title from cover.	
CCM 17.4.4c	525		Has occasional accompanying CD-ROMs other than the annual, Jane's year of defence.	AACR2 12.7B8g
17.4.4c	525		Some issues accompanied by supplements which are also supplements to Jane's defence weekly.	12.7B8g
17.4.4c	580		Issued 1997- with the annual CD-ROM: Jane's year of defence.	12.7B8g
17.4.4c	580		Selected articles also available 1997- in the annual CD-ROM: Jane's year of defence.	12.7B8g
17.4.4c	580		Includes bound in supplement: Defense electronics & computing, <1996>- , as separately titled section every second month (later titled: Defense, Science & Technology, <2001->).	12.7B8g
	650	0	Military art and science ǂv Periodicals.	
14.3.4 17.4.4a	770	0	ǂt Jane's IDR extra ǂw (DLC)sn 96038043 ǂw (OCoLC)34258043	12.7B8g
14.3.4 17.4.4a	770	0	ǂt Jane's international defense review. Quarterly report ǂw (DLC)sn 98033863 ǂw (OCoLC)34689017	12.7B8g
14.3.6	777	1	ǂt Jane's year of defence ǂg 1997- ǂw (DLC)sn 97032449 ǂw (OCoLC)38095468	12.7B22
	780	0 0	ǂt International defense review ǂx 0020-6512 ǂw (DLC)sf 77000189 ǂw (OCoLC)1893800	
14.3.7	787	1	ǂt Jane's year of defence ǂg 1997- ǂw (DLC)sn 97032449 ǂw (OCoLC)38095468	12.7B8
17.4.4b2	740	0 2	Defense electronics & computing.	21.30M1
17.4.4b2	740	0 2	Defense science & technology.	21.30M1

AACR2

12.7B8 - Make notes on the bibliographic history and relationships with other resources

12.7B8g - If a resource is a supplement to another resource, give the name of the main resource. If a resource has supplement(s) that are described separately, make notes identifying the supplement(s). Make brief general notes on irregular, informal, numerous, or unimportant supplements that are not described separately

12.7B22 - If the description is of a resource issued with one or more other resources, make a note beginning *Issued with*: and listing the other resource(s)

21.30M1 - Make an analytical added entry under the heading for a work contained within the item being catalogued

RDA

24.4 - Record relationships between works, expressions, manifestations, and items using one or more of the conventions described under 24.4.1 rda (identifier), 24.4.2 rda (authorized access point), or 24.4.3 rda (description)

24.5.1.3 - Record an appropriate term from the list in appendix J rda to indicate the nature of the relationship more specifically than is indicated by the defined scope of the relationship element itself

CCM

14.3.4 - When a supplement is cataloged separately from its parent serial, link from the supplement to the parent serial, and vice versa. When cataloging the supplement, give an added entry for the parent serial, unless the supplement has a common title that is identical to the title proper of the related serial

14.3.6 - When a separately cataloged serial is "issued with" (i.e., included in) the serial being cataloged, use field 777 to link the two records. Due to the complexity of most "issued with" relationships, field 580 is usually input to provide the note

14.3.7 - Companions, summaries, and other related resources (Field 787): a resource that is related to a serial in a manner that is not expressed by one of the other linking entry fields and that is separately cataloged falls into this category

17.4.4a - Use linking entry fields 772 (Supplement to) and 770 (Has supplement) when the supplement is cataloged separately

17.4.4c - A note for a supplement is recorded in field 772 or 580 when the supplement is cataloged separately and in field 525 when the supplement is not cataloged separately

17.4.4b2 - If the title of the supplement is significantly different from that of the main work, give the title in the note and give an added entry

Cover

OCLC #928149

EXERCISE 1

The serial *International Review of Cytology* has a supplement called *International Review of Cytology. Supplement.* Record the relationship between the parent publication and its supplement by creating appropriate 770 and 772 fields with correct indicators and subfields (‡t, ‡x, and/or ‡w).

Type a	ELvl	Srce d	GPub	Ctrl	Lang eng
BLvl s	Form	Conf 0	Freq	MRec	Ctry nyu
S/L 0	Orig	EntW	Regl x	Alph a	
Desc	SrTp m	Cont	DtSt d	Dates 1952	, 2008

010		52005203
022		0074-7696 ‡2 1
037		‡b Academic Press, 525 B Street, Suite 1900, San Diego, California 92101-4495
042		nsdp ‡a lc
210	0	Int. rev. cyt.
222		0 International review of cytology
245	0 0	International review of cytology.
260		New York, ‡b Academic Press, ‡c 1952-2008.
300		v. ‡b ill. ‡c 24 cm.
310		Irregular
362	0	v. 1-265.
500		Editor: v. 1- G.H. Bourne.
510	2	Chemical abstracts ‡x 0009-2258
515		Vol. 137 issues in parts.
550		Vols. issued under the auspices of the International Society for Cell Biology.
555		Cumulative title index: v.1-30 with v.30.
555		Cumulative subject index: v.1-9 with v.10; v.11-22 with v.22; v. 138 (1992)-176 (1997). 1 v.
650		0 Cytology.
650		2 Cytology ‡v Periodicals.
653		Cytology ‡a Serials.
700	1	Bourne, Geoffrey H. ‡q (Geoffrey Howard), ‡d 1909-1988.
710	2	International Society for Cell Biology.
770		
776	0 8	‡i Issued also online: ‡t International review of cytology (Online) ‡w (OCoLC)56993324
785	0 0	‡t International review of cell and molecular biology ‡x 1937-6448 ‡w (DLC) 2007213895 ‡w (OCoLC)174222860

OCLC #3226959

Type a	ELvl	Srce c	GPub	Ctrl	Lang eng
BLvl s	Form	Conf 0	Freq	MRec	Ctry nyu
S/L 0	Orig	EntW	Regl x	Alph a	
Desc a	SrTp	Cont	DtSt d	Dates 1969	, 1987

010			sf 90017608 ǂz 90645665 ǂz sn 80001655
022			0074-770X ǂl 0074-770X ǂ2 1
042			pcc ǂa nsdp
245	0	0	International review of cytology. ǂp Supplement.
260			New York : ǂb Academic Press,
300			17 v. : ǂb ill. ; ǂc 24 cm.
362	1		Began with 1 (1969); ceased with 17 (1987).
500			Each volume has also a distinctive title.
500			Description based on: 6, published in 1977.
510	2		Chemical abstracts ǂx 0009-2258
650		0	Cells ǂv Periodicals.
650		2	Cytology ǂv Periodicals.
650		6	Cytologie ǂv Collections.
772			

Cover

OCLC #8610701

EXERCISE 2

From 1991–1998, the serial *Casa del Tiempo* had a monthly supplement containing poetic works, entitled *Margen de Poesía*. This supplement was issued as a tear-out insert to the main serial and had its own numbering. On the following records—one for the parent publication and the other for the supplement—use appropriate 770 and 772 fields, with correct indicators and subfields (‡t, ‡x, and/or ‡w), to show the relationship between the parent publication and the supplement. The 580 notes fields provide useful information about the parent publication and the supplement.

Type a	ELvl	Srce	GPub	Ctrl	Lang spa
BLvl s	Form	Conf 0	Freq m	MRec	Ctry mx
S/L 0	Orig	EntW	Regl r	Alph b	
Desc a	SrTp p	Cont o	DtSt c	Dates 1980	, 9999

022		0185-4275 ‡y 0185-2417 ‡2 q
037		‡b Medellín 28, Col. Roma, C.P. 06700, México, D.F.
042		lc
043		n-mx— ‡a cl—
245	0 0	Casa del tiempo.
260		[México] : ‡b Universidad Autónoma Metropolitana, ‡c 1980-
300		v : ‡b ill. ; ‡c 28-30 cm.
310		Monthly
362	0	Vol. 1, no. 1 (sept. 1980)- ; nueve época, v. 11, no. 1 (oct. 1991)-nueve época, v. 11, no. 7 (abr. 1992) ; época 2, v. 11, no. 8 (mayo 1992)-época 2, v. 14, no 82/83 (dic. 1998/enero 1999) ; época 3, v. 1, no. 1 (feb. 1999)-época 3, v. 9, no. 100 (jul./sept. 2007); época 4, v. 1, no. 1 (oct./nov. 2007)-
500		Title from cover.
500		Latest issue consulted: época 4, v. 1, no. 5/6 (marzo/abr. 2008).
515		Some issues published in combined form.
515		Issues for <enero-feb. 1988-marzo-abr. 1991> also called no. <75-100>
515		Vols. for oct. 1991-abr. 1992 also called v. 11, nueva época no. 1-v. 11, nueve época, no. 7; mayo 1992- also called v. 11, época 2, no. 8-
580		Has supplement: Margen the poesía, <1993->
550		Issued by the Dirección de Difusión Cultural.
651	0	Mexico ‡v Periodicals.
651	0	Mexico ‡x Civilization ‡v Periodicals.

650		0	Latin American literature ‡x History and criticism ‡v Periodicals.
710	2		Universidad Autónoma Metropolitana. ‡b Dirección de Difusión Cultural.
730	0		Margen de poesía.
770			
776	0	8	‡i Also available online: ‡t Casa del tiempo (Online) ‡w (OCoLC) 168254760
856	4	1	‡u http://www.difusioncultural.uam.mx/revista/index.html

OCLC #26249073

Type a	ELvl I	Srce d	GPub	Ctrl	Lang spa
BLvl s	Form	Conf 0	Freq m	MRec	Ctry mx
S/L 0	Orig	EntW	Regl r	Alph b	
Desc a	SrTp m	Cont	DtSt d	Dates 1991	, 1998

245	0	0	Margen de poesía.
260			México : ‡b Universidad Autónoma Metropolitana, ‡c 1991-
300			v. ; ‡c 21 cm.
310			Monthly
362	0		1 (1991)-
362	1		Ceased with 71, published 1998?
500			Each issue is devoted to the poetry of a single author.
580			Issued as a tear-out supplement to: Casa del tiempo.
650		0	Mexican poetry ‡y 20th century ‡v Periodicals.
710	2		Universidad Autónoma Metropolitana.
730	0		Casa del tiempo.
772			

Cover

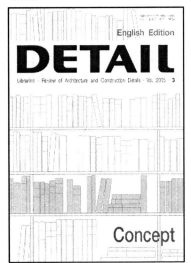

EXERCISE 3

The bimonthly architectural journal *Detail* has a semiannual supplement on sustainable architecture called *Detail Green*. The supplement is issued under separate cover and has its own numbering system. Create linking fields within the records for the main serial and the supplement by using appropriate 770 and 772 fields, with correct indicators and subfields (‡t, ‡x, and/or ‡w).

OCLC #58804304

Type a	ELvl	Srce d	GPub	Ctrl	Lang eng
BLvl s	Form	Conf 0	Freq b	MRec	Ctry gw
S/L 0	Orig	EntW	Regl r	Alph a	
Desc a	SrTp p	Cont	DtSt c	Dates 2004	, 9999

010			2006214569
022			1614-4600 ‡2 6
042			nsdp ‡a lcd
130	0		Detail (English ed.)
245	1	0	Detail : ‡b Review of architecture and construction details.
250			English ed.
260			München: ‡b Institut für Internationale Architektur-Dokumentation, ‡c 2005-
300			v. : ‡b ill. ; ‡c 30 cm.
310			Bimonthly
362	0		Vol. 2005, 1 (Jan./Feb. 2005)-
500			Title from cover.
500			Some issues have also a thematic title.
500			Latest issue consulted: Vol. 2006, 3 (May/June 2006).
580			Semiannual supplement: Detail green, issued from 2009-
650		0	Architecture ‡v Periodicals.
650		0	Architecture ‡x Details ‡v Periodicals.
650		0	Building ‡v Periodicals.
650		0	Building ‡x Details ‡v Periodicals.
710	2		Institut für Internationale Architektur-Dokumentation.
770			

OCLC #330765419

Type a	ELvl I	Srce d	GPub	Ctrl	Lang eng
BLvl s	Form	Conf 0	Freq f	MRec	Ctry gw
S/L 0	Orig	EntW	Regl r	Alph	
Desc a	SrTp p	Cont	DtSt c	Dates 2009	, 9999

022			1868-3843
245	0	0	Detail green.
250			English ed.
260			München : ‡b Institut für Internationale Arkitektur-Dokumentation
310			Semiannual
362	0		Began with 01/09, [i.e. 2009/1].
500			Description based on 01/09; title from cover.
500			Latest issue consulted: 01/09.
650		0	Architecture ‡v Periodicals.
650		0	Architecture ‡x Details ‡v Periodicals.
650		0	Building ‡v Periodicals.
650		0	Building ‡x Details ‡v Periodicals.
650		0	Sustainable architecture ‡v Periodicals.
710	2		Institut für Internationale Arkitektur-Dokumentation.
772			
775	0		‡t Detail green ‡b German ed. ‡w (DLC) 2009264114 ‡w (OCoLC) 402062249

Notes

CHAPTER 8

Uniform Titles

There are two primary purposes for the creation of uniform titles in serials cataloging: to differentiate between two serials with identical titles and, less commonly, to gather together related works. The second of these is the purpose for which uniform titles were originally created: to collocate related works with different titles. This includes different manifestations, such as editions or translations. However, with the exception of translations or language editions, uniform titles for serials are usually created as a means of resolving a conflict in the catalog between works that have the same title.

Because serials are usually cataloged under the title as the main entry (unless the serial emanates from a corporate body that falls into one of the categories specified in AACR2 21.1B2), conflict resolution is especially important.[1] Many serials, including corporate publications that fall outside of the categories specified in AACR2 21.1B2, have generic titles that must be entered under the title. Generic titles are those that consist solely of an indication of type of publication and/or periodicity, such as "Annual Report," "Publication," or "Review." These are less distinctive than most and therefore need qualifiers to uniquely identify them. Guidelines for deciding when to use uniform titles are detailed in the beginning of Chapter 25 of AACR2 (25.1A).[2]

In this chapter, we will review some typical scenarios to show when uniform titles need to be created and the form those titles can take. The examples will illustrate the following:

- Types of qualifiers
- The use of multiple qualifiers
- Changes affecting uniform titles
- Creation of the uniform title when the title proper is the added entry (use of the 240 field)

The category of uniform title created to differentiate between works with the same title was, according to Module 5 of the CONSER Cataloging Manual, "devised shortly after the adoption of AACR2 in 1981." Because most serials under AACR2 are entered under title, these rules increased the likelihood of identical titles and thus the need to distinguish between them. According to Glasby, the Library of Congress realized this "during the period between publication of AACR2 and its implementation."[3] LCRI 25.5B, which provides for the entry of serials with nonunique titles under a uniform title created by the addition of a qualifier to the title, was written to address this problem.

The AACR2 1988 revision incorporated "the rules revised since publication of AACR2 but not the rule interpretations."[4] The same article reported in 1992 that the Canadian Committee on Cataloguing and the ALA Committee to Study Serials Cataloging proposed revisions to incorporate into the rules themselves provisions for the use of uniform titles for serials with identical titles proper. This would make the AACR2 rules *explicitly* state the use of uniform titles for serials."[5] The

1998 revision of AACR2 added examples of uniform titles used to address conflict resolution of serial titles.

When a serial title conflicts with another already in the catalog, a uniform title is created by adding a qualifier (in parenthesis) to the title proper in order to distinguish it from the cataloged title. Generic titles (those that indicate either the type of publication or the periodicity of issuance, such as "Bulletin" or "Occasional Paper") entered under title are usually qualified by the name of the issuing or publishing corporate body. In other situations, serials catalogers will need to exercise their judgment in determining the most appropriate qualifier for the serial title being cataloged. It should be noted that when called for, uniform titles are only assigned to a new record being created. *Do not retrospectively assign uniform titles to pre-existing records.* LCRI 25.5B lists possible qualifiers catalogers can use to create uniform titles:

- Corporate body
- Date of publication—choose the date of publication of the first issue published or the earliest issue in hand, in that order of preference (not date from chronological designation)
- Descriptive data elements (e.g., edition statement, GMD, physical medium)
- Place of publication—if the serial/series is published in more than one place, choose as the qualifying term the place that would be named first in the publication, distribution, etc., area for the first issue published, the earliest issue for which a place is known, or the earliest issue in hand, in that order of preference. If the name of the local place has changed, use in the qualifier the name the place had at the time the first/earliest issue was published

This listing is not prescriptive and is not in priority order. If none of these qualifiers are appropriate, catalogers can also use any other words that will serve to distinguish one serial from another. It may also be the case that the use of more than one qualifier is sometimes needed to make the uniform title unique (LCRI 25.5B). Qualifiers that use either place names or corporate bodies should take the AACR2 form of the name as found in the authority file.

If the uniform title is the main entry, it is encoded in MARC field 130. However, if a uniform title is needed for a serial entered under a corporate body or personal name main entry, the uniform title is entered in the 240 field following the 1XX field. Authority records are not generally created for serial uniform titles.

The instructions governing the choice of qualifier have changed over time. "Cataloging Service Bulletin no. 5 (Summer 1979) stated the rationale for using uniform titles to distinguish between two or more otherwise identical serials and gave six guidelines for their construction (under rule 25.5B)."[6] Included in these guidelines was a preference for use of the issuing corporate body as qualifier. However, CSB no. 23 (Winter 1983) introduced a dramatic change when the LC announced the intention to qualify in general by place of publication instead of issuing body.[7] This change was introduced in order to reduce unnecessary successive entry cataloging that resulted when the corporate body changed.[8]

The issues are stated well by Maxwell:

"The choice between using the issuing body as the qualifier for the uniform title and other qualifiers is important because it may determine whether a new record is needed when a change occurs. Under AACR2 principles, when a corporate body changes its name, it becomes a new entity. Therefore, if a serial uniform title has been qualified by the name of the issuing body and the body changes, this is significant enough to require a new record with a new uniform title, *even if the serial continues and the title proper of the serial does not change* (cf. LCRI 25.5B, "Change in qualifier: Body used as qualifier")." He continues: "[T]his argues against using the name of the issuing body to qualify if there is a choice, except in the case of generic titles. . . ."[9]

With the implementation of CSR in 2007, uniform titles are only required for monographic series and "generic" titles (i.e., those cases where the title consists solely of a word or words indicating the type of resource or the periodicity of the resource, such as "monthly newsletter," "journal," "biennial working papers").[10]

In RDA, the term "uniform title" has been replaced with the "preferred title for the work," a core element defined in RDA 6.2.2.1 as "the title or form of title chosen as the basis for the authorized access point representing that work." The guidelines at RDA 5.5 give instructions for constructing an authorized access point to represent the work based on the preferred title. RDA Chapter 6.0 provides general guidelines for choosing and recording preferred titles for works and points out the purposes for using authorized access points representing works and expressions:

(a) bringing together all descriptions of resources embodying a work when various expressions or manifestations of the work have appeared under various titles

(b) identifying a work when the title by which it is known differs from the title proper of the resource being described

(c) differentiating between two or more works with the same title

(d) organizing hierarchical displays of descriptions for resources embodying different expressions of a work

(e) referencing a related work or a related expression

NOTES

1. In determining whether a serial should be entered under corporate body main entry, the rules of AACR2 Chapter 21 are applied in the same manner as for monographs.

2. In Chapter 25, conditions for the use of uniform titles and the basic rules are followed by special rules for certain materials. The materials given special treatment include manuscripts and incunabula, laws and treaties, sacred scriptures and other religious works liturgical works, and music. The rules for construction of uniform titles for these materials are not illustrated here because they are outside the scope of this book. These rules are intended to meet the first purpose of uniform titles, which is that of collocating related works, although multiple qualifiers can be added if serials in these areas need to be distinguished. For additional information, see the cataloging manuals specific to these areas—for example, *Cataloging Legal Literature*, *List of Uniform Titles for Liturgical Works*, and *Uniform Titles for Music*.

3. Dorothy J. Glasby, "The Descriptive Cataloging of Serials: Library of Congress' Application of AACR2," in *Serials Cataloging: The State of the Art*, Jim E. Cole and Jackie Zajanc, eds. (New York: Haworth Press, 1987). Published simultaneously as *Serials Librarian*, v. 12 no. 1/2 (1987).

4. Mitch L. Turitz, "Presentation of Holdings Data in Union Lists and Uniform Titles: A View of Two Problem Areas in Serials Cataloging." *Serials Librarian* (0361-526X) v. 22 no. 1/2 (1992).

5. *Ibid.*

6. James W. Williams, "Serials Cataloging With AACR2: The Primary Problems and Concerns," in *Serials Cataloging: The State of the Art*, Jim E. Cole and Jackie Zajanc, eds. (New York: Haworth Press, 1987). Published simultaneously as *Serials Librarian*, v. 12 no. 1/2 (1987).

7. *Ibid.*

8. Turitz (1992).

9. Robert L. Maxwell, *Maxwell's Guide to Authority Work*. (Chicago: American Library Association, 2002).

10. *CONSER Standard Record Documentation*, July 22, 2010: http://www.loc.gov/catdir/cpso/conserdoc.pdf.

RESOURCES CONSULTED

AACR2

21.14 Entry of translation under appropriate headings

25.5B Uniform Title Additions: Conflict resolution when two different works share a common title

25.5C Uniform Title Additions: Translations of a work

LCRI

25.5B LC conflict resolution

RDA

6.2.2 Preferred title for the work

6.3 Form of work

6.4 Date of work

6.5 Place of origin of the work

6.6 Other distinguishing characteristic of the work

6.9 Content type

6.11 Language of expression

6.12 Other distinguishing characteristics of the expression

CCM

Module 5 Uniform Titles (fields 130 and 240)

Uniform Title Qualified by Place of Publication

Title: Theoria

Uniform Title: Theoria (Denton, Tex.)

Title Page

Supervising Editor
John Covach

Managing Editors   *Assistant Editor*
Robin Miller   Sean Finnegan
Donna Dupuy

                Graphics Edito
                David Carson B

                        Advisory Board
Ian Bent
Thoms Christensen
Sarah Fuller
Kevin Korsyn
Harold Krebs
Joel Lester

                        Acknowledgeme

When there is another serial with the same name in the catalog, a uniform title is assigned. The uniform title can be qualified by the initial place of publication. The established form of the place's name is used, with the higher jurisdiction separated from the city by a comma.

Table of Contents

Theoria

Historical Aspects of Music Theory   **Volume 7, 1993**

Contents

DAVID E. COHEN
Metaphysics, Ideology, Discipline: Consonance, Dissonance, and
    the Foundations of Western Polyphony 1

JOEL LESTER
Composition Made Easy: Bontempi's *Nova methodus* of 1660 87

DENIS COLLINS
Zarlino and Berardi as Teachers of Canon 103

JANE PIPER CLENDINNING
Review of *Compositional Theory in the Eighteenth Century*
    by Joel Lester 125

GRAHAM H. PHIPPS
The "Nature of Things" and the Evolution of Nineteenth-Century
    Musical Style: An Essay on Carl Dahlhaus's *Studies on the
    Origin of Harmonic Tonality* 141

Theoria is published annually by the College of Music, University of North
    Texas, Denton, TX 76203

The publication location can generally be found on the title page or the title page verso (here, it is found at the bottom of the title page verso, which also serves as the journal's table of contents). When constructing a uniform title, always use the location of the first issuance (i.e. , the location that is recorded in the 260 MARC field).

OCLC #12979399

Type: a	ELvl:	Srce: d	GPub:	Ctrl:	Lang: eng
BLvl: s	Form:	Conf: 0	Freq: a	MRec:	Ctry: txu
S/L: 0	Orig:	EntW:	Regl: r	Alph: a	
Desc: a	SrTp:	Cont:	DtSt: c	Dates: 1985,	9999

	022	0	1554-1312 ‡2 1
	037		‡b University of North Texas, College of Music, Theoria, POB 311367, Denton, Tex. 76203-1367
	042		lc ‡a nsdp
CCM 5.3.1	130	0	Theoria (Denton, Tex.)
	245	0 0	Theoria / ‡c [compiled and edited annually by graduate students at the School of Music, North Texas State University]
	260		[Denton, Tex.] : ‡b The School, ‡c [c1985-
	300		v. : ‡b music ; ‡c 24 cm.
	310		Annual
	362	0	Vol. 1 (1985)-
	500		Title from cover.
	500		"Historical aspects of music theory."
	650	0	Music theory ‡v Periodicals.
	650	0	Music theory ‡x History ‡v Periodicals.
	710	2	North Texas State University. ‡b School of Music.

(AACR2 25.5B1)

AACR2

25.5B1 - Add a qualifying term or phrase (in parentheses) to the uniform title in order to distinguish identical or similar publications

LCRI

25.5B - When creating a bibliographic record for a serial, construct a uniform title made up of the title proper plus a parenthetical qualifier to distinguish the serial from another with the same title proper in a bibliographic record

- For choice of cataloging terms, catalogers should use judgment in determining the most appropriate qualifier for the serial being cataloged

- Some possible qualifiers are date of publication, physical medium, and place of publication

- If the serial is published in more than one place, choose as the qualifying term the place that would be named first in the publication, distribution, etc. area for the first issue published, the earliest issue for which a place is known or the earliest issue in hand, in that order of preference

- If the name of the local place has changed, use in the qualifier the name the place had at the time the first/earliest issue was published

- As for the form of the place of publication, use the AACR2 form from the name authority record for the place minus any cataloger's addition (cf. AACR2 24.6); record the name of the larger place preceded by a comma (cf. AACR2 23.4A1)

RDA

6.27.1.9 - For additions to access points representing works, add one or more of the following, as appropriate:

a) a term indicating the form of work (see 6.3)

b) the date of the work (see 6.4)

c) the place of origin of the work (see 6.5), and/or

d) a term indicating another distinguishing characteristic of the work (see 6.6)

CCM

5.3.1 - The place used for this type of uniform title is that of the publication of the earliest issue

– This place name will match the location identified in the 260 field and should be at the city level

– If the exact city is unknown, it is appropriate to use a higher jurisdiction

– Punctuation should follow the rules spelled out in AACR2 23.4A1. Make all additions to place names used as entry elements in parentheses). If the place name is being used as an addition, precede the name of a larger place by a comma

Uniform Title Qualified by Corporate Body

Title: Rocky Mountain review

Uniform Title: Rocky Mountain review (Rocky Mountain Modern Language Association)

Title Page

A search in OCLC's WorldCat catalog resulted in several serials titled *Rocky Mountain Review*. In this case, because the name of the issuing corporate body is located on the title page and the title page verso, it makes sense to use the corporate body as the qualifying term in the uniform title.

ROCKY MOUNTAIN REVIEW

THE JOURNAL OF THE ROCKY MOUNTAIN MODERN LANGUAGE ASSOCIATION

2 0 0 8 ✦ VOLUME 62 ✦ NUMBER

Title Page Verso

ROCKY MOUNTAIN MODERN LANGUAGE ASSOCIATION

BOARD OF DIRECTORS

EDITORIAL AND EXECUTIVE STAFF AT WASHINGTON STATE UNIVERSITY

PRESIDENT
Albrecht Classen
University of Arizona

VICE PRESIDENT
Sura Rath
Central Washington University

PAST PRESIDENT
Liahna Armstrong
Central Washington University

DELEGATES
David H. Chisholm
University of Arizona

Beverly Zimmerman
Brigham Young University

Joy Landeira
University of Northern Colorado

GRADUATE STUDENT DELEGATES
Javier F. Gonzalez
University of Colorado, Boulder

Katie Arosteguy
Washington State University

EXECUTIVE DIRECTOR
Joan Grenier-Winther
Washington State University

EDITORS
Michael Delahoyde
Washington State University

Sabine Davis
Washington State University

MANAGING EDITOR
Nathanael Whitworth
Washington State University

ADMINISTRATIVE ASSISTANT
Jennifer Schewe
Washington State University

RMMLA SECRETARIAT
Washington State University
PO Box 642610
Pullman, WA 99164-2610
Phone: 509-335-4198

The Secretariat of the Rocky Mountain Modern Language Association is hosted by the Department of Foreign Languages and Cultures and the Department of English at Washington State University. Correspondence regarding membership in the association and the annual convention should be addressed to the Secretariat.

Annual dues for individual membership in the association are $35. Graduate students, independent scholars, and emeritus/a annual dues are $25. The annual fee for departments is $100 (which includes one individual member), and for institutions is $200 (includes two to four individual members from different departments on the same campus). Discounted three year membership and lifetime membership rates are also available. Check the website for these.

Neither the Association nor the Editors, nor the sponsoring institution, assumes responsibility for statements of fact or opinion made by contributors.

Copyright ©2008 by the Rocky Mountain Modern Language Association. Printed in the USA. Simultaneously published in Canada. All rights reserved.

ISSN 0361-1299

RMMLA is a member of the
Council of Editors of Learned Journals

CELJ

2 ✦ ROCKY MOUNTAIN REVIEW ✦ SPRING 2008

For determining the form of the qualifying term, LCRI 25.5B tells catalogers to use the AACR2 form of the name exactly as it appears in the name authority file, which can be accessed either by subscription through the OCLC Connexion website at http://connexion.oclc.org or for free from the Library of Congress website at http://authorities.loc.gov.

The name of the issuing corporate body is located on either the title page or the title page verso (here, it is clearly identified on both). Transcribe the name exactly as it appears in the name authority file.

OCLC #228008429

Type: a	ELvl:	Srce: d	GPub:	Ctrl:	Lang: eng
BLvl: s	Form:	Conf: 0	Freq: a	MRec:	Ctry: wau
S/L: 0	Orig:	EntW:	Regl: r	Alph:	
Desc: a	SrTp: p	Cont: o	DtSt: c	Dates: 2008,	9999

	022	0		‡y 0361-1299	
	042			lcd	
CCM 5.3.2	130	0		Rocky Mountain review (Rocky Mountain Modern Language Association)	AACR2 25.5B1
	245	1	0	Rocky Mountain review.	
	246	1		‡i Issues for <fall 2008- > have earlier title on cover and spine: ‡a Rocky Mountain review of language and literature	
	260			Pullman, Wash. : ‡b Rocky Mountain Modern Language Association	
	300			v. : ‡b ill. ; ‡c 26 cm.	
	310			Semiannual	
	362	1		Vol. 62, no. 1 (2008)-	
	500			Description based on first issue.	
	500			Also issued online.	
	650		0	Philology, Modern ‡v Periodicals.	
	710	2		Rocky Mountain Modern Language Association.	
	780	0	0	‡t Rocky Mountain review of language and literature ‡x 0361-1299 ‡w (DLC) 76641242 ‡w (OCoLC)1910486	
	856	4	1	‡u http://rmmla.wsu.edu/ereview/issueindex.asp	

AACR2

25.5B1 - Add a qualifying term or phrase (in parentheses) to the uniform title in order to distinguish identical or similar publications

LCRI

25.5B - Use judgment in determining the most appropriate qualifier for the serial/series being cataloged. Possible qualifiers include corporate body, date of publication, place of publication, as well as descriptive data elements, such as edition statement, GMD, physical medium

RDA

6.6 - Other distinguishing characteristic of the work is a core element when needed to differentiate a work from another work with the same title or from the name of a person, family, or corporate body

6.6.1.1 - Other distinguishing characteristic of the work is a characteristic other than form of work, date of work, or place of origin of the work that serves to differentiate a work from another work with the same title or from the name of a person, family, or corporate body

(Continued on next page)

CCM

5.3.2 - Use a corporate body as a qualifier when the title proper consists solely of very general words that indicate the type of publication and/or periodicity

- Use when the place of publication as a qualifier has already been used by another serial publication of the same name

- Use when it is known that more than one serial with the same title is published in the same place

- If there is more than one corporate body associated with the serial work, use the issuing body as qualifier rather than the publisher

- If there is more than one body equally responsible for issuing the serial, use the one that appears first

- Give the corporate body in the qualifier exactly as it is found in the name authority record (i.e., as it appears in the 110 field in the name authority record) or as it would be established as a heading

- If the authority file name is qualified, retain the parentheses

Uniform Title Qualified by Date

Title: Tightwire

Uniform Title: Tightwire (1979)

Cover

The literary publication *Tight-wire* changed its title to *Tightwire Publications* in 1978. It changed its title back to *Tightwire* in 1979. To assist in user access to the new title, a uniform title was created by using the date of publication as the qualifier, thus distinguishing it from the *Tight-wire* published earlier.

Title page

When using the date of publication as a qualifying element, be certain to use the date of first known issuance (i.e., the date found in the 260 field).

OCLC #3439502 for the original title | **OCLC #10809794 for the first title change**

022			0822-9945		022			0832-5650
245	0	0	Tightwire.		245	0	0	Tightwire publications.
260			Kingston, Ont. ‡b [s.n.]		260			Kingston, Ont. : ‡b [Tightwire Publications, ‡c 1978-1979]
362	0		-v. 3, ed. 1; -Jan./Feb. 1978.		362	0		[Vol. 3, no. 2] (Mar./Apr. 1978)-[v. 4, no. 1/2/3/4] (Jan./Feb./Mar./Apr. 79).
785	0	0	‡t Tightwire publications ‡x 0832-5650 ‡w (OCoLC)10809794		780	0	0	‡t Tightwire ‡x 0822-9945 ‡w (OCoLC)3439502
					785	0	0	‡t Tightwire (1979) ‡x 0702-9004 ‡w (OCoLC)18110446

The name of the issuing corporate body is located on either the title page or the title page verso (here, it is clearly identified on both). Transcribe the name exactly as it appears in the name authority file.

OCLC #18110446 for the second title change

Type: a	ELvl:	Srce: d	GPub:	Ctrl:	Lang: eng
BLvl: s	Form:	Conf: 0	Freq: b	MRec:	Ctry: onc
S/L: 0	Orig:	EntW:	Regl: r	Alph: a	
Desc: a	SrTp: p	Cont:	DtSt: c	Dates: 1979,	9999

022		0702-9004	
042		nlc ‡a isds/c	

CCM 5.3.3 | 130 | 0 | Tightwire (1979) | AACR2 25.5B1

245	0	0	Tightwire.
260			[Kingston, Ont. : ‡b Tightwire Publications, ‡c 1979]-
300			v. : ‡b ill. ; ‡c 28 cm.
310			Bimonthly
362	0		Vol. 5, no. 5/6 (May/June [1979])-
500			At head of title: Prison for women.
500			Title from cover.
650		0	Women prisoners ‡z Ontario ‡z Kingston ‡v Periodicals.
780	0	0	‡t Tightwire publications. ‡x 0832-5650 ‡w (OCoLC)10809794 ‡w (DLC)cn 84030776

AACR2

25.5B1 - Add a qualifying term or phrase (in parentheses) to the uniform title in order to distinguish identical or similar publications

LCRI

25.5B - Use judgment in determining the most appropriate qualifier for the serial being cataloged. Date of publication is one of the possible qualifiers given here in the list to be used to construct a uniform title

RDA

6.4 - Date of work is a core element when needed to differentiate a work from another work with the same title or from the name of a person, family, or corporate body

6.4.1.1 - Date of work is the earliest date associated with a work

– Date of work may be the date the work was created or the date the work was first published or released

6.4.1.3 - Record dates in terms of the calendar preferred by the agency creating the data

– Record the date of the work by giving the year or years alone

CCM

5.3.3 - Dates, as qualifiers, may be used alone or with the place or corporate body

– When a second qualifier is needed to supplement a place or corporate body qualifier, the date of publication is given

– The date given as a qualifier is the publishing date found in field 260 subfield c, not the chronological designation

– When basing the description on a later issue and the beginning date of publication is unknown, use the publication date or assumed publication date of the issue upon which the description is based

– Punctuation should follow the rules spelled out in AACR2 23.4A1

Uniform Title Qualified by Physical Medium

Title: Tissue Engineering

Uniform Title: Tissue engineering (Online)

OCLC #3045376 (Print version)

022	0		1076-3279 ǂl 1076-3279 ǂ2 1
245	0	0	Tissue engineering.
260			Larchmont, NY : ǂb Mary Ann Liebert, ǂc c1995-
300			v. : ǂb ill. ; ǂc 28 cm.
310			Bimonthly, ǂb 1999
362	1		Vol. 1, no. 1 (spring 1995)-vol. 13, no. 12 (Dec. 2007).
530			Also available to subscribers via the World Wide Web.
776	1		ǂt Tissue engineering (Online) ǂx 1557-8690 ǂw (DLC) 2005214595 ǂw (OCoLC)45193934

The journal *Tissue Engineering* is available in print and online formats. Because the print version of the serial was cataloged first, no uniform title was applied to the record. When new and back issues of *Tissue Engineering* were made available online, a new record was created, with the uniform title qualified by "online" to distinguish it from the print version.

Note that LCRI 25.5B instructs the cataloger to "generally avoid use of the terms 'print' and 'text' as qualifiers because they are vague and there is not a consensus as to their appropriate use." When breaking the conflict between separate headings for the same title published in multiple physical media, add a qualifier to the heading for the physical medium that is not printed text on paper (even if that means assigning a qualifier to a heading in an existing record). However, it is worth pointing out that under CSR practice, uniform titles are no longer created for this purpose. Catalogers are only required to create uniform titles for monographic series and generic titles, such as *Newsletter*, *Annual Report*, and *Journal*.

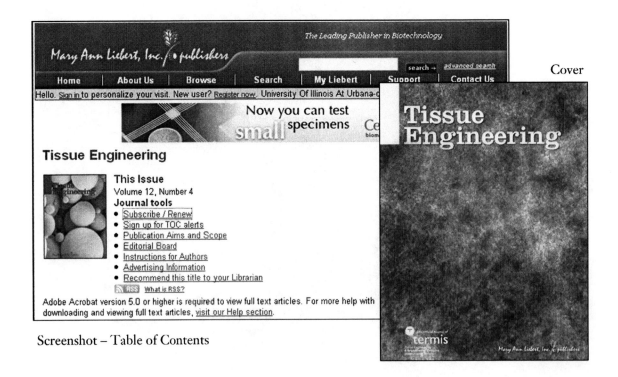

Cover

Screenshot – Table of Contents

OCLC #45193934 (Online version)

Type: a	ELvl:	Srce: d	GPub:	Ctrl:	Lang: eng
BLvl: s	Form: s	Conf: 0	Freq: q	MRec:	Ctry: nyu
S/L: 0	Orig: s	EntW:	Regl: r	Alph: a	
Desc: a	SrTp: p	Cont:	DtSt: d	Dates: 1995	2007

022	0		1557-8690 ‡y 1076-3279 ‡2 1
042			lcd ‡a nsdp
130	0		Tissue engineering (Online)
245	1	0	Tissue engineering ‡h [electronic resource].
260			New Rochelle, NY: ‡b Mary Ann Liebert, Inc., ‡c [1995-2007]
310			Monthly, ‡b 2004-2007
321			Bimonthly, ‡b 1999-2003
321			Quarterly, ‡b 1995-1998
362	0		Vol. 1, no. 1 (Mar. 1995)-v. 13, no. 12 (Dec. 2007).
500			Title from article PDF (publisher's Web site, viewed May 29, 2008).
515			Some issues combined.
530			Also issued in print.
538			Mode of access: World Wide Web.
650		0	Tissue engineering ‡v Periodicals.
650		0	Biomedical engineering ‡v Periodicals.
650		0	Biomedical materials ‡v Periodicals.
776	1		‡t Tissue engineering ‡x 1076-3279 ‡w (DLC)sn 94005129 ‡w (OCoLC)30453761
856	4	0	‡u *http://www.liebertonline.com/loi/ten*

CCM 5.3.4 (left of 130); AACR2 25.5B1 (right of 130)

AACR2

25.5B1 - Add a qualifying term or phrase (in parentheses) to the uniform title in order to distinguish identical or similar publications

LCRI

25.5B - Use judgment in determining the most appropriate qualifier for the serial being cataloged. Possible qualifiers given here include descriptive data elements (e.g., edition statement, GMD, physical medium)

RDA

6.3 - Form of work is a core element when needed to differentiate a work from another work with the same title or from the name of a person, family, or corporate body

(Continued on next page)

CCM

5.3.4 - Prefer a more specific term when using the medium as qualifier (i.e. "online" or "CD-ROM" is preferred over more general terms such as "electronic resource", which is the GMD)

- Uniform titles are not created to differentiate different physical manifestations of a serial when one is a republication of the other (e.g., a microfilm reproduction, a reprint)
- Since CCM treats most remote electronic serials as simultaneous editions rather than electronic reproductions, a uniform title qualified by the physical medium is used if the online and print version titles conflict

31.5 - Uniform titles (created according to LCRI 25.5B)

Uniform Titles for Serials With Later Title Changed Back to an Earlier Title

Titles: Lotus; Lotus International; Lotus

Uniform Titles: Lotus (Venice, Italy: 1965); Lotus (Milan, Italy: 1991)

Title Page

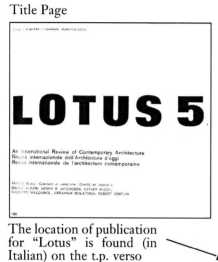

The location of publication for "Lotus" is found (in Italian) on the t.p. verso

The journal *Lotus* began its publication in Venice, Italy, in 1965. Around 1974, it changed its title to *Lotus International* and then reverted back to its original title *Lotus* in 1991 when it began publication in Milan, Italy. Records with uniform titles were created to reflect these changes. The qualifiers in the uniform titles are constructed from the publication location as well as the initial date of publication for the titles. The two qualifiers are separated by a space-colon-space.

Title Page Verso

> LOTUS
> An international Review of contemporary Architecture
> Rivista internazionale dell'architettura contemporanea
> Revue internationale de l'architecture contemporaine
> Direttore responsabile: Bruno Alfieri.
> Collaboratori / Contributors: Esther McCoy, Alberto Rosselli, Giulia Verd
> Dorfles, Margit Staber, Angelo Mangiarotti, Mario Galvagni, Giuseppe Ma
> Allan Temko, David Gebhard, Christopher Alexander, Henry R. Hitchco
> Redazione: Venezia, san Marco 2291, telefono 38731.
> Fotografo: Gianni Berengo Gardin.

According to the basic principles guiding uniform title creation, a uniform title is usually assigned to the title being cataloged and it is not necessary to retrospectively add a qualifier to a heading in an existing record. However, if records for all the titles are being created or edited at the same time, a uniform title may be constructed for each (CCM 5.2.1). In this case, separate uniform titles have been assigned to the earlier *Lotus* and the later *Lotus*.

OCLC #1783117 for the original title

Type: a	ELvl:	Srce:	GPub:	Ctrl:	Lang: eng
BLvl: s	Form:	Conf: 0	Freq: a	MRec:	Ctry: it
S/L: 0	Orig:	EntW:	Regl: r	Alph: a	
Desc: a	SrTp:	Cont:	DtSt: d	Dates: 1965,	1970

022		0076-101X ‡2 z	
041	0	Engfregeritaspa	
042		Lc	
CCM 5.3.6 → 130	0	Lotus (Venice, Italy : 1965)	← AACR2 25.5B1
245	0 0	Lotus : ‡b architectural annual.	
260		Venezia : ‡b B. Alfieri, ‡c [1965?-	
300		7 v. : ‡b ill. (some col.), plans ; ‡c 24 x 25 cm.	
362	0	1964/1965-	
362	1	Ceased publication with no. 7, 1970.	
500		Stamped on t.p.: Distributed by Wittenborn, New York, 1964/65-<1966/67>	
530		Also issued online.	
546		English, French, German, Italian, or Spanish.	
650	0	Architecture ‡v Periodicals.	
650	0	Industrial design ‡v Periodicals.	
785	0 0	‡t Lotus international ‡w (DLC) 77659330 ‡w (OCoLC)3076558	

(Continued on next page)

OCLC #3076558 for the first title change

245	0	0	Lotus international.
260			Milano : ‡b Industrie grafiche editoriali, ‡c [1974?-c1990]
300			59 v. : ‡b ill. (some col.) ; ‡c 26 cm.
310			Quarterly
362	0		8-67.
780	0	0	‡t Lotus (Venice, Italy : 1965) ‡x 0076-101X ‡w (DLC) 64056568 ‡w (OCoLC)1783117
785	0	0	‡t Lotus (Milan, Italy : 1991) ‡w (DLC) 2002205262 ‡w (OCoLC)49888329

Cover

Title Page Verso

OCLC #49888329 for the second title change with the uniform title

Type: a	ELvl:	Srce:	GPub:	Ctrl:	Lang: eng
BLvl: s	Form:	Conf: 0	Freq: q	MRec:	Ctry: it
S/L: 0	Orig:	EntW:	Regl: r	Alph:	
Desc: a	SrTp: p	Cont:	DtSt: c	Dates: 1991,	9999

	042			Lc
	041	0		Engita
CCM 5.3.6	130	0		Lotus (Milan, Italy : 1991)

AACR2 25.5B1

	245	0	0	Lotus : ‡b quarterly architectural review.
	246	1	3	Lotus international
	260			Milan, Italy : ‡b Elemond Periodici, ‡c c1991-
	300			v. : ‡b ill. (some col.) ; ‡c 28 cm.
	310			Quarterly
	362	0		68-
	500			Cover title.
	546			English and Italian.
	650		0	Architecture ‡v Periodicals.
	650		0	City planning ‡v Periodicals.
	780	0	0	‡t Lotus international ‡w (OCoLC)3076558 ‡w (DLC) 77649330

AACR2

25.5B1 - Add a qualifying term or phrase (in parentheses) to the uniform title in order to distinguish identical or similar publications

LCRI

25.5B - For multiple qualifiers: if more than one qualifier is needed, separate the qualifiers with a space-colon-space within one set of parentheses. Exception: if one of the qualifiers is "(Series)," give that qualifier first and enclose each qualifier in its own set of parentheses

RDA

6.27.1.9 - For additions to access points representing works, add one or more of the following, as appropriate:

a) a term indicating the form of work (see 6.3)

b) the date of the work (see 6.4)

c) the place of origin of the work (see 6.5), and/or

d) a term indicating another distinguishing characteristic of the work (see 6.6)

CCM

5.3.6 - Multiple qualifiers may be combined (separate qualifiers by a space, colon, space)

Uniform Titles When the Title Remains the Same but the Name of a Corporate Body Used as Qualifier Changes

Titles: Publication - Extension Division, Virginia Polytechnic Institute; Publication Uniform Titles: Publication (Virginia Polytechnic Institute. Extension Division); Publication (Virginia Polytechnic Institute and State University. Extension Division)

Cover

Cover

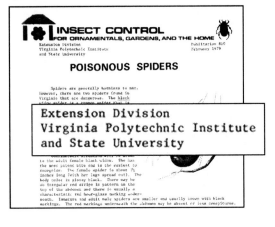

The name of the issuing body for the Extension Division's generic title *Publication* changed three times over the course of this serial's run, although the title *Publication* itself did not change. Because the corporate body is used as qualifier in the uniform title, and the name of the body has changed, a new record for the serial has been created with each corporate body name change. The following three examples show the different records created to reflect the changes.

The serial was first issued under the name *Virginia Polytechnic Institute. Extension Division*, and the uniform title was *Publication (Virginia Polytechnic Institute. Extension Division)*.

The title proper *Publication* and the name of the issuing body "Virginia Polytechnic Institute, Extension Division" can be found on the cover and the cover verso.

When the name of the issuing body changed to "Virginia Polytechnic Institute and State University. : Extension Division," a new record was created with the uniform title *Publication (Virginia Polytechnic Institute and State University. Extension Division)*. The established form of the corporate body's name as found in the authority record was used as the qualifier.

Because the title of the publication is still the generic term *Publication*, the name of the issuing body is used as the qualifier.

OCLC #4401162

	Type: a	ELvl:	Srce: d	GPub:	Ctrl:		Lang: eng
	BLvl: s	Form:	Conf: 0	Freq:	MRec:		Ctry: vau
	S/L: 0	Orig:	EntW:	Regl: x	Alph: a		
	Desc:	SrTp: m	Cont:	DtSt: d	Dates: 1968,	1970	

	022	1	0083-6478 ‡2 1
	042		Nsdp
	043		n-us-va
CCM 5.3.2	**130**	**0**	**Publication (Virginia Polytechnic Institute. Extension Division)**
	245	0 0	Publication - Extension Division, Virginia Polytechnic Institute.
	260		Blacksburg, Va., ‡b Virginia Polytechnic Institute, Extension Division, ‡c 1968-1970.
	362	0	no. 1-
	650	0	Agriculture ‡z Virginia.
	785	0 0	‡t Publication - Extension Division, Virginia Polytechnic Institute and State University ‡x 0093-2809 ‡w (OCoLC)4403300

(AACR2 25.5B1 marginal note beside the 130 field)

AACR2

25.5B1 - Add a qualifying term or phrase (in parentheses) to the uniform title in order to distinguish identical or similar publications

LCRI

25.5B - If corporate body is used as qualifier in the uniform title, and then the name of the body changes or the body is no longer involved with the serial, create a new record for the serial

- If the name of the body changes but one name authority record is used for both forms of name or if the heading on the one name authority record is revised, do not create a new record for the serial

- Change the form of name in the qualifier, as necessary, to match the heading in the name authority record

RDA

1.6.2.4 - Create a new description if there is a change in responsibility that requires a change in the identification of the serial as a work

6.1.3.2 - If there is a change in responsibility, and the change affects the name of a person, family, or corporate body used as an addition to the authorized access point representing the work (see 6.27.1.9), then the change requires the construction of an authorized access point representing a new work

CCM

5.3.2 - Use a corporate body as a qualifier when the title proper consists solely of very general words that indicate the type of publication and/or periodicity; give the corporate body in the qualifier exactly as it is found in the 110 field in the name authority record or as it would be established as a heading

(Continued on next page)

OCLC #4403300

Type: a	ELvl:	Srce: d	GPub: s	Ctrl:	Lang: eng
BLvl: s	Form:	Conf: 0	Freq:	MRec:	Ctry: vau
S/L: 0	Orig:	EntW:	Regl: x	Alph: a	
Desc: a	SrTp: m	Cont:	DtSt: d	Dates: 1970,	198u

	022	0	0093-2809 ‡2 1
	042		Nsdp
	043		n-us-va
CCM 5.3.2	130	0	Publication (Virginia Polytechnic Institute and State University. Extension Division) AACR2 25.5B1
	245	0 0	Publication / ‡c Extension Division, Virginia Polytechnic Institute and State University.
	260		[Blacksburg, Va.] : ‡b The Division
	300		v. : ‡b ill. ; ‡c 28 cm.
	310		Irregular
	362	1	Began in 1970?
	500		Description based on: 390 (Aug. 1970); title from cover.
	650	0	Agricultural extension work ‡z Virginia.
	650	0	Agriculture ‡z Virginia.
	710	2	Virginia Polytechnic Institute and State University. ‡b Extension Division.
	780	0 0	‡t Publication (Virginia Polytechnic Institute. Extension Division) ‡x 0083-6478 ‡w (DLC)sn 79009689 ‡w (OCoLC)4401162
	785	0 0	‡t Publication (Virginia Cooperative Extension Service) ‡w (OCoLC) 14580861

The final name change (to Virginia Cooperative Extension Service) required the creation of a third bibliographic record with a new uniform title.

Uniform Titles When the Title Changes Back and Forth

Title: California cultivator

Uniform Title: California cultivator (Los Angeles, Calif. : 1932)

The farm journal *California Cultivator and Poultry Keeper* began its publication in the 1890s and has changed its name multiple times: to *California Cultivator* in 1900; to *California Cultivator and Livestock and Dairy Journal* in 1918; and back to *California Cultivator* in 1932. The final change returned the publication to an earlier name—*California Cultivator*—when the journal was published from 1900 to 1918.

OCLC #36035425 for the original title

245	0	0	California cultivator and poultry keeper.
260			Los Angeles, Cal. : ǂb Goodwin & Thompson, Props.
362	0		-v. 13, no. 12 (Dec. 1899).
785	0	0	ǂt California cultivator ǂw (DLC) sn2007060107 ǂw (OCoLC)1552538

OCLC #1552538 for the first title change

245	0	0	California cultivator.
260			Los Angeles, Cal. : ǂb G.H.A. Goodwin
362	0		Vol. 14, no. 1 (Jan. 1900)-v. 50, no. 8 (Feb. 23, 1918).
780	0	0	ǂt California cultivator and poultry keeper ǂw (DLC)sn2007060109 ǂw (OCoLC)36035425
785	0	0	ǂt California cultivator and livestock and dairy journal ǂw (DLC)sn2007060110 ǂw (OCoLC)123905819

OCLC #123905819 for the second title change

245	0	0	California cultivator and livestock and dairy journal.
260			Los Angeles, Cal. : ǂb Cultivator Pub. Co., Inc.
310			Weekly
362	0		Vol. 50, no. 9 (Mar. 2, 1918)-v. 79, no. 6 (Aug. 6, 1932).
780	0	0	ǂt California cultivator ǂw (DLC)sn2007060107 ǂw (OCoLC)1552538
785	0	0	ǂt California cultivator (Los Angeles, Calif. : 1932) ǂw (DLC)sn2007060111 ǂw (OCoLC) 123905861

Cover

Cover

Cover

Cover

In order to distinguish the later *California Cultivator* (1932) from the earlier *California Cultivator* (1900), a uniform title was created for the later publication by using dates combined with the place. According to LCRI 25.5B, a cataloger should not predict a conflict. However, if a conflict does occur, it should be resolved by the addition of a uniform title heading in the bibliographic record being created. A uniform title heading is generally not added to the existing record (exceptions have been noted in the previous example). Therefore, the uniform title is only present in the bibliographic record for the later *California Cultivator*, published in 1932 (OCLC #123905861), and not in the bibliographic record for the earlier *California Cultivator*, published from 1900 to 1918 (OCLC #1552538).

OCLC #123905861 for the third title change

Type: a	ELvl:	Srce: d	GPub:	Ctrl:		Lang: eng
BLvl: s	Form:	Conf: 0	Freq: w	MRec:		Ctry: cau
S/L: 0	Orig: e	EntW:	Regl: r	Alph: a		
Desc: a	SrTp: p	Cont:	DtSt: d	Dates: 1932,		19uu

	042		Lcd	
	043		a-bg---	
CCM 5.3.6	130	0	California cultivator (Los Angeles, Calif. : 1932)	AACR2 25.5B1
	245	0 0	California cultivator.	
	260		Los Angeles, [Calif.] : ‡b Cultivator Pub. Co., Inc.	
	310		Weekly	
	362	0	Vol. 79, no. 7 (Aug. 13, 1932)-	
	650	0	Agriculture ‡z California ‡v Periodicals.	
	651	0	Los Angeles (Calif.) ‡v Periodicals.	
	651	0	San Francisco (Calif.) ‡v Periodicals.	
	752		United States ‡b California ‡c Los Angeles ‡d Los Angeles.	
	780	0 0	‡t California cultivator and livestock and dairy journal ‡w (DLC) sn2007060110 ‡w (OCoLC)123905819	

AACR2

25.5B1 - Add a qualifying term or phrase (in parentheses) to the uniform title in order to distinguish identical or similar publications

LCRI

25.5B - Resolve the conflict by using a uniform title heading or name heading/uniform title in the bibliographic or series authority record being created. Do not also add a uniform title heading or a name heading/uniform title to the existing record

RDA

6.27.1.9 - For additions to access points representing works, add one or more of the following, as appropriate:

a) a term indicating the form of work (see 6.3)

b) the date of the work (see 6.4)

c) the place of origin of the work (see 6.5), and/or

d) a term indicating another distinguishing characteristic of the work (see 6.6)

CCM

5.3.6 - Multiple qualifiers may be combined (separate qualifiers by a space, colon, space)

Uniform Title With Corporate Body as Main Entry

Title: Annual Report

Uniform Title: Annual report (1998)

The annual report issued by American Museum of Natural History started its title as *The . . . Annual Report of the American Museum of Natural History* in 1870. The title changed to *Biennial Report* in 1997 and changed again to *Annual Report* in 1998. The search results in the OCLC bibliographic utility included other records for *Annual Report* issued by the same corporate body. Therefore, a uniform title was created for *Annual Report* (1998).

OCLC #20691637

110	2		American Museum of Natural History.
245	1	8	The . . . annual report of the American Museum of Natural History.
260			New York : ‡b American Museum of Natural History, ‡c 1870-1994.
300			v. : ‡b ill. ; ‡c 22-29 cm.
310			Annual
362	0		1st (Jan. 1870)-1993/1994.
785	0	0	American Museum of Natural History. ‡t Biennial report ‡w (DLC)sn 98053067 ‡w (OCoLC) 39791419

Cover

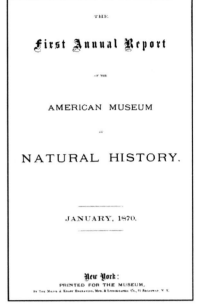

OCLC #39791419

110	2		American Museum of Natural History.
245	1	0	Biennial report / ‡c American Museum of Natural History.
260			New York, N.Y. : ‡b The Museum, ‡c c1997.
300			1 v. : ‡b ill. ; ‡c 28 cm.
310			Biennial
362			1994-95/1995-96.
776	0	8	‡i Also issued online: American Museum of Natural History. ‡t Biennial report ‡w (DLC) 2009252136 ‡w (OCoLC)316122998
780	0	0	American Museum of Natural History. ‡t Annual report of the American Museum of Natural History ‡w (DLC) 2004249039 ‡w (OCoLC)20691637
785	0	0	American Museum of Natural History. ‡s Annual report (1998) ‡w (DLC)sn 99044510 ‡w (OCoLC) 41281786

Cover

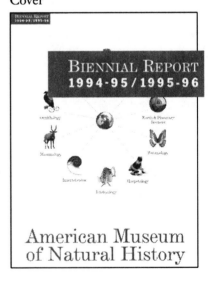

Because the corporate body American Museum of Natural History is the main entry in the 110 field, the uniform title is entered in a 240 field (rather than a 130 uniform title main entry field). It is made up of the title proper—*Annual Report*—plus a parenthetical qualifier (1998).

Please note: The date used as qualifier is the publishing date in the 260 field, not the chronological designation in the 362 field.

Cover

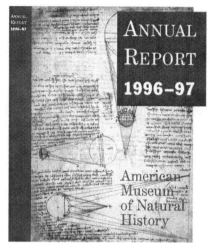

OCLC #41281786

Type: a	ELvl:	Srce: d	GPub:	Ctrl:	Lang: eng
BLvl: s	Form:	Conf: 0	Freq: a	MRec:	Ctry: nyu
S/L: 0	Orig:	EntW:	Regl: r	Alph:	
Desc: a	SrTp: p	Cont:	DtSt: d	Dates: 1997,	200u

	042		lcd	
	043		n-us-ny	
	110	2	American Museum of Natural History.	AACR2 21.1B2
CCM 5.3.3	240	1 0	Annual report (1998)	25.5B1
	245	1 0	Annual report / ‡c American Museum of Natural History.	
	260		New York : ‡b American Museum of Natural History, ‡c 1998-	
	300		v. : ‡b ill. ; ‡c 31 cm.	
	310		Annual	
	362		1996/97-	
	500		Title from cover.	
	500		Last issue consulted: 1997/98.	
	610	2 0	American Museum of Natural History ‡v Periodicals.	
	650	0	Natural history museums ‡z New York (State) ‡z New York ‡v Periodicals.	
	776	0 8	‡i Also issued online: American Museum of Natural History. ‡s Annual report (1998). ‡t Annual report ‡w (DLC) 2009252137 ‡w (OCoLC)316122990	
	780	0 0	American Museum of Natural History. ‡t Biennial report ‡w (DLC)sn 98053067 ‡w (OCoLC)39791419	
	785	0 0	American Museum of Natural History. ‡t Report for fiscal years ... ‡w (DLC) 2007223150 ‡w (OCoCL)64283101	

(Continued on next page)

AACR2

21.1B2 - Works emanating from a single corporate body that are of an administrative nature dealing with the corporate body itself

25.5B1 - Add a qualifying term or phrase (in parentheses) to the uniform title in order to distinguish identical or similar publications

LCRI

25.5B - For serials entered under name heading, use judgment in determining the most appropriate qualifier for the serial/series being cataloged. Possible qualifiers are

– Date of publication: choose the date of publication (not date from chronological designation) of the first issue published or the earliest issue in hand, in that order of preference

– Descriptive data elements (e.g., edition statement)

RDA

6.4 - Date of work is a core element when needed to differentiate a work from another work with the same title or from the name of a person, family, or corporate body

6.4.1.1 - Date of work is the earliest date associated with a work

– Date of work may be the date the work was created or the date the work was first published or released

6.4.1.3 - Record dates in terms of the calendar preferred by the agency creating the data

– Record the date of the work by giving the year or years alone

CCM

5.2.3 - Entry under corporate body (Fields 110/240 or 111/240): create a uniform title for a serial entered under corporate body when both the corporate body and title are the same as that found on another serial record

5.3.3 - Dates, as qualifiers, may be used alone or with the place or corporate body. The date given as a qualifier is the publishing date found in field 260 subfield c

Uniform Title for Different Language Editions

Title: Annual Report

Uniform Title: Memoria anual de labores. English.

Cover

Cover

In addition to differentiating serials, uniform titles also bring serials together. They are used to show an association between different language editions of the same serial. When creating uniform titles for publications in different language editions, one should first decide which language edition can serve as the primary edition, as it will provide the title used to create the uniform title on all other editions. The rules in AACR2 25.3C1-C3 set out criteria to help catalogers decide which edition serves as the "primary edition."

In this example, the publication is available in Spanish and English. Because the Spanish title—*Memoria Anual de Labores*—is in the same language as the main entry—*Banco Centroamericano de Integración Económica*—the Spanish is chosen as the primary edition. It therefore needs no uniform title. For all other editions, the title of the primary edition is entered in subfield ‡a of the uniform title field and the language of the item is added in subfield ‡l. Subfield ‡l is preceded by a full stop. Uniform titles with language qualifiers can be input in either fields 130 or 240 depending on the entry. In our record, because there is already a corporate body as main entry in the 110 field, the uniform title is entered as an added entry in the 240 field.

Under CSR practice, it is not required to create a uniform title either in 130 field (as a main entry) or in 240 field (in conjunction with a personal or corporate name main entry) for translations or language editions. Instead, an added entry in fields 730/740 (in addition to any 765 or 775 linking field) should be made to provide collocation with the original language edition. The name of the language of the resource being cataloged is coded in subfield ‡l of the 730 field.

OCLC #55689377

Type: a	ELvl:	Srce: c	GPub:	Ctrl:	Lang: eng
BLvl: s	Form:	Conf: 0	Freq: a	MRec:	Ctry: ho
S/L: 0	Orig:	EntW:	Regl: r	Alph:	
Desc: a	SrTp:	Cont: s	DtSt: c	Dates: 199u,	9999

	042	lcd
	043	nc----
	110 2	Banco Centroamericano de Integración Económica.
CCM 5.6.2	240 1 0	Memoria anual de labores. ‡l English
	245 1 0	Annual report.
	260	Tegucigalpa, Honduras : ‡b Central American Bank for Economic Integration
	300	v. : ‡b col. ill. ; ‡c 28-35 cm.
	310	Annual
	500	Description based on: 37 (1997/1998 fiscal year)
	500	Latest issue consulted: 42 (fiscal year 2002/2003).
	530	Also issued online.
	580	Also issued in Spanish, with title: Memoria anual de labores.
	610 2 0	Banco Centroamericano de Integración Económica ‡v Periodicals.
	651 0	Central America ‡x Economic integration ‡v Periodicals.
	650 0	Banks and banking ‡z Central America ‡v Periodicals.
	775 1	Banco Centroamericano de Integración Económica. ‡t Memoria anual de labores ‡w (DLC) 2004240543 ‡w (OCoLC)46862891
	780 0 0	Banco Centroamericano de Integración Económica. ‡s Memoria anual. English. ‡t Annual report ‡w (DLC) 94645349 ‡w (OCoLC)31714026

(marginal note, right of 240: AACR2 25.5C)

AACR2

25.5C - When the publication is issued in a language that is other than the original (i.e., the primary edition), add the name of the language of the item to the uniform title

– Precede the language subfield by a full stop

25.3C2 - If a work entered under the heading for a corporate body is published simultaneously in different languages and under different titles, none of which is known to be the original language or title, use as the uniform title the title in the language in which the name of the corporate body is entered in the catalogue

LCRI

25.5C - When naming a language in a uniform title, base the name on the form found in the current edition of the MARC Code List for Languages (and the updates published in Cataloging Service Bulletin and at http://www.loc.gov/marc/languages)

RDA

6.11 - Language of expression is a core element when needed to differentiate an expression of a work from another expression of the same work

6.11.1.3 - Record the language or languages of the expression using an appropriate term or terms in the language preferred by the agency creating the data. Select terms from a standard list of names of languages, if available

CCM

5.6.2 - One edition is chosen according to various criteria to serve as the "primary edition" (see AACR2 25.3C1-C3) and the title of that edition is used in the uniform title on all other editions

– Do not create a uniform title for the primary edition (unless needed for other reasons)

– For editions other than the primary edition, add the language of the publication to the uniform title in subfield ‡l

– Use fields 130 or 240, depending on the entry

Uniform Titles for Both the Original Title and the Changed Title

Title: Space news; Space news international

Uniform Title: Space news (Springfield, Va.); Space news international (Springfield, Va.)

Title from Caption

Title from Caption

The title of the periodical *Space News* changed to *Space News International*, resulting in a new record. Because both titles are not unique (i.e., there are other publications bearing the same titles), uniform titles are created for the original title and the changed title.

Note that because title changes are involved, linking fields 780 and 785 are needed. The titles in subfield ‡t in these linking fields are taken from the uniform title in the 130 field rather than from the title proper in the 245 field of the related record.

OCLC #20496753

Type: a	ELvl:	Srce: d	GPub:	Ctrl:	Lang: eng
BLvl: s	Form:	Conf: 0	Freq: w	MRec:	Ctry: vau
S/L: 0	Orig: e	EntW:	Regl: r	Alph: a	
Desc: a	SrTp: p	Cont:	DtSt: d	Dates: 1990,	2001

	022	0	1046-6940 ‡2 1
	037		‡b Space News, Springfield, VA 22159-0500
	042		nsdp ‡a lc
CCM 5.3.1	130	0	Space news (Springfield, Va.) *AACR2 25.5B1*
	245	1 0	Space news.
	260		Springfield, Va. : ‡b Times Journal Co., ‡c [1990]-2001.
	300		v. : ‡b ill. (mostly col.) ; ‡c 37 cm.
	310		Weekly
	362	0	Vol. 1, no. 1 (Jan. 15-21, 1990)-vol. 12, no. 38 (Oct. 8, 2001).
	500		Title from caption.
	500		Final issue consulted.
	515		First issue preceded by 2 preview issues dated: Sept. 18, 1989 and Nov. 13, 1989.
	530		Also issued online by subscription.
	650	0	Astronautics ‡v Periodicals.

650		0	Aerospace industries ǂv Periodicals.
740	0		Spacenews.com
776	1		Microfilm. ǂb Washington, D.C. : ǂd Library of Congress Preservation Microfilming Program ǂw (DLC)sf 94093463 ǂw (OCoLC)30953548
785	0	0	ǂt Space news international (Springfield, Va.) ǂx 1937-1462 ǂw (DLC) 2007202074 ǂw (OCoLC)48386660
856	4	1	ǂz Username and password required for access: ǂu *http://www.space.com/ spacenews/*

AACR2

25.5B1 - Add a qualifying term or phrase (in parentheses) to the uniform title in order to distinguish identical or similar publications

LCRI

25.5B - When creating a bibliographic record for a serial, construct a uniform title made up of the title proper plus a parenthetical qualifier to distinguish the serial from another with the same title proper in a bibliographic record

- For choice of cataloging terms, catalogers should use judgment in determining the most appropriate qualifier for the serial being cataloged

- Some possible qualifiers are date of publication, physical medium, and place of publication

- If the serial is published in more than one place, choose as the qualifying term the place that would be named first in the publication, distribution, etc. area for the first issue published, the earliest issue for which a place is known or the earliest issue in hand, in that order of preference. If the name of the local place has changed, use in the qualifier the name the place had at the time the first/earliest issue was published

- As for the form of the place of publication, use the AACR2 form from the name authority record for the place minus any cataloger's addition (cf. AACR2 24.6); record the name of the larger place preceded by a comma (cf. AACR2 23.4A1)

RDA

6.27.1.9 - For additions to access points representing works, add one or more of the following, as appropriate:

a) a term indicating the form of work (see 6.3)

b) the date of the work (see 6.4)

c) the place of origin of the work (see 6.5), and/or

d) a term indicating another distinguishing characteristic of the work (see 6.6)

CCM

5.3.1 - The place used for this type of uniform title is that of the publication of the earliest issue

- This place name will match the location identified in the 260 field and should be at the city level

- If the exact city is unknown, it is appropriate to use a higher jurisdiction

- Punctuation should follow the rules spelled out in AACR2 23.4A1

(Continued on next page)

OCLC #48386660

Type: a	ELvl:	Srce: d	GPub:	Ctrl:	Lang: eng	
BLvl: s	Form:	Conf: 0	Freq: w	MRec:	Ctry: vau	
S/L: 0	Orig: e	EntW:	Regl: r	Alph: a		
Desc: a	SrTp: p	Cont:	DtSt: c	Dates: 2001,	9999	

	022	0	1937-1462 ǂy 1046-6940 ǂ2 1
	037		ǂb Space.com, 6883 Commercial Dr., Springfield, VA 22159-0500
	042		lccopycat ǂa nsdp
CCM 5.3.1	130	0	Space news international (Springfield, Va.) AACR2 25.5B1
	245	1 0	Space news international.
	246	1 7	Space news
	260		Springfield, Va. : ǂb Space.com
	310		Weekly
	362	1	Began with vol. 12, no. 39 (Oct. 15, 2001).
	500		Published: Imaginova Corp., <Apr. 2007->
	500		Description based on: Vol. 13, no. 3 (Jan. 21, 2002); title from caption.
	500		Latest issue consulted: Vol. 18, no. 16 (Apr. 23, 2007).
	530		Also issued online by subscription.
	580		Issued in conjuction with: International space directory and industry source book.
	650	0	Astronautics ǂv Periodicals.
	776	1	ǂt Space news international (Springfield, Va. : Online) ǂw (OCoLC) 60640230
	780	0 0	ǂt Space news (Springfield, Va.) ǂx 1046-6940 ǂw (DLC)90659023 ǂw (OCoLC)20496753
	787	1	ǂt International space directory and industry source book ǂx 1937-1470 ǂw (DLC) 2006242085 ǂw (OCoLC)68728224
	856	4 1	ǂu http://www.space.com/spacenews/

Cover

volume I
trespass

architecture and landscape architecture
faculty and graduate student work at the University of Virginia School of Architecture

EXERCISE 1

You are about to catalog the architectural journal *Lunch*, but there are other publications called *Lunch*. To make the title unique, create a uniform title by using the place of publication (CCM 5.3.1) as the qualifier.

lunch volume 1: *trespass* is published with support from the Arts Council and The School of Architecture Foundation at the University of Virginia.

Copyright © 2006 University of Virginia School of Architecture, Charlottesville, VA
All rights reserved

Library of Congress Card Catalog Number is available.

Editors: Kevin J Bell, Matthew Ibarra, and Ryan Moody
Printed in the United States by Carter Printing, Richmond, VA

University of Virginia School of Architecture
Campbell Hall
P.O. Box 400122
Charlottesville VA 22904-4122
434.924.3715
http://www.arch.virginia.edu

ISBN # 0-9771024-2-4

Cover Verso

OCLC #68225692

Type: a	ELvl:	Srce: c	GPub:	Ctrl:	Lang: eng
BLvl: s	Form:	Conf: 0	Freq: a	MRec:	Ctry: vau
S/L: 0	Orig:	EntW:	Regl: r	Alph: a	
Desc: a	SrTp:	Cont:	DtSt: c	Dates: 2006,	9999

022	0		1931-7786 ‡2 1
037			‡b University of Virginia School of Architecture, Campbell Hall, PO Box 400122, Charlottesville, VA 22904-4122
042			lccopycat ‡a nsdp
130	0		
245	1	0	Lunch.
260			Charlottesville, Va. : ‡b University of Virginia School of Architecture, ‡c c2006-
300			v. : ‡b ill. ; ‡c 26 cm.
310			Annual
362	0		Vol. 1-
500			Title from cover.
500			Some issues also have a distinctive title.
650		0	Architecture ‡v Periodicals.
650		0	Landscape architecture ‡v Periodicals.
710	2		University of Virginia. ‡b School of Architecture.

Title page

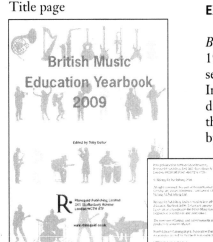

EXERCISE 2

British Music Education Yearbook began publication in 1984. In 1994, it changed its title to *Music Education Yearbook* and subsequently changed to *Rhinegold Guide to Music Education* in 2004. In 2009, it changed back to *British Music Education Yearbook*. To distinguish the latest title *British Music Education Yearbook* from the earlier *British Music Education Yearbook*, create a uniform title by using the initial publication date of the latest title (CCM 5.3.3) as the qualifier.

Title Page Verso

OCLC #270773195

Type: a	ELvl: I	Srce: d	GPub:	Ctrl:	Lang: eng
BLvl: s	Form:	Conf: 0	Freq: a	MRec:	Ctry: enk
S/L: 0	Orig:	EntW:	Regl: r	Alph:	
Desc: a	SrTp:	Cont: r	DtSt: c	Dates: 2009,	9999

022	0		1758-3667
130	0		
245	1	0	British music education yearbook.
260			London : ‡b Rhinegold Pub., ‡c 2009-
300			v. : ‡b ill. (some col.) ; ‡c 30 cm.
310			Annual
362	1		Began with 2009 issue.
500			Description based on first issue.
650		0	Music ‡x Instruction and study ‡z Great Britain ‡v Periodicals.
650		0	Music ‡z Great Britain ‡v Directories.
710	2		Rhinegold Publishing Limited.
780	0	0	‡t Rhinegold guide to music education ‡x 1744-277X ‡w (DLC) 2004204920 ‡w (OCoCL)56394150

Cover

How to Own Gold

Gold has no official monetary role but central banks and individuals hold it for good reason. It serves as a store of value, a means of investment diversification, and as protection from economic or political crises.

by the AIER Research Staff

The history of fiat currencies is that they eventually become worthless. Their decrease in value but usually been accompanied by increasingly severe restrictions on personal economic freedom rationing or seizures of assets and debt new and old. Fiat order relics on promises to redeem depreciate gist currency.

Currencies originated in coins of a fixed weight and fineness. However, today all use fiat currencies. Because a limited amount of gold exists in the world, used paper money can be created without limit, gold is the ultimate protection against the decline in value of currency.

That the current experiment with fiat currency has continued for many decades that price inflation has abated from the peak of the 1970s and 1980s, or that the benefits of increased freedom are increasingly undervalued and accepted around the world, are not, in our view, sufficient reasons to ignore the lesson of history, one of which is that gold has held its value down through the ages.

Paper is paper, gold is money. As a financial asset, gold is unique because it is "no one else's liability." This is the situation with anything tangible that might work, but tables, art, antiques, fine art, jewelry, or other collectibles, the spread between the bid and asked prices for gold is narrow. That is, the price that a person can sell gold for at a given moment in time is usually close to the price that he can buy gold for at that moment. Moreover, gold does not rust or decay, and a relatively large amount of value can be stored in a relatively small space. This means that holding it costs little.

Finally, the value of gold is less dependent on economic and political conditions than any other tangible asset and much less so than stocks, bonds, and other paper investments.

The most frequently cited reason to hold gold, therefore, is to obtain protection for a portion of one's wealth against the possibility of serious economic, monetary, and political disruptions that lead to a breakdown of payment and credit mechanisms based on fiat currency. Gold in one's physical possession cannot default or otherwise have its value decreased in the stroke of a pen.

What most miners produce are bullion bars of approximately 400 troy ounces. That is also what central banks hold, and what is traded at the daily London gold fixings, which set the price of gold for the rest of the world.

But gold ingots are not the best way for individuals to hold gold because they must be assayed whenever they change hands. The expense of an assay cannot be justified for smaller bars, and the difficulties, even if one could afford them, are immense for an individual's purposes.

Gold coins are better; they do not require an assay—their weight, mineral content, quality values are exact.

> The value of gold is less dependent on economic and political conditions than any other tangible asset and much less so than are stocks, bonds, and other paper investments.

This article is updated from AIER's February 2005 *Economic Education Bulletin* by the same authors.

OCLC #300429310

Type: a	ELvl:	Srce:	GPub:	Ctrl:	Lang: eng
BLvl: s	Form:	Conf:	Freq:	MRec:	Ctry: mau
S/L: 0	Orig:	EntW:	Regl:	Alph:	
Desc:	SrTp: p	Cont:	DtSt: c	Dates: 2009,	9999

022	0		ǂy 0424-2769
042			lcd
130	0		
245	1	0	Economic bulletin
246	1	3	AIER economic bulletin
260			Great Barrington, Mass. : ǂb American Institute for Economic Research
300			ǂb ill. ǂc 28 cm.
310			Monthly
362	1		Began with v. 49, no. [1] (Jan. 2009).
500			Description based on: Vol. 49, no. [1] (Jan. 2009); title from caption.
650		0	Finance, Personal ǂv Periodicals.
710	2		American Institute for Economic Research.
780	0	0	ǂt Economic education bulletin ǂx 0424-2769 ǂw (DLC) 79002143 ǂw (OCoLC)2250348

EXERCISE 3

The publication *Economic Bulletin*, issued by the American Institute for Economic Research, has a generic title. In order to make it uniquely identifiable, create a uniform title by using the name of the corporate body (CCM 5.3.2) as the qualifier.

Cover

EXERCISE 4

The *Journal of the Illinois State Historical Society* changed its name to the *Illinois Historical Journal* and then later changed its name back to the *Journal of the Illinois State Historical Society*. A uniform title should be created for the latest title by using the date of publication (CCM 5.3.3) as the qualifier. Fill in the 130 field with the correct uniform title.

Cover Verso

Articles appearing in the *Journal of the Illinois State Historical Society* are abstracted and indexed in both *Historical Abstracts* and *America: History and Life*. The *Journal* is a member of the Conference of Historical Journals.

Neither the editors nor the Illinois State Historical Society assume any responsibility for statements, whether of fact or opinion, made by contributors.

The *Journal of the Illinois State Historical Society* (ISSN 1522-1067) is published four times a year (Spring, Summer, Autumn, and Winter) by The Illinois State Historical Society, 210-1/2 South Sixth Street, Suite 200, Springfield, Illinois 62701-1503, and is printed by William Street Press, Decatur, Illinois.

A copy of the Society's publications list is available upon request.

Copyright 2008 The Illinois State Historical Society

OCLC #40058087

Type: a	ELvl:	Srce: d	GPub: s	Ctrl:	Lang: eng
BLvl: s	Form:	Conf: 0	Freq: q	MRec:	Ctry: ilu
S/L: 0	Orig:	EntW:	Regl: r	Alph: a	
Desc: a	SrTp: p	Cont: o	DtSt: c	Dates: 1998,	9999

022	0	1522-1067 ǂ2 1
037		ǂb Illinois State Historical Society, 1 Old State Capitol Plaza, Springfield, IL 62701-1507
042		nsdp ǂa lc
130	0	
245	1 0	Journal of the Illinois State Historical Society.
260		Springfield, Ill. : ǂb Illinois State Historical Society, ǂc 1998-
300		v. ; ǂc 23 cm.
310		Quarterly
362	0	Vol. 91, no. 2 (summer 1998)-
500		Title from cover.
500		Latest issue consulted: Vol. 92, no. 4 (winter 1999).
650	0	Illinois ǂx History ǂv Periodicals.
710	2	Illinois State Historical Society.
780	0 0	ǂt Illinois historical journal ǂx 0748-8149 ǂw (DLC) 84650610 ǂw (OCoLC)11010786

Title page

BANGLADESH JOURNAL OF PUBLIC ADMINISTRATION
Volume XIV Nmuber I and II 2005

BPATC : P 31/EJ (725)/94
BPATC : LIBRARY : 05035

ISSN 1563-5032

2005
Bangladesh Public Adrmnistration Training Centre
Savar, Dhaka, Bangladesh

All business correspondence should be addressed to the Publication Officer
Bangladesh Public Administration Training Centre
Savar, Dhaka, Bangladesh

Rates of Subscription :
Bangladesh: Tk. 180.00 per issue, Tk. 360.00 per year

EXERCISE 5

The *Bangladesh Journal of Public Administration* has had its title changed back and forth (beginning as the *Bangladesh Journal of Public Administration*, changing to the *Bangladesh Public Administration Journal*, and then reverting back to the *Bangladesh Journal of Public Administration*). In order to be uniquely identified, the latest title should be assigned a uniform title. Enter the uniform title for this publication by using the place of publication and the date of initial publication (CCM 5.3.6) as the qualifiers.

OCLC #42857143

Type: a	ELvl:	Srce: d	GPub:	Ctrl:	Lang: eng
BLvl: s	Form:	Conf: 0	Freq: f	MRec:	Ctry: bg
S/L: 0	Orig:	EntW:	Regl: r	Alph:	
Desc: a	SrTp: p	Cont:	DtSt: c	Dates: 1996,	9999

022		‡y 1563-5032
042		Lcd
043		a-bg---
130	0	
245	0 0	Bangladesh journal of public administration.
260		Savar, Dhaka : ‡b Bangladesh Public Administration Training Centre
300		v. ; ‡c 24 cm.
310		Semiannual
362	1	Began with vol. 5, no. 1 (annual issue 1996).
500		Description based on first issue; title from title page.
515		Some issues combined.
500		Latest issue consulted: Vol. 15, no. 1 & 2 (2006).
651	0	Bangladesh ‡x Politics and government ‡y 1971- ‡v Periodicals.
650	0	Public administration ‡v Periodicals.
650	0	Public administration ‡z Bangladesh ‡v Periodicals.
710	2	Bangladesh Public Administration Training Centre.
710	2	Virginia Cooperative Extension Service.
780	0 0	‡t Bangladesh public administration journal ‡w (DLC)sn 95021439 ‡w (OCoLC)31526872

Notes

CHAPTER 9

Notes

The dynamic nature of serials requires a variety of notes in catalog records. These notes include title-related notes, issuing body notes, notes about the availability of different formats of the resource, notes about numbering irregularities, supplements, complex title changes, etc. While some notes are required and others are optional, they all provide important and useful information not recorded elsewhere in the description. If the bibliographic record contains several notes, they are usually input in 5xx numeric tag order, according to CCM. This chapter will describe some common notes used in serials and explain what they mean and when they should be used. Examples with explanations will be included. Frequency notes have been covered in Chapter 5, so further discussion has been omitted here.

The most commonly used note is the general note recorded in the 500 field, such as:

500 _ _ Vols. for <2000- > have annual supplements.
500 _ _ Each volume also has a distinctive title.
500 _ _ Title from cover.

Prior to May 2010, the 500 note field was also used for "Description based on" (including when it was combined with source of title information) and "Latest issue consulted" notes. In May 2010, OCLC published *Technical Bulletin 258: OCLC-MARC Format Update 2010 Including RDA Changes* (TB 258). One of the new MARC coding fields introduced is the 588 Source of Description Note field, to be used to record these two notes. CONSER has subsequently implemented this field. When following CSR guidelines, catalogers are required to add description based on (DBO) information and combine it with the source of title information in all CSR records, even if cataloging is based on the first issue and even if the source of title is the title page. Catalogers are also required to input a separate 588 note to record latest issue consulted (LIC) information in all CSR records, even when the issue is already cited in a DBO note.

Most other notes are optional. Although serials notes are not prescriptive, catalogers should try to make them as useful and to the point as possible so they help catalog users find, identify, and select the resource they seek.

RESOURCES CONSULTED

AACR2

12.7 Note Area

RDA

2.20 Note

CCM

Module 13 Notes

CONSER Editing Guide (CEG)

Variable Data Fields—5XX Notes

MARC21

5XX fields for notes
500 General Note
515 Numbering Peculiarities Note
525 Supplement Note
530 Additional Physical Form Available Note
546 Language Note
550 Issuing Body Note
580 Linking Entry Complexity Note
588 Source of Description Note
59X Local Note

Genereux, C., and Paul Moeller. (2009). *Notes for Serials Cataloging* (3rd ed.). Santa Barbara, CA: Libraries Unlimited.

Online Audiovisual Catalogers

Source of Title Notes for Internet Resources: http://www.olacinc.org/drupal/?q=node/20

Notes for Source of Title, Description Based On, and Latest Issue Consulted

Title: Algebra & number theory

Cover

When cataloging a serial, a cataloger should document the primary source of information if using a source other than the chief source of information outlined in AACR2 12.0B2 and the specific issue used in creating the record.

According to AACR2 12.0B3, the prescribed source of information for the title and statement of responsibility of a print journal is the title page. When an alternate source of information is utilized, a note must be made. In this example, the journal *Algebra & Number Theory*, a quarterly publication that began in 2007, is issued without a formal title page and the cover is chosen as a title page substitute and thus used as the chief source of information. A 500 note "Title from cover" is used to indicate this.

The first issue Vol. 1, no. 1 (2007) was used as the basis of description when the record was created. AACR2 12.7B23 tells us to make a note only if the description is not based on the first issue or part or on the first iteration. However, according to the (CSR) Metadata Application Profile (MAP), it is mandatory to provide the description based on (DBO) information, even if it is the first issue, and the source of title, even if it is the title page, on all records. This information should be combined (separated by a semicolon) into one 500 note.

Additionally, AACR2 12.7B23 states that if more than one issue or part has been consulted, a cataloger should make a note of the latest issue or part used in making the description. CSR guidelines also require latest issue consulted (LIC) information on all CSR records, so a second 500 field has been added for the "Latest issue consulted" note.

Because the new MARC field 588 for source of description is now available, the issue used as the basis of description and the source of title should be combined and coded in one 588 field, while the latest issue consulted should be given in a separate 588 note. The pair should be kept in this order: DBO always precedes the LIC note.

588 _ _ Description based on: Vol. 1, no. 1 (2007); title from cover.
588 _ _ Latest issue consulted: Vol. 2, no. 2 (2008).

However, if cataloged according to AACR2 rather than CSR guidelines, some records may have stand-alone source of title notes (e.g., when a cataloger has the first issue in hand when cataloging). If this is the case, the 500 field will continue to be used rather than the 588 field. The rational for using the new 588 field is the convenience of the user. The notes for DBO and LIC are more useful for catalogers than for library patrons. Because it is CCM practice to input 5XX notes in numeric tag order, coding this information in 588 fields will move the notes further down in the record. As a result, other important notes will be displayed more prominently in the OPAC display for library patrons.

As of this writing, OCLC has started converting 500 DBO and LIC fields to 588 fields, but it is likely that there will continue to be records with 500 DBO and LIC fields in your local database. Therefore, it is helpful to be familiar with both practices.

OCLC #124075925

	Type a	ELvl	Srce c	GPub	Ctrl	Lang eng
	BLvl s	Form	Conf 0	Freq q	MRec	Ctry cau
	S/L 0	Orig	EntW	Regl r	Alph a	
	Desc a	SrTp p	Cont	DtSt c	Dates 2007	, 9999

	022	0		1937-0652 ‡2 1
	042			lcd ‡a nsdp
	245	0	0	Algebra & number theory.
	246	3		Algebra and number theory
	260			Berkeley, CA : ‡b Mathematical Sciences Publishers, ‡c c2007-
	300			v. ; ‡c 26 cm.
	310			Quarterly
	362	1		Began with v.1, no. 1 (2007).

CCM 13.2.1 8.1.1c	500	Description based on: Vol. 1, no. 1 (2007); title from cover.	AACR2 12.7B3 12.7B23
	500	Latest issue consulted: Vol. 2, no. 2 (2008).	12.7B23

	650		0	Algebra ‡v Periodicals.
	650		0	Number theory ‡v Periodicals.
	776	0	8	‡i Also issued online: ‡t Algebra & number theory (Online) ‡w (OCoLC)162197509
	856	4	1	‡u http://pjm.math.berkeley.edu/ant/about/journal/about.html

AACR2

12.7B3 - Make a note on the source of the title proper if a title page substitute is used as the chief source of information

12.7B23 - Make a note if the description is not based on the first issue or part or on the first iteration... If more than one issue or part has been consulted, make a note of the latest issue or part consulted in making the description

RDA

2.20.2.3 - Make a note on the source from which the title proper is taken if it is a source other than: a) the title page. . . .

2.20.13 - Make a note on issue, part, or iteration used as the basis for identification of the resource

CCM

13.2.1 - Note when a title page substitute is used as the chief source of information

8.1.1c - Provide the numbering for the earliest available issue in a 500 field when the first issue is not in hand. Precede this information with the words "Description based on:". It is an LC/CCM best practice to combine the "Description based on" note with the "source of information" note when both are given

Notes Concerning Title, Source of Title, and History of the Journal Publication

Title: Granta

Cover

The many functions of the 500 note field include the recording of an alternate source of title information or the variable nature of a magazine's subtitle. A 500 field may also be used—at a cataloger's discretion—to add information to the record in the form of quoted notes that may be useful to a researcher who is unclear as to the nature of the publication.

In this example, a cataloger has added a quoted historical note—culled from the magazine's website—to provide a brief history of the magazine and its importance within the literary realm. The source for the quoted note is provided in a parenthetical statement at the end of the quoted passage.

Other notes (e.g., "Title from caption," "Subtitle varies," and "Each issue has also a distinctive title") all provide information relating to the title and the source of title information.

Additionally, please observe that because "Title from caption" is not used together with the "Description based on" note, this note should remain coded in the 500 field rather than in the 588 field.

As identified with in the record, the quoted text used within the 500 field can be found on the publication's "About Us" webpage.

Screenshot – 'About Us' Webpage

OCLC #6619122

Type a	ELvl	Srce d	GPub	Ctrl	Lang eng
BLvl s	Form	Conf 0	Freq q	MRec	Ctry nyu
S/L 0	Orig	EntW	Regl x	Alph a	
Desc a	SrTp p	Cont	DtSt c	Dates 1889	, 9999

	022		0017-3231 ‡y 0017-3232 ‡y 0-14-0017-3231 ‡2 z
	042		lc ‡a nsdp
	245	0 4	The Granta.
	260		[London : ‡b Printed and published for the proprietor by King, Sell, & Railtor, Ltd., ‡c 1889]-
	300		v. : ‡b ill. ; ‡c 21-27 cm.
	310		5 issues per year, ‡b 2009-
	321		Weekly, ‡b Jan. 1889-[1978]
	321		Quarterly, ‡b [1979]-2008
	362	0	Vol. 1, no. 1 (Jan. 18, 1889)- ; [new ser., 1 (1979)]-
CCM 13.2.6	500		"Granta's first incarnation was as a student magazine at Cambridge University. It began in 1889 and published the early work of writers as various as E.M. Forster and A.A. Milne, Ted Hughes and Sylvia Plath. Granta's second incarnation took it out of Cambridge and into the wider world. It began in 1979." (a brief history from the Granta web page)
13.2.1	500		Title from caption.	AACR2 12.7B3
6.7.1	500		Subtitle varies: 1889-19, A college joke to cure the dumps; <autumn 2000>- , The magazine of new writing.	12.7B6.2.a)
7.2.2f	500		In the new series, each issue has also a distinctive title.	12.7B4.1
	500		Published <2000>- by Granta Publications in London and by Granta USA in New York.
	500		Latest issue consulted: 106 (2009).
	530		Issued also online.
	650	0	Literature ‡v Periodicals.
	856	4 1	‡u http://www.granta.com/

AACR2

1.7A3 - Give quotations from the item or from other sources in quotation marks. Follow the quotation by an indication of its source

12.7B3 - Make a note if a title page substitute is used as the chief source of information

12.7B6.2.a - Make notes on changes in other title information that occur after the first/earliest issue or part if considered to be important. If the changes have been numerous, a general statement may be made

12.7B4.1 - Make notes on titles other than the title proper borne by the resource, and changes to such titles, if considered to be important

RDA

1.10.3 - Record quotations from the resource or from other sources in quotation marks. Follow the quotation by an indication of its source

2.20.2.3 - Make a note on the source from which the title proper is taken if it is a source other than: a) the title page

2.20.2.4 - If scattered issues have different titles proper or other title information, and the differences are not considered important for identification or access, make a note indicating that the title, etc., varies

CCM

6.7.1 - Make a "Subtitle varies" note to document changes/variations in a serial's subtitle that does not constitute a major change

7.2.2f - Make a note indicating the use of distinctive titles. Do not enumerate distinctive titles in 246 fields

13.2.1 - Note when a title page substitute is used as the chief source of information

13.2.6 - Quoted notes may be used in fields 500; cite the source of a quoted note if it is taken from a source other than the chief source of the item

Notes for Numbering Peculiarities and Linking Entry Complexity

Title: News and notes

Title from Caption

In conjunction with the information given in the 362 field, which is used to record the beginning and ending alphabetic, numeric, and chronological designations of the issue (i.e., the initial date and number of the serial and, if known, the date and number of the ceasing issue), the 515 field is used for recording peculiarities in a serial's numbering. For example, the duplication or skipping of numbers within a serial's run is recorded in the 515 note field.

In this example, the newsletter of the International Correctional Education Association—*News & Notes*—repeated numbering because both the Apr./May and Aug./Sept. 1994 issues were numbered Vol. 16, no. 2. To record this irregularity, a note was made to provide information about this numbering duplication.

Furthermore, in 2008, the newsletter ceased publication in print format and began to be issued online. The field 580 (linking entry complex note) is used here to describe the presence of another format/relationship—in this case, the online newsletter.

It is interesting to note that although the format change necessitates the creation of a new record, none can be found in OCLC for the online newsletter as of this writing. Because of this, no corresponding linking entry field (i.e., no 785 field) is present in the existing record for *News & Notes*. Additionally, because of differing priorities and differing levels of available resources, it is up to each library to decide whether to catalog free resources found on the Internet.

OCLC #30607754

Type a	ELvl	Srce d	GPub	Ctrl	Lang eng
BLvl s	Form	Conf 0	Freq b	MRec	Ctry cau
S/L 0	Orig	EntW	Regl r	Alph	
Desc a	SrTp p	Cont	DtSt d	Dates 1994	, 2008

042			lcd
043			n-us---
110	2		Correctional Education Association (U.S.)
245	1	0	News and notes / ‡c International Correctional Education Association.
246	1	7	CEA news and notes
260			Downey, Ca. : ‡b Los Angeles County Office of Education, ‡c 1994-2008.
300			v. ; ‡c 28 cm.
310			Bimonthly, ‡b 2008-
321			Quarterly
362	0		Vol. 16, no. 1 (Jan. 1994)-
362	1		Ceased with: May 2008.
500			Title from caption.

CCM 13.4.2 → 515 Vol. 16, no. 2 repeated in numbering of issues for Apr./May and Aug./Sept. 1994. ← **AACR2 12.7B10.2**

14.1.6 → 580 Ceased in print; continued online by publication with same title. ← **12.7B16**

610	2	0	Correctional Education Association (U.S.) ‡v Periodicals.
650		0	Corrections ‡v Periodicals.
710	1		Los Angeles County (Calif.). ‡b Office of Education.
780	0	0	Correctional Education Association (U.S.). ‡t CEA news & notes ‡w (DLC)sn 91028415 ‡w (OCoLC)19068652

AACR2

12.7B10.2 - Make notes documenting complex or irregular numbering not already specified in field 362

12.7B16 - Make notes documenting other formats in which the content of the serial is, or has been, issued

RDA

2.20.5.4 - Make notes on complex or irregular numbering of a serial, or numbering errors, not already specified in the numbering of serials element if they are considered to be important for identification

27.1.1.3 - Reference related manifestations through examples, including unstructured description of the related manifestation

CCM

13.4.2 - Make a field 515 note to document numbering peculiarities that cannot be fully expressed in the 362 field or the 500 "Description based on" note

14.1.6 - Make a field 580 note to explain a change in physical medium that requires a new entry

Notes for Additional Physical Form Available as well as Different Language Editions Available

Title: Trade policy review. Bahrain

Cover – Print edition

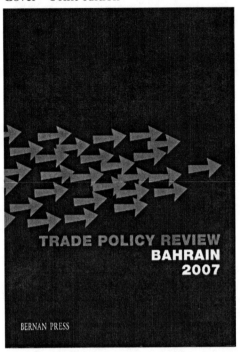

Title Page – Print edition

Trade Policy Review

Bahrain
2007

World Trade Organization
Geneva, October 2007

When a serial is issued in several different formats (such as online or CD-ROM), note fields are used to record the alternate forms on the main serial record. In this example, the serial *Trade Policy Review Bahrain* is available in two different formats, each of which is recorded in a separate 530 field for additional physical format available note.

The first of the two 530 field notes relates to a compilation CD-ROM that includes the serial *Trade Policy Review Bahrain*, along with several other reports dealing with trade policy, issued by the World Trade Organization. The compilation CD-ROM, which is issued annually under the title *Trade Policy Review*, is further linked to this record by a 776 additional physical form entry linking field.

The second 530 note lets users know that the report is also available online, and a corresponding link to the serial is provided in an 856 field to help users locate and access the electronic version of the resource. The 856 field can be used in a bibliographic record when either the resource or a subset of it is available online.

This serial is also issued in Spanish and French editions. The existence of these alternate language editions is recorded in a 580 linking complex entry note to alert users to the availability of other language editions. AACR2 12.7B8f instructs serials catalogers to give the name of the other edition(s) for simultaneous language editions but to make a general note if the name of the other edition is not readily available. In this example, the following note is included:

580 Issued also in Spanish and French editions.

OCLC #46668782

	Type a	ELvl	Srce d	GPub i	Ctrl	Lang eng
	BLvl s	Form	Conf 0	Freq	MRec	Ctry sz
	S/L 0	Orig	EntW	Regl x	Alph	
	Desc a	SrTp	Cont s	DtSt c	Dates 2000	, 9999

	042		lc
	043		a-ba---
	245	0 0	Trade policy review. ‡p Bahrain.
	246	3 0	Bahrain
	260		Geneva : ‡b World Trade Organization ; ‡a Lanham, MD : ‡b Bernan Associates, ‡c 2000-
	300		v. : ‡b ill. ; ‡c 30 cm.
	310		Irregular
	362	0	-2000

CCM 14.3.5	530		Also available in the CD-ROM compilation of the WTO reports on specific countries, issued under the title: Trade policy review.	AACR2 12.7B16
14.3.5	530		Also issued online.	12.7B16
14.1.6c	580		Issued also in Spanish and French editions.	12.7B8f

	650	0	Foreign trade regulation ‡z Bahrain ‡v Periodicals.
	651	0	Bahrain ‡x Commerce ‡v Periodicals.
	651	0	Bahrain ‡x Commercial policy ‡v Periodicals.
	710	2	World Trade Organization.
	776	1	‡t Trade policy review (World Trade Organization) ‡w (DLC)sn 98034735 ‡w (OCoLC)40430547
	856	4 1	‡u http://bibpurl.oclc.org/web/18082 ‡u http://www.wto.org/english/ tratop_e/tpr_e/tp_rep_e.htm ‡z Choose country from dropdown menu and select type of document, or scroll to chronological list

AACR2

12.7B8f - Generate a note if the serial is issued in two or more editions that differ in partial content or language

12.7B16 - Generate notes documenting other formats in which the content of the serial is, or has been, issued

RDA

28.1.1.3 - Reference a related item applying the general guidelines on referencing related works, expressions, manifestations, and items given under 24.4

26.1.1.3 - Reference a related expression applying the general guidelines on referencing related works, expressions, manifestations, and items given under 24.4

27.1.1.3 - Reference a related manifestation applying the general guidelines on referencing related works, expressions, manifestations, and items given under 24.4

25.1.1.3 - Reference a related work applying the general guidelines on referencing related works, expressions, manifestations, and items given under 24.4

(Continued on next page)

CCM

14.1.6c - Generate a linking note when other editions of the publication (such as translations of which the original title is unknown) are not given a linking entry field

14.3.5 - Generate a field 530 note to document the availability of other physical media (such as CD-ROMs or electronic formats)

Notes Related to Direct Access Electronic Resources and Format Change

Title: Proceedings of the . . . Conference of the American Academy of Advertising

CD-ROM

When creating a record for a serial issued in CD-ROM format, catalogers usually make a 500 field note for the source of title proper information and a 538 field note for system requirements. These notes assist user access to the resources they need.

As outlined in the CCM, a note is always created to record the source of the title proper information for electronic resources, including CD-ROMs. In this example, the title is taken from the disc label and is noted in the 500 field. When making notes about CD-ROMs, a cataloger should use the spelling of "disc" for optical media.

When the information is readily available, the system requirements note (field 538) should be used to record system details needed to access the resource. In this example, the CD-ROM *Proceedings of the . . . Conference of the American Academy of Advertising* requires a computer that is "IBM PC compatible" and has a "CD-ROM drive."

If a system does not meet the requirements noted in the 538 field, a user may not be able to access the information from the resource. The rule in AACR29.7B1b specifies the order of characteristics to be listed when recording the details of the system requirements and the punctuations within the note (i.e., precede each characteristic, other than the first, by a semicolon). A more detailed note might look like this:

"IBM PC or compatible; 80486 or Pentium processor; 8 MB RAM; 10 MB hard drive space; Microsoft Windows 3.1 or higher; Windows 95 or Windows NT; VGA monitor; CD-ROM drive."

Because system requirements information becomes outdated quickly and is difficult to keep up to date in records, CCM 30.14.1 reminds serial catalogers to "at a minimum provide the make and model of the computer and the operating system" and to "consider omitting specific data such as versions of software or memory requirements."

Because the CD-ROM in this example continues the print version of the serial, a 580 note is created to explain the change in physical medium that requires a new entry. CCM14.1.6b states that in this situation, the nature of the change is better expressed in a 580 note because the titles are usually the same, and the display constant generated from a link entry field 780 or 785 is not sufficient.

When a 580 note is used, the first indicator in the linking entry field should be set to 1 (i.e., do not produce a display constant). However, because this practice can interfere with hyperlinking to related records in many systems, catalogers should take into consideration their local needs and system capabilities when setting the indicator value. In this example, even with the 580 note, the first indicator in the 780 field is set to the value 0 in order to print the display constant "Continues:" in the online catalog. This also allows users to navigate links between bibliographic records in the catalog for related resources. For further discussion on this issue, see *Standing Committee on Automation Task Group on Linking Entries: Final Report, Feb. 2005*, at http://www.loc.gov/catdir/pcc/archive/tglnkentr-rpt05.pdf.

```
OCLC #76810990
```

Type a	ELvl	Srce d	GPub	Ctrl	Lang eng
BLvl s	Form s	Conf 1	Freq a	MRec	Ctry txu
S/L 0	Orig s	EntW	Regl r	Alph	
Desc a	SrTp	Cont	DtSt c	Dates 2006	, 9999

	022		‡y 0883-2404
	042		lcd
	043		n-us---
	110	2	American Academy of Advertising. ‡b Conference.
	240	1 0	Proceedings of the . . . Conference of the American Academy of Advertising (CD-ROM)
	245	1 0	Proceedings of the . . . Conference of the American Academy of Advertising ‡h [electronic resource]
	260		Austin, TX : ‡b American Academy of Advertising, ‡c c2006-
	300		CD-ROMs ; ‡c 4 3/4 in.
	310		Annual
	362	0	2006-

CCM				AACR2
CCM 30.3.3	500		Title from disc label.	AACR2 9.1B2 9.7B3
30.14.1	538		System requirements: IBM PC compatible; CD-ROM drive.	9.7B1b
14.1.6 16.4.1a	580		Continues a print publication with the same title: Proceedings of the . . . Conference of the American Academy of Advertising.	LCRI 21.3B

	650	0	Advertising ‡z United States ‡v Congresses.
	780	0 0	American Academy of Advertising. Conference. ‡t Proceedings of the . . . Conference of the American Academy of Advertising (1985) ‡x 0883-2404 ‡w (DLC)sn 85007561 ‡w (OCoLC)12096045

AACR2

9.1B2 - Always give the source of the title proper in a note for electronic resources

9.7B1b - Make a note on the system requirements of the resource if the information is readily available. Begin the note with "System requirements:". Give the following characteristics in the order in which they are listed below and precede each characteristic, other than the first, by a semicolon:

– the make and model of the computer(s) on which the resource is designed to run; the amount of memory required; the name of the operating system; the software requirements (including the programming language); the kind and characteristics of any required or recommended peripherals; the type of any required or recommended hardware modifications

9.7B3 - Always give the source of the title proper for electronic resources

LCRI

21.3B - Other conditions for making a new entry for a serial: the physical medium in which the serial is issued changes as expressed in the specific material designation in the physical description area, such as a change from paper to microfiche, from paper to online, etc.

RDA

2.20.2.3 - Make a note on the source from which the title proper is taken if it is a source other than the title page, title sheet, or title card (or image thereof) of a resource consisting of multiple pages, leaves, sheets, or cards (or images thereof)

3.20.1.3 - Record any equipment or system requirements beyond what is normal and obvious for the type of carrier or type of file (e.g., the make and model of equipment or hardware, the operating system, the amount of memory, or any plug-ins or peripherals required to play, view, or run the resource)

27.1.1.3 - Reference a related manifestation applying the general guidelines on referencing related works, expressions, manifestations, and items given under 24.4

CCM

14.1.6 - Make a 580 note to explain a change in physical medium that requires a new entry

16.4.1a - In general, a change in the physical medium of the serial is a major change. The new record is necessary because of differences in the fixed fields and description (particularly the physical description, field 300)

30.3.3 - A note on the source of the title proper must always be given for electronic resources, even if the title is taken from the prescribed chief source (e.g., disc label)

30.14.1 - Make a note, using field 538, to record any hardware and software requirements necessary to read or utilize an electronic resource

Notes Related to Remote Access Electronic Resources

Title: Wool technology and sheep breeding

Screenshot – PDF Cover

Screenshot – Journal Homepage

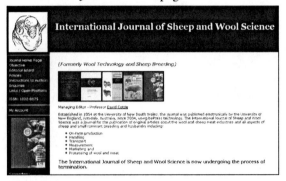

When a cataloger creates a record for a remote access electronic resources, the source of the title proper must always be documented in a 500 field note or in a 588 field if it is combined with the description based on note. As discussed in the earlier example *Algebra & Number Theory*, the description based on note and the source of title are combined and coded in one 588 field in CSR. However, in a record created according to AACR2, the stand-alone source of title proper note should still be recorded in the 500 field rather than the 588 field.

AACR2 9.7B22 tells catalogers creating new records to give the date viewed in parentheses following the source of title. The content provider version used for the basis of description should also be added to the title source note.

In this example, the online edition of the journal *Wool Technology and Sheep Breeding* was viewed and cataloged on July 12, 2007. The publication is made available as a PDF document, and the title of the publication was taken from the PDF title page.

As this resource is available via the Internet, a 538 note was used to describe the mode of access for the resource, although under CSR guidelines, this note is only needed if the mode of access is unusual (i.e, other than through the World Wide Web).

OCLC #155249238

	Type a	ELvl I	Srce d	GPub	Ctrl	Lang eng
	BLvl s	Form s	Conf 0	Freq f	MRec	Ctry at
	S/L 0	Orig s	EntW	Regl r	Alph	
	Desc	SrTp	Cont	DtSt d	Dates 1958	, 1997

	022		ǂy 0043-7875
	130	0	Wool technology and sheep breeding (Online)
	245	0 0	Wool technology and sheep breeding ǂh [electronic resource].
	246	1	ǂi Some online sources list issues under title: ǂa International journal of sheep and wool science
	260		Sydney : ǂb School of Wool Technology, University of New South Wales; Australian Association of Stud Merino Breeders, ǂc [1958-1997]
	310		Semiannual
	362	0	Vol. 5, issue 1 (1958)-

				AACR2
CCM 31.3.4	500		Title from PDF title page (University of New South Wales, viewed on July 12, 2007).	9.1B2 9.7B3 9.7B22
31.14.5	538		Mode of access: World Wide Web.	9.7B1c
	588		Latest issue consulted: Vol. 50, issue 4 (2002)	

	650	0	Sheep ǂz Australia.
	650	0	Wool ǂx Research.
	710	2	University of New South Wales.
	776	0 8	ǂi Also issued in print: ǂt Wool technology and sheep breeding ǂx 0043-7875 ǂw (DLC)sn 86012517 ǂw (OCoLC)6245366
	780	0 0	ǂt Wool technology (Online) ǂw (OCoLC)155248998
	785	0 0	ǂt International journal of sheep and wool science ǂx 1832-8679 ǂw (OCoLC)62119493
	856	4 0	ǂu http://bibpurl.oclc.org/web/19046 ǂu http://sheepjournal.une.edu.au/sheepjournal/

AACR2

9.1B2 - Always give the source of the title proper in a note for electronic resources

9.7B1c - If a resource is available only by remote access, always specify the mode of access. Begin the note with "Mode of access:"

9.7B3 - Always give the source of the title proper for electronic resources

9.7B22 - For remote access resources, always give the date on which the resource was viewed for description

RDA

2.20.2.3 - Make a note on the source from which the title proper is taken if it is a source other than the title page, title sheet, or title card (or image thereof) of a resource consisting of multiple pages, leaves, sheets, or cards (or images thereof)

(Continued on next page)

2.20.13.5 - For online resources, make a note identifying the date on which the resource was viewed for description

3.20.1.3 - Record any equipment or system requirements beyond what is normal and obvious for the type of carrier or type of file (e.g., the make and model of equipment or hardware, the operating system, the amount of memory, or any plug-ins or peripherals required to play, view, or run the resource)

CCM

31.3.4 - Always give in a note the source of title for an online serial. To cite the source of title, use a term that is as specific as possible to describe the source. In new records, give the date viewed in parentheses following the source of title. In general, do not add the date viewed to the source of title note in existing records.

31.14.5 - A mode of access note (field 538) must be given in all records for remote access serials to explain the means by which the serial can be accessed. Begin the note with the phrase "Mode of access:" following the system requirements note, if present

Notes for Place of Publication Change

Title: Yearbook of the College Reading Association

Title Page

Title Page Verso

Title Page

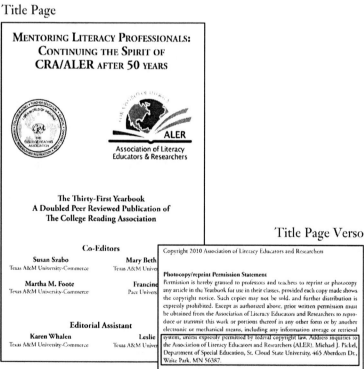

Title Page Verso

When a place of publication changes due to a change in editorial control of the publication, as often happens with publications issued by committees or associations that have rotating or changing editorial committee memberships, a general 500 field note may be made to avoid cluttering the record with insignificant changes.

In this example, the *Yearbook of the College Reading Association* has different places of publication, with Pittsburg, Kansas, as the original place of publication recorded in the 260 field. Other places of publication include Arlington, Texas, as shown in the title page verso of the 30th *Yearbook*, and Waite Park, Minnesota, as found on the title page verso of the 31st *Yearbook*. Because the place of publication changes frequently, a general note is made to reflect this change:

> 500 _ _ Place of publication
> varies.

Because some issues also have distinctive titles in addition to carrying the serial title *Yearbook*, the record contains a general note about the title. For example, the 30th *Yearbook* also has the title *Literacy Issues During Changing Times* and the 31st *Yearbook* is also titled *Mentoring Literacy Professionals: Continuing the Spirit of CRA/ALER After 50 Years*. A general 500 note is made to record this:

> 500 _ _ Some issues have also
> distinctive titles.

OCLC #23859969

Type a	ELvl	Srce d	GPub	Ctrl	Lang eng
BLvl s	Form	Conf 0	Freq a	MRec	Ctry txu
S/L 0	Orig	EntW	Regl r	Alph	
Desc a	SrTp	Cont	DtSt c	Dates 1990	, 9999

	042		lcd
	245	0 0	Yearbook of the College Reading Association.
	246	1	‡i Issues for <2004-> have title: ‡a College Reading Association yearbook
	246	1	‡i Issues for <2001-2003> have title: ‡a Yearbook
	260		Pittsburg, KS : ‡b College Reading Association
	300		v. : ‡b ill. ; ‡c 22 cm.
	310		Annual
	362	1	Began with v. 12 (1990).
	500		Some issues have also distinctive titles.	AACR2 12.7B4.1
	500		Description based on: 13th (1991).
CCM 10.6	500		Place of publication varies.	12.7B11.2
	500		Twenty-fourth Yearbook incorrectly called twenty-third on title page.
	500		Latest issue consulted: 30th.
	515		Year dropped with 29th.
	650	0	Reading (Higher education) ‡v Periodicals.
	710	2	College Reading Association.
	780	0 0	College Reading Association. ‡t Proceedings of the College Reading Association ‡w (DLC) 67003259 ‡w (OCoLC)2058969

AACR2

12.7B4.1 - Make notes on titles other than the title proper borne by the resource, and changes to such titles, if considered to be important

12.7B11.2 - Makes notes on changes in the place and/or name of publisher that occur after the first/earliest issue if considered important. If the changes have been numerous, a general statement may be made

RDA

2.8.1.5.2 - If the place of publication changes on a later issue or part of a serial, make a note on the change if considered to be important

2.20.7.5.2 - Makes notes on changes in place of publication and/or publishers' names that occur after the first/earliest issue of a serial if they are considered to be important for identification or access

CCM

10.6 - With the exception of the final date of publication, significant changes appearing on later issues may be recorded in notes. Do not clutter the record with minor changes, particularly those that involve commercial publishers. Notes relating to changes in place of publication, commercial publisher, or date are given in a 500 field

Notes for Numbering Peculiarities

Title: Mome

Cover

When peculiarities in the numbering of a serial are too complex to be accurately reflected in the 362 field, one or more 515 notes may be created to explain the irregularities.

In this example, some issues of the graphic novel serial *Mome* have been issued in combined form, necessitating a "Some issues combined" note. The note is intentionally general to indicate that the combining of issues has occurred numerous times. A second, more specific note was created to highlight an irregularity in the recorded numbering pattern for the serial.

OCLC #61704290

Type a	ELvl	Srce d	GPub	Ctrl	Lang eng
BLvl s	Form	Conf 0	Freq q	MRec	Ctry wau
S/L 0	Orig	EntW	Regl r	Alph a	
Desc a	SrTp p	Cont	DtSt c	Dates 2005	, 9999

022	0		1933-5652 ǂ2 1
037			ǂb Fantagraphics Books, 7563 Lake City Way NE, Seattle, WA 98115
042			lcd ǂa nsdp
222		0	Mome
245	0	0	Mome.
260			Seattle, Wash. : ǂb Fantagraphics, ǂc 2005-
310			Quarterly
362		0	Summer 2005-
500			Title from cover.
500			Latest issue consulted: Vol. 9 (fall 2007).

CCM			AACR2
13.4.1 13.4.2	515	Some issues combined.	12.7B10.2
13.4.1-2	515	Issues for summer and fall 2005 lack issue numbering but constitute v. 1 and 2. Issues for winter 2006- also called v. 3-	12.7B10.2

530			Also issued online.
650		0	Comic books, strips, etc. ǂv Periodicals.
650		0	Graphic novels ǂv Periodicals.
710		2	Fantagraphics Books.

AACR2

12.7B10.2 - Make notes on complex or irregular numbering not already specified in the numbering area if considered to be important. Make notes on issuing peculiarities if considered to be important

RDA

2.20.5.4 - Make notes on complex or irregular numbering of a serial, or numbering errors, not already specified in the numbering of serials element if they are considered to be important for identification

CCM

13.4.1 - The numbering peculiarities note is used to explain changes, irregularities, or complex situations relating to the numbering

13.4.2 - Make a field 515 note to document numbering peculiarities that cannot be fully expressed in the 362 field or the 500 "Description based on" note

Language Notes

Title: West African journal of archaeology

Cover

Title Page

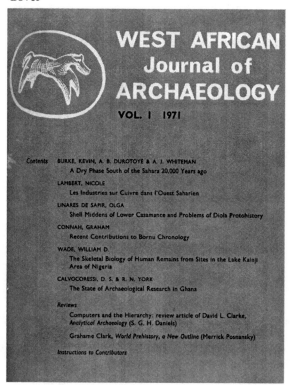

Since 1977, the publication *West African Journal of Archaeology* has been available in English and French. This is recorded in a language note, found in field 546. Some examples of language notes include:

"Chiefly in Urdu; some text in French and English."
"Text in English and French, with French text on inverted pages." (this note is very common for Canadian government documents)
"In Japanese and Korean, with summaries in Chinese, English, and French."

The languages of issuance are indicated in the fixed field element Lang (language code) and the variable field 041 (language code). Field 041 contains codes for the language of the text, summaries, abstracts, and/or original language of the work. Codes are assigned from the MARC Code List for Languages, available at http://www.loc.gov/marc/languages/langhome.html. For more information on the use of the 041 field, consult the *CONSER Editing Guide* available by subscription from http:desktop.loc.gov.

OCLC #1633851

Type a	ELvl	Srce c	GPub	Ctrl		Lang eng
BLvl s	Form	Conf 0	Freq f	MRec		Ctry nr
S/L 0	Orig	EntW	Regl x	Alph a		
Desc a	SrTp	Cont	DtSt u	Dates 1971		, uuuu

022			0331-3158 ‡y 0083-8160
041	0		eng ‡a fre
042			lc
043			fw-----
210	0		West Afr. j. archaeol.
222		0	West African journal of archaeology
245	0	0	West African journal of archaeology.
246	1		‡i Title also in French, 1977- : ‡a Revue ouest africaine d'archéologie
246	3	0	WAJA
246	1	3	W.A.J.A.
260			Ibadan : ‡b Published for the editorial board of WAJA by Oxford University Press, ‡c [1971]-
300			v. : ‡b ill., maps : ‡c 22-27 cm.
310			2 issues a year, ‡b 1995-
321			Annual, ‡b 1971-1994
362	0		Vol. 1 (Jan. 1971)-
500			Published on behalf of the editorial board of WAJA by Ibadan University Press, 1976-1979; on behalf of the West African Archaeological Association by the editorial board, 1980/81-
500			Latest issue consulted: 31 (2) (2001).
546			In English, 1971-1976; in English and French, 1977-
650		0	Prehistoric peoples ‡z Africa, West ‡v Periodicals.
650		0	Antiquities, Prehistoric ‡z Africa, West ‡v Periodicals.
651		0	Africa, West ‡x Antiquities ‡v Periodicals.
650		0	Archaeology ‡v Periodicals.
710	2		West African Archaeological Association.
780	0	0	‡t West African archaeological newsletter ‡x 0083-8160 ‡w (OCoLC) 2192555

CCM 13.6.1 13.6.2 (beside 546)

AACR2 12.7B2 (beside 546)

AACR2

12.7B2 - Make notes on the language(s) of the resource unless this is apparent from the rest of the description

RDA

6.11.1.4 - If a single expression of a work involves more than one language, record each of the languages

CCM

13.6.1 - The language or languages of the item are not apparent from the title data, when the title appears in more than one language but the text is only in one language, when summaries and/or titles of contents are given in languages different from that of the text

13.6.2 - When including more than one language in the note, give first the predominant language of the text. If there is no predominant language, give the languages in alphabetic order. Separate the languages by the word "and" in all cases. The language note is given in conjunction with field 041 (Language code)

Issuing Body Notes in 550

Title: Historia

Cover

The serial *Historia* was originally published by Eastern Illinois University's Department of History. Between 1999 and 2001, the journal was jointly issued with Epsilon Mu, a chapter of Phi Alpha Theta. Because this second issuing body is not otherwise mentioned in the descriptive part of the cataloging record, an issuing body note is made in the 550 field to show the relationship between the issuing body and the publication. It also justifies the use of an added entry for the Epsilon Mu Chapter of Phi Alpha Theta, in the 7xx fields as an additional access point.. This aids user access because a search for the name of either issuing body would identify the journal.

Commonly used wording in issuing body notes include:

"Published under the auspices of..."

"Some issues published in association with..."

"Issuing body varies..." (used when there are too many issuing body changes to independently document)

"Official publication of..."

Screenshot – Journal Home

Note that corporate bodies whose sole function is that of publishing should only be cited in a 500 field general note.

OCLC #34007607

Type a	ELvl	Srce d	GPub	Ctrl	Lang eng
BLvl s	Form	Conf 0	Freq a	MRec	Ctry ilu
S/L 0	Orig	EntW b	Regl r	Alph a	
Desc a	SrTp p	Cont	DtSt c	Dates 1992	, 9999

022	0		1537-2189 ‡2 1
042			lc
130	0		Historia (Charleston, Ill.)
245	0	0	Historia / ‡c Department of History, Eastern Illinois University.
260			Charleston, Ill. : ‡b Dept. of History, Eastern Illinois University, ‡c 1992-
300			v. : ‡b ill. ; ‡c 22 cm.
310			Annual
362	0		Vol. 1, no. 1 (spring/summer 1992)-
500			Latest issue consulted: Vol. 10 (2001).
530			Tables of contents and recent vols. also available via Internet from the EIU web site. Address as of 03/05/03: http://www.eiu.edu/historia/.

CCM
13.5.1
13.5.3

| 550 | Vols. for 1999-<2001> issued jointly with Epsilon Mu Chapter, Phi Alpha Theta. |

AACR2
12.7B7.1
12.7B7.2

650		0	History ‡v Periodicals.
710	2		Eastern Illinois University. ‡b Dept. of History.
710	2		Phi Alpha Theta. ‡b Epsilon Mu Chapter (Eastern Illinois University)
856	4	1	‡u http://www.eiu.edu/%7Ehistoria/

AACR2

12.7B7.1 - Make notes on statements of responsibility that do not appear in the title and statement of responsibility area if considered to be important

12.7B7.2 - Make notes on changes in statements of responsibility that occur after the first/earliest issue or part if considered to be important

RDA

2.20.3.5 - Make notes on other details relating to a statement of responsibility if they are considered to be important for identification or access

2.20.3.6.2 - Make notes on changes in statements of responsibility that occur after the first/earliest issue or part of a serial if they are considered to be important for identification or access

CCM

13.5.1 - In general, give an issuing bodies note to cite a corporate body that is not already mentioned in the body of the entry for which an added entry is desired

13.5.3 - Generally, give the corporate body in the note as it appears on the piece; it need not be given as it is established in the name authority file

Notes for Editors (500), Numbering Peculiarities (515), and Additional Physical Format (530)

Title: Frontiers in neuroendocrinology

Cover   Title Page

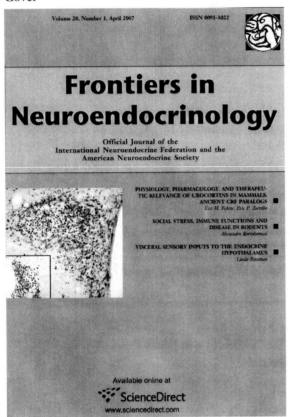

For serials, it is very rare to have personal authors or editors as the main entry. If an editor is considered important, a 500 field note is made for the editor, thus providing justification for the added entries in 7xx fields. In this example, William F. Ganong and Luciano Martini have been the editors of *Frontiers in Neuro-endocrinology* since its inception, and it is possible that users may try to find this journal by searching the names of the editors.

Commonly used wording for editor notes includes:

"Compiled and edited by . . . "
"Vols. for 2000– edited by: . . . "

Other notes in this example are:

515 *Numbering peculiarities note*
530 *Additional physical form available note*

OCLC #1388525

Type a	ELvl	Srce d	GPub	Ctrl	Lang eng
BLvl s	Form	Conf 0	Freq q	MRec	Ctry nyu
S/L 0	Orig	EntW	Regl r	Alph a	
Desc	SrTp	Cont	DtSt c	Dates 1969	, 9999

022	0	0091-3022 ‡z 0532-7466 ‡2 1	
042		nsdp ‡a lc	
245	0 0	Frontiers in neuroendocrinology.	
260		New York, ‡b Raven Press [etc.]	
300		v. ‡b ill., ports. ‡c 24 cm.	
310		Quarterly, ‡b Jan. 1990-	
321		Biennial, ‡b 1969-1989	
362	0	v. [1]- 1969-	

CCM			AACR2
13.8.1 13.8.2	500	Editors: 1969- W.F. Ganong and L. Martini.	12.7B7.1
13.4.2	515	Volume numbering begins with v. 4.	12.7B10.2
14.3.5	530	Also available to subscribers via the World Wide Web.	12.7B16

650	0	Neuroendocrinology ‡v Periodicals.	
700	1	Ganong, William F.	
700	1	Martini, Luciano, ‡d 1927-	
776	1	‡t Frontiers in neuroendocrinology (Online) ‡x 1095-6808 ‡w (DLC)sn 97006905 ‡w (OCoLC)36980284	
856	4 1	‡u http://www.sciencedirect.com/science/journal/00913022	
856	4 1	‡u http://www.idealibrary.com/links/toc/frne	

AACR2

12.7B7.1 - Give the name of any editor considered to be an important means of identifying the serial (e.g., if a particular person edited the serial for all or most of its existence; if the person's name is likely to be better known than the title of the serial)

12.7B10.2 - Make notes documenting complex or irregular numbering not already specified in field 362

12.7B16 - Make notes documenting other formats in which the content of the serial is, or has been, issued

RDA

2.20.3.5 - Make notes on other details relating to a statement of responsibility if they are considered to be important for identification or access

2.20.5.4 - Make notes on complex or irregular numbering of a serial, or numbering errors, not already specified in the numbering of serials element if they are considered to be important for identification

(Continued on next page)

27.1.1.3 - Reference a related manifestation applying the general guidelines on referencing related works, expressions, manifestations, and items given under 24.4

CCM

13.4.2 - Make a field 515 note to document numbering peculiarities that cannot be fully expressed in the 362 field or the 500 "Description based on" note

13.8.1 - Editors are not given in the statement of responsibility but may be given in a note. Inclusion of an editor note should be limited to those cases where the same editor has been responsible for most of the serial or when the editor is better known than the title of the serial, and an added entry will be given

13.8.2 - Begin the note with "Editor:" or "Editors:". When there is more than one editor covering different time spans, give the corresponding dates preceding the name. Give the name as it appears on the piece

14.3.5 - Make a note in the 530 field on the record for the original to note the availability of other physical media, such as the existence of electronic versions

Index Note and Linking Complexity Note

Title: Rick Steves' Great Britain

If individual issues contain indexes, a 500 field note is created to record the presence of the index. However, if the index is an annual and cumulative index, it would be recorded in the 555 field, as shown below:

555 _ _ Index published separately each year.
555 _ _ Dec. issue includes a cumulative index.

In this example, the annual issue of *Rick Steves' Great Britain* includes an index, which is recorded in a 500 note. Because some of the content from *Rick Steves' Great Britain* also appears in *Rick Steves' England*, a note is created in the 580 field (linking complexity note) to record that fact. The nonspecific relationship between the two publications is indicated by the corresponding linking entry field 787.

Some commonly seen linking entry complexity notes include:

580 _ _ Merged with: . . . , to form: . . .
580 _ _ Continues print publication of the same name.
580 _ _ Also available as part of CD-ROM: . . .

Title Page

Note that when a 580 field is used in conjunction with a linking entry field, the first indicator in the linking field should be set to 1 to suppress the display of the print constant (CCM 14.1.6). In this example, the first indicator in the 787 field is set to 1 so the print constant "Related item" is suppressed from display.

Title Page Verso

Avalon Travel
a member of the Perseus Books Group
1700 Fourth Street
Berkeley, CA 94710

Text © 2009 by Rick Steves
Maps © 2009 by Europe Through the Back Door. All rights reserved.

Printed in the USA by Worzalla
Second printing May 2009

ISBN (10) 1-59880-111-2
ISBN (13) 978-1-59880-111-8
ISSN 1090-6843

Thanks to my wife, Anne, for making home my favorite travel destination. Thanks also to Cameron Hewitt for his original work on several of the Scotland chapters (particularly St. Andrews and the Isle of Skye), to Jennifer Hauseman for the original version of the Glasgow chapter, and to friends listed in this book who put the "Great" in Britain.

For the latest on Rick's lectures, guidebooks, tours, public radio show, and public television series, contact Europe Through the Back Door, Box 2009, Edmonds, WA 98020, 425/771-8303, fax 425/771-0833, www.ricksteves.com, rick@ricksteves.com.

OCLC #48541421

Type a	ELvl	Srce d	GPub	Ctrl	Lang eng
BLvl s	Form	Conf 0	Freq a	MRec	Ctry cau
S/L 0	Orig	EntW	Regl r	Alph a	
Desc a	SrTp	Cont	DtSt c	Dates 2002	, 9999

022	0	1541-1621 ‡y 1090-6843 ‡2 1	
042		lc ‡a nsdp	
043		e-uk---	
130	0	Rick Steves' Great Britain (2002)	
245	1	0	Rick Steves' Great Britain.
246	3	Great Britain	
260		Emeryville, CA : ‡b Avalon Travel Pub., ‡c c2002-	
300		v. : ‡b maps ; ‡c 21 cm.	
310		Annual	
362	0	-2002	

CCM 17.5.3	500	Includes index.	AACR2 12.7B17
	500	Latest issue consulted: 2009.	
14.3.7	580	Some content also published in: Rick Steves' England, 2006-	12.7B
	651	0	Great Britain ‡v Guidebooks.
	700	1	Steves, Rick, ‡d 1955-
	780	0	1	‡t Rick Steves' Great Britain & Ireland ‡x 1090-6843 ‡w (DLC) 97649766 ‡w (OCoLC)35392473
	787	1	‡t Rick Steves' England ‡x 1930-4617 ‡w (DLC) 2006213615 ‡w (OCoLC)64548242

AACR2

12.7B17 - Make notes on the presence of cumulative indexes

12.7B - Notes may include information not appropriate to other areas of the description

RDA

7.16.1.1 - Supplementary content is content (e.g., an index, a bibliography, an appendix) designed to supplement the primary content of a resource

7.16.1.3 - If the resource contains supplementary content, record the nature of that content (i.e., its type, extent, location within the resource, etc.), if it is considered important for identification or selection

CCM

17.5.3 - Depending on the type, an index may be noted in the bibliographic record, cataloged separately, or noted only on the check-in record

14.3.7 - Other related resources (field 787): a resource that is related to a serial in a manner that is not expressed by one of the other linking entry fields and that is separately cataloged falls into this category. Because there are many types of relationships that can be included in field 787, most systems programs do not include a display constant for field 787. Instead subfield ‡i is used to include the display text or field 580 is used

Cover

EXERCISE 1

You are cataloging a new serial called *Getty Research Journal*. You have two issues: Number 1 (2009) and Number 2 (2010). The title appears on the cover. Follow CSR guidelines to record the information in the 362 and 588 fields—if applicable—including the correct indicators.

OCLC #239617254

Type a	ELvl	Srce c	GPub	Ctrl	Lang eng
BLvl s	Form	Conf 0	Freq f	MRec	Ctry cau
S/L 0	Orig	EntW	Regl r	Alph a	
Desc a	SrTp p	Cont	DtSt c	Dates 2009	, 9999

022	0	1944-8740 ‡2 1
037		‡b Getty Publications Distribution Center, P.O. Box 49659, Los Angeles, CA 90049-0659
042		lcd ‡a nsdp
245	0 0	Getty research journal.
260		Los Angeles, Calif. : ‡b Getty Research Institute
300		v. : ‡b ill. ; ‡c 26 cm.
310		Semiannual
362		
588		
588		
650	0	Art ‡x History ‡v Periodicals.
650	0	Art ‡x Archival resources ‡v Periodicals.
650	0	Rare books ‡v Periodicals.
650	0	Art ‡z California ‡z Los Angeles ‡v Periodicals.
650	0	Rare books ‡z California ‡z Los Angeles ‡v Periodicals.
610	2 0	Getty Research Institute ‡v Periodicals.
610	2 0	J. Paul Getty Trust ‡v Periodicals.
710	2	Getty Research Institute.
710	2	J. Paul Getty Trust.

Cover

EXERCISE 2

The journal *Avian Biology Research* is available in print and on-line. On the record for the print version, provide a note about the availability of the online version.

Screenshot – Table of Contents

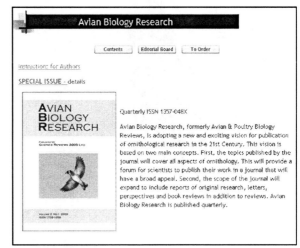

OCLC #244981611

Type a	ELvl	Srce d	GPub	Ctrl	Lang eng
BLvl s	Form	Conf 0	Freq q	MRec	Ctry enk
S/L 0	Orig	EntW	Regl r	Alph a	
Desc a	SrTp p	Cont	DtSt c	Dates 2008	, 9999

022			1758-1559
042			lcd
245	0	0	Avian biology research.
260			St. Albans : ǂb Science Reviews 2000 Ltd., ǂc 2008-
300			v. : ǂb ill. ; ǂc 30 cm.
310			Quarterly
362	1		Began with vol. 1, no. 1 (2008).
588			Description based on vol. 1, no. 1 (2008); title from cover.
588			Latest issue consulted: Vol. 1, no. 3 (2008).
530			
650		0	Ornithology ǂv Periodicals.
650		0	Birds ǂx Research ǂv Periodicals.
780	0	0	ǂt Avian and poultry biology reviews ǂx 1470-2061 ǂw (OCoLC) 44313824
856	4	1	ǂu http://umd.library.ingentaconnect.com/content/stl/abr

EXERCISE 3

The journal *Studies in Ethnicity and Nationalism* is published jointly by the Association for the Study of Ethnicity and Nationalism and the London School of Economics and Political Science. Make a note for the joint issuing body.

Cover

Cover Verso

OCLC #50525160

Type a	ELvl	Srce c	GPub	Ctrl	Lang eng
BLvl s	Form	Conf 0	Freq t	MRec	Ctry enk
S/L 0	Orig	EntW	Regl r	Alph	
Desc a	SrTp p	Cont	DtSt c	Dates 2001	, 9999

022			1473-8481
042			lcd
245	0	0	Studies in ethnicity and nationalism / ‡c Association for the Study of Ethnicity and Nationalism.
260			London : ‡b Association for the Study of Ethnicity and Nationalism, ‡c 2001-
310			Three times a year, ‡b 2008-
321			Semiannual, ‡b 2002-<2007>
362	0		Vol. 1, no. 1 (2002)-
550			
500			Latest issue consulted: Vol. 8, no. 3 (2008).
650		0	Nationalism ‡v Periodicals.
650		0	Ethnicity ‡v Periodicals.
610	2	0	Association for the Study of Ethnicity and Nationalism ‡v Periodicals.
710	2		Association for the Study of Ethnicity and Nationalism.
710	2		London School of Economics and Political Science.
776	0	8	‡i Online version: ‡t Studies in ethnicity and nationalism ‡x 1754-9469 ‡w (DLC) 2008242151 ‡w (OCoLC)170924159
780	0	0	‡t ASEN bulletin ‡x 1353-8004 ‡w (DLC)sn 97032462 ‡w (OCoLC)36150091
856	4	1	‡u http://www.blackwell-synergy.com/loi/sena

Cover

EXERCISE 4

The publication *La Revue des Musées de France* is published in French but has abstracts in English and German. Make a language note to give this information.

Table of Contents

OCLC #55677534

Type a	ELvl	Srce d	GPub	Ctrl	Lang fre
BLvl s	Form	Conf 0	Freq q	MRec	Ctry fr
S/L 0	Orig	EntW	Regl x	Alph	
Desc a	SrTp p	Cont	DtSt c	Dates 2004	, 9999

022		1962-4271 ‡y 0035-2608
041	0	fre ‡b eng ‡b ger
042		lcd
043		e-fr---
245	0 3	La revue des musées de France : ‡b revue du Louvre.
246	3 0	Revue du Louvre
260		Paris : ‡b Publiée sous les auspices du Conseil des musées nationaux, ‡c [2004]-
300		v. : ‡b ill. (some col.) ; ‡c 29 cm.
310		Five no. a year
362	0	54. année, 1 (févr. 2004)-
500		Title from cover.
500		Latest issue consulted: 57. année, 5 (déc. 2008).
546		
610	2 0	Musée du Louvre ‡v Periodicals.
650	0	Art museums ‡z France ‡v Periodicals.
650	0	Art ‡v Periodicals.
710	2	Conseil des musées nationaux (France)
780	0 0	‡t Revue du Louvre ‡w (DLC)sn 92038036 ‡w (OCoLC)23957378

Screenshot – Issues List

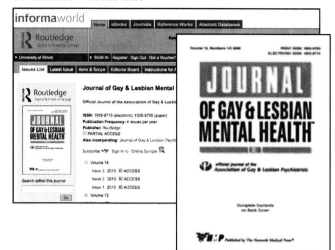

EXERCISE 5

The publication *Journal of Gay & Lesbian Mental Health* is available in print and online. It began with vol. 12, no. 1/2 (2008) because of the title change from the earlier title *Journal of Gay & Lesbian Psychotherapy*. The new title appears on the publisher's home page. On the following record for the online version, please make a "Description Based On" note and "Mode of Access Note." In addition, make a note for the availability of the print version.

OCLC #83832445

Type a	ELvl	Srce c	GPub	Ctrl	Lang eng
BLvl s	Form s	Conf 0	Freq q	MRec	Ctry nyu
S/L 0	Orig s	EntW	Regl r	Alph a	
Desc a	SrTp p	Cont	DtSt c	Dates 2008	, 9999

022	0	1935-9713 ‡2 1
037		‡b Haworth Medical Press, an imprint of the Haworth Press, 10 Alice Street, Binghamton, NY 13904-1580
042		lcd ‡a nsdp
130	0	Journal of gay & lesbian mental health (Online)
210	0	J. gay lesbian ment. health ‡b (Online)
222	0	Journal of gay & lesbian mental health ‡b (Online)
245	1 0	Journal of gay & lesbian mental health ‡h [electronic resource].
246	3	Journal of gay and lesbian mental health
260		New York, N.Y. : ‡b Haworth Medical Press
310		Quarterly
362	1	Began with vol. 12, no. 1/2 (2008).
530		
538		
588		
650	0	Gays ‡x Mental health ‡v Periodicals.
650	0	Lesbians ‡x Mental health ‡v Periodicals.
650	0	Bisexuality ‡v Periodicals.
710	2	Association of Gay & Lesbian Psychiatrists.
776	1	‡t Journal of gay & lesbian mental health ‡x 1935-9705 ‡w (DLC) 2007214197 ‡w (OCoLC)83831862
780	0 0	‡t Journal of gay & lesbian psychotherapy (Online) ‡x 1540-7128 ‡w (DLC) 2002214457 ‡w (OCoLC)50103807
856	4 0	‡u http://jglp.haworthpress.com

Notes

Standard Numbers and Control Numbers

In the same way that books are assigned unique numbers for identification (International Standard Book Numbers, or ISBNs), serials are assigned International Standard Serial Numbers (ISSNs). These standard numbers, together with control numbers, such as the LCCN (Library of Congress Control Number) and the OCLC control number, are useful access points. They serve as resource identifiers that can help with discovery and retrieval. They are critical to showing relationships in the serials bibliographic world, where they help to identify related resources in linking fields—whether between earlier and later titles, a parent publication and supplements, or print and online versions.

This chapter will explain what standard numbers and control numbers are and how to record them correctly in serials bibliographic records. Examples with explanations will be included to show how ISSNs, LCCNs, and OCLC control numbers are used as identifiers for resource discovery and retrieval.

The ISSN is "the international identifier for serials and other continuing resources, in the electronic and print world."[1] It contains eight digits (two groups of four digits separated by a hyphen). ISSN numbers are assigned by the ISSN National Centers and are recorded in the ISSN database: the ISSN Register.

The ISSN is an important mechanism for identifying serials as well as for linking and retrieving related serials. As more and more serials are available in multiple formats and manifestations, or "medium versions," the ISSN becomes increasingly important for identifying the various versions of a serial and for collocating or linking these versions. For the former, separate ISSN numbers are assigned to the different medium versions of a serial, while for the latter, the linking ISSN (ISSN-L) has been defined in the new ISO Standard on ISSN.[2]

An ISSN-L is an ISSN designated by the ISSN Network to group the different media versions of a serial. Only one ISSN-L is designated and associated with a serial.[3] ISSN-Ls have been assigned retrospectively to all journals in the ISSN registry, and they can be seen in many bibliographic records in the subfield "l" of the MARC field 022 for the ISSN. For more information on ISSN and ISSN-L, see "All About ISSN" and "What Is an ISSN-L" at http://www.issn.org/2-22636-All-about-ISSN.php.

The Library Congress Control Number (LCCN) and the OCLC Control Number are also important data elements and record identifiers that are useful for resource identification and access. Like the ISSN, they are used in linking fields for the retrieval of related resources, such as earlier and later titles, main title and supplements, print and online versions, etc.

An LCCN is the "unique number assigned to a MARC record by the Library of Congress."[4] More specifically, it is the unique number assigned to an authenticated CONSER record.[5] LCCNs should be recorded in bibliographic records with the correct length and structure. The LCCN is 12 characters in length and consists of three basic elements: the prefix, year, and serial number. When present, the alphabetic prefix is used to distinguish between different series of LC control numbers. The year in an LCCN reflects the year in which the control number was assigned, which is often the same year the bibliographic record was created. For LCCNs created before January 2001, the year portion consists of the last two digits of the year. For LCCNs created after January 1, 2001, all four digits of the year are included. LCCNs are recorded in the MARC field 010, with the valid LCCN entered in the subfield ‡a and a cancelled or invalid LCCN in subfield ‡z.

The OCLC control number is a unique number generated by the system when a bibliographic record is created in the OCLC bibliographic utility. The standard format includes prefixes, with the choice determined by which field is being used, as well as the number of digits in the control number. When found in MARC field 001, the OCLC control number is prefixed by "ocm" or "ocn." The "ocm" prefix is used for OCLC numbers 1 through 99,999,999. The OCLC control number is a fixed-length eight-digit number, so leading zeros are added to control numbers that are less than eight digits to create the fixed length. Beginning with the OCLC number 100,000,000, the OCLC control number becomes nine digits or higher and the "ocn" prefix is used. The 100 millionth WorldCat record was assigned the first nine-digit number. When seen in the MARC 035 field, the OCLC control number is a variable-length numeric string with no leading zeros and is preceded by "(OCoLC)." This is also the format used in linking fields in serials bibliographic records.

This chapter uses examples to illustrate how ISSN, LCCN, and OCLC control numbers are recorded in bibliographic records to help patrons retrieve and access serials resources. Guidelines and instructions from AACR2 and RDA are cited to help with decision making. Because RDA places great emphasis on showing the relationships between the FRBR entities of work, expression, manifestation, and item, it is increasingly important to record identifiers correctly to indicate the relationships. This enables users to find works, expressions, manifestations, and items related to the resources being sought. RDA 17.4.2.1 instructs a cataloger to provide an identifier for the work, expression, manifestation, or item, formulated according to the instructions given under RDA 6.8, relating to identifiers for works, RDA 6.13 for expressions, RDA 2.15 for manifestations, and RDA 2.19 for items.

NOTES

1. "ISSN International Centre." Retrieved on October 4, 2010, from http://www.issn.org.

2. Oliver Pesch. (2009). "ISSN-L: A New Standard Means Better Links." *The Serials Librarian*, 57, no.1/2, pp. 40–47.

3. "What Is an ISSN-L?" Retrieved on April 22, 2012, from http://www.issn.org/2-22637 -What-is-an-ISSN-L.php.

4. "MARC 21 Format for Bibliographic Data." Retrieved on April 22, 2012, from http:// www.loc.gov/marc/bibliographic.

5. *CONSER Editing Guide (CEG)*. Retrieved on June 28, 2011, available by subscription from http://desktop.loc.gov.

RESOURCES CONSULTED

AACR2

1.8 Standard Number and Terms of Availability Area

RDA

2.15 Identifier for the Manifestation

2.19 Identifier for the Item

6.8 Identifier for the Work

6.13 Identifier for the Expression

MARC

MARC 21 Format for Bibliographic Data: http://www.loc.gov/marc/bibliographic

OCLC

Bibliographic Formats and Standards: http://www.oclc.org/bibformats

Different ISSNs, LCCNs, and OCLC Control Numbers for Title Changes

Title: Rick Steves' best of Europe

Cover

The ISSN for *Rick Steves' Best of Europe* appears on the title page verso as 1096-7702. It is recorded in the 022 field in the bibliographic record, with the first indicator value 0, meaning the title is of international interest. This value may only be assigned by the ISSN Centers. Other institutions usually code it blank to show that the level of international interest is unknown or not specified. The linking ISSN is input in the subfield ‡l—used to link together various media versions of this resource.

The subfield ‡2 of the 022 field is used to record the code for the ISSN Center that assigned the ISSN. For example, 0 indicates ISSN International Center, 1 indicates United States, etc. The full list of Country and ISSN Center Codes is available at: http://www.issn.org/files/issn/Documentation/list-country-and-issn-centre-codes-jun2008.pdf.

When the serial changes its title, a new ISSN is assigned to the new title. In this example, *Rick Steves' Best of Europe* has the ISSN 1096-7702, and its immediately preceding title—*Rick Steves' Europe*—has the ISSN 1085-939X.

Title Page Verso

Avalon Travel
a member of the Perseus Books Group
1700 Fourth Street
Berkeley, CA 94710, USA

Text © 2009, 2008, 2007, 2006, 2005, 2004, 2003, 2002, 2001, 2000 by Rick Steves
Cover © 2009, 2008, 2007, 2006, 2005, 2004, 2003 by Avalon Travel. All rights reserved.

Maps © 2009, 2008, 2007 by Europe Through the Back Door
Printed in the US by Worzalla
First printing August 2009

For the latest on Rick Steves' lectures, guidebooks, tours, public television series, and public radio show, contact Europe Through the Back Door, Box 2009, Edmonds, WA 98020, 425/771-8303, fax 425/771-0833, www.ricksteves.com, rick@ricksteves.com.

ISBN-13: 978-1-59880-282-5
ISSN: 1096-7702

OCLC #37874880 (later title)

Type a	ELvl	Srce d	GPub	Ctrl	Lang eng
BLvl s	Form	Conf 0	Freq a	MRec	Ctry nmu
S/L 0	Orig	EntW	Regl r	Alph a	
Desc a	SrTp	Cont	DtSt c	Dates 1998	, 9999

010		99111511 ‡z sn 97001489
022	0	1096-7702 ‡l 1096-7702 ‡2 1
042		nsdp ‡a lc
130	0	Rick Steves' best of Europe (Santa Fe, N.M. : 1998)
210	0	Rick Steves' best of Europe ‡b (1998)
222		0	Rick Steves' best of Europe ‡b (1998)
245	0	0	Rick Steves' best of Europe.
260		Santa Fe, NM : ‡b John Muir Publications, ‡c c1998-
300		v. : ‡b maps ; ‡c 21 cm.
310		Annual
362	0	-1998
500		Title from cover.
651		0	Europe ‡v Guidebooks.
700	1	Steves, Rick, ‡d 1955-
780	0	0	‡t Rick Steves' Europe ‡x 1085-939X ‡w (DLC) 97649769 ‡w (OCoLC)33454933

Linking fields, such as fields 780/785, contain subfields with identifiers for the earlier and/or later titles. These include subfield ‡x for the ISSN and a separate subfield ‡w for each of the record control numbers (the OCLC control number and the LCCN). The data elements are taken from the subfield ‡a of the 010 and 022 fields in the records for the related titles rather than from subfield ‡z of field 010 (cancelled/invalid LC control number), subfield ‡y of field 022 (incorrect ISSN), or ‡z of field 022 (cancelled ISSN). The OCLC number recorded in subfield ‡w is preceded by the prefix (OCoLC).

OCLC #33454933 (earlier title)

Type a	ELvl	Srce d	GPub	Ctrl	Lang eng
BLvl s	Form	Conf 0	Freq a	MRec	Ctry nmu
S/L 0	Orig	EntW	Regl r	Alph a	
Desc a	SrTp	Cont	DtSt d	Dates 1996	, 1997

010		97649769 ‡z sn 95005712
022	0	1085-939X ‡2 1
042		nsdp ‡a lc
245	0 0	Rick Steves' Europe.
260		Santa Fe, N.M. : ‡b John Muir Publications, ‡c c1996-
300		v. : ‡b maps ; ‡c 21 cm.
310		Annual
362	0	-1996
362	1	Ceased with 1997.
500		Title from cover.
651	0	Europe ‡v Guidebooks.
700	1	Steves, Rick, ‡d 1955-
780	0 0	‡t Rick Steves' best of Europe ‡x 1078-7992 ‡w (DLC) 95641049 ‡w (OCoLC)31194882
785	0 0	‡t Rick Steve's best of Europe (Santa Fe, N.M. : 1998) ‡x 1096-7702 ‡w (DLC) 99111511 ‡w (OCoLC)37874880

AACR2

1.8A2 - Take information included in this area from any source. Do not enclose any information in brackets

1.8B1 - Give the International Standard Book Number (ISBN), or International Standard Serial Number (ISSN), or any other internationally agreed standard number for the item being described. Give such numbers with the agreed abbreviation and with the standard spacing or hyphenation

12.8B1 - Give the International Standard Serial Number (ISSN) or International Standard Book Number (ISBN) assigned to a resource as instructed in 1.8B

RDA

2.15 - Identifier for the Manifestation: CORE ELEMENT
   If there is more than one identifier for the manifestation, prefer an internationally recognized identifier, if applicable. Additional identifiers for the manifestation are optional

2.15.1.1 - An identifier for the manifestation is a character string associated with a manifestation that serves to differentiate that manifestation from other manifestations

(Continued on next page)

2.15.1.2 - Take identifiers for the manifestation from any source

2.15.1.4 - Recording Identifiers for Manifestations: if the identifier for the manifestation is one for which there is a prescribed display format (e.g., ISBN, ISSN, URN), record it in accordance with that format

2.15.1.6 - Incorrect Identifiers: if an identifier is known to be incorrectly represented in the resource, record the number as it appears and indicate that the number is incorrect, cancelled, or invalid, as appropriate

6.8.1.3 - Record an identifier for the work

6.13.1.3 - Record an identifier for the expression

Different ISSNs, LCCNs, and OCLC Control Numbers for Different Formats

Title: Journal of thermal science and engineering applications

Cover of Print Version   Screenshot – Journal Information Page

Cover Verso

In this example, the *Journal of Thermal Science and Engineering Applications* is available in print and online. Each has its own ISSN: 1948-5085 for the print version and 1948-5093 for the online version. To link the two manifestations of this serial (that is, to show the horizontal relationship), the 776 field is used to record information about another format of the same title. The subfields should be coded carefully with the correct ISSN (‡x), LCCN (‡w (DLC)), and OCLC (‡w (OCoLC)) in the 776 field.

OCLC #320088264 (print version)

Type a	ELvl	Srce c	GPub	Ctrl	Lang eng
BLvl s	Form	Conf	Freq q	MRec	Ctry nyu
S/L 0	Orig	EntW	Regl r	Alph a	
Desc a	SrTp p	Cont	DtSt c	Dates 2009	, 9999

010		2009202683
022	0	1948-5085 ‡2 1
042		pcc ‡a nsdp
245	0 0	Journal of thermal science and engineering applications.
260		New York, N.Y. : ‡b American Society of Mechanical Engineers
310		Quarterly
362	1	Began with v. 1, no. 1 (Mar. 2009).
490	1	Transactions of the ASME
500		Description based on: Vol. 1, no. 1 (Mar. 2009); title from cover.
650	0	Heat engineering ‡v Periodicals.
650	0	Thermodynamics ‡v Periodicals.
710	2	American Society of Mechanical Engineers.
776	0 8	‡i Also issued online: ‡t Journal of thermal science and engineering applications (Online) ‡x 1948-5093 ‡w (DLC) 2009202684 ‡w (OCoLC)320089028
830	0	Transactions of the ASME (1959)
856	4 1	‡u http://asmedl.aip.org/TSEA

(Continued on next page)

AACR2

1.8A2 - Take information included in this area from any source. Do not enclose any information in brackets

1.8B1 - Give the International Standard Book Number (ISBN), or International Standard Serial Number (ISSN), or any other internationally agreed standard number for the item being described. Give such numbers with the agreed abbreviation and with the standard spacing or hyphenation

12.8B1 - Give the International Standard Serial Number (ISSN) or International Standard Book Number (ISBN) assigned to a resource as instructed in 1.8B

RDA

2.15 - Identifier for the Manifestation: CORE ELEMENT
If there is more than one identifier for the manifestation, prefer an internationally recognized identifier, if applicable. Additional identifiers for the manifestation are optional

2.15.1.1 - An identifier for the manifestation is a character string associated with a manifestation that serves to differentiate that manifestation from other manifestations

2.15.1.2 - Take identifiers for the manifestation from any source

2.15.1.4 - Recording Identifiers for Manifestations: if the identifier for the manifestation is one for which there is a prescribed display format (e.g., ISBN, ISSN, URN), record it in accordance with that format

2.15.1.6 - Incorrect Identifiers: if an identifier is known to be incorrectly represented in the resource, record the number as it appears and indicate that the number is incorrect, cancelled, or invalid, as appropriate

6.8.1.3 - Record an identifier for the work

6.13.1.3 - Record an identifier for the expression

OCLC #320089028 (online version)

Type a	ELvl	Srce c	GPub	Ctrl	Lang eng
BLvl s	Form s	Conf 0	Freq q	MRec	Ctry nyu
S/L 0	Orig s	EntW	Regl r	Alph a	
Desc a	SrTp p	Cont	DtSt c	Dates 2009	, 9999

006		m d
007		c ǂb r
010		2009202684
022	0	1948-5093 ǂ2 1
042		pcc ǂa nsdp
130	0	Journal of thermal science and engineering applications (Online)
245	1 0	Journal of thermal science and engineering applications ǂh [electronic resource].
260		New York, N.Y. : ǂb American Society of Mechanical Engineers
310		Quarterly
362	1	Began with: Vol. 1, issue 1 (Mar. 2009).
490	1	Transactions of the ASME

500			Description based on: Vol. 1, issue 1 (Mar. 2009); title from contents page (ASME Digital Library website, viewed Jan. 8, 2010).
500			Latest issue consulted: Vol. 1, issue 3 (Sept. 2009) (ASME Digital Library website, viewed Jan. 8, 2010).
650		0	Heat engineering ‡v Periodicals.
650		0	Thermodynamics ‡v Periodicals.
710	2		American Society of Mechanical Engineers.
776	0	8	‡i Also issued in print: ‡t Journal of thermal science and engineering applications ‡x 1948-5085 ‡w (DLC) 2009202683 ‡w (OCoLC) 320088264
830		0	Transactions of the ASME (1959)
856	4	0	‡u http://www.asmedl.org/TSEA
856	4	0	‡u http://scitation.aip.org/dbt/dbt.jsp?KEY=JTSEBV

Correct and Incorrect ISSNs, LCCN, OCLC Control Number

Title: Photo district news; Photo district news (Midwestern ed.)

Front Page

Front Page

The serial *Photo District News* was preceded by the earlier title *New York Photo District News* and was later split into four regional editions: *Photo District News (Southern ed.)*; *Photo District News (Midwestern ed.)*; *Photo District News (Western ed.)*; and *Photo District News (Eastern ed.)*. Its ISSN 0883-766X is encoded in subfield ‡a of 022 field, while an incorrect ISSN is input in subfield ‡y of 022 field. In this case, the ISSN in subfield ‡y 1274-7731 was for the earlier title: *New York Photo District News*.

When recording identifiers, be sure to use the correct ISSN, LCCN, and OCLC control numbers in all linking fields for earlier titles, later titles, different versions, and different editions.

OCLC #12206141 (earlier Title)

Type a	ELvl 7	Srce d	GPub	Ctrl	Lang eng
BLvl s	Form	Conf 0	Freq m	MRec	Ctry nyu
S/L 0	Orig e	EntW	Regl n	Alph a	
Desc a	SrTp p	Cont	DtSt d	Dates 198u	, 1987

010		sn 85009271
022	0	0883-766X ‡y 1274-7731 ‡2 1
042		nsdp
245	0 0	Photo district news.
260		New York, NY : ‡b Visions Unlimited Corp.,
300		v. : ‡b ill. ; ‡c 41 cm.
310		Monthly (except 2 issues in May and Nov.), ‡b <Jan. 1987->
321		Monthly, ‡b <Dec. 1984->
321		Monthly (except 2 issues in Mar., May, and Oct.), ‡b <Feb. 1986->
362	1	Ceased with v. 7, issue 14 (Dec. 1987).
500		Description based on: Vol. 5, issue 12 (Dec. 1985); title from cover.
500		Final issue consulted: Vol. 7, issue 14 (Dec. 1987).
580		Split into four regional editions: Photo district news (Southern ed.); Photo district news (Midwestern ed.); Photo district news (Western ed.); and: Photo district news (Eastern ed.)
650	0	Commercial photography ‡v Periodicals.
780	0 0	‡t New York photo district news ‡x 0274-7731 ‡w (DLC)sn 80001440 ‡w (OCoLC)6582873
785	1 6	‡t Photo district news (Southern ed.) ‡x 1048-0153 ‡w (DLC)sn 90004326 ‡w (OCoLC)20841207
785	1 6	‡t Photo district news (Midwestern ed.) ‡x 1048-0161 ‡w (DLC)sn 90004327 ‡w (OCoLC)20841363
785	1 6	‡t Photo district news (Western ed.) ‡x 1048-0145 ‡w (DLC)sn 90004325 ‡w (OCoLC)20840851
785	1 6	‡t Photo district news (Eastern ed.) ‡x 1045-8158 ‡w (DLC)sn 89007763 ‡w (OCoLC)20254856

AACR2

1.8A2 - Take information included in this area from any source. Do not enclose any information in brackets

1.8B1 - Give the International Standard Book Number (ISBN), or International Standard Serial Number (ISSN), or any other internationally agreed standard number for the item being described. Give such numbers with the agreed abbreviation and with the standard spacing or hyphenation

12.8B1 - Give the International Standard Serial Number (ISSN) or International Standard Book Number (ISBN) assigned to a resource as instructed in 1.8B

RDA

2.15 - Identifier for the Manifestation: CORE ELEMENT
  If there is more than one identifier for the manifestation, prefer an internationally recognized identifier, if applicable. Additional identifiers for the manifestation are optional

(Continued on next page)

2.15.1.1 - An identifier for the manifestation is a character string associated with a manifestation that serves to differentiate that manifestation from other manifestations

2.15.1.2 - Take identifiers for the manifestation from any source

2.15.1.4 - Recording Identifiers for Manifestations: if the identifier for the manifestation is one for which there is a prescribed display format (e.g., ISBN, ISSN, URN), record it in accordance with that format

2.15.1.6 - Incorrect Identifiers: if an identifier is known to be incorrectly represented in the resource, record the number as it appears and indicate that the number is incorrect, cancelled, or invalid, as appropriate

6.8.1.3 - Record an identifier for the work

6.13.1.3 - Record an identifier for the expression

OCLC #20841363 (Midwestern ed.)

Type a	ELvl 7	Srce d	GPub	Ctrl	Lang eng
BLvl s	Form	Conf 0	Freq m	MRec	Ctry nyu
S/L 0	Orig	EntW	Regl n	Alpha a	
Desc a	SrTp p	Cont	DtSt d	Dates 1988	, 199u

010		sn 90004327
022	0	1048-0161 ǂy 0883-766X ǂ2 1
042		nsdp ǂa msc
130	0	Photo district news (Midwestern ed.)
245	1	0	Photo district news.
250		Midwestern ed.
260		New York, NY : ǂb Visions Unlimited Corp.,
300		v. : ǂb ill. ; ǂc 41 cm.
310		Monthly (except for May & Oct. when 1 extra issue is printed)
362	0	Vol. 8, issue 1 (Jan. 1988)-
500		Description based on: Vol. 10, issue 1 (Jan. 1990); title from caption.
650		0	Commercial photography ǂv Periodicals.
775	0	ǂt Photo district news (Western ed.) ǂx 1048-0145 ǂw (DLC)sn 90004325 ǂw (OCoLC)20840851
775	0	ǂt Photo district news (Southern ed.) ǂx 1048-0153 ǂw (DLC)sn 90004326 ǂw (OCoLC)20841207
775	0	ǂt Photo district news (Eastern ed.) ǂx 1045-8158 ǂw (DLC)sn 89007763 ǂw (OCoLC)20254856
780	0	1	ǂt Photo district news ǂx 0883-766X ǂw (DLC)sn 85009271 ǂw (OCoLC)12206141
785	0	5	ǂt PDN (New York, N.Y.) ǂx 1543-0294 ǂw (DLC)sn 96044133 ǂw (OCoLC)34499521

ISSN, LCCN, OCLC Control Number in Linking Fields for Related Resources

Title: Population

Print Cover

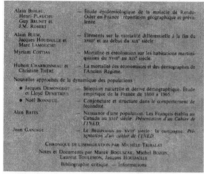

Screenshot–Journal Homepage

The serial *Population* is a French publication, but some of its content is also available in English issued under the titles *Population. English Selection*, 1989–2001, and *Population. English*, 2002–. These relationships are recorded in the 787 (Other Relationship Entry) and 775 fields (Other Edition Entry), respectively. Additionally, the 776 field is used because this periodical also has an online version.

In these linking fields, the most common subfields are input in this order: ǂt, ǂx, and ǂw, where the ISSN is input in subfield ǂx, the LCCN in subfield ǂw (preceded by LC's MARC code DLC in parenthesis), and the OCLC control number in a separate subfield ǂw (preceded by OCLC's MARC code OCoLC in parenthesis). There should be no space between "(OCoLC)" and the OCLC control number. Note that the ISSN in ǂx is taken from the 022 field subfield ǂa of the related record, while the LCCN and OCLC control numbers are taken from the 001 and 010 fields, respectively, of the related record.

There are differences in recording the post-2000 and pre-2001 (LCCNs assigned from 1898 to 2000) formats of LCCN in subfield ǂw. According to the *CONSER Editing Guide* (CEG), post-2000 records have 12 character positions: 2 character positions for the alphabetic prefix, 4 character positions for the year, and 6 character positions for the number portion of the LCCN. If the number portion has fewer than six digits, leading zeroes are added to fill in the positions (e.g., ǂw (DLC) 2002261159, ǂw (DLC)sn2001061303). Pre-2001 LCCNs have the following format: 3 character positions for the alphabetic prefix, 2 character positions for the year, and 6 character positions for the number portion. Three leading blank spaces are input between the symbol "(DLC)" and the two-digit year if the LCCN has no prefix. If the LCCN has a prefix of fewer than three characters, leave the appropriate number of blank spaces following the prefix; input the two-digit year information; do not input a hyphen; and input the six-digit number last. Add leading zeros where necessary. Do not include a trailing blank following the number. The following are examples of the pre-2001 LCCNs: ǂw (DLC) 72000153, ǂw (DLC)sn 90025063.

OCLC #1762663

Type a	ELvl	Srce	GPub	Ctrl	Lang fre
BLvl s	Form	Conf 0	Freq q	MRec	Ctry fr
S/L 0	Orig	EntW	Regl r	Alph	
Desc	SrTp p	Cont	DtSt c	Dates 1946	, 9999

010		49051872
022		0032-4663
042		lc
245	0 0	Population.
260		Paris, ‡b Institut national d'études démographiques [etc.]
300		v. ‡b maps, diagrs. ‡c 25 cm.
310		Quarterly, ‡b 2007-
321		Bimonthly ‡b <, nov./déc. 1978-2006>
321		Quarterly, ‡b 1946-
362	0	1.- année; jan./mars 1946-
500		Latest issue consulted: Vol. 62, no 1 (2007).
530		Also issued online.
550		"Revue bimestrielle de l'Institut national d'études démographiques."
555		1946-59. 1 v.
580		Issued also in English under the titles: Population. English selection, 1989-2001; and later: Population. English, 2002-.
650	0	Population ‡v Periodicals.
710	2	Institut national d'études démographiques (France)
775	0	‡t Population. English ‡x 1634-2941 ‡w (DLC) 2002261159 ‡w (OCoLC)49898107
776	1	‡t Population (Institut national d'études démographiques (France) : Online) ‡x 1957-7966 ‡w (DLC) 2005237378 ‡w (OCoLC)60627536
787	1	‡t Population. English selection ‡x 1169-1018 ‡w (DLC)sn 90025063 ‡w (OCoLC)21028583
856	4 1	‡u http://www.jstor.org/journals/00324663.html
856	4 1	‡u http://bibpurl.oclc.org/web/25736 ‡u http://www.persee.fr/web/revues/home/prescript/revue/pop

AACR2

1.8A2 - Take information included in this area from any source. Do not enclose any information in brackets

1.8B1 - Give the International Standard Book Number (ISBN), or International Standard Serial Number (ISSN), or any other internationally agreed standard number for the item being described. Give such numbers with the agreed abbreviation and with the standard spacing or hyphenation

12.8B1 - Give the International Standard Serial Number (ISSN) or International Standard Book Number (ISBN) assigned to a resource as instructed in 1.8B

RDA

2.15 - Identifier for the Manifestation: CORE ELEMENT
If there is more than one identifier for the manifestation, prefer an internationally recognized identifier, if applicable. Additional identifiers for the manifestation are optional

2.15.1.1 - An identifier for the manifestation is a character string associated with a manifestation that serves to differentiate that manifestation from other manifestations

2.15.1.2 - Take identifiers for the manifestation from any source

2.15.1.4 - Recording identifiers for manifestations: if the identifier for the manifestation is one for which there is a prescribed display format (e.g., ISBN, ISSN, URN), record it in accordance with that format

2.15.1.6 - Incorrect identifiers: if an identifier is known to be incorrectly represented in the resource, record the number as it appears and indicate that the number is incorrect, cancelled, or invalid, as appropriate

6.8.1.3 - Record an identifier for the work

6.13.1.3 - Record an identifier for the expression

ISSN Not Changed With Title Change

Title: Insight into diversity

Cover

Masthead

Masthead

Cover

A major title change requires a new ISSN, but sometimes, the ISSN found on the serial may not be the correct one. For example, when a journal goes through a title change, a new ISSN may not have been obtained in time to be printed in the first new issue under the later title. This happened with the serial Affirmative Action Register, which changed its title to Insight Into Diversity with Vol. 74, no. 3 (Nov. 2009) but kept the existing ISSN 0146-2113 until a few issues later. The new ISSN 2154-0349 first appeared with Vol. 75, no. 3 (June 2010).

The correct ISSN is entered in subfield ‡a of the MARC 022 field. An incorrect ISSN (i.e., one that has already been assigned to an earlier title) is recorded in subfield ‡y and cancelled ISSNs are recorded in subfield ‡z.

When there are questions, it is best to verify the ISSN so the correct information will be recorded in the bibliographic record. Sources of verification include two subscription websites: the ISSN Portal (found at http://www.issn.org) or Ulrich's International Periodical Directory (http://ulrichsweb.serialssolutions.com).

OCLC #460107918 (later title)

Type a	ELvl	Srce c	GPub	Ctrl	Lang eng
BLvl s	Form	Conf 0	Freq m	MRec	Ctry mou
S/L 0	Orig	EntW	Regl r	Alph	
Desc a	SrTp p	Cont	DtSt c	Dates 2009	, 9999

010			2009257195
022			2154-0349 ‡y 0146-2113
042			pcc
043			n-us---
245	0	0	Insight into diversity.
246	3	0	Insight
260			St. Louis, Mo. : ‡b Potomac Pub., Inc., ‡c c2009-
300			v. ; ‡c 28 cm.
310			Monthly
362	1		Began with v. 74, no. 3 (Nov. 2009).
500			"Connecting diverse professionals to diverse careers."
500			Description based on: Vol. 74, no. 3 (Nov. 2009); title from cover.
500			Latest issue consulted: Dec. 2009.
650		0	Minorities ‡x Employment ‡v Periodicals.
650		0	Help-wanted advertising ‡v Periodicals.
650		0	Affirmative action programs ‡v Periodicals.
780	0	0	‡t Affirmative action register ‡x 0146-2113 ‡w (DLC)sc 77000990 ‡w (OCoLC)2273613

AACR2

1.8A2 - Take information included in this area from any source. Do not enclose any information in brackets

1.8B1 - Give the International Standard Book Number (ISBN), or International Standard Serial Number (ISSN), or any other internationally agreed standard number for the item being described. Give such numbers with the agreed abbreviation and with the standard spacing or hyphenation

12.8B1 - Give the International Standard Serial Number (ISSN) or International Standard Book Number (ISBN) assigned to a resource as instructed in 1.8B

RDA

2.15 - Identifier for the Manifestation: CORE ELEMENT
   If there is more than one identifier for the manifestation, prefer an internationally recognized identifier, if applicable. Additional identifiers for the manifestation are optional

2.15.1.1 - An identifier for the manifestation is a character string associated with a manifestation that serves to differentiate that manifestation from other manifestations

2.15.1.2 - Take identifiers for the manifestation from any source

2.15.1.4 - Recording identifiers for manifestations: if the identifier for the manifestation is one for which there is a prescribed display format (e.g., ISBN, ISSN, URN), record it in accordance with that format

(Continued on next page)

2.15.1.6 - Incorrect identifiers: if an identifier is known to be incorrectly represented in the resource, record the number as it appears and indicate that the number is incorrect, cancelled, or invalid, as appropriate

6.8.1.3 - Record an identifier for the work

6.13.1.3 - Record an identifier for the expression

OCLC #2273613 (earlier title)

Type a	ELvl	Srce c	GPub	Ctrl	Lang eng
BLvl s	Form	Conf 0	Freq m	MRec	Ctry mou
S/L 0	Orig	EntW	Regl r	Alph a	
Desc	SrTp p	Cont	DtSt d	Dates 19uu	, 2009

010			sc 77000990
022	0		0146-2113 ‡2 1
042			nsdp ‡a lc
043			n-us---
245	0	0	Affirmative action register.
246	3	0	AAR/EEO, Affirmative action register
246	1	3	AAR, Affirmative action register
260			St. Louis, Mo. ‡b Potomac Pub., Inc.
300			v. ‡c 28 cm.
362	1		Ceased with v. 74, no. 2 (Oct. 2009).
500			At head of title: AAR/EEO, Aug. 1984-<June 1994>
500			Published <-Mar. 1977> by Affirmative Action, Inc.
530			Also issued online.
650		0	Minorities ‡x Employment ‡v Periodicals.
650		0	Help-wanted advertising ‡v Periodicals.
650		0	Affirmative action programs ‡v Periodicals.
785	0	0	‡t Insight into diversity ‡w (DLC) 2009257195 ‡w (OCoLC) 460107918
856	4	1	‡u http://www.aar-eeo.com/

Cover

EXERCISE 1

World Future Review is a journal formed by the merger of two earlier titles—*Future Research Quarterly* and *Future Survey*—as shown in the cataloging records. These are OCLC #11276457 and OCLC #4693322, respectively (see the following pages for complete records). Based on the information provided, complete the cataloging record for the new title *World Future Review* by using the correct ISSN, OCLC control number, and LCCN in the two 780 fields.

World Future Review
A Journal of Strategic Foresight

Volume 1, Number 1   February-March 2009

Towards a Future Global Science:
Axioms for Modeling a Living Universe
By Elisabet Sahtouris, Ph.D.

Ensuring Strategic Direction: Using
Principles-Based Strategy and Scenarios Together
By Robert E. Neilson

Ethnography in Robotics: Measuring Learning
Through Qualitative Analysis in the
Robotics-for-Theater Project
By Gerardo del Cerro Santamaria

The Future Evolution of the Ecology of Mind
By Tom Lombardo, Ph.D.

Plus:

Featured Futurist: Don Tapscott

Book Review

Abstracts of Books and Journals

Table of Contents

WORLD FUTURE REVIEW (ISSN 8755-3317) is published bimonthly by the World Future Society, 7910 Woodmont Avenue, Suite 450, Bethesda, Maryland 20814, U.S.A. Included with Professional membership in the World Future Society (dues. $275 per year). Subscriptions for libraries and other institutions are $330 annually. Application to Mail at Periodicals Postage Prices is Pending at Bethesda, Maryland, and at Additional Mailing Offices. • POSTMASTER: Send address changes to WORLD FUTURE REVIEW, 7910 Woodmont Avenue, Suite 450, Bethesda, Maryland 20814. • OWNERSHIP: WORLD FUTURE REVIEW is owned exclusively by the World Future Society, a nonpartisan educational and scientific organization incorporated in the District of Columbia and recognized by the U.S. Internal Revenue Service as a nonprofit tax-exempt organization under section 501(c)3 of the Internal Revenue Code. • CHANGE OF ADDRESS: Write or call Membership Department at the Society. 1-800-989-8274.

OCLC #301795864

Type a	ELvl	Srce c	GPub	Ctrl	Lang eng
BLvl s	Form	Conf 0	Freq b	MRec	Ctry mdu
S/L 0	Orig	EntW	Regl r	Alph a	
Desc a	SrTp p	Cont	DtSt c	Dates 2009	, 9999

010			2009207441
022	0		1946-7567 ‡2 1
042			nsdp ‡a lcd
245	0	0	World future review.
260			Bethesda, MD : ‡b World Future Society
310			Bimonthly
362	1		Began with: Vol. 1, no. 1 (Feb.-Mar. 2009).
500			Description based on 1st issue; title from title page.
500			Latest issue consulted: Vol. 1, no. 3 (June–July 2009).
580			Merger of: Future survey, and: Futures research quarterly.
650		0	Forecasting ‡v Periodicals.
650		0	Forecasting ‡x Study and teaching ‡v Periodicals.
710	2		World Future Society.

780	1	4	‡t Futures research quarterly ‡x	‡w (DLC)	‡w (OCoLC)
780	1	4	‡t Future survey ‡x	‡w (DLC)	‡w (OCoLC)

OCLC #11276457 (earlier title: *Futures Research Quarterly*)

Type a	ELvl	Srce c	GPub	Ctrl	Lang eng
BLvl s	Form	Conf 0	Freq q	MRec	Ctry mdu
S/L 0	Orig	EntW	Regl r	Alph a	
Desc a	SrTp p	Cont o	DtSt d	Dates 1985	, 2008

010			87644223
022	0		8755-3317 ‡l 8755-3317 ‡y 0049-8092 ‡2 1
042			nsdp ‡a pcc
245	0	0	Futures research quarterly.
260			Bethesda, MD : ‡b World Future Society, ‡c c1985-
300			v. : ‡b ill. ; ‡c 24 cm.
310			Quarterly
362	0		Vol. 1, no. 1 (spring 1985)-
362	1		Ceased in 2008.
500			Title from cover.
500			Latest issue consulted: vol. 24, no. 1 (spring 2008).
580			Merged with: Future survey to form: World future review.
650		0	Forecasting ‡v Periodicals.
650		0	Forecasting ‡x Study and teaching ‡v Periodicals.
710	2		World Future Society.
780	0	0	‡t World Future Society bulletin ‡x 0049-8092 ‡w (DLC) 87644228 ‡w (OCoLC)3302525
785	1	7	‡t Future survey ‡w (OCoLC)4693322
785	1	7	‡t World future review ‡x 1946-7567 ‡w (DLC) 2009207441 ‡w (OCoLC)301795864

OCLC #4693322 (earlier title: *Future Survey*)

Type a	ELvl	Srce d	GPub	Ctrl	Lang eng
BLvl s	Form	Conf 0	Freq m	MRec	Ctry dcu
S/L 0	Orig	EntW a	Regl r	Alph a	
Desc a	SrTp p	Cont	DtSt d	Dates 1979	, 2008

010			81649971 ǂz sn 79001912
022	0		0190-3241 ǂ2 1
042			lc ǂa nsdp
245	0	0	Future survey.
260			Washington, D.C. : ǂb World Future Society, ǂc c1979-c2008.
300			v. ; ǂc 28 cm.
310			Monthly
362	0		Vol. 1, no. 1 (Jan. 1979)-v. 30, no. 12 (Dec 2008).
500			"A monthly abstract of books, articles and reports concerning forecasts, trends, and ideas about the future."
500			Title from cover.
580			Merged with: Futures research quarterly to form: World future review
650		0	Social prediction ǂv Abstracts ǂv Periodicals.
650		0	Social indicators ǂv Abstracts ǂv Periodicals.
710	2		World Future Society.
776	0	8	ǂt Future survey (Online) ǂw (OCoLC)60626134
780	0	0	ǂt Public policy book forecast ǂx 0197-9035 ǂw (DLC)sc 79004758
785	1	7	ǂt Futures research quarterly ǂw (OCoLC)11276457
785	1	7	ǂt World future review ǂw (OCoLC)301795864

Cover

EXERCISE 2

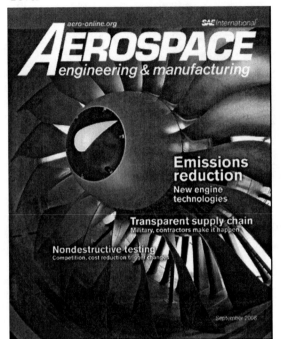

In 2008, *Aerospace Engineering* changed its title to *Aerospace Engineering & Manufacturing* and became available in print and online formats. The bibliographic records for the earlier title *Aerospace Engineering* (OCLC #9090151) and for the online version of the new title *Aerospace Engineering & Manufacturing* (OCLC #166398436) are found on the following pages. Based on the information provided, update the linking fields 776 and 780 for the print version of the new title *Aerospace Engineering & Manufacturing* (OCLC #162634811). You will need to enter the ISSN, LCCN, and OCLC control numbers.

OCLC #162634811

Type a	ELvl	Srce c	GPub	Ctrl	Lang eng
BLvl s	Form	Conf 0	Freq m	MRec	Ctry pau
S/L 0	Orig	EntW	Regl r	Alph a	
Desc a	SrTp p	Cont	DtSt c	Dates 2008	, 9999

022	0	1937-5212 ‡2 1
037		‡b Society of Automotive Engineers, Inc., 400 Commonwealth Dr., Warrendale, PA 15096
042		lcd ‡a nsdp
210	0	Aerosp. eng. manuf.
222	0	Aerospace engineering & manufacturing
245	0 0	Aerospace engineering & manufacturing.
246	1 3	Aerospace engineering and manufacturing
260		Warrendale, PA : ‡b SAE International, ‡c c2008-
300		v. : ‡b ill. ; ‡c 28 cm.
310		Ten no. a year
362	1	Began with Vol. 28, no. 1 (Jan./Feb. 2008).
500		Description based on first issue; title from cover.
650	0	Airplanes ‡x Design and construction ‡v Periodicals.
650	0	Space vehicles ‡x Design and construction ‡v Periodicals.
710	2	Society of Automotive Engineers.
776	0 8	‡i Also available online: ‡t Aerospace engineering & manufacturing ‡x ‡w (DLC) ‡w (OCoLC)
780	0 0	‡t Aerospace engineering (Society of Automotive Engineers) ‡x ‡w (DLC) ‡w (OCoLC)
856	4 1	‡u http://www.aero-online.org

OCLC #9090151 (earlier title: *Aerospace Engineering*)

Type a	ELvl	Srce d	GPub	Ctrl	Lang eng
BLvl s	Form	Conf 0	Freq m	MRec	Ctry pau
S/L 0	Orig	EntW	Regl r	Alph a	
Desc a	SrTp p	Cont	DtSt d	Dates 1983	, 2007

010		83644639 ǂz sn 82008061
022	0	0736-2536 ǂ2 1
042		lc ǂa nsdp
130	0	Aerospace engineering (Society of Automotive Engineers)
245	0 0	Aerospace engineering / ǂc SAE.
260		Warrendale, Pa. : ǂb Society of Automotive Engineers, ǂc -c2007.
300		25 v. : ǂb ill. ; ǂc 28 cm.
310		10 no. a year, ǂb -Nov./Dec. 2007.
321		Monthly ǂb <, Jan. 1986- >
321		Quarterly
321		Bimonthly, ǂb 1984-198
362	0	[Vol. 3, no. 1] (Mar. 1983)-v. 27, no. 10 (Nov./Dec. 2007).
650	0	Airplanes ǂx Design and construction ǂv Periodicals.
650	0	Space vehicles ǂx Design and construction ǂv Periodicals.
710	2	Society of Automotive Engineers.
780	0 0	ǂt SAE in aerospace engineering ǂx 0730-3017 ǂw (DLC) 81649451 ǂw (OCoLC)7780391
785	0 0	ǂt Aerospace engineering & manufacturing ǂx 1937-5212 ǂw (DLC) 2007212608 ǂw (OCoLC)162634811

OCLC #166398436 (Online version: *Aerospace Engineering & Manufacturing*)

Type a	ELvl 7	Srce c	GPub	Ctrl	Lang eng
BLvl s	Form s	Conf	Freq	MRec	Ctry pau
S/L 0	Orig s	EntW	Regl	Alph a	
Desc a	SrTp p	Cont	DtSt c	Dates 2008	, 9999

006		m d
007		c ǂb r
010		2007215491
022	0	1939-6694 ǂ1937-5212 ǂ2 1
042		nsdp ǂa lcd
245	0 0	Aerospace engineering & manufacturing ǂh [electronic resource].
246	3	Aerospace engineering and manufacturing
260		Warrendale, PA : ǂb SAE International
310		Ten no. a year.
362	1	Began in 2008.
500		Description based on: Aug. 2008; title from title screen.
710	2	Society of Automotive Engineers.
776	0 8	ǂi Also available in print: ǂt Aerospace engineering & manufacturing ǂx 1937-5212 ǂw (DLC) 2007212608 ǂw (OCoLC)162634811
856	4 0	ǂz to suscribe ǂu http://www.aero-online.org

Cover

EXERCISE 3

The journal *Integrative Physiological and Behavioral Science*—available in print and online formats—had the earlier title Pavlovian Journal of Biological Science and the later title Integrative Psychological & Behavioral Science. Based on the information found in the OCLC records for the related titles provided on the following two pages, update the record (OCLC #22684607) for Integrative Physiological and Behavioral Science with linking fields 776, 780, and 785. Make sure to include the ISSN, LCCN, and OCLC control numbers for the earlier title, later title, and online version of the title.

OCLC #22684607

Type a	ELvl	Srce d	GPub	Ctrl	Lang eng
BLvl s	Form	Conf 0	Freq q	MRec	Ctry nju
S/L 0	Orig	EntW	Regl r	Alph a	
Desc a	SrTp p	Cont	DtSt d	Dates 1991	, 2005

022	0	1053-881X ‡2 1
037		‡b Transaction Periodicals Consortium, Dept. 4010, Rutgers Univ., New Brunswick, NJ 08903
042		nsdp ‡a lc
245	0 0	Integrative physiological and behavioral science : ‡b the official journal of the Pavlovian Society.
260		New Brunswick, NJ : ‡b Transaction Periodicals Consortium, Rutgers University, ‡c c1991-
300		v. : ‡b ill. ; ‡c 26 cm.
310		Quarterly
362	0	Vol. 26, no. 1 (Jan.-Mar. 1991)-
362	1	Ceased with Vol. 40, no. 4 (Oct./Dec. 2005).
500		Title from cover.
510	2	Chemical abstracts ‡x 0009-2258
530		Also issued online.
650	0	Psychology ‡v Periodicals.
650	0	Conditioned response ‡v Periodicals.
710	2	Pavlovian Society of America.
776	1	‡t Integrative physiological and behavioral science ‡w (DLC) ‡w (OCoLC)
780	0 0	‡t Pavlovian journal of biological science ‡x ‡w (DLC) ‡w (OCoLC)
785	0 0	‡t Integrative psychological & behavioral science ‡x ‡w (DLC) ‡w (OCoLC)
856	4	‡u http://firstsearch.oclc.org ‡z Address for accessing the journal using authorization number and password through OCLC FirstSearch Electronic Collections Online. Subscription to online journal required for access to abstracts and full text

OCLC #1793503 (earlier title: *Pavlovian Journal of Biological Science*)

Type a	ELvl	Srce	GPub	Ctrl	Lang eng
BLvl s	Form	Conf 0	Freq q	MRec	Ctry pau
S/L 0	Orig	EntW	Regl r	Alph a	
Desc	SrTp p	Cont	DtSt d	Dates 1974	, 1990

010		74644014
022		0093-2213 ‡2 1
042		lc ‡a nsdp
245	0 4	The Pavlovian journal of biological science.
260		Philadelphia, ‡b J.B. Lippincott.
300		v. ‡b ill. ‡c 26 cm.
310		Quarterly
362	0	v. 9-25; Jan./Mar. 1974-Oct.-Dec. 1990.
500		Official journal of the Pavlovian Society of America.
510	2	Chemical abstracts ‡x 0009-2258 ‡b -1988
530		Also issued online.
650	0	Psychology ‡v Periodicals.
650	0	Conditioned response ‡v Periodicals.
710	2	Pavlovian Society of America.
780	0 0	‡t Conditional reflex ‡x 0010-5392 ‡w (DLC) 66009911 ‡w (OCoLC) 1564659
785	0 0	‡t Integrative physiological and behavioral science ‡x 1053-881X ‡w (DLC) 91657030
856	4 1	‡u http://www.springerlink.com/content/120815/

OCLC #70254151 (later title: *Integrative Psychological & Behavioral Science*)

Type a	ELvl	Srce c	GPub	Ctrl	Lang eng
BLvl s	Form	Conf 0	Freq q	MRec	Ctry nyu
S/L 0	Orig	EntW	Regl r	Alph a	
Desc a	SrTp p	Cont	DtSt c	Dates 2007	, 9999

010		2006213445
022	0	1932-4502
042		lcd
245	0 0	Integrative psychological & behavioral science.
246	3	Integrative psychological and behavioral science
260		New York : ‡b Springer Science + Business Media, ‡c 2007-
263		701
300		v. : ‡b ill. ; ‡c 24 cm.
310		Quarterly
362	1	Began with Vol. 41, no. 1 (Mar. 2007).
500		Description based on first issue; title from cover.
650	0	Psychology ‡v Periodicals.
650	0	Conditioned response ‡v Periodicals.
776	0 8	‡i Online version: ‡t Integrative psychological & behavioral science ‡w (OCoLC)189869595

(Continued on next page)

| 780 | 0 | 0 | ‡t Integrative physiological and behavioral science ‡x 1053-881X ‡w (DLC) 91657030 ‡w (OCoLC)22684607 |
| 856 | 4 | 1 | ‡u http://www.springerlink.com/openurl.asp? genre=journal&issn=1932-4502 |

OCLC #44653757 (Online version: *Integrative Physiological and Behavioral Science*)

Type a	ELvl K	Srce d	GPub	Ctrl	Lang eng
BLvl s	Form s	Conf 0	Freq q	MRec	Ctry nju
S/L 0	Orig s	EntW	Regl r	Alph a	
Desc a	SrTp p	Cont	DtSt c	Dates 1991	, 2005

006		m d
010		2010247821
022		‡y 1053-881X
042		pcc
130	0	Integrative physiological and behavioral science (Online)
245	1	0	Integrative physiological and behavioral science ‡h [electronic resource] : ‡b the official journal of the Pavlovian Society.
260			New Brunswick, NJ : ‡b Transaction Periodicals Consortium, Rutgers University, ‡c c1991-
310			Quarterly
362	0		Vol. 26, no. 1 (Jan.-Mar. 1991)-
500			Title from cover.
530			Also issued in print.
538			Mode of access: World Wide Web.
588			Description based on: v. 26, no. 1 (Jan./Mar. 1991); title from article PDF (SpringerLink Web site, viewed Sept. 16, 2010).
588			Latest issue consulted: v. 40, no. 4 (Oct./Dec. 2005) (viewed Sept. 16, 2010).
650		0	Psychology ‡v Periodicals.
650		0	Conditioned response ‡v Periodicals.
710	2		Pavlovian Society of America.
776	1		‡t Integrative physiological and behavioral science ‡x 1053-881X ‡w (DLC) 91657030 ‡w (OCoLC)22684607
780	0	0	‡t Pavlovian journal of biological science ‡x 0093-2213 ‡w (DLC) 74644014 ‡w (OCoLC)1793503
856	4		‡u http://firstsearch.oclc.org ‡z Address for accessing the journal using authorization number and password through OCLC FirstSearch Electronic Collections Online
856	4		‡u http://firstsearch.oclc.org/journal=1053-881x;screen=info;ECOIP ‡z Address for accessing the journal from an authorized IP address through OCLC FirstSearch Electronic Collections Online

Answer Key

CHAPTER 1: TITLE

1.

245	0	0	People & strategy : ǂb journal of the Human Resource Planning Society.
246	1		People and strategy

2.

246	1		ǂi Also known as: ǂa Connection

3.

246	1		Johns Hopkins University Center for Alternatives to Animal Testing
246	1		Center for Alternatives to Animal Testing newsletter

4.

246	1	3	Black women, gender and families
246	1	3	Black women, gender plus families
246	1	3	BWGF

5.

246	1	1	Revue de musique folklorique canadienne

CHAPTER 2: MAJOR CHANGES

1.
The record is pre-AACR2:
- "Desc" fixed field is blank. (If the record followed AACR2 standards, this fixed field would be coded "a.")
- "S/L" fixed field is 1, indicating that the record follows the latest entry convention.
- 245 field is updated with the current title.
- Multiple 247 fields are used to document the history of title changes in chronological order.
2.
A title change is considered to be "major" if the change occurs within the first five words of the title. While there are nine exceptions to the rule (see AACR2 21.2C2bi – 21.2Cbix), the word change of "Genetical" to "Genetics" is not covered by one of the exceptions.
3.

785	0	0	ǂt Attention, perception & psychophysics (print) ǂx 1943-3921 ǂw (DLC) 2008212295 ǂw (OCoLC)235533099
780	0	0	ǂt Perception & psychophysics ǂx 0031-5117 ǂw (DLC) 74201512 ǂw (OCoLC)1762090

4a.

580			Merger of: Future survey, and: Futures research quarterly.
780	1	4	ǂt Futures research quarterly ǂx 8755-3317 ǂw (DLC) 87644223 ǂw (OCoLC) 11276457
780	1	4	ǂt Future survey ǂx 0190-3241 ǂw (DLC) 81649971 ǂw (OCoLC)4693322

4b.

580			Merged with: Futures research quarterly, to form: World future review.
785	1	7	‡t Futures research quarterly ‡x 8755-3317 ‡w (DLC) 87644223 ‡w (OCoLC) 11276457
785	1	7	‡t World future review ‡x 1946-7567 ‡w (DLC) 2009207441 ‡w (OCoLC) 301795864

4c.

580			Merged with: Future survey, to form: World future review.
785	1	7	‡t Future survey ‡x 0190-3241 ‡w (DLC) 81649971 ‡w (OCoLC)4693322
785	1	7	‡t World future review ‡x 1946-7567 ‡w (DLC) 2009207441 ‡w (OCoLC) 301795864

5a.

785	0	4	‡t Journal of social psychology ‡x 0022-4545 ‡w (DLC) 33021284 ‡w (OCoLC)1782304

5b.

780	0	5	‡t Genetic, social, and general psychology monographs ‡x 8756-7547 ‡w (DLC) 85647127 ‡w (OCoLC)11659641

CHAPTER 3: CORPORATE BODY AS MAIN ENTRY

1.

110	2		Society of the Friendly Sons of Saint Patrick in the City of New York.
245	1	0	Yearbook of the Society of the Friendly Sons of Saint Patrick in the City of New York.

2.

130	0		Statistical abstract (Kenya. Central Bureau of Statistics)
245	1	0	Statistical abstract.
710	1		Kenya. ‡b Central Bureau of Statistics.

3.

110	2		Michigan Entomological Society.
245	1	0	Newsletter / ‡c Michigan Entomological Society.
246	1		‡i Some issues have title: ‡a Newsletter of the Michigan Entomological Society

CHAPTER 4: PUBLISHER

1a. Past Practice
Fixed Field: Ctry: tz

260	Dar es Salaam, Tanzania : ‡b Ministry of Education, ‡c 1985-1995.
550	Issued by: Ministry of Education, 1980/1984-1985/1989; by: Ministry of Education and Culture, 1986/1990-1990/1994.

1b. Present Practice
Fixed Field: Ctry: tz

260		‡3 1980/1984-1984/1989: ‡a Dar es Salaam, Tanzania : ‡b Ministry of Education
260	3	‡3 1986/1990-1990/1994: ‡a Dar es Salaam, Tanzania : ‡b Ministry of Education and Culture

2a. Past Practice
Fixed Field: Ctry: flu

260	Westport, CT : ‡b GP Subscription Publications, ‡c c1992-
500	Published: Tampa, FL : The Goldman Group, <Mar. 2003->

2b. Present Practice
Fixed Field: Ctry: flu

260		‡3 Jan. 1992- : ‡a Westport, CT : ‡b GP Subscription Publications, ‡c c1992-
260	3	‡3 <Mar. 2003->: ‡a Tampa, FL : ‡b The Goldman Group

3a. Past Practice
Fixed Field: Ctry: ug

260		Geneva, Switzerland : ‡b Isis-WICCE, ‡c 1984-
500		Place of publication varies: Kampala, Uganda, <1996-2001>

3b. Present Practice
Fixed Field: Ctry: ug

260		‡3 1984-1995 : ‡a Geneva, Switzerland : ‡b Isis-WICCE, ‡c 1984-
260	3	‡3 <1996-2001>: ‡a Kampala, Uganda : ‡b Isis-WICCE

CHAPTER 5: FREQUENCY / NUMBERING

1.
Fixed Fields: Freq: BLANK – no Freq is recorded Regl: x Dates: 1925 , 1944

310	Irregular

2.
Fixed Fields: Freq: t Regl: r Dates: 2002 , 9999

310		Three times a year, ‡b 2008-
321		Semiannual, ‡b 2002-2007
362	0	Vol. 1, no. 1 (2002)-

3.
Fixed Fields: Freq: q Regl: r Dates: 2008 , 9999

310		Four issues per year
362	1	Began with: No. 388 (2008).

4.
Fixed Fields: Freq: a Regl: r Dates: 1921 , 9999

310		Annual, ‡b 1980-
321		Frequency varies, ‡b 1921-1979
362	0	No. 1 (May 1921)-no. 2 (May 1949) ; n.s., no. 1 (June 1966)-

5.
Fixed Fields: Freq: q Regl: r Dates: 1995 , 9999

310		Four issues yearly
362	0	Vol. 1, no. 1 (summer 1995)-v. 14, no. 3 (autumn 2008) ; [new ser.] v. 1, no. 1 (winter 2008/2009)-

CHAPTER 6: DIFFERENT FORMATS

1a.

776	0	8	‡i Also issued in print: ‡t Wasafiri ‡x 0269-0055 ‡w (DLC)sn 86023450 ‡w (OCoLC)14929302

1b.

776	0	8	‡i Issued also online: ‡t Wasafiri (Online) ‡x 1747-1508 ‡w (DLC) 2010250523 ‡w (OCoLC)67618880

2a.

776	0	8	‡i Online version: ‡t ACM journal of data and information quality (Online) ‡x 1936-1963 ‡w (DLC) 2007214263 ‡w (OCoLC)85776286

2b.

776	0	8	‡i Also available in print: ‡t ACM journal of data and information quality ‡x 1936-1955 ‡w (DLC) 2007214262 ‡w (OCoLC)85776277

3a.

776	0		‡t Applied stochastic models and data analysis (Online) ‡x 1099-0747 ‡w (DLC) 2001212357 ‡w (OCoLC)43969746
785	0	0	‡t Applied stochastic models in business and industry ‡x 1524-1904 ‡w (DLC) sn 99008399 ‡w (OCoLC)40963631

3b.

776	0	8	‡i Print version: ‡t Applied stochastic models and data analysis ‡x 8755-0024 ‡w (DLC) 86643430 ‡w (OCoLC)11241541
785	0	0	‡t Applied stochastic models in business and industry (Online) ‡x 1526-4025 ‡w (DLC)sn 99009168 ‡w (OCoLC)42212556

3c.

776	0	8	‡i Online version: ‡t Applied stochastic models in business and industry (Online) ‡x 1526-4025 ‡w (DLC)sn 99009168 ‡w (OCoLC)42212556
780	0	0	‡t Applied stochastic models and data analysis ‡x 8755-0024 ‡w (DLC) 86643430 ‡w (OCoLC) 11241541

3d.

776	0	8	‡i Print version: ‡t Applied stochastic models in business and industry ‡x 1524-1904 ‡w (DLC)sn 99008399 ‡w (OCoLC)40963631
780	0	0	‡t Applied stochastic models and data analysis (Online) ‡x 1099-0747 ‡w (DLC) 2001212357 ‡w (OCoLC) 43969746

4a.

Fixed Fields: Dates: <u>1990</u> , <u>2009</u>

580			Continued online only, July 2009-
776	0	8	‡i Also available online, <March 2002>-May 2009: ‡t CAA news (Online) ‡x 1942-4892 ‡w (DLC) 2007236533 ‡w (OCoLC)52717321
785	1	0	‡t CAA news (Online) ‡x 1942-4892 ‡w (DLC) 2007236533 ‡w (OCoLC) 52717321

4b.

776	0	8	‡i Also issued in print, 1990-May 2009: ‡t CAA news ‡x 1557-511X ‡w (DLC)sn 90033514 ‡w (OCoLC)21009074
780	0	0	‡t CAA news ‡x 1557-511X ‡w (DLC)sn 90033514 ‡w (OCoLC)21009074

CHAPTER 7: SUPPLEMENTS

1a.

770	0	‡t International review of cytology. Supplement ‡x 0074-770X ‡w (DLC)sf 90017608 ‡w (OCoLC)3226959

1b.

772	0	‡t International review of cytology ‡x 0074-7696 ‡w (DLC) 52005203 ‡w (OCoLC)928149

2a.

770	1	‡t Margen de poesía ‡w (OCoLC)26249073

2b.

772	1	‡t Casa del tiempo ‡x 0185-4275 ‡w (OCoLC)8610701

3a.

770	1	‡t Detail green ‡x 1868-3843 ‡w (OCoLC)330765419

3b.

772	0	‡t Detail (English ed.) ‡x 1614-4600 ‡w (DLC) 2006214569 ‡w (OCoLC) 58804304

CHAPTER 8: UNIFORM TITLES

1.
130	0	Lunch (Charlottesville, Va.)

2.
130	0	British music education yearbook (2009)

3.
130	0	Economic bulletin (American Institute for Economic Research)

4.
130	0	Journal of the Illinois State Historical Society (1998)

5.
130	0	Bangladesh journal of public administration (Savar, Bangladesh : 1996)

CHAPTER 9: NOTES

1.
362	1	Began with: Number 1 (2009).
588		Description based on: Number 1 (2009); title from cover.
588		Latest issue consulted: Number 2 (2010).

2.
530	Also available online.

3.
550	Published jointly with the London School of Economics and Political Science.

4.
546	Text in French; abstracts in English and German.

5.
530	Also available in print.
538	Mode of access: Internet.
588	Description based on first issue; title from publisher's homepage (viewed June 5, 2008).

CHAPTER 10: STANDARD NUMBERS

1.
780	1	4	‡t Futures research quarterly ‡x 8755-3317 ‡w (DLC) 87644223 ‡w (OCoLC)11276457
780	1	4	‡t Future survey ‡x 0190-3241 ‡w (DLC) 81649971 ‡w (OCoLC)4693322

2.
776	0	8	‡i Also available online: ‡t Aerospace engineering & manufacturing ‡x 1939-6694 ‡w (DLC) 2007215491 ‡w (OCoLC)166398436
780	0	0	‡t Aerospace engineering (Society of Automotive Engineers) ‡x 0736-2536 ‡w (DLC) 83644639 ‡w (OCoLC)9090151

3.
776	1		‡t Integrative physiological and behavioral science ‡w (DLC) 2010247821‡w (OCoLC)44653757
780	0	0	‡t Pavlovian journal of biological science ‡x 0093-2213 ‡w (DLC) 74644014 ‡w (OCoLC)1793503
785	0	0	‡t Integrative psychological & behavioral science ‡x 1932-4502 ‡w (DLC) 2006213445 ‡w (OCoLC)70254151

Index

About the Authors

FANG HUANG GAO is a supervisory librarian for the U.S. Government Printing Office. Fang was previously the manager of Serials Services at the University Library at the University of Illinois at Urbana-Champaign and an adjunct faculty member for the Graduate School of Library and Information Science at the University of Illinois at Urbana-Champaign. She is a trainer for the National Serials Cooperative Cataloging Training Program (SCCTP), a trainer for Fundamentals of Series Authorities, and a trainer for the Cataloging for the 21st Century Program: Rules and Tools for Cataloging Internet Resources.

HEATHER TENNISON holds an MLS and a certificate in Special Collections Librarianship from the University of Illinois at Urbana-Champaign. Heather currently resides in Champaign, where she is pursuing an advanced degree in art history.

JANET A. WEBER began her library career at the Lincoln Trail Libraries System, a regional Illinois library system, where she gained a diverse amount of library experience, including a good understanding of how libraries work together. She joined the University of Illinois Library 16 years ago, primarily cataloging monographs, serials, and electronic resources as well as supporting electronic resources management. She has more recently been involved in the redesign of technical services workflows.

CPSIA information can be obtained at www.ICGtesting.com
Printed in the USA
LVOW09s0012240813

349198LV00009B/117/P